Welcome

Frederica Mathewes-Green, through her writing, has become the "Greeter" for every person who begins to seek out and explore the "other Christianity" which is the Eastern Orthodox Church. Few authors can take the mystery, beauty and often-daunting complexities of Orthodoxy and transform them in such an inviting path of spiritual journey as this author has done with this book.

—THE VERY REV. DR. CHAD HATFIELD,
Chancellor, St. Vladimir's Orthodoxy Seminary, New York

How do you introduce (Eastern) Orthodoxy? Frederica Mathewes-Green suggests we treat it as a large, and much-loved, family house. She takes us round it, showing us all the rooms and what goes on in them. Her conversational style is completely accessible, but utterly honest; there is lots of information, and she deals directly with problems to be encountered. It feels a bit like Mussorgsky's *Pictures at an Exhibition*. This is a wonderful book.

—FR. ANDREW LOUTH,
Professor of Patristic and Byzantine Studies at Durham University

In her own warm and engaging way, Frederica takes you on a journey into a strange and exotic world for those unfamiliar with it but a spiritual refuge and oasis for those who have embraced it. This just may be the Church you have been looking for and didn't even know it existed.

—JOHN MADDEX,
CEO, Ancient Faith Ministries

This beginner's guide to Orthodoxy can be described as a work of superb hospitality. While guiding her guests through a fictitious but true-to-life Orthodox house of worship and introducing them to its parish family, Frederica Mathewes-Green serves up a lavish feast of Orthodox architecture, art, theology, history, and devotional practices, all seasoned with tangy anecdotes and nuggets of wisdom. Even longstanding Orthodox believers will find nourishment here.

—CAROLE MONICA BURNETT,
Editor, Fathers of the Church Series, Catholic University of America Press, Washington, DC

No one alive today has done more to introduce ordinary Americans to the wonders of the ancient faith than Frederica Mathewes-Green. If not for her, I doubt I would be Orthodox. Hers was one of the greatest and most surprising gifts anyone has ever given me, and it's thrilling to think of how many others will receive it through this book.

—ROD DREHER,
author of *The Little Way of Ruthie Leming*

Beautifully written and carefully explained with a heart for the non-Orthodox. As an evangelical who grew up in the Greek Orthodox Church, until being shipped off to boarding school in England, I found myself longing to revisit the liturgy and traditions of my youth.

—EMMANUEL KAMPOURIS,
Former Chairman & CEO of American Standard Companies,
Founder of www.biblemesh.com

Frederica Mathewes-Green is one of the most engaging interpreters of the Eastern Christian way in our time. In this book she takes us by the hand as it were and introduces us to something of the mystery, wisdom, worship, and beauty—in short, the life—of Eastern Christianity. A rich, illuminating introduction.

—TIMOTHY GEORGE,
Founding Dean of Beeson Divinity School of Samford University
and Chair of the Doctrine and Christian Unity Commission
of the Baptist World Alliance.

Frederica Mathewes-Green has given us a warm and inviting defense of Orthodox Christianity without being defensive. This wonderful book explains the roots of the ancient truths and traditions of the Church in a conversational style to a broad audience of both believers and those still searching, while avoiding pedantic language which can be off-putting: a great book about the great Church.

—ANDREW NATSIOS,
Professor, George H.W. Bush School of Government and
Public Service, Texas A&M University

Welcome
TO THE
ORTHODOX CHURCH
AN INTRODUCTION TO
Eastern Christianity

Frederica
Mathewes-Green

PARACLETE PRESS
BREWSTER, MASSACHUSETTS

2016 Second printing
2015 First printing

Welcome to the Orthodox Church: An Introduction to Eastern Christianity

Copyright © 2015 by Frederica Mathewes-Green

ISBN 978-1-55725-921-9

Unless otherwise indicated, Scripture quotations are taken from the *Revised Standard Version of the Bible*, copyright 1952 [2nd edition, 1971] by the Division of Christian Education of the National Council of the Churches of Christ in the United States of America. Used by permission. All rights reserved.

Scripture quotations marked NRSV are taken from the *New Revised Standard Version Bible*, copyright 1989, 1993, Division of Christian Education of the National Council of the Churches of Christ in the United States of America. Used by permission. All rights reserved.

The index is courtesy of Robert Weaver.

The Paraclete Press name and logo (dove on cross) are trademarks of Paraclete Press, Inc.

Library of Congress Cataloging-in-Publication Data

Mathewes-Green, Frederica.
  Welcome to the Orthodox Church : an introduction to Eastern Christianity / Frederica Mathewes-Green.
    pages cm
  ISBN 978-1-55725-921-9 (paperback)
  1. Orthodox Eastern Church. I. Title.
  BX320.3.M38 2015
  281.9—dc23   2014041905

10 9 8 7 6 5 4 3 2

Published by Paraclete Press
Brewster, Massachusetts
www.paracletepress.com
Printed in the United States of America

To my husband, Father Gregory Mathewes-Green,
on our fortieth anniversary.
You are my one true love, both now and ever and unto ages of ages.

Contents

Part Two: Inside the Liturgy

Part Three: Inside the Community

Introduction

How to Learn About Orthodoxy

*M*y husband is an Orthodox priest, so he regularly teaches a class to introduce newcomers to the faith. It's trickier than you'd think. At the first class he writes on the board:

What you will not learn in this class: Orthodoxy.
What you will learn: About Orthodoxy.

What's the difference? Like so many important things in life, Orthodox Christianity is not something you can grasp from the outside. From the outside, it looks simply like a grand, historic institution—the ancient Christian church of the East, outside the bounds of Western Europe. (We could just as well call it "Eastern Christianity," though it is, of course, a worldwide faith, like every form of Christianity.)

Orthodoxy is a rich faith, abounding in treasures of arts and architecture, liturgical poetry and music, and profound works of theology and spirituality. Even after joining the church, a person can go on making new discoveries, year after year. There is plenty to learn *about* Orthodoxy.

But to learn Orthodoxy itself is a different matter. Because once you're on the inside, you find that Orthodoxy is not primarily a religious institution, but a spiritual path. The institution exists for the sake of the path. Every element you meet has the same purpose: to help you be filled more completely with the life and presence of Christ. There is an undercurrent of dynamism, liveliness, and a frank expectation of action and growth. When asked, "What's different about Orthodoxy?" people who have converted to Orthodoxy keep returning to the word *challenging*.

So those who join the Church find that each beautiful new thing they encounter contains a note of exhortation. Each bears persistent questions: How are you applying this in your life? Have you forgiven everyone you should? How is your humility today? How is your self-control? There's a great deal of talk about sin and repentance, even though that's currently unfashionable; yet self-reflection and change are indispensable if there's going to be any growth. There are frequent reminders to be vigilant against temptation—as if that was something that really *mattered*, as if it had some effect on our ability to practice God's presence.

The icons that fill a church may initially look like nice religious paintings, but they have an unsettling way of coming to life. You begin to feel like the people depicted are looking back at you, looking *through* you. "Here we are," they seem to say. "We lived for Christ. How about you?"

So Orthodoxy is a path of continual transformation, and people who join the church are always discovering more of what it "is," and not just what it "is about."

But if it's so hard to grasp Orthodoxy without actually living it, how are you supposed to get to know it in the first place? The curious can hardly be told to come back when they're ready to sign up. In today's theological free market, those who are considering a change want to know a great deal about a faith before making a decision. Others don't expect ever to join the church, but would still like to know more about it. Perhaps they have a relative or friend who has become Orthodox, and they wonder what all the fuss is about. Perhaps they've been invited to a wedding or liturgy and wonder what they're in for. A book that sorts it all out would help.

And that's exactly where I ran into a problem.

When I started trying to organize this work, I found the material isn't very amenable to sorting. All the dynamic elements slide into one another, so you can't (at least I can't) separate a chapter on sacraments from a chapter on theology from a chapter on history. Some living quality gets lost in the process. It's resistant to categorization, and many of the familiar categories don't quite work anyway.

In part this is because there's a lot about Orthodoxy that just never got put into words. Historically, the Orthodox haven't spent much time explaining their faith to other Christians. Descendants of Christian Europe inherit many centuries of interdenominational debate and verbal sparring, but those living in traditionally Orthodox lands (Africa, Asia, the Middle East, and Eastern Europe, mostly) had less experience of that. They had lots of unsettling experiences with *non*-Christians—Persians, Mongols, Muslims, Communists—and knew well how life in Christ differs from life without him. But the long-running arguments among Western Christians, the countless terms with precise and prickly meanings (e.g., works, merits, atonement), just didn't play a part in the Eastern Christian story.

I can tell you how we went about it, when my family joined the Orthodox Church some twenty years ago. We mostly got to know Orthodoxy by *experience*. Our journey preceded development of the Internet, and we went quickly through the few books then available on the subject. So if we wanted to understand what the church teaches on a particular topic, we made sure to look at how it was handled in worship.

Say we wondered how Orthodox understand Christ's Ascension. We would look up the prayers and hymns that are used that day; we'd study the icon of the Ascension (which, no matter where or when it's painted, shows the same characters arranged in similar ways). As the years passed and the liturgical cycle kept turning, our comprehension kept expanding. We learned how the meaning of the Ascension connects to the meaning of the Incarnation, and the Transfiguration, and even to the creation of the human race in Genesis. We kept building and correcting our understanding.

At first, a lot of things were startling. I kept hearing theological
ideas, or combinations of ideas, or ways of expressing them, that I'd
never heard before. After some years those surprises were less frequent, and then came a period of noticing that there were things I
didn't hear about anymore. It wouldn't have surprised me if the concept of God's wrath had cropped up in Orthodox spirituality, since I
knew it was a thoroughly premodern church. But I found that, on the
rare occasions it was mentioned, it was always when stressing that
God is *not* wrathful. Prayers would say, in so many words, "Though
we deserve your wrath, you instead always give us compassion."

Another example was the "problem of evil," the question of why
there is suffering in the world, and in particular why the innocent
suffer. This is a tormenting puzzle in the West, for Christians
and non-Christians alike. However (and it took me several years
to notice this), in Orthodoxy it just doesn't come up. Orthodox
Christians suffer as much as people do anywhere, and grieve as
deeply. But there isn't the confusion and bitterness about it that
infects the discussion in the West. It took me quite a while to fully
grasp the reason why.

This time of learning and discovering was exciting, to tell the
truth. My husband and I had completed our seminary degrees some
years before, and exploring Orthodoxy sent us back to revisit and
rethink a multitude of topics. Many a settled concept had to be
revised. Many a Scripture we'd thought obvious had to be seen in a
different light.

Often, that was a light that better reflected the original Greek
text. European theology was built upon a foundation of reading the
Bible in Latin translation, and as we went along we learned that
there are gaps in what Latin can convey. For example, there was
no equivalent for the New Testament term "energy" (*energeia*), used
some thirty times by St. Paul. That's another intriguing, perspective-
changing element we'll get to later.

From the beginning, there was something about Orthodoxy
that struck me as really *different*. It was hard to put into words. It
wasn't only the explicit theological differences, but also some basic

assumptions about who we are, and how God is known, and what Christianity is supposed to do. There was an unnamable underlying *something* that was different from any form of Christianity I'd ever known, and grasping it was a multiyear project.

Since I learned Orthodoxy in this unpredictable way, it was not obvious how I should pass it on to others. Compare and contrast might seem the most obvious course; start with what people already know about Christian faith and make adjustments. If you'd never heard of baseball, you'd ask, "Is it like bowling this way? Is it like soccer that way?" After I give a talk about Orthodoxy, the audience's questions often follow that line, comparing what I've said with the denominations they already know.

But that can result in more confusion. Some points that initially look similar can turn out not to be so, on closer inspection. Sometimes the same biblical term is understood in a different way. Some Eastern Christian concepts lie outside Western categories entirely. It's not just that the answers are different; even the *questions* are different.

Strange as it sounds, Catholic and Protestant look a lot alike from an Eastern perspective. Those two cousins grew up in the same family; they share a common geography, a common history, and have argued over common questions.

But the Orthodox weren't part of that Western story. They had little role in the Crusades (besides defending themselves from invading crusaders); they had no Avignon popes, no sale of indulgences, no scholastic movement, no Reformation, no substitutionary atonement theory, no Enlightenment, no modernism. It's a whole different story.

On the other hand, describing and exploring differences between East and West in a forthright way might just seem like making trouble (and, as you'd guess, I'm partial to Orthodoxy). Why focus on differences, some might ask, when Christians need to stick together?

But if you're reading this book, you must be at least a *little* curious about the differences. With almost anything it's the differences that are most interesting. Men and women are mostly alike—both have sinuses, elbows, and spleens—but it's the differences that have traditionally been most intriguing.

Unfortunately, I couldn't treat each topic with the thoroughness it deserves. There just wasn't room. In the bibliography you'll find many recommendations for further reading that will increase your understanding. There are now many more books about Orthodoxy available than there were when my family joined the church.

Yet the best way to understand anything is not to read about it, but to experience it firsthand. Some people seem to do nothing *but* read books, gathering ever-more-detailed opinions. Don't do that. Nobody can understand how the Orthodox spiritual path works without digging in and practicing it seriously and with self-discipline. The ancient Orthodox prayers, the hymns and visual arts, are designed to communicate directly to the worshiper. They've spoken to Christians of all lands and cultures and somehow transcended their borders. They have the power of art and beauty; they go directly to the heart.

If you think about it, reading is an impoverished way to learn anything. We can learn to read the squiggles on a page, but we are made to read people. We watch how people move, listen to how they use their voices, watch what they say and do. From that we learn about the thing they are doing, and what it means to them.

That's how most people got to know the Christian faith in ages past: not by reading books, but by joining a community. They learned by keeping their eyes and ears open during worship, listening to the Scriptures and sermons, and thinking about the words of hymns. They participated in the fasting seasons, benefiting from the advice and support of the "old hands" who knew it well. They watched the people around them, seeing what they did and listening to how they spoke about the faith—not just the words, but also the quality of reverence in their voices. Over time, they soaked things up.

In the midst of a community like that, "thrown in the deep end" so to speak, you wouldn't learn things in any particular order. You'd learn important things alongside less-important things (though you wouldn't know the difference at the time). You'd keep running into the same thing over and over from different angles, and have to keep correcting first impressions. Gradually, you'd see how all the elements fit together, and how they work in practice.

Having pled for the superiority of direct experience over reading a book, here we are—at the beginning of a book. I've attempted to overcome some of the medium's limitations, and simulate that "deep end" experience, by constructing an imaginary parish, St. Felicity Orthodox Church. (You'll find out more about the name in chapter 2.) We'll get acquainted with Orthodoxy by making a series of visits there, dealing with a full range of topics as they might arise naturally, in a context of places and relationships.

In part 1, we begin on a weekday when the church is empty. There are a lot of things to look at in an Orthodox church, and a preliminary visit when it's quiet can help you get your bearings. We'll learn about architecture, icons, prayer, saints, and more. Not every church is arranged exactly like St. Felicity, but what we see here is typical and will orient us for things to come.

In parts 2 and 3 we'll come back to the church for some of the events you might experience in real life: a Vespers service, a typical Sunday-morning liturgy, a wedding, a funeral, and so on. We'll also go to a parishioner's home for a house blessing, and sit in on coffee hour. These parts doesn't aim to tell a story; they just present a series of snapshots, to show how things might look in practice. While the characters I introduce are fictitious, they're intended to be realistic and typical, and to resemble people you might meet in any Orthodox church—or anywhere else, for that matter.

Orthodox Christianity is a spiritual path. It is that rather than an organization, or even a set of theological propositions. Eastern Orthodoxy is a comprehensive program of inner transformation; it is a journey, a way, even "the Way" (see, e.g., Acts 9:2; 19:9; 22:4).

This path *has* an institution, like a hospital has an administrative board. Still, the life of a hospital will always be its healing mission. You hope that those board members were carefully selected, but even glaring failures would not be able to damage medical science itself.

Orthodox Christians are grateful for the church, which has preserved and offered this spiritual path century after century, but can't be too surprised if flaws appear in the earthly institution. There will always be weeds among the wheat; as Jesus said, "an enemy has done this" (Matt. 14:24–30). Yet the time-tested process of spiritual healing continues to be effective, no matter how humans mess things up.

Not every Orthodox leader is a saint. Not every church member is devout. People go to church for all different reasons. Not every congregation is full of people urgently seeking transformation in Christ (though it can be hard to tell, because the most diligent are often the most quiet). In some Orthodox congregations this way of transformation has been forgotten, and is neither taught nor sought.

But even in a congregation that appears dull and distracted, the Way itself is still effective, waiting to be tried, like an unopened Bible. All the Orthodox "tribes and tongues" hold this treasure in common—even when they follow it badly, even when they fail in visible ways, even when they practice it in parallel observance, grumbling at the guys in the church across the street.

If Orthodoxy were a worldly organization, it wouldn't be an efficient one. If it claimed infallible leadership, it would be greeted with laughter. But Orthodoxy is not a set of propositions, not a mere organization. It is a Way—a way to be immersed in the presence of God, through our Creator and Savior, the only Lord, Jesus Christ.

Interior of a Typical Orthodox Church

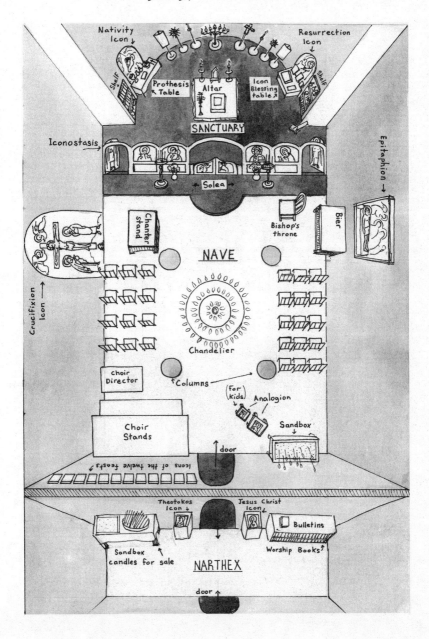

Sanctuary of a Typical Orthodox Church

PART

One

INSIDE THE
TEMPLE

Though Orthodox Christians refer to the building as "the church" like everyone else, they also call it "the temple." Our trip to St. Felicity will familiarize you with the different areas in the temple, what happens there and why.

We'll look at the narthex (the front lobby), the nave (the congregation's worship space), the iconostasis (a screen that holds icons, at the front end of the nave), and the altar (the whole area behind the iconostasis). As we do, we'll spend some time looking at practices such as praying with icons and making the sign of the cross. We'll also talk about concepts such as the prayers of the saints, the atonement, theosis, and the place of the Virgin Mary. The conversation around these ideas and practices will lay a foundation as we move deeper into the life of the Orthodox Church.

1

"Enter His Gates"

(Ps. 99/100:4)

The Narthex, Praying with Icons, Venerating Them, Making the Sign of the Cross

*L*et's drop in on St. Felicity Orthodox Church on a weekday morning, when things are quiet and no worship is going on. As we come through the front doors, we find ourselves in a little foyer called a *narthex*. Here we see the same things you'd find in the lobby of any church: service bulletins, newsletters, forgotten umbrellas, a basket of canned goods for a local soup kitchen, pinned-up notices for retreats and events, and, on a Sunday morning, greeters. But in the narthex of an Orthodox church you find a few more things as well.

There's also a basket of candles, mostly taper-style candles made of beeswax, and depending on the parish, votive candles in small or large glass containers. There may be a donation basket—you'd be surprised how much those candles cost the church—or, during services, someone on hand to receive donations and make change. In some churches there are also slips of paper on which you can write the names of those you'd like prayed for during the service (in two columns, for the living and the dead).

The narthex is more than just a lobby, though. It's actually part of the liturgical space, and some services, or preliminary parts of services, were traditionally held here. For example, before a wedding the priest would meet the bride and groom here and ask formally if they had come of their own free will, and whether they had promised themselves to anyone else. He'd ask a series of questions here before a baptism, too. These days those preliminaries are more likely to be held inside the nave, the main worship space, but you'll sometimes see the narthex used in its traditional way.

When people arrive for worship, most will take a candle and go to an icon here in the narthex to pray, mentally offering some words of greeting and recalling their prayer needs. (They'll greet icons this way inside the nave, too.) The custom when entering an Orthodox church is to pause in front of an icon and pray; if there is a nearby candle stand, you might light your candle and leave it here.

Depending on your background, you might think that sounds like idolatry. You're not the first person to have such thoughts, and sorting out the meaning of icons took over a hundred years, and cost the lives of hundreds of icon-defenders. We'll talk in more detail about that in chapter 8; in fact, we'll keep learning more about icons as we go along, answering questions and learning what icons have to teach.

But, here at the start, it helps to keep in mind that what Orthodox Christians chiefly feel when they look at icons is *love*. Maybe you have a photo of someone you love who has departed this life. You might keep it framed in your home, someplace where you'll see it frequently. When you see it, your thoughts fly to this person; you might give thanks that he or she is alive in Christ now, and no doubt praying for you.

If you can picture feeling that way toward the photo of a loved one, then you're very close to understanding how Orthodox Christians feel toward the saints, and the icons that bear their images.

Icons are never the object of worship; we don't pray to them. We don't even pray in a different *way* in the presence of icons; there is no distinct form of "spirituality" for icons. To us, icons are more like companions—more like that photo of a loved one. They remind us that the unseen "great cloud of witnesses" (Heb. 12:1) is surrounding us whenever we pray, and when we don't, as well.

Icons are treated with respect, the kind of respect you would give to your favorite Bible. A leather-bound, gilt-edged, red-letter bible is not *the* Bible; if it were lost in a fire, the Bible would still exist. And yet, because it is a copy of the Holy Bible, it deserves respect. Your familiar, favorite Bible probably wins your reverence and affection as well. You wouldn't worship it, but you would always handle it with respect. That's because you think of it as a place of encounter with God. Icons are a similar place of encounter, and have often been called "windows into heaven."

Christians made use of the visual arts from the faith's earliest years. Images depicting people and events from the Bible and Christian history were invaluable during the long centuries when most Christians were illiterate. They served a purpose much like the pictures in a children's Bible, filling a church's walls with images depicting the people and events of salvation history. In those days all Bibles were copied by hand, and were astronomically expensive; think of how much it would cost today to have a calligrapher make you a copy of the Bible. So a parish was likely to have only one copy, and people would encounter the Scriptures most often by hearing them read aloud. If someone wanted to refresh his memory of a story that might not come around for another six months, he could seek out its picture on the wall. (Missionaries also found portable icons useful when conveying the gospel story across a language barrier.)

Icons depict the characters and events of Scripture in wood and paint, rather than paper and ink; for this reason they are often said to be "written" rather than "painted" (though the distinction in English doesn't occur in Greek). Most icons are unsigned, in humility, but if the painter's name appears, it's phrased as "by the hand of" the painter. This means that the true source of the image is the united prayers of the community, and it was delivered through the iconographer's hand.

Why light a candle? Because it reminds us of the light of Christ ("I am the light of the world," John 8:12). When we go to the evening prayer service, Vespers, in part 2, we'll encounter an ancient hymn that was sung when the evening lamps were lit, one that praises Christ as the "joyous light of the holy glory of the immortal Father."

But we light candles for a practical reason as well. For the many centuries before electric wiring was invented, churches were pretty dark. Lighting a candle in front of an icon would make that beloved face bloom out of the darkness. Throughout the service it would remain visible, a reminder of invisible reality: all the saints who have ever lived are here, praying with us. Although candles don't much serve that practical function anymore, it is still our custom—our "family tradition," you might say—to place them there, as we'd light candles on a dinner table. It is a gesture of respect and affection.

Either here in the narthex, or just inside the nave, there will be an icon that represents the name of the church. If the church is called "Holy Ascension," the icon will depict Christ's Ascension. If the church is called "St. Paul," the icon will be of their patron saint, St. Paul. (And by the way, an Orthodox church is called "St. Paul" rather than "St. Paul's," the form more common with Western churches.)

Some of these patronal images may surprise you: in a church named "Holy Trinity" you are likely to see an icon of the three angels who visited Abraham and Sarah and told them that they would have a son.* A church named "Holy Resurrection" will have an icon showing Christ, not at the garden tomb, but in the cavernous realm of death, setting the captives free. The icon of a church named "Holy Cross" would not show the Crucifixion, but a man in clerical robes holding the cross high in the midst of a gathering of worshipers, a snapshot from church history. In the foreground stands St. Helena, mother of the emperor Constantine, who recovered the cross of Christ from beneath the foundations of a Jerusalem temple to Venus, where it had lain buried for three centuries.

---

* This image is called "The Old Testament Trinity." The version by St. Andrei Rublev, AD 1360–1427, is one of the best-loved icons in the world.

Icons tell stories and teach theology; they summarize and convey things that can't be readily expressed in words. It is a great responsibility to teach theology, so the form and content of icons follow standardized patterns. An icon of Christ's Transfiguration, for example, will always depict the same characters, arranged in the same ways. We don't want the artist's personal opinions popping up in icon-painting any more than we'd want them in Bible-translating.

So, unlike contemporary artists, an iconographer doesn't seek self-expression in her work. Her job is to accurately pass on the faith she has received, following in the footsteps of icon-painters throughout the ages. But her icon will vary just enough from anyone else's to reveal the uniqueness of God's work in her soul. The depth of her prayer life, and her wrestling with fasting and prayer while painting it, will shine from the completed icon.

It is the custom to venerate a church's patronal icon before going into the nave, and if you watched people doing this, you'd soon conclude that "venerate" means "kiss." It's a gesture of reverence, honor, and even affection. They are greeting the person depicted in the icon, and in many Orthodox cultures friends exchange a kiss when they meet. So as members of the church come through on Sunday morning, they will pick up a candle and then pause before the patronal icon. They will make the sign of the cross (usually with a bow), pray silently, and kiss the icon—on the hands or feet of the person depicted, preferably. If there are also icons of Christ and the Virgin Mary in the narthex, they will venerate them, too. (A liturgical kiss, by the way, is silent; a gentle pressure of the lips, but no "smack." Children's kisses excepted, of course.)

There may also be an icon on a low stand for children to venerate. Everyone enjoys watching little ones as they learn how to make the sign of the cross. That right hand goes flying all over the place. It looks like a random one-handed version of "Head, Shoulders, Knees, and Toes."

To make the sign of the cross, Eastern Christians lift the right hand and touch the forehead, the lower chest or abdomen, the right shoulder, and the left shoulder. That movement from shoulder to shoulder is the opposite of the custom in the West, where the hand goes from left to right. I had to relearn this when I became Orthodox, and it helped me to think, "Push, don't pull."

Some Christians mistrust the sign of the cross, thinking of it as a relic of medieval superstition. It's a gesture that goes back much earlier, though, even to the years of Roman persecution. Tertullian (AD 160–225) cautions Christian women not to marry unbelievers: "Will you escape notice when you sign your bed, your 'dear little body'?"[1] He warns that the husband who sees this and realizes his wife is a Christian might use it against her, threatening her with arrest and execution. This was still the age of martyrs.

It's interesting that Tertullian doesn't then say, "So stop making the sign of the cross." To refuse to bear the cross of Christ, to conceal it even for personal safety, was simply not possible. "Far be it from me to glory except in the cross of our Lord Jesus Christ" (Gal. 6:14).

To the early Christians the sign of the cross was not a merely symbolic gesture, but a way to invoke the immediate presence and power of Jesus Christ. St. Athanasius (about AD 320) invited skeptics to test this for themselves: "Let him who would test this by experience, in the presence of lying demons and fraudulent oracles and magic, let him use this sign of the cross which they laugh at. He will see how it makes demons take flight, oracles cease, and all magic and witchcraft is ended."[2]

Trusting in such power, the early Christians made the sign of the cross frequently. "Let the Cross, as our seal, be boldly made with our fingers upon our brow and on all occasions," says St. Cyril of Jerusalem (AD 313–386), "over the bread we eat, over the cups we drink, in our comings and in our goings, before sleep, on lying down and rising up, when we are on the way and when we are still."[3]

When Westerners see Eastern Christians make the sign of the cross, they are often impressed with the accompanying seriousness of intent. Even as settled a nonliturgical evangelical as Charles Colson, founder of Prison Fellowship, could say:

> After praying with an Orthodox sister, Irina Ratushinskaya [who survived Communist prison], . . . I said my "Amen" and then watched her make the sign of the Cross with such depth of feeling that I had a powerful urge to make the sign myself. I resisted—for fear it might be a betrayal of my Baptist tradition. How foolish I felt when I later discovered that believers since the very beginning and through the centuries have made the sign of the Cross, signifying that they have been crucified with Christ.[4]

In the West, all five fingers are loosely held together; some say this represents the five wounds of Christ. In the East, it's more complicated. I almost hate to tell you. This is the sort of thing that I resented when I was initially (and somewhat uncertainly) following my husband into Orthodoxy. Some of the Orthodox customs I was learning seemed overly detailed, and struck me as fussy and complicated.

One thing that helped me through was the gradual realization that Orthodox worship is rarely self-conscious. The beloved Anglican author C. S. Lewis noticed this when visiting Orthodox churches, and liked it very much. "Some sit, some lie on their faces, some stand, some kneel, some walk about, . . . and *no one takes the slightest notice of what anyone else is doing*," he said in one letter.[5]

People behave in a way that is devout and respectful, of course—we all face the altar and pray—but if you feel like you can't lift your arm for one more sign of the cross, no one will gasp. In Orthodox worship, your personal expressions of devotion are your own business, and not a matter for others' scrutiny.

When Orthodox Christians make the sign of the cross, they position the thumb and first two fingers of the right hand together at the tip, to represent the Trinity. This is what you use to touch forehead, abdomen, shoulder, and shoulder. The ring and little finger are held together, to represent the two natures of Christ; they are bent down to touch the palm, to represent his descent to earth.

When I first began attending Orthodox worship, I found it very hard to scramble my fingers into this position on short notice. So I would form them correctly at the beginning of the service and just try to keep them that way till the end. I never knew when it was going to be time to make the sign of the cross again; it seemed like we were doing it every few minutes.

I grew up thinking of the sign of the cross as something you do at the beginning and end of a prayer, like bookends. But Orthodox Christians cross themselves with great frequency during worship: when entering or leaving a church, when kissing a cross, an icon, or the Gospel book, at each mention of the Trinity or of the cross, before and after a reading from Scripture, during the Nicene Creed, during the Communion prayers, at the end of the Lord's Prayer, before and after receiving Communion—really, just about any time. Even outside of church I cross myself when I hear an ambulance siren, and when I hear something I should pray about. In such cases it is the gesture that seals a flying prayer: "Lord, help."

When we cross the nave of the church from one side to the other, we show respect to the altar by stopping in the middle to bow toward it and cross ourselves. I absorbed this habit so completely that I automatically start to do it whenever I cross a large room. If I'm walking across a movie theater, I have to remember not to stop in the middle, cross myself, and bow to the screen.

Those who come from a Western liturgical background have been looking around the narthex for a holy water font, so they can dip their fingers and make the sign of the cross. We don't have these in the Eastern Orthodox Church; we do have holy water, but it is used for sprinkling and (this was a surprise to me) drinking. We'll encounter the holy water font inside the nave.

And the sharp-eyed have noticed there is something here they don't usually see in a narthex: worship books. Why are they out here, and not on the little shelves on the backs of the pews? Wait and see. Next we enter the nave.

2

"The House of God"

(GEN. 28:17)

Church Architectural Styles, Wraparound Iconography,
Why No Pews?, The Saint of the Day

We'll spend the next few chapters in the nave, the worship space proper. But before we enter, let's stand here in the narthex a minute more, in front of the doors to the nave. What will we see when we open them?

My mind flies over the hundreds of Orthodox churches I have seen. I have been to Hagia Sophia, the magnificent temple built in Istanbul (then Constantinople) in AD 537. It is one of the largest churches in the world—eighty thousand square feet—and its "floating" dome is still an architectural wonder. I've been to many, many American churches built in the nineteenth and twentieth centuries by the hard work and devotion of immigrants from Russia, Syria, Greece, or other nations. I've been to churches that were entirely covered, walls and ceiling, with magnificent icons, a veritable jewel box. I have been to the ruins of many ancient Orthodox churches in Turkey. Our brothers and sisters in Christ may have run there, and died there, when the invaders came sweeping in; now the stones, some of which still bear crosses, are tumbled about, worn by wind and rain.

I've been to many American Orthodox churches that occupy buildings originally built by Protestant or Catholic congregations.

Since Orthodox prefer to worship facing east (I'll explain why below), the worship space has sometimes been turned sideways, or even completely around, such that today's worshipers face the side where the original congregation came in the door.

I've been to Annunciation Orthodox Cathedral in Milwaukee, Wisconsin, designed by Frank Lloyd Wright and variously described as "the flying saucer" or "the floating hamburger." I have been to a church in an industrial park, where a flat plywood disk bearing an icon of Christ was attached to the metal ceiling twenty-two feet overhead. I've worshiped in a church in a strip mall, between a Chinese buffet and a nail salon. I have been to a start-up church that was meeting in the priest's home, where the worship space took a sharp right on its way from the front door to the end of the living room. (My friend commented, "It's the first time I've ever seen an L-shaped nave.") I've been to churches where a borrowed room, available only on Sunday, was converted into a holy place, the throne of God and an outpost of heaven, by setting out a couple of icons on folding easels and a homemade wooden altar.

Is there any particular way that an Orthodox church should look? The earliest congregations gathered in people's homes (Rom. 16:5; 1 Cor. 16:9), and sometimes houses would be set apart more permanently as churches. Once Christianity became legal, in AD 313, believers could start building structures specifically designed for worship. The earliest were based on the Greek and Roman architectural design known as a basilica; *basil* means "king" in Greek, and the basilica was the king's law court.* (If you're thinking, "I thought *basil* was an herb," you're right. Remember that St. Helena found the cross of Christ's crucifixion in Jerusalem? It's said that she found a delicious herb growing over the site, and named it "basil." Basil plants decorate the nave on the Feast of the Exaltation of the Cross, September 14.)

A basilica has a simple design: a rectangle with an entry door at one end, and at the other a semicircle capped by a half-dome called an apse. Sometimes the main body of the rectangle was divided

---

* I'm using the term *basilica* here in its architectural sense alone; in the Roman Catholic Church, a church is called a basilica only when it has received that honorary title from the pope.

into three long aisles, with two rows of columns running down its length. When the center aisle was built higher than the side aisles, the top walls could be pierced with windows, letting in a great deal of light.

In the fourth century, a number of basilica-style churches were built by St. Helena and her son St. Constantine. He was the first Roman emperor to embrace Christianity, and his works included the original St. Peter's in Rome and the Church of the Resurrection in Jerusalem (in the West it's called the Church of the Holy Sepulchre). Churches in such important cities endured a great deal of renovation over the centuries—hostile, benign, or well-intentioned-but-regrettable. The Church of the Resurrection was completely demolished by Jerusalem's Muslim conquerors in the eleventh century, but in the rebuilt church, patches of St. Helena's original mosaic floor can still be seen.

If you wonder what it would have been like to worship in an ancient, intact basilica, you can't do better than visiting the Church of St. Apollinare Nuovo in the Italian city of Ravenna. It was built about AD 500, and even in photos you can get a feel for the wonderful light brought in through the high windows, which sets the great expanses of golden mosaic shimmering. (Sometimes gold tiles are inlaid at different angles so reflected light will shift and twinkle.) Though we usually think of icons as paintings, some of the best-preserved ancient icons were crafted of mosaic tiles, tiny squares of glass containing a layer of color. Mosaics never fade, and can be cleaned of candle smoke and grime, so they give us the best idea of what ancient Christian art looked like.

In the West, the basilica design was expanded by adding a *transept*, another aisle running horizontally across the nave, just below the apse; this gave the whole building the shape of a cross. As these long, narrow buildings grew taller (the fourteenth-century Cathedral of Notre Dame in Paris is a great example), the ceilings would soar to high pointed arches, creating for the worshiper a sense of heaven's endless reach and God's transcendent power. This is a beautiful design, very graceful, which draws the worshiper's eyes to the delicate play of arches crossing overhead. If there's a drawback, it is that such a long nave puts the worshiper far from the altar, and such a high ceiling can make him feel isolated, alone in a crowd.

Church architecture developed differently in the East. Some early churches were built at the site of a martyr's tomb, as a square structure (representing the earth) with a domed roof (representing heaven). Then the apse was borrowed from the basilica design, which bumped out the eastern wall into a semicircle, providing room for an altar. Worshipers would enter through doors on the west and face east, toward the altar, as they prayed.

Why east? Because Christ told us that's where we will see him when he comes again: "As the lightning comes from the east and shines as far as the west, so will be the coming of the Son of man" (Matt. 24:27). He is the "bright morning star" (Rev. 22:16). As early as the fourth century, St. Basil the Great could refer to eastward worship as a custom so ancient that no one knew its origin.[6] While the Jewish tradition was to face Jerusalem to pray, and Muslims face Mecca, Christians have always faced east; even in Japan, Orthodox Christians face east.

A central dome was an early characteristic of Eastern Christian churches—but there's a problem. A dome can only be made so wide. What if you need a bigger church? The building could be enlarged by setting the dome upon four pillars, and expanding the square around it on all sides. You could make the square as large as necessary, and the encompassing dome would still unite the space visually. This design is called "cross-in-square." (We'll see why in a minute.) Just as the Gothic church design spread throughout the Christian West, the cross-in-square is found in all Orthodox lands.

By the way, I found it confusing at first that there were so many different Orthodox lands and churches: Russian, Greek, Romanian, Antiochian, and so on. I assumed that they were all different denominations, like the variety of viewpoints among churches that share the name "Baptist." I learned, though, that all are members of the same worldwide Orthodox Church. Every land should have its own national church, but here in America waves of immigrants set up their own parishes and administrative bodies before that could be organized. The process to create a single American Orthodox Church is under way, though not with brisk American efficiency. There's a saying, "I don't believe in organized religion. I'm Orthodox."

Administrative unity won't make a dramatic difference on the local level, since such churches are already one in the important ways. In a big city a hundred years ago you could have seen an Irish Catholic church, a Polish Catholic church, and an Italian Catholic church, but they knew themselves to be members of a common faith. As those immigrants made America their home, such distinctions melted away, and hopefully the same will happen here. Whether administrative wheels turn quickly or slowly, unity already exists in local parishes, where people from many lands come together and share their traditions.

In the meantime, these different groups (Greek Orthodox, Antiochian Orthodox, and so on) are termed *jurisdictions*, not denominations. They share the same liturgies, faith, and spiritual path, and are in communion with each other. In the United States most worship is in English. (Our fictional St. Felicity Orthodox Church doesn't represent any particular ethnic background; I've intentionally given it elements from many different lands.)

As we step into the nave, we find ourselves in a room that feels much larger than would seem possible, due to the airy height of the ceiling and its dome far overhead. It is hard to get a sense of the shape of this room. Everywhere around us there are curves: round arches, cylindrical pillars, and a generous half-shell ceiling to crown the altar.

As we walk to stand in the center of the church, under that dome, we find ourselves at a crossroads. Extensions (called "bays") reach in all four directions, each framed by two columns. Before us is the bay that extends to the altar, and behind us is the bay that goes back to the church's narthex and front door. If we look left or right, the pairs of columns now enclose the bays on those sides, extending the nave left and right.

These four bays form a cross with arms of equal length, which is the reason for the name "cross-in-square." Churches built on this plan look square from the outside (more or less, allowing for additions), but inside, thanks to the four columns marking off the space, it feels like a cross—one that, nevertheless, has a round ceiling. This is an interesting contrast, and creates a feeling of being gathered together "as a hen gathers her brood under her wings" (Matt. 23:37). Instead of soaring to a heavenly point, such a ceiling "mothers" the congregation and unites it.

Orthodox churches can be built in many different styles, but the cross-in-square is most traditional. It can gain extra bays, till it looks octagonal or even round; these bays can be topped with their own, smaller domes. When those domes are of different heights, sometimes even painted with different designs, the exterior view can be baffling. St. Basil Cathedral (built 1555–1561), in Moscow's Red Square, has a cross-in-square at its center, but with its extra bays and cluster of multihued, snow-shedding "onion domes" it has been described as resembling a bonfire.[7]

It's expensive to complete the icon program in a church, but since St. Felicity has the advantage of being imaginary, we can cover every inch of walls, ceiling, and columns with scenes and people from the Bible and church history. Now it's even harder to get a sense of the shape of the interior space. Yet there is an intimate feeling, thanks to the sheltering dome and the room's gently rounded lines. The full-length saints on the walls and columns are about our size, and might be taken for fellow worshipers—as the saints they represent really are.

The most eye-catching thing in the nave is the wooden screen, like a room divider, that stands between the main worship space and the altar. It is adorned with icons and is called the *iconostasis*, a Greek word meaning "icon stand." The iconostasis developed from a smaller structure, a low wall called a *templon*, which separated the altar area from the worship space in churches of the early centuries. The templon was very like the communion rail in a Western church. (There is no communion rail in an Orthodox church, since we stand to receive Communion.) With time, as the interiors of churches were painted with images of saints and Bible stories, icons were attached to the templon as well. With even more time, it grew larger and higher, to hold more icons, and eventually became our modern-day iconostasis. (We'll examine the iconostasis in more detail in chapter 8.)

The next thing we're likely to notice, as we look around, is that there are no pews. There are short rows of chairs along each side wall, but the main body of the church is open, with oriental rugs spanning the floor. That's why the service books are kept in the narthex. No shelves on pew backs. No pew backs. No pews.

If you've been to the great cathedrals of Europe, you probably noticed that they don't have pews either. Sitting down in church is a fairly recent idea. Recall that, for the first fifteen hundred years, the universal expectation on Sunday morning was that God was going to appear in a tangible way, an *edible* way, of all things, turning ordinary bread and wine into his body and blood. You can understand why people would be standing at attention for that. That God is offering his body as food—offering it even to the lowliest sinner—is astounding, when you think about it. It's a good idea to think about it, because it goes a long way toward explaining the tone of Orthodox worship.

If the focus of worship was instead on the sermon, and helping the people to understand the Scriptures and how to live a Christian life, it would make sense to give them a place to sit down. Pews began to appear after the Protestant Reformation, in the sixteenth century, and their obvious usefulness made them ubiquitous in time.

Now we expect people to sit down while the pastor stands to preach, but the ancient way was the reverse: the teacher alone would sit (we still speak of a "chair" at a university), while students stood respectfully around him, or perhaps "sat at his feet" (Lk. 10:39; Acts 22:3). Chairs, in fact, came into common household use only about five hundred years ago. Not that people didn't sit down, but they sat on stools and benches; a chair with a back was a fancy thing, an emblem of authority. (Those early chairs and thrones were uncomfortable, too; it took some time for people to figure out that the back did not have to be at exactly a ninety-degree angle.) The Greek word for "chair" is *kathedra*, and a cathedral is the building where the bishop keeps his chair.

One functional result of a church not having pews is that it doesn't have kneelers either. Surprisingly, Orthodox worship doesn't involve much kneeling. It's standing up, almost all the time. Most people sit for the sermon—finding one of the chairs or just sitting on the floor, if that's most convenient.

Newcomers shouldn't feel anxious about all this standing. It is always all right to sit down if you need to. The "don't watch your neighbor" guideline applies here, too. The most important times to stand, if you're able, are during the reading of the Gospel and the Eucharistic prayers. Other than that, if everybody else stands up, go ahead and do the same.

Though St. Felicity follows the Old World style, you'll see pews in many (perhaps most) Orthodox churches. A building purchased from another denomination may have come with pews, and some new Orthodox churches are even built with them. That's an instance of cultural sensitivity: when Orthodox immigrants observed that it was the American custom to have pews, they adapted to it. For the same reason the church may have an organ, though Orthodox worship is nearly always sung a cappella, without accompaniment. Even when an organ is used, it only undergirds the melody in a simple way. Every parish needs a choir director, but it may not need an organist.

Near the narthex door, where we just came in, we see a stand with a slanting top, like a lectern, made to hold a single icon. The role of this stand—it's called an *analogion*—is like that of the blackboard at a restaurant, the one that lists "Today's Specials." The icon placed here will show who or what is special today. If it is the feast of St. George, we'll see an icon of that young man, on horseback in his military array. If it is January 6, the Feast of the Theophany—Epiphany in the West—we'll see Christ standing in the River Jordan, as St. John baptizes him. Sometimes the icon changes daily, but when there's a major feast the corresponding icon might hold this place for a week or more. (In some churches you'll find this icon-stand in the middle of the nave, rather than just inside the door as here.)

It's not likely that a church would own an icon for every day of the year and every saint on the calendar—there could be dozens of saints each day. When the specific icon isn't available, an icon of the parish's patron, St. Felicity in this case, will be the default placeholder, and we see her here today.

I chose St. Felicity for this imaginary church because she is my patron saint. She was a North African slave, killed in the Carthage arena in AD 203 as part of the birthday celebration for the emperor's son. She appears in the icon as a slender young woman holding a cross (the emblem of a martyr) and a scroll. Felicity was arrested along with several other members of her church. She was pregnant at the time, and feared that, because the Romans did not execute pregnant women, she would be separated from her companions, held back to die later in the company of criminals. Everyone prayed for her labor to begin, and she gave birth in her prison cell to a little girl, who was adopted by a family in her congregation.

In labor, Felicity cried out in pain. A prison guard mocked her, saying in so many words, "You're screaming now? Just wait." In her icon, St. Felicity holds an open scroll that gives her reply: "Now I suffer; but in the arena another will suffer for me, because I will be suffering for him."

Felicity was only a slave, but the leader of these Christian prisoners, St. Perpetua, was a brilliant and educated young woman, herself mother of an infant son. Perpetua kept a prison diary during the days leading up to their martyrdom, and it is one of the treasures of early Christian writing. You can find it, and most of the other ancient documents I'll mention, online.

Orthodox don't think of St. Felicity as merely a historical figure. We expect that she is alive in heaven now, and continually worshiping before God's throne. We ask her to pray for us, just as we would ask any friend.

Beside St. Felicity's icon stands a rectangular box, table-height, of sand. This is for candles; many people, after venerating the icon on the stand, will light their candle and place it here. There are several other places in the church where candles could be placed—brass stands in front of Christ and the Virgin Mary on the iconostasis, and near other icons elsewhere in the church.

I find that the topic of prayer and the saints is one of the things that makes nonliturgical Christians nervous. Their objections have a realistic basis, because prayer to the saints has at times gotten completely out of hand. We'll cover that topic in the next chapter.

3
"So Great a Cloud"
(HEB. 12:1)

Loving the Theotokos, The Prayers of the Saints

n the Middle Ages, in Europe, an idea arose that one should go through appropriate channels with a prayer need: bring it to your patron saint, who would then carry it to Mary, who would then submit it to Christ, who would then present it to the Father. A chain of command, so to speak—a pattern familiar from feudal society.

Of course, that was the only society medieval people knew. A peasant could never hope to tell a king his troubles. Christianity was a thrilling liberation from such bonds, because that peasant could go right over the king's head. But our peasant would not expect to go straight to the top. He would think himself blessed that he could catch the ear of a heavenly underling, and put the petition in motion. Unfortunately, this led to some very bad ideas about the allocation of power in heaven, most notably in the case of the Virgin Mary, the *Theotokos.**

---

*   The title *Theotokos,* which Orthodox Christians commonly and constantly use, means "Birthgiver of God." It was in use by AD 250, and probably arose in reaction against an idea that Jesus had not always been God. To say that Mary is the Theotokos is to say that Christ was God even in his mother's womb; the theological point is about him rather than her.

Because "Birthgiver of God" is unwieldy, Theotokos is often translated "Mother of God," which is all right as long as you understand it doesn't mean she gave birth to God the Father or the Trinity. Mary does not precede the eternal God, of course. But from the moment she responded to the angel, God was fully present in her womb.

I once saw a small comic-book tract (maybe you've encountered those Jack Chick publications) that showed the Virgin Mary kneeling before God's throne; she was praying that he would forgive those Christians who treat her like an idol. Funnily enough, that's exactly what liturgical Christians believe she does—she prays for us. She must pray especially for those who have misunderstood her role, and "worshiped and served the creature rather than the Creator" (Rom. 1:25). Misguided affection may have been offered with the best of intentions, and in simple ignorance or exuberant-but-misguided love; but it is, all the same, a very serious sin and must grieve her profoundly.

It's a shame that inappropriately extreme adoration of the Theotokos has made some Christians wary of her altogether. If we didn't have those excesses before our eyes, we'd find it natural to accord her at least as much admiration as we give to the apostle Paul—and more, in fact, considering her unique and tender role in Jesus' life. He must have loved her very much, and would want us to love and honor her as well.

We don't preach the Virgin Mary; we preach only Christ. But when we're at home in the family of the Lord, we cherish her companionship. Likewise, you might discover on a visit to a friend's home that you like his parents and siblings, too. That would not diminish your affection for your friend, but enhance it.

But how do you find the line between love for the Virgin that is appropriately warm and appreciative, and idolatry?

We can start by looking for clues in Christian practice of the early centuries, before the medieval era. For example, the Scriptures tell us that, when Mary knew she had conceived the Messiah, she said, "All generations will call me blessed" (Lk. 1:48). She foretold that all generations would rejoice with her at the news of this great blessing, that she was invited to be the mother of the Son of God. Perhaps it is all right to do that, to call her blessed?

The Theotokos holds a unique and dramatic role in history, since she was the one on whom all the universe waited, in that silent moment after the angel spoke. She said, "Let it be to me according to your word," and all salvation history flows forward from that point. Christ's story begins with that small, private moment and broadens and increases until the end of time. We rejoice with her, and praise her for her willingness and courage, for her "Yes."

Next, we can take a look at how the earliest Christians regarded her. I sometimes hear people speak of the European church of AD 1000 or 1200 as if it were the early church, but that's a thousand years later; it's halfway through the story. It's also a different continent and a different culture. When we instead look at Christians in the earliest centuries, living in the greater neighborhood of Christ's birthplace, we don't find excessive adulation of the Virgin Mary, or speculation about her rank and power, but instead simple, warm affection. She was dearly loved. She was viewed with great fondness as *one of us*—a fellow human being, born as we are, who responded to God's calling with extraordinary faith.

The flavor of this affection comes through strongly in a story that was immensely popular in the Christian East—copies and fragments have been found in eight ancient languages—that tells her story from her conception through the birth of Christ. When this work was first translated into Latin, in AD 1522, it was given the bulky title *The Protevangelium of James.*† Scholars think this story was in written form by AD 150, and as I studied it I came to think that it sounded like the kind of story that was originally passed on by word of mouth, as the Gospels were. It appears to come from a distinctly Jewish context since as there are references to practices only Jewish hearers were likely to know about (for example, Exod. 28:36–38). It's not a careful work of literature, but a straightforward and charming tale that reveals how much curiosity early Christians had about Jesus' life. You could call it a "prequel": What was his mom like? What was his grandmother like? Where did they live? Were they pious? Were they poor?

---

† In my book *Mary As the Early Christians Knew Her*, I provide a fresh annotated translation. *Protevangelium* means "pre-Gospel" ("proto-evangelium").

The story tells us how Mary took her first steps, and describes the party her parents gave on her first birthday. It says that, after her third birthday, her parents brought her to the temple, where the high priest welcomed and kissed her, and sat her down on the third step of the altar; "and she danced with her feet, and all the house of Israel loved her." That this early Christian audience found it easy to believe that a little girl could be so doted on seems, to me, significant; in too many cultures, little girls have been regarded as worthless, and in hard times they are the first to go. Not so among the early Christians.

So in the *Protevangelium* you can observe the natural warmth that the early Christians felt toward Christ's mother, and such love can be entirely appropriate. If you are one of those who are cautiously tiptoeing up to Mary, be assured that you can feel that same appreciation without making a leap to something more grandiose.

Some Protestant Christians have trouble with the title "Ever-Virgin," envisioning Mary and Joseph as a young couple in love, who would have reasonably begun marital relations after the Virgin Birth of Jesus. Before becoming Orthodox, I assumed that the ever-virginity of Mary was one of those traditions that arose in the Middle Ages, attributable to an unhealthy discomfort with matters of sex and the body. I found out that's not the case, though. The tradition that Mary remained virgin before, during, and after the birth of Christ goes all the way back to the beginning. It's there in the *Protevangelium*, for instance.

Why would the early Christians claim that Mary remained a virgin all her life? It wasn't a concern they would have inherited from Judaism; that faith did not especially admire lifelong virginity, but took marital love and resultant children as a blessing. The only reason the early Christians would have included this detail in Christ's story was because they believed it was true.

Some who reject her ever-virginity point to a line in Matthew's Gospel which says that Joseph "knew her not until [*heos*] she had borne a son" (Matt. 1:25). They infer that this means he "knew" her (had sexual intercourse with her—it's an Old Testament euphemism) after the birth.

But the text doesn't say that; it speaks only of what happened *before* Christ was born. The same construction occurs when Jesus says, "Lo, I am with you always, until [*heos*] the close of the age" (Matt. 28:20). He wasn't warning us that after the end of the age we'll be on our own.

Others challenge Mary's ever-virginity with the Scriptures that refer to Jesus' brothers (e.g., Matt. 13:55); those are siblings born to Mary and Joseph after Jesus' birth, they say, and were his half brothers. (No one claims they were Jesus' full brothers, for Jesus had a unique Father.) In reply, Western Christians who believe in Mary's ever-virginity usually say that the term embraces those who are cousins as well; they were children of Joseph's siblings.

But Eastern Christians have preserved a different and very ancient story, in which those brothers are not Jesus' half brothers but his stepbrothers. It's told in the *Protevangelium*. There Joseph is an old man, a widower, who was chosen by lot to be Mary's guardian. He has children of his own, perhaps not much younger than Mary herself. So he objects strenuously—"I have sons and I am an old man, but she is a young girl! I will appear a laughingstock to the children of Israel!"—but the high priest prevails on him to accept her.

Mary came into Joseph's home as stepmother to the children from his first marriage. Jesus, generally thought to be Joseph's youngest son, and the only offspring of his second marriage, would have grown up running and playing with those siblings in the streets of Nazareth. Villagers would naturally call them his brothers and sisters.

The early Christians understood these children to be his step-brothers; Protestants who reject Mary's ever-virginity understand them to be his half brothers. Scripture doesn't compel us to either understanding. We have to choose whose interpretation of the Scriptures we're going to trust.‡

---

‡ It's worth considering that, for the first fifteen hundred years, Christians interpreted these Scriptures to support Mary's ever-virginity. Even Reformers such as Luther and Zwingli held that view.

Which brings us to a fundamental issue: How can we know which Bible interpretation is right?

Though all Christians look to the authority of the Bible, we don't regard each book and verse equally. There are many people who could quote John 3:16 ("God so loved the world . . ."), but would have no idea what John 3:15 or 3:17 say. Might as well admit it: when it comes to the Scriptures, we play favorites. There are passages in the Bible that we read and reread with ever-deepening wonder, and other passages that we read occasionally, dutifully, and without registering much illumination.

That might sound shocking—to claim that we presume to judge between Bible verses. Yet we do it all the time, and could scarcely function otherwise. If you tried to esteem every single verse to be the equal of all others, you'd be unable to make sense of the Scriptures at all. So we read it through an interpretive screen.

What's more, we acquire that interpretation before we ever open the Bible for ourselves. Before we read it, we've already been taught how to understand what we'll read. We're taught which verses to value most highly, how to understand difficult verses, and what themes we should expect to find. There's a saying that "there is no Bible reading without Bible interpretation," and we are given an interpretation before we start to read.

So how should you approach this extraordinary book? You might decide that you're going to read the Scriptures for yourself, pray about them, listen to your heart, and then decide what's right. That's how we end up with, some say, twenty thousand different Christian denominations.

Or you might reflect that "no prophecy of scripture is a matter of one's own interpretation" (2 Pet. 1:20), and acknowledge that you need guidance. You might say, "I'm going to follow the teachings of the church that is founded on the Bible."

But they *all* believe they're founded on the Bible. Sincere Scripture-reading people can come up with a lot of different ways of sincerely reading the Scriptures.

Perhaps you decide to study theology and the different approaches to Scripture, and follow the teacher you think gets it right. This was a popular approach even in the first century: "Each one of you says, 'I belong to Paul,' or 'I belong to Apollos,' or 'I belong to Cephas,' or 'I belong to Christ'" (1 Cor. 1:12). Some people even choose a teacher alive today, and accept his original interpretations of Scripture; but a person who claims, in the twenty-first century, to have found something in the Bible that no one ever saw before has probably found something that is not really there.

A friend told me in an e-mail that he worked diligently to acquire the skills to interpret the Scriptures, going through Bible college, seminary, and graduate school, learning the ancient languages. "I expected to dig my way down to the foundation and confirm everything I'd been taught," he wrote. "Instead, the further down I went, the weaker everything seemed." He eventually realized that "I had only acquired the ability to manipulate the Bible to say pretty much anything I wanted it to." He concluded that "if the Bible was meant to say anything, it was meant to say it within a community, and this was the only alternative to cynicism."

A community. Being a Christian means being a member of a community; you just can't do it on your own.

It's tempting to view the Bible as an object, pristine and perfect, that each person can confidently approach on a private basis, like the machine you face when you enter a voting booth. But that confidence hasn't been well proved over the centuries, has it? How can there be so many different interpretations of the same book? When you look at the cacophony of Christian beliefs around the world, all rooted in different views of the same Scriptures, it looks as if "that they all may be one" (John 17:21) is not going to happen on a spontaneous basis.

For me, any time there is a difference of opinion in interpreting Scripture, the early church's viewpoint wins out. Not because they were better Christians (though they did handle persecution more courageously than we would, I suspect). No, it's because they were the New Testament's original authors, and its original audience. They wrote it, and they were its intended readers. That just gives them an edge when it comes to understanding what St. Paul or St. Luke is talking about. Someone living in those times, in the neighborhood of Bible lands (maybe even a relative or descendant of Bible authors and characters), speaking New Testament Greek every day, simply has a natural advantage.

Likewise, scholars could beat their heads against a contested line of Shakespeare for centuries, while a London laborer in 1600 could explain it to you right away. It doesn't mean he's smarter than the professors; it's just that he's talking about his own familiar world.

A French monk, St. Vincent of Lérins (AD 380–445), came up with a useful guideline for understanding the Scriptures. He wrote, "All possible care must be taken that we hold that faith which has been believed everywhere, always, and by all."[8] That means holding the interpretation that is found most widely in the church, geographically; which has been held from the earliest times; and which has been most affirmed by church fathers and councils. (This is called "the Vincentian Canon.")

When some people hear that definition, they picture the pathetically tiny list of beliefs that all self-identified Christians of today would affirm. That's not it, for that leaves out the "always." Wherever there is division among Christians, it can be traced back to someone, at some point in history, walking away from an earlier consensus.

But how can you find out what the early church believed? You might think there's a hole in the record; a graduate from a Lutheran seminary told me that, when he went back to check his classroom notes on church history, he found that the years between the apostles and the sixteenth-century Reformation had been covered in three pages. But in reality there is no such gap in Christian history. Believers taught believers from one generation to the next, all down the line.

There's no gap in Christian writing either. In the decades after Christ's resurrection, St. Paul wrote his letters, and the Evangelists wrote their Gospels, but they were far from being the only Christian writers. Then and ever after believers wrote all sorts of things: letters to other Christians, commentaries, collections of sermons, accounts of spiritual experiences, prayers and hymns—a range much like that found in a bookstore's Christian section today. Most of these early works are available online, and you're welcome to plunge in and enjoy.

But it wouldn't make sense to try to grasp the ancient understanding by reading all of the church fathers. Even if it were possible to digest such a vast number of works (my hardback edition runs to thirty-eight hefty, small-print volumes), the Fathers don't always agree with each other. Sometimes they make mistakes, for even the saints aren't perfect. (There's a saying that "100 percent of the Fathers are right 80 percent of the time.") After all, the early Christians didn't learn their faith by studying the writings of the church fathers. Neither did the Fathers, for that matter.

Everyone, from eminent theologians down to shepherdesses, learned the faith through worship. That is where they encountered the Scriptures—not as a book to study in private, but read aloud in the midst of the community. A church's Gospel book is beautiful, clad in gold, held aloft in procession, treated with honor; at some services, worshipers line up to venerate it with a kiss. It wasn't a private relationship with a printed text, but a communal relationship with the Word of God, a living word spoken aloud in their midst.

Those Scripture readings did not stand alone, but were surrounded with beauty: hymns, icons, processions, homilies, and sacraments. The entire worship experience taught the faith, echoing and reinforcing the Scriptures in multiple forms. Saturated in the faith this way, children and fishermen could know the Bible as well as any scholar.

The Bible was an organic part of the community's life from the start. The same Holy Spirit who inspired the Scriptures has accompanied the body of Christ all these centuries, guiding it "into all the truth," as Christ promised (John 16:13).

The early church wrote the New Testament. They were the first readers of the New Testament—the people the authors were picturing as they sat down to write. The early church chose which books would be *in* the New Testament, discerning where the Holy Spirit had spoken and where he had not. (Some books they enjoyed very much, like the *Protevangelium*, didn't make the cut.) We trust them to have decided wisely. Any time we open the New Testament we show the confidence we already have in the early church's discernment.

When it comes time to decide which interpretation of a Scripture verse is correct, how do you choose? For me, the consensus of the early church, which is expressed in their common worship, will always have the edge. Throughout this book we will be looking at and listening to worship,§ to grasp that ancient and continuing faith.

Orthodox Christians look to Mary as our best example for living a Christian life. She is hailed in our hymns as our "Captain," our "Champion Leader," an active and vigorous heavenly friend. She is more than a role model, for Christ told St. John at the Cross, and us through him, "Behold, your mother" (John 19:27). We are invited to love her with the affection of a child, and she prays for us as a mother would.

Having said that, you might be shocked by some of the language addressed to her and other saints in Orthodox worship, for it does tend to be effusive. Worship language is often exuberant; it's not always careful and precise, like the language of theological description or a creed would be. It's more like the speeches made at a

---

§   The word "Orthodox" joins the Greek *ortho*, "straight" or "correct" (as in orthodontics, straight teeth), with *doxa*, a word that lies behind both "doctrine" and "doxology" (which means glory or praise). "Orthodoxy" means both the right theology and the right worship.

   That's when the word has a capital "O," and refers to the Eastern Orthodox Church. Small-o "orthodox" can refer to anything in its classic form— orthodox medical treatment, an orthodox karate stance, even orthodox (traditional) Christian beliefs held by someone who's not a member of the capital-O Orthodox Church.

rollicking testimonial dinner, where the guests of honor are praised beyond all bounds. When you have something big to express—especially when it's gratitude—words are bound to fall short. What most people do is add more words. Add more *extravagant* words.

As I was writing this book the feast day of the apostle James rolled around—not the brother of St. John the Evangelist, but the one who doesn't get much attention, called "James the Less." Nevertheless, the hymn for his feast referred to him as "the most venerable of Jesus' disciples." If you asked an Orthodox person, "Who do you think is the most venerable of the disciples? St. James the Less, right?" she'd be perplexed. Even if she'd just sung this line, she might reply, "Why would you think that?"

So our worship sometimes sounds over the top ("Save us, O Virgin," "You are our only hope"), but we know what we mean. Mostly, we mean, "Pray for us." We *don't* mean that Mary has the power to grant eternal salvation, that she was created differently than other humans, or that she supplied some additional saving factor at the Cross. It doesn't mean that she can (or would) do anything independently from the will of her Son.¶

I think that's where things went wrong in Western Christianity. A thread of devotion took shape that saw Mary as an independent operator, with her own allotment of power. In Tim Perry's book *Mary for Evangelicals,* I ran across a clue about when this began. Perry reviews many writings about Mary, starting from the very beginning of church history, and eventually comes to a passage by St. Peter Damian, a saintly abbot who was born in Ravenna, Italy, in AD 1007.

St. Peter Damian recounts a legend that there was a cleric who, having behaved badly all his life, felt anxiety as death drew near. He appealed to Mary for help, reminding her that, despite his dissolute and negligent life, he had at least faithfully performed her prayers. "You are my witness," he said, "that 'seven times a day I praised

¶ Some Orthodox translators have used "Mediatress" in reference to the Virgin Mary, wholly unaware of how explosive that term is in Western Christian history. They just meant that she prays for us, for anyone who intercedes is in a sense a mediator. (It could also be a reference to her body being the *medium*, the matter, from which Christ took flesh.)

you' [Ps. 118/119:164**], and although I am a sinner, although I am
unworthy, I did not cheat you any of the canonical hours in your
honor."⁹

St. Peter says that he doesn't know whether the story is true, but
he affirms its message: no matter how much a person ignores God's
will and worship, if he consistently offers the appointed prayers
to Mary, he "will have the mother of the Judge as his helper and
advocate in his day of need."

I don't know about that. If he's saying only that Mary will *pray*
for such a one, maybe she does. But the point of the story seems to
be that Mary can award salvation to her servants by her own will,
independently of God's judgment.

That is where the trouble crept in, when Mary began to be seen as
having power apart from the Trinity. That idea may reflect guesses
people made about heaven based on what they knew of earthly
empires—that sometimes the mother of the king was even more
powerful than he was, and could enact her will over his objections.
Not so in heaven, though. Mary is great in heaven precisely because
she did, and still does, the will of the Father in all things.

** Should that be Ps. 118 or 119? The Jewish Scriptures (the Old Testament)
used by the first Christians numbered the Psalms differently from ours
today; usually, but not always, it's one number lower. Here's the backstory. A
couple of centuries before Christ's birth, the Hebrew language was passing
out of common use, so Jewish scholars produced a translation into Greek,
the most widely used language of the time. It's called "the Septuagint"
(abbreviated LXX), because it was said to be the work of seventy Jewish
scholars. Nearly all Old Testament quotations in the New Testament are
from the LXX. Orthodox Christians have continued using the LXX as their
Old Testament all these years.

Oddly enough, the LXX is older than any complete Hebrew text of the
Jewish Scriptures. While the LXX was produced around 250 BC, the Hebrew
"Masoretic text" (abbreviated MT), the basis of most English Bible translations today, was produced a thousand years later, between the seventh and
tenth centuries AD. The two texts are mostly identical, of course, but when
there are differences, they can be interesting; for example, the LXX renders
Isaiah's prophecy as "a virgin will conceive," while the MT says "a young
woman will conceive" (Isa. 7:14). Again, the LXX is a pre-Christian *Jewish*
translation, made centuries before Christ's birth.

What about that present tense, though? Even to assume that the Virgin is *active* in heaven, aware of life on earth and capable of hearing our prayers, requires some groundwork. So let's ask: Where are the saints now? What are they up to?

It's often said that Western Christianity focuses on the Cross and Eastern Christianity on the Resurrection. Indeed, the most significant truth, to Orthodox Christians, is "Christ is risen!" We cry out these words hundreds of times, in dozens of languages, in the weeks following Easter Sunday.[††]

It was our own sins that enslaved us. "The wages of sin is death" (Rom. 6:23), and every child of Adam and Eve has since been born with a fatal susceptibility to sin, bound to pass through the door of death and into the shadowy realm of Hades. There could be no return to Paradise, for a cherub with a flaming sword stood to guard the gates (Gen. 3:24).

But God could not bear to see his beloved creatures, made in his own image and likeness (Gen. 1:26), damaged and dying. Christ came to rescue us, putting on our human nature and following our common course, even into the realm of Death. (It's the strategy we see in some action movies, where the hero rescues his imprisoned friend by first getting himself arrested.)

- "So will the Son of Man be three days and three nights in the heart of the earth" (Matt. 12:40).
- "He . . . descended into the lower parts of the earth" (Eph. 4:9).
- "[Christ was] . . . made alive in the spirit; in which he went and preached to the spirits in prison, who formerly did not obey" (1 Pet. 3:18–20).
- "The gospel was preached even to the dead, that though judged in the flesh like men, they might live in the spirit like God" (1 Pet. 4:6).

---

†† The Orthodox call this feast *Pascha*, pronounced "Pahs-kah." The term comes from the Hebrew *Pesach*, meaning Passover.

- "They shall gather them into a prison . . . and after many generations they shall be visited" (Isa. 24:22 LXX; this is one of the
  rare times that the Septuagint differs from the Masoretic text.)

Christ went into Hades in the guise of a corpse—but, once there,
he revealed his divinity. He flooded the darkness with his light and
power, vanquishing the evil one and setting the captives free.

The icon of the Resurrection (in Greek, the *Anastasis*) shows Christ
victorious in the realm of Death, and one of the most compelling
examples is a fourteenth-century fresco in the Church of Chora, near
Istanbul. Christ is centered in the image, robed in radiant white, standing
on the broken gates of Hades. He is braced and striding, pulling Adam
and Eve from their stony tombs, and they come up flying; he grasps them
by their wrists, not their hands, for all power streams from him. On one
side, King David, King Solomon, and St. John the Forerunner (called
"the Baptist" in the West) marvel at this wondrous sight; on the other,
the righteous of all ages await their turn, with Abel first in line behind his
mother. Below Christ's feet, beneath the fallen gates, is a black pit strewn
with broken chains and locks, and there we see the evil one bound in his
own fetters. "The reason the Son of God appeared was to destroy the
works of the devil" (1 John 3:8).‡‡

This victory over death has an immediate, practical implication.
It means that the departed in Christ are actually *not dead*. Even now,
at this moment, they are in God's presence, worshiping before his
throne (Rev. 7:9). We on earth still stumble on this continuing
battlefield, but they are participating in a brilliant peace, illuminated
by the light of the Lamb (Rev. 21:23). They see reality more clearly
than we do. Their prayers are more effortlessly in tune with God's
will. They are continuously before God's throne, holding "golden
bowls of incense, which are the prayers of the saints" (Rev. 5:8).

---

‡‡ Make a mental note of that, because it will keep coming up: in the Christian
East, Christ's work is understood primarily as defeating death and the devil,
and rescuing us from their bonds. In the West a different idea emerged about
a thousand years ago, that Christ's suffering paid the Father the debt for our
sin. From rescue to repayment. It made a world of difference, and we'll talk
more about it later.

Those are the simple yet exhilarating thoughts that caused early believers to turn to the holy departed and ask their intercession. But the idea of "praying to" saints is still very troubling to many Christians, and I think part of the trouble is precisely in that little word "pray."

If you had a big prayer need coming up—say, a job interview—you might ask others to pray for you. When you ask for the prayers of family and friends, you convey the request by phone or e-mail. When you ask the saints, you send the request by prayer. Like talking, e-mailing, or phoning, praying is a means of communication; instead of spoken words or typed letters it takes the form of a directed thought. So a prayer is like an envelope, and you can put different sorts of content inside. If the intended recipient is God, the content may well be worship; if the recipient is a friend among the saints, the content is most likely a request for them to support you in prayer.

The English word *prayer* used to refer to any sort of request. A previous generation might well say to a dinner companion, "I pray thee, pass the broccoli." But with time, the word became restricted to requests made of those in heaven. You're not worshiping a saint when you make these requests any more than you're worshiping your friends when you ask for their earthly prayers.

It's like we're standing in a circle of friends before Christ. Usually we speak to him directly, but sometimes we'll turn to another member of the circle and ask for support: "Put in a good word for me" or "Help me out here." Such connections don't diminish our relationship with Christ; if anything, the friendships we form with others who love him, whether living or departed, enrich and strengthen our faith.

I explained this to a friend once, and she responded, "Thanks all the same, but I'm still going to go to the Lord directly." I said, "All right; if that's what you want, I won't pray for you anymore." You see, if the question is "directness," asking heavenly prayers is no different from asking earthly prayers. The question then becomes: Why should anybody pray for *anybody*? We could send all our prayers directly to the Lord, and not bother with fellow humans.

You could even go back another step, and ask why we should pray for *ourselves*. After all, "Your Father knows what you need before you ask him" (Matt. 6:8). Since God already knows what's best for us, why should we pester him with our requests?

When you start thinking about the whole matter of prayer, you run into many such tangles. You might feel that you got that job because so many people were praying for you—but that can't mean you *wouldn't* have gotten it if some of them slacked off. It can't mean that people who have no one to pray for them never receive any blessings. It can't mean that God won't listen to prayers until the request-counter rings up a certain number of unique petitioners.

And yet we know that we *should* pray for our needs; we have no doubt about that. We can see that our Lord praised the widow who would not stop importuning a judge for justice (Lk. 18:1–8). We are also supposed to pray for others, since St. James told the sick to call the church elders to come and minister prayer and anointing (Jas. 5:13–16).

If someone asked you, "Why do you ask friends to pray for you? Why don't you just go to the Lord directly?" or, "Why do you pray at all, since God already knows best?" you might have trouble putting an answer into words. Still, it's clear, if just from the urging in our hearts, that we should come to our Lord with all our worries, for ourselves and others. He could certainly deal with every case "directly," without anybody's help, without anyone's asking, but we're not meant to be solo Christians. "We go to heaven together and to hell alone," a Romanian saying goes.

All that sounds fine, but you may still wonder why we should ask the saints in glory to pray for us. The reason goes back to that earlier point—that they are not dead, but alive in heaven, and already in constant prayer.§§ We ask them to pray for us because we believe in the Resurrection.

---

§§ Incidentally, the Orthodox custom is to say that someone "reposed" rather than "died."

Imagine that you had a dear friend who was going through his final illness, who had always been diligent in praying for others. While sitting at his bedside you might say, "When you come before the throne of God, please pray for me. Don't stop praying for me." Likewise, when you imagine yourself, after death, entering God's presence, don't you see yourself praying for those you left behind?

The whole universe is more porous than we think. The saints are always before the throne of God, but in a mystery, they're also *with us.* "Since we are surrounded by so great a cloud of witnesses" (Heb. 12:1), we are never alone. The "great cloud" accompanies us in our daily lives and supports us in our spiritual combat. They are our unseen companions, our older brothers and sisters in the faith, whose prayers help us wend our way through this fallen world.

If there is a Christian of ages past whom you particularly admire, whom you feel close to, you can reflect upon the fact that he is alive in the presence of God now and praying with all the company of the saints. You might keep his companionship in mind as you go through the day, and feel encouraged by it. You could ask for his prayers, and thank him for that help. As with our earthly friends, the company of other believers doesn't compete with our faith in God, but rather enhances it.

However, don't focus on that relationship in an unhealthy way; the saint is your fellow companion in Christ, and not a substitute for praying "directly." The Old Testament warnings about necromancy and séances are there for a reason. If you keep trying to get information out of the departed, such as knowledge of the future, you will surely experience something sooner or later—something counterfeit. Earthly and heavenly friends join us in intercession, but our main focus is always on the Lord.

4

"Upon This Rock"

(MATT. 16:18)

Quick History Lesson, East and West Divide, Filioque, Conciliarity

No matter how familiar you are with the range of churches and practices in Western Christianity, Eastern Orthodoxy can be full of surprises. In fact, you may still wonder how there can even *be* such a thing as "Eastern Christianity." Isn't this a Western religion? Let's have a quick history lesson.

Picture where the Christian faith began, on a hilltop outside Jerusalem. It immediately started spreading in all directions at once: south into Ethiopia and through the Sinai Peninsula, east through Iraq and to India and beyond, north through modern-day Lebanon, Syria, and Turkey, west across Bulgaria, Macedonia, Greece, on into Italy, and throughout all Europe. The known world was a network of trade routes stretching from China to Ireland, and missionaries went farther and faster than you might think. Christians in southern India say the apostle Thomas brought them the gospel in AD 52 (and they don't think of that great evangelist and martyr as "Doubting").

From the Euro-American perspective, Christianity next set up a central office in Rome, and lapsed into spindly dependence elsewhere. Christians of the East see it differently, though. For many centuries, Christianity was actually more robust in Eastern and Southern lands than it was in Western Europe.

Every history lesson needs a map, and for this we will use your left hand. Open it, palm toward you, tilted slightly so that thumb points northwest and index finger northeast. Now assign your thumb to Rome. That's where they speak Latin, and their culture is characterized by all the military and administrative precision we associate with the Roman Empire. Now, over on your fingertips, you see a half-moon string of cities. Constantinople (pointing northeast) is farthest north, sitting at the pinpoint juncture of Asia and Europe. Next comes Antioch of Syria (where "the disciples were for the first time called Christians," Acts 11:26), then Jerusalem. Christians in the Middle East knew the culture, language, and history of the Bible like it was their own backyard. Because it *was* their own backyard. Finally, furthest south, is the city of Alexandria, capital of Egypt, home to many flavors of mysticism and spirituality. Christian monasticism got its start here.

These five cities are called the *Pentarchy* ("Five Rulers"), and were the great centers of early Christianity. But you'll notice that the four Eastern cities have more in common with each other than they do with Rome. They all speak Greek, for one thing, since it was the common trade language of the time, as English is today. (That's why the New Testament was written in Greek.) You can see how the Christians of Rome and those farther East might gradually grow apart. Misunderstandings, once they began, would be hard to clear up. Geographic distance, language differences, and cultural variations all played a part in a gradual estrangement between the churches East and West.

The most divisive issue had to do with the authority of the pope. Christians of the East recognized Rome as the foremost of the five great cities, because it was the most powerful metropolis of the ancient world, the New York City of its day. Jerusalem was the biblical Holy City and homeland of the faith, but it was small in worldly terms. Rome, as the saying goes, was where all roads led. The bishop of Rome, the pope, was considered "first among equals."

But over the years East and West developed different ideas of what that meant. In the East, all bishops were seen as equal in authority, no matter how small or remote the city they ruled (their *diocese*). The bishop of Rome held honorary precedence, but they didn't think this empowered him to rule the whole church. We could liken their understanding of "first among equals" to the office of chief justice of the Supreme Court: it's a genuine honor, but doesn't empower him to hire and fire the other justices, or tell them how to vote. So Eastern Christians did not think the bishop of Rome had the power to govern Christians worldwide, or to make changes within another bishop's diocese, or to issue theological opinions that everyone else had to accept.

The first millennium was a rough time for the Western Roman Empire—Goths and Vandals, Huns and Vikings, kingdoms rising and falling, alliances ever shifting. In that time of extreme political instability there were plenty of good practical reasons for the Roman Church to insist on its own politics-transcending authority. All across Europe, over the course of several centuries, there was chaos, carnage, and significant cultural loss.

The Roman emperor Constantine the Great (AD 274–337), recognizing how things stood, moved the empire's capital far away from volatile Rome. He chose a strategically placed town at the eastern end of the Mediterranean, Byzantium, and built it into a great city. It was called Constantinople, "City of Constantine," and hailed as the "Second Rome."*

It was this emperor, St. Constantine, who legalized Christian faith in AD 313, putting an end to centuries of persecution. After that, a stable Christian culture took shape in the East and flourished for over a thousand years. (The fall of Constantinople to the Ottoman

---

* To be clear, Constantinople was the capital of the *Roman* Empire. There never was a Byzantine Empire. That term was created a few centuries ago by a German historian, and it can be useful when discussing history. But it would have baffled its citizens; though culturally Greek, they called themselves Romans (in Turkey today Christians are still called "Rum").

invaders in AD 1453 is generally seen as the sunset of that great era, though Christians live in those lands still, sometimes under persecution.) We could arguably call Christianity an "Eastern religion," given its first-millennium strength in the Holy Land, the Middle East, Asia Minor, and Africa.

In the (comparative) peace of the Eastern Roman Empire, the faith had room to thrive. I've already mentioned the extensive writings of the early church, which include a great deal of preaching and Bible commentary. It's impressive how thoroughly those writers knew the Scriptures, given that they had very little in the way of concordances and other study tools that we take for granted. I've read the Bible through a number of times, but when I read these early works I keep running into verses that I had never noticed.†

Their love of Scripture was also evident in the beautiful handmade Bibles they produced. I've seen Bibles lettered in gold ink on vellum dipped in the purple dye of royalty. Constantine himself commissioned fifty richly made copies of the Bible, two of which are preserved in museums today.

All seven of the great ecumenical councils, held between AD 325 and 787, took place in the East. ("Ecumenical" here means "of the whole household," that is, a council attended by bishops from the entire Christian world.) Most of the church fathers lived in the East, and most early writings are in Greek; even in Rome, Christians worshiped in Greek until about AD 380.[10] Though St. Augustine looms large in the West, he's only one of a very large company of writers (and his theology comes in for some criticism in the East, as we'll see later).

---

† For example, the Syrian poet St. Romanos (AD 475–556) wrote a hymn, "On the Victory of the Cross," in which the devil and Hades argue about whether the Crucifixion means their triumph or defeat. The devil tells Hades that if he's scared of a wooden cross, he must have been terrified when Haman was hung on a wooden gallows (Esther 7:10), Jael pierced Sisera's temple with a wooden stake (Judg. 4:21), Joshua hung five enemy kings from trees (Josh. 10:26), and Adam ate fruit from the tree in Eden (Gen. 3:6). Even with my nifty Bible software, I wouldn't have come up with all those biblical examples of death by means of wood. Orthodox hymnography revels in the patterns and paradoxes of Scripture, a dexterity that was possible only for writers who knew the Bible very, very well.

Most important to me personally is that the Christian East mapped out a way for ordinary people to stay always in the presence of God, to "pray constantly" (1 Thess. 5:17). This is what I had longed for ever since I became a Christian, though it seemed an impossible goal. But very early in Christian history, starting in the second century, the Desert Fathers and Desert Mothers went into the wilderness to devote themselves to prayer alone. Over the centuries a great deal of wisdom and practical experience has accumulated, resulting in a Way of prayer that can be used by ordinary people living in the world, not just monks and mystics. We'll explore this more in chapter 6.

Eastern Christians established the first Christian hospitals, orphanages, and homes for the poor and the elderly. They debated and defeated pagan and philosophical religion throughout the empire. They sent out missionaries with the gospel to the ends of the known world. They died for their faith by the hundreds of thousands. And their great devotion to Christ was met with miracles, healings, and direct guidance from God, a treasury of stories that are told and retold (and still occurring) to this day.

Even though the West largely ignored Eastern Christianity, that didn't stop them. They were over there having two thousand years of history, whether we were looking or not.

So at the beginning there was a single united church, East and West. (There were breakaway and heretical groups, too, but we'll be tracing the path of the central, continuing church.) As time passed, the understanding of the pope's authority gradually expanded in the West, but in the East that expansion was generally ignored. And there things stood for a very long time.

But in the eleventh century some controversies that had simmered for centuries came to a rolling boil. The issue historians most often cite was the addition of a single word, *filioque* (Latin, "and the Son"), to the Nicene Creed. This creed, a summary of Christian beliefs (Orthodox call it "the Symbol of Faith"), was hammered out at the first two ecumenical councils, at Nicaea (AD 325) and Constantinople (AD 381). Since that time worshipers had always said, "I believe in the Holy Spirit . . . who proceeds from the Father." But under the *filioque* revision they would say, "from the Father *and the Son.*"

This addition had been in intermittent use in Europe for several centuries (oddly enough, it was not adopted at Rome until AD 1014), and had been criticized in the East by theologians and church leaders. You might be puzzled by that because, in the Scriptures, the Holy Spirit clearly comes through the Son; the Gospel of John says that, when Jesus appeared to his apostles after his resurrection, "he breathed on them, and said to them, 'Receive the Holy Spirit'" (John 20:22).

The creed, however, first speaks of each member of the Trinity in eternity, then in earthly history. "I believe in one God, the Father Almighty—Creator of heaven and earth"; "I believe in one Lord, the Only-Begotten Son, Jesus Christ . . . who for us and our salvation came down from heaven"; "I believe in the Holy Spirit . . . who has spoken by the prophets." In eternity, the Spirit "proceeds" from the Father alone; after the creation of the world, he is breathed into human history by the Son. Theologians of the East saw the *filioque* as promoting the Son to a position above the Spirit, endangering the balance of the Trinity.

While the Eastern Church had theological reasons for objecting to the *filioque*, there was another reason you might not expect: the belief that, when a text has been approved by the whole council of bishops, it cannot be changed by one bishop acting alone. This principle is called conciliarity. It means that when all the bishops come together in council, and prayerfully address a controversy, they can count on the Holy Spirit to lead them to agreement. Christ had said to expect that guidance, for the Holy Spirit would "guide you into all the truth" (John 16:13).

When the gathered bishops find consensus, they give thanks for the Holy Spirit's guidance; but there's one more step to go, for the rest of the Church, back home, must confirm their decision. The bishops return home, their decision is released, and the clergy, laypeople, and monastics hear it and weigh it. If they accept it (or, as it's said, "receive" it), that seals the truth of the bishops' decision.

So in the East, theology is not defined by a powerful leader or a panel of experts. The guarding of the Christian faith is the responsibility of every member of the body of Christ, right down to a circle of grannies in a remote rural parish.

This, obviously, makes it hard to change anything. How are you going to convince those grannies? They're going to stick with what *their* grannies taught *them*.‡ A friend of mine draws an analogy to fence posts on a prairie; if you've set them correctly, when you look down the row, they will all line up.

So the faith is preserved by community memory, a present-tense "memory" that is ever alive in the Holy Spirit. That's why Orthodox believe they have kept unchanged the "faith which was once for all delivered to the saints" (Jude 1:3), the faith that was first preached by the apostles.

It's possible for the laity to reject and thereby void a council's decision. In the fifteenth century, at a council in Florence, all but one of the Eastern delegates agreed to sign a document placing the Orthodox Church under the authority of Rome. The delegates' hope was that, in return, Rome would supply military aid against the Ottoman Empire, which was then at Constantinople's gates.

But when this agreement was carried back to the Orthodox faithful, it was emphatically rejected. The agreement was made void; the West did not send help; and the East was overrun by Muslim conquerors, who still control much of those lands to this day. The Orthodox Church recognizes as a saint the single delegate who refused to sign: St. Mark of Ephesus.

Conciliarity means that we discern God's will as a community, as people in communion with God and each other. The first such

‡   This is one of the starkest differences between East and West, for the assumption over here is that we always need something *new*. The habit of seeking the new means looking for differences, looking for things you can change, so it tends to separate believers rather than draw them together.

council appears in Acts 15, when missionaries and Church leaders gathered in Jerusalem to settle how much of the Jewish purity code Gentile converts should observe. After discussion St. James, the bishop of Jerusalem, who presided at the council, identified and pronounced the group's consensus. The letter announcing this decision said, "It has seemed good to the Holy Spirit and to us . . ." (Acts 15:28).

But while the East embraced conciliarity, Western Christianity tended toward a monarchical view, where the pope had king-like authority over all. Think of the chaos of those centuries in Europe; stable, central authority was a desperate need.

The "Great Schism" between East and West was a long and gradual process, and it's debatable what exactly constitutes the moment of division. Historians have found it handy to point to an event that took place in AD 1054. Representatives of the pope came to Constantinople with a letter for the patriarch there, Michael Cerularius, insisting that he recognize Rome's authority over the worldwide Church.§ When Michael refused, those representatives laid a document of excommunication upon the altar of his cathedral, the great church of Hagia Sophia. Patriarch Michael excommunicated the delegates in turn, and the two historic churches have been separate ever since.

But who left whom? There's a subtle distinction here, and it has to do with what you think the Church *is.*

From a Western perspective, the Church constitutes the faith. Christians are held together by common membership in that Church, as if it were an exoskeleton (skeleton on the outside, like a lobster). To the West it was the Orthodox who left, because they abandoned the authority of the Church's head, the pope.

---

§ A *patriarch,* by the way, is a bishop, and there is no higher clerical rank than bishop. There are higher *administrative* ranks—an archbishop has authority over assistant bishops, and a patriarch even more—but each bishop is otherwise the equal of any other bishop. A bishop is identified by the city where he presides, and the bishops of certain historic cities are given the title "patriarch," likening their office to that of the patriarchs of the Old Testament. Since the bishop of Rome, the pope, is no longer in communion with the Orthodox Church, the role of "first among equals" is held by the patriarch of Constantinople.

But from an Eastern perspective, the faith constitutes the Church. Christians are held together by their common beliefs, as if it were an endoskeleton (skeleton on the inside, like a salmon). To the East it was the Western Christians who left, because they abandoned the common ancient faith, embracing new ideas like the *filioque* and increased papal authority.

I regret having to dig up this old history, because all Christians are now under such siege from opponents of our faith that it's better to put aside differences and stand together at every point we can. But this part of Christian history, a very significant part, is largely unfamiliar in the West, and helps us understand why the Christian East can seem so very different.

5

"A Sacrifice of Praise"
(HEB. 13:15)

*Baptism, Holy Water, The Perils of Service Books,
Beauty in Worship, Music, Tradition*

s we continue to stand just inside the entrance of the nave, we see to our left a silver-colored baptismal font, shaped like a huge chalice. It's about three and a half feet high, and large enough to dip a year-old baby. Orthodox baptize by immersion, and this font is brought to the center of the church for the occasion. Since there are no pews, little children can stand around it and watch with wide eyes.

When the candidate for baptism is an adult, it takes a much larger font, of course. In ancient times, baptism was done outside the church or in the narthex, and some exterior baptisteries took the form of a cross-shaped pit cut into the bedrock. A candidate would enter it by walking down a few stairs along the western arm, kneeling and being dipped below the water three times by the priest, then ascending on stairs leading to the east. (We'll look at the rite of baptism in part 3.) At St. Felicity, they use a watering trough for adult baptism—the kind you'd find on a farm, for cattle and horses. They haul it out of storage and put it in the middle of the nave, but even after it's wrapped in white flounces it still looks like a horse trough.

There has been a wave of adult conversions to Orthodoxy in recent years, one of many effects of a general fascination with the early church; other examples are the popularity of the "Lost Gospel" books, *The Da Vinci Code*, and the 2004 movie *The Passion of the Christ*. That movie would have been an impossible sell in my college days. Movies in the 70s portrayed Jesus as a hippie, as in *Godspell* and *Jesus Christ Superstar*. At the time, there was strong feeling that the faith had to be presented in "relevant" ways, and couched in terms that contemporary hip people would find appealing. A movie that aimed instead for historical accuracy, and was filmed in Latin and Aramaic, could never have been made. But that sure was what people were craving in 2004.

So a lot of people are curious about the ancient church, and some of them end up becoming Orthodox. The percentage of church membership represented by converts has grown dramatically in recent decades. A 2008 survey found that, in the United States, 29 percent of the Greek Orthodox Archdiocese and 51 percent of the Orthodox Church in America (Russian roots) joined the Church as adults.[11] The percentage is even higher among clergy; in the Antiochian Archdiocese (Arab roots), an astonishing 70 percent of the clergy are converts.[12] In general, well-informed and enthusiastic converts have given American Orthodoxy a shot of energy, but that kind of enthusiasm can admittedly be wearying. Those who grew up in the Church have had ample opportunity to practice hospitality, as well as patience.

Beside the chalice-shaped font is a similar vessel, one designed for holy water. It has a tap at the bottom, and can hold a couple of gallons. There's a collection of glass jars on the shelf underneath. Orthodox Christians take holy water home and keep it in their family prayer corner (usually called an "icon corner"). They might sip a little each day with their morning prayers, or sprinkle it on a sick child.

Every year on the day that commemorates Christ's baptism, the Feast of Theophany (January 6), the priest consecrates the holy water that will be used in the coming year. The evocative and stirring prayers, written by St. Sophronius of Jerusalem (AD 560–638), proclaim that Jesus' descent into the Jordan means that he is reclaiming all of creation as his own. The water of the Jordan, and all water, and all the physical world, is being filled with the presence of God; the death of death has begun.

This water is also used in house blessings, and when a family moves into a new home the priest will come over and bless it. (We'll go to a house blessing in chapter 23.) Many denominations do house blessings, but the unusual thing about Orthodox practice is that a house is reblessed every year, sometime between Theophany and the beginning of Lent. The pastor goes with the family through every room in the house—basement, attic, garage, bathrooms—sprinkling holy water on the walls. (This isn't the full-length blessing service that is done when a family moves to a new home, but an annual "booster shot.") Everyone sings the Theophany hymn, as they go through the house bearing icons and candles.

O Lord, when you were baptized in the Jordan
You revealed the worship that is due the Trinity;
For the Father's voice bore witness, calling you his beloved Son,
And the Spirit appeared as a dove,
Proving the truth of his words.
O Christ our God, you revealed yourself and gave light to the
    world!
Glory to you!

There's probably good pastoral wisdom in having the pastor walk, praying, through every room of every home once a year. As you'd guess, it's very time-consuming, and during those weeks a parish priest gets little done besides house blessings. Most families want to serve him a meal as well, or at least see him have some coffee and cake, all of which means that the pounds put on over the Christmas holidays aren't coming off anytime soon.

Above the holy water dispenser there is a cluster of twelve icons on wooden plaques. They tell the story of salvation: the Annunciation, the birth of Christ, his baptism in the Jordan, and the rest. The church year is a cycle of feasts, and as the months pass each icon will be taken down from the wall and have a turn on the *analogion* near the door, replacing the icon of St. Felicity there now.* There's no icon here of Pascha, the feast of feasts, for it stands above all the rest.

Over here, in a back corner of the nave, there is a cluster of music stands, where the choir will stand during the Sunday-morning liturgy. Nearly all of the service is chanted or sung, mostly by the choir or by the congregation following the lead (it is hoped) of the choir. There are stretches where the priest has no audible role, and can participate in worship (or pray in silence) like everybody else.

At St. Felicity they use small binders as worship books, so the choir director can change the melodies as the year goes by—more somber tunes for Lenten seasons, more joyous for the great feasts. But a newcomer trying to follow along in one of these books can easily get lost. There are pages that repeat the same prayers with different music, or present a set of prayers of which only one will be used. For example, there is a series of eight short, standard hymns about Christ's resurrection, and we sing only one of them each Sunday, rotating through in order. There will be other hymns that are used only in certain liturgical seasons—perhaps one or two of them this week, or none. On any Sunday, the saint of the day will also have his or her own hymn, but it won't be in the binder at all. So it can be confusing.

That's why newcomers are often told: don't try to follow in the book. Just watch and listen, and join in when you can. "Look and listen" is how everybody learned Christian worship, for a very long time.

The service books in an Orthodox church don't separate prayers from hymns; instead they show a single Sunday-morning service that runs from beginning to end, with the hymns embedded as you

---

*   Surprisingly enough, though the Western church year begins in November or December, on the first Sunday of Advent, the Eastern church year begins on September 1. This is close to the date the Roman Empire began a new year, the day taxes were set, after the summer harvest had been appraised. Orthodox still call this day by its old name, "the Indiction."

go along. There's actually no firm distinction between "hymn" and "prayer," since all the prayers are sung. They're *all* hymns.

I should explain that when I say, "hymn," I don't mean four rhymed lines and a chorus. An Orthodox hymn is usually unrhymed and without meter (in English translation, anyway), but uses poetic language. Most are about a paragraph long; the Theophany hymn, above, is a typical example. Pretty much everything on Sunday morning is either sung or chanted, including the Scripture readings. (The sermon, thank goodness, is spoken.)

Orthodox hymns, then, aren't songs that the pastor or worship leader can select and plug into empty spots in the service. Instead, the whole service is composed of sung prayers, the same ones sung at every Orthodox church on that day, varying, if at all, in the translations and melodies used. Once the liturgy begins, it goes on without a break, carrying you along. ("See you at the end!" a choir friend used to say.)[†] Very little of the service changes from week to week, and even the hymns that do change—the ones saluting a particular feast or person—are designated for that day, appearing at their appointed places.

So the choir director doesn't have the job of choosing hymns that worshipers will enjoy or find moving. Hopefully he'll provide a well-rehearsed choir that is ready to do its best, but even when that is not the case there's no feeling that the day's worship was a failed performance. It's not a performance. It's worship. The focus is on God, not the congregation.

For example, if the choir is botching a hymn, the director will signal them to stop, give each part its proper pitch, and start again. Somehow, this is not embarrassing. Like people working together to do anything well, we stop and make corrections when needed. "Liturgy" comes from the Greek *leitourgos*, meaning the "laity-work," the work of the people.

I expect this attitude is another reason for that lack of self-consciousness that C. S. Lewis noted. Even though Orthodox

---

† An advantage of having a set liturgy, like this, is that worship has nothing to do with your emotions. Everyone gets on the train at the station in the valley and it carries us to the top, regardless of our subjective state.

worship is the most elaborate and sense-saturating I've ever seen, it's not formal in the sense of "stuffy."

The first time my family attended an Orthodox service, the usher was so genuinely delighted with us that he insisted that our sons put on vestments and serve as altar boys. *The first time.* (This was an Orthodox church with Arab roots, and that's a culture that's hard to beat when it comes to overflowing hospitality.) Under great smiling pressure the boys acquiesced, and the result could have been in a Buster Keaton movie, but nobody worried about it. Meanwhile, at the extra-pointy liturgical churches we usually attended, altar servers did not participate until they had been thoroughly drilled, trained to bow to the same angle, and matched for height.

Since we associate "fancy" with "fussy" when it comes to worship, this combination of extravagant beauty and unforced behavior sounds surprising. But it's something we've all seen at a wedding reception. In that situation, extravagance feels right; we want everything to be as beautiful as possible, and the bride gloriously adorned. But we don't then sit at the table acting stiff and self-conscious. Great beauty doesn't intimidate, but rather heightens our joy, and draws us forward in communion.

Some people mistrust beauty in worship, though, picturing poor medieval peasants dazzled and manipulated by liturgical theater. Yet the tradition of liturgical beauty goes back much further than that, to the time of Moses. In the book of Exodus we see God giving Moses very detailed instructions on creating and furnishing the worship space. For example, he tells Moses that he must make a box to hold the tablets of the law—a storage container, basically. When we picture a storage container, we think of a roomy plastic box with a snap-on lid.

But God required much more from Moses. He instructed him to make the box from acacia, or thorn-tree wood, which already sounds like a challenge. Moses was then to overlay it with gold— not only on the exterior but inside as well, even though the inside would never be seen. The interior had to be beautiful because it was being made for God. The rings and poles for the ark were to be golden, too. God commanded a "mercy seat" to be placed on top of the ark, and two cherubim, also made of hammered gold, to face each other atop it, their wings touching.

That's rather a lot of cost and effort to expend on a storage container, especially one that the Israelites would need to pack up and carry through the desert. Yet it's only *one* of the items God required. He gave similar orders for the table, the lamp stand, the tabernacle, the veil, the altar, and the priestly vestments. All of these were likewise to be beautified with gold, silver, embroidery, and precious stones.

The Lord was specific even about small details. Around the hem of the priests' garments there were to be embroidered pomegranates of purple, blue, and red, interspersed with golden bells: "a golden bell and a pomegranate, a golden bell and a pomegranate, round about on the skirts of the robe" (Exod. 28:34). Even though the children of Israel were refugees, wandering in the desert and living in tents, God commanded Moses to use extravagant resources to make worship beautiful. All of it portable, too, so that an impoverished people could carry that beauty with them, as they crossed and recrossed the desert over the course of four decades.

Beauty must mean something. God must know something about how beauty works on the human heart. He must have made us that way.

When the first Christians were expelled from Jewish congregations, they didn't need to create a whole new style of worship. They already knew how God wanted to be worshiped; he had told Moses in great detail. They knew he'd required the use of incense, for example. It was costly and rare, but I don't think there is an incident of formal worship in the Old Testament that does not include incense: "From the rising of the sun to its setting my name is great among the nations, and in every place incense is offered to my name" (Mal. 1:11).

The early Christians continued that practice, as we see in the book of Revelation, which records the vision that came to St. John during a Communion liturgy: "Another angel came . . . and he was given much

incense to mingle with the prayers of all the saints . . . and the smoke
of the incense rose with the prayers of the saints from the hand of the
angel before God" (Rev. 8:3–4). From ancient times, rising incense
was associated with prayer: "Let my prayer be counted as incense
before you, and the lifting up of my hands as an evening sacrifice"
(Ps. 140/141:2, NRSV).

The first Christians were Jews, and they were used to two main
forms of corporate worship: a service of Scripture readings and
intercessions (offered in the Jerusalem temple and in synagogues
everywhere) and a service of sacrifices (offered only in the temple).
At first Christians worshiped with their fellow Jews for Scripture
and prayers, but held the Communion service, which replaced
the temple sacrifice, in their homes. For a time, these were held as
two separate services: "And day by day, [1] attending the temple
together and [2] breaking bread in their homes, they partook of
food with glad and generous hearts (Acts 2:46).

Pliny the Younger (AD 61–112), governor of a Roman province
on the Black Sea, reported to the emperor Trajan that he had
tortured two Christian deaconesses and learned that the community met "to sing responsively a hymn to Christ as to a god.
. . . When this was over, it was their custom to depart and to
assemble again to partake of food, but ordinary and innocent
food."[13] (There was a rumor that Christians ate evil food—that
they were cannibals. Christians were persecuted in ancient Rome
not only because they would not worship Roman gods but also
because they were accused of terrible things.)

Before long the two services were joined, so that the prayer-and-
Scripture service was immediately followed by the Communion
service, with no break.‡ This synthesis continues to be the Sunday-
morning worship that Orthodox and other liturgical Christians

---

‡   The first part of the Divine Liturgy is called the Liturgy of the Catechumens,
    and the second the Liturgy of the Faithful; anyone could attend the first and
    hear the Scriptures and prayers, but the unbaptized would depart before the
    celebration of the Eucharist, which was for church members only. (Western
    churches call these instead the Liturgy of the Word and the Liturgy of the
    Table.)

offer today. Western Christians call it "the Mass" or "the Eucharist," while Orthodox call it "the Divine Liturgy." The earliest version of the combined service is ascribed to St. James ("the Lord's brother," Gal. 1:19, first bishop of Jerusalem, chair of the first church council, and author of the Epistle of St. James). But St. James's work "seemed very long to later Christians,"[14] and shorter, edited versions were produced both by St. Basil the Great (AD 329–379) and St. John Chrysostom (AD 347–407).

Eastern Orthodox churches use the Chrysostom liturgy on most Sundays, and the Basil version during Lent and on occasional feasts. Both of these services would be termed "Byzantine Rite" (or "Eastern Rite"), but some Orthodox churches use a "Western Rite" instead, one that bears a resemblance to traditional Roman Catholic or Anglican worship. While you can focus on the differences between Western and Eastern Rite, on a spectrum of all the varieties of Christian worship available today they look a great deal alike. An Orthodox parish will stick to one Rite or the other, but both belong to the larger Orthodox Church and hold the same faith. When I get to attend a Western Rite service I'm struck by the clarity, humility, and tranquility of the worship. (Such a discussion also demonstrates the difficulty of describing any church as "Eastern" or "Western," since, by now, everyone is everywhere. The terms are useful to indicate a lineage, like "French fries," and sometimes lineage is interesting to explore.)

A Jewish friend of mine told me that when he first became a Christian he attended a "Messianic Jewish" service. That worship has an evangelical style, and he found it noisy and strange. But when he came to a Divine Liturgy he recognized it as much like the worship he'd grown up with. It's been said that, if a first-century Christian were to step out of a time machine, he'd feel right at home in an Orthodox service.

But aren't there seductive dangers in all this sensual beauty? A few years ago I was interviewed on NPR, and the woman who hosted the program asked me, "All this fancy stuff you do in church, the icons and candles and incense, doesn't it get in the way? Doesn't it distract you from worshiping God?"

"Imagine that it's your anniversary," I answered, "and your husband has taken you to a nice restaurant. There's a white tablecloth, and roses and candles, and violin music playing in the background. Does that distract you from feeling romantic?"

Now, it's true that it's possible to have all this beauty and take it for granted. That couple could plow through a fancy restaurant meal without looking each other in the eye. But it wouldn't be the restaurant's fault. Likewise, you could yawn your way through the liturgy without paying attention. You could read the Bible without paying attention, too, but it wouldn't be the fault of the Bible.

Why make a priority of beauty in worship? Because it is what God deserves. He is of ultimate worth, and deserves to receive from us as much honor as we can give. From the first, he directed his people to worship him with gold, incense, embroidery, carved wood, vestments, "a golden bell and a pomegranate."

Yes, he deserves it—but it's just as true that we need to give it. God doesn't *need* these costly things, for he already owns everything that is.

Every beast of the forest is mine,
the cattle on a thousand hills. (Ps. 49/50:10)

It is we who need to offer such things; we need to keep giving him beauty and honor, so we can understand what worship means. Beauty makes things happen within us that can't be conveyed in words. Beauty sets the heart aright, and opens it to God.

Though most of the hymns are led by the choir, some are trickier, like the ones that pop up only once a year for a particular saint or event. That's a job for a soloist or a small group, a category known as the chanters. So up front, near the left end of the iconostasis, is the chanters' stand—a rotating lectern on top of a packed bookcase, one that stores all the books they would consult to find the hymns for the day. Hardworking chanters supplement the choir's work when needed, and handle the worship entirely at services where there is no choir.

When the Feast of the Prophet Elijah rolls around, on July 20, the chanters might be called on for the hymns that occur only that day, hymns that aren't likely to be familiar to the choir and congregation. (Those hymns would be unfamiliar, that is, unless the church is named "St. Elijah" or, more likely, "St. Elias," the Greek pronunciation. Congregations get to know the hymns of their church's patron saint because they sing them every Sunday.) If chanters are preparing for worship on St. Elias's feast, they'll look in these books for the hymns of the day. During the service, one of the chanters will sing the troparion.

> Elijah was like an angel among men and a leader among
>   prophets,
> And like Moses proclaimed the coming of Christ.
> In glory, he sent to Elisha grace from on high,
> To heal diseases and cleanse all afflictions.
> He still pours out healings on all who honor his festival.

(That's a bit of shorthand: Elijah "pours out healings" by praying to God for our healing.) Then she or another chanter will sing St. Elijah's kontakion.

> Prophet Elijah, greatly renowned,
> Who foresaw God's works of might,
> You held back the rain by your prayers.
> Pray now for us to the only God, who loves mankind.

Historically there is a difference between a troparion and a kontakion; the first is a short summary hymn for a saint or feast (analogous to a *collect* in the West), while a kontakion is the first verse of a rarely sung, much longer hymn. In practice, though, they sound about the same. Feasts and saints usually have both a kontakion and a troparion. The Theophany hymn we sing at a house blessing, which I mentioned above, is actually the troparion of the feast. Here is the kontakion.

O Lord, on this day you revealed yourself to the universe
And signed us with your light.
We praise you with understanding,
Singing, "You have come, you have revealed yourself,
O Light Unapproachable."

By the way, you'll sometimes find "thee-thou" language used in Orthodox hymns—"O Lord, on this day thou didst reveal thyself." When Orthodox began coming to this country in numbers a century or more ago, translations were phrased that way because it was the current practice. Some jurisdictions have updated their translations, while others continue to use the traditional style, which has its own loveliness.

What's more frustrating in practice, though, is that there are by now a great many different English versions in circulation. When churches from different jurisdictions get together for a joint service, every hymn is dotted with midair collisions. Perhaps most frustrating is when a hymn looks like it's going to be familiar—it's the same translation and the same familiar ancient melody—but it turns out that the syllables have been *assigned to different notes*. In this book I mostly use my own translations and paraphrases, doing my bit to contribute to the confusion.

So how do you fit melodies to these flowing, meterless lines? We use chant, but it's not like the Gregorian chant you might be familiar with—that flowing, stately, hushed unison with a soft pause after each line. Byzantine chant, instead, sounds to Western ears like it's in a minor key, and often has a vigorous rhythm. It's frequently solo-chanted, with the other singers giving support on a single low note (the *ison*), which creates a drone effect and sounds rather unearthly.

Traditionally, a chanter has some freedom to add embellishments to the melody, and to vary the rhythm (kind of like jazz). There is a given underlying melody, but each solo chanter will sing it in his or her own way, gliding around with wavering notes and melisma, as was the grand style in the Byzantine Middle Ages.§

---

§   *Melisma* means singing the same syllable on a series of different notes, as we do with the long "Glo-o-o-o-ria" in the Christmas carol "Angels We Have Heard on High."

Worshipers who want to join in will hum or sing along quietly,¶ or sing the *ison;* they might stop or start singing at any time. At first it seems strange that other worshipers are joining in unpredictably, not paying any attention to those around them, but actually they're *not* paying any attention to those around them.

There are eight basic melodies, and these are called the eight Tones. Earlier I mentioned that there is a series of eight hymns (or troparia) of the Resurrection, one of which is sung each week; each of these has its own Tone, and that Tone will predominate at services all week. After a while you get these eight hymns memorized, and know the tunes, or rather Tones, by heart.

So imagine that you were standing at the chanters' stand during worship, and were called on to solo-chant a hymn you'd never seen before. The *protopsalti* (director of the chanters) points to a paragraph in one of those big books, points at you, and you're on.

Not to worry. You notice that it's marked "Tone 4," or perhaps you recall that this week we are singing the Resurrection troparion that's in Tone 4. You could think, "*Hmm,* Tone 4, that's the one that starts, 'When the women disciples of the Lord. . . .'" Keeping that melody in mind, you would then sort the words of the hymn at hand generally into that pattern; you'd do this however you like, and another chanter might do it differently. You'd sing it through to the end, pacing yourself so that words and melody come out more or less together, and panic later.

Byzantine Tones are a challenge to Western worshipers for several reasons, a significant one being that the Byzantine scale has different notes than those in the Western scale.** It's difficult to get the hang of it, but Byzantine music can sure grow on you. The

---

¶ Match the volume level of those around you; if you can hear yourself, you're singing too loudly.

** Though it sounds minor-key to me, apparently it's much more complicated than that. I've heard Byzantine music explained a number of times, but it's completely over my head. A friend writes, "What gives the tones an unusual flavor is that they use eharmonic and chromatic scales." Awhile later he concludes, "So in the West the plagal follows the main mode, while in the East the plagals come after the four main modes." There were a lot of other words in the middle. Also a chart.

(apparent) minor key, combined with strong rhythm, is a combination we don't hear much in Western hymnography.

As Orthodox Christianity spread around the world the Tones were sometimes reshaped into more culturally accessible music. The Russian version of the eight Tones, influenced by European music, sounds more familiar to Western ears. The words of the ancient prayers cannot be changed, but the melodies can. New prayers continue to be written, too; if a contemporary person is recognized as a saint, a new troparion and kontakion will be written for her feast day, and then sung to some form of the Tones, or to a new melody. At St. Felicity they use both Byzantine and Russian Tones, as well as melodies composed in Greece, the Middle East, Finland, the republic of Georgia, France, and America.

Given that all this sounds pretty flexible, a newcomer can be justly frustrated by claims that the Orthodox Church never changes. The reason my husband and I became Orthodox was that our mainline denomination was energetically revising its theology; church leaders were teaching that Jesus wasn't born of a virgin, he didn't do any miracles, and he didn't rise from the dead.†† After some reading, visiting churches, praying, and a whole lot of talking, we decided to join the Orthodox Church. We had heard that it was the communion that kept most closely to the faith and practice of the early church; in fact, that it claimed to *be* the early church, continuing unchanged over the centuries.

But, once in, we found that newer things kept cropping up. For example, there is a hymn form called an *akathist* that runs to many pages and can be done as a stand-alone service. Orthodox people continue to write new akathists in honor of new saints, or, for example, asking Mary's prayers for children, or giving thanks

†† Apparently his pals just decided to spread that story so his teachings wouldn't be forgotten. That fails to explain their willingness to die for their belief that he had returned to life.

for the beauty of nature and the environment. One of my favorites is addressed to "Jesus, Light to those in Darkness," and speaks for those who struggle with sorrow, fear, and loss.

But these hymns are obviously not ancient, and the akathist form itself goes back only to AD 500. So what is "unchanging" supposed to mean?

It's a fair question. Once I'd given a talk at an Orthodox church, and explained that we'd joined the faith because we wanted to belong to a church that doesn't change. An aged Greek priest stopped me afterward and said that I must not say that, because the Church *does* change. Surprised, I asked what he meant. He said, "In the Divine Liturgy we pray for those who travel by land, sea, *and air*. Do you think St. John Chrysostom knew about air travel?"

So it's worth thinking about what "change" means. When somebody refers to a church that "never changes," that adheres to "ancient tradition," we picture one that requires strict adherence to correct forms and behavior—sort of like people who reenact historic battles, but this time wearing Byzantine outfits. The motivation might be fear of the new, and fixation on the old simply because it is old. The desired result would be something like a museum diorama.

But think instead about what "unchanging" and "tradition" mean in a family—say, Christmas traditions. Every family that celebrates Christmas has its own traditions. In one family, everyone knows that it's the angel, not the star, that goes on top of the tree. They know that everyone must wear one of Great-Grandma's homemade scarves to the midnight church service. They know that you can open one, and only one, present on Christmas Eve. At Christmas dinner, they know to set the table with the now-faded red and green napkins.

But they also know that it doesn't matter who gets what color. If Grandpa had a red one last year and gets a green one now, no one would even notice. An outsider might say, "Aha! You broke your tradition!" But those inside the family know, instinctively it seems, how to handle variations. There's not only a tradition; there's a tradition *about* the tradition. You couldn't figure it out by looking from the outside. You'd think they were always breaking their own rules. But those who are inside a community learn by living, it seems, where tradition is stretchy and where it is not.

That's the kind of tradition people follow willingly. It's not a dead tradition, but a living, life-giving tradition. It can be called "living" even though it doesn't change. In fact, its unchanging quality is somehow part of its strength, as those alive today link arms with all who went before.

Christmas traditions aren't maintained for the sake of tradition, but for the sake of the family. Traditions are kept because they *do* something. They foster love and joy, and bind people together. Family members don't complain that a Christmas tradition is old-fashioned, or that it's the same thing they did last year. Old, familiar traditions seem fresh and lively, because they renew the family's life.

Imagine that a member of this family wanted to add a new tradition—say, that on Christmas Eve they'd all watch the movie *A Christmas Story* together. That new tradition might fit right into the old, overarching tradition. It wouldn't feel like it was challenging or revising that tradition, but like an enhancement, a bonus.

But now imagine that, after a few years, people have had more than enough of *A Christmas Story*. They start coming late to the Christmas gathering just so they don't have to watch it again. That new tradition failed; it didn't pass the test of generating life and joy. A custom could slide into, then out of, a family's Christmas traditions without much fanfare either way.

Orthodoxy is likewise designed to *do* something. Its purpose is to make saints—to provide all things necessary (community, spiritual disciplines, prayers, sacraments, and so on) to help a person be filled with the light and presence of Christ. That transformed person can then be used for God's work in this world, a work that includes bringing other people to Christ; the whole beautiful thing is in continuous, elegant motion. To that extent, the various traditions of the Church are like the implements in a glorious toolbox.

When something new is added to the toolbox, it has to prove itself; it must be shown effective in the transformation process. Here's an example. Tsar Peter the Great of Russia (1672–1725) greatly admired the Western European arts. Under his authority, traditional Byzantine church music (emphatically rhythmic, minor-sounding, solo-chanted) was displaced by grand, polyphonic Western music (the kind that sounds like Handel's *Messiah*). Traditional icons— austere, golden, stylized—were destroyed or repainted in a lush, naturalistic European style, which showed beautiful people doing dramatic things.

Time passed. It gradually became apparent that the new iconography wasn't working. Since icons are "windows into heaven," their job is to draw us from this world's fleeting worries and desires toward the golden and shadowless kingdom of God. Icons should affect us the way seeing Christ's Transfiguration affected his disciples, radically transforming our sense of reality.

The new-style icons weren't doing that. Their earthly beauty left them earthbound. They could depict this world quite faithfully, but you can look out your window and see *this* world. What's needed instead is iconography that stirs in the viewer a hunger for "the homeland of my heart's desire" (as a prayer in the funeral service says). All over Russia ancient icons are being restored, and the interloping "modern" style discarded.

The new music, on the other hand, did just fine. Though very different from the Byzantine style, its gorgeous fullness complemented the ancient texts well. The music facilitated worship and spiritual growth, and proved itself compatible with the ancient hymns. The new-style icons had to go, but the new-style music stayed, and the church is richer for it.

You'll sometimes hear it said that there are big-*T* Traditions that are observed everywhere, and little-*t* traditions that are more flexible. That is sometimes a useful distinction, but not always, I think; the gradations can be so much more subtle than that, and there are also times when people disagree about whether something is a big or small *T*.

Such disagreements don't always have to be resolved. Sometimes we can just wait them out, while the healing mission of the Church continues unimpeded. The Russians were able to "wait out" the new icon style because, though it was curiously inadequate, it did not undermine that mission. Millions of Russian Christians suffered and died for their faith under Soviet rule, and they had been raised mostly on the new icons.

That points to a general principle that's hard to express, that there's a core to Orthodoxy, a central mission, that remains the same in every time and place. It's there beneath the stamps of different cultures: icons painted in Ethiopia have a different style than ones painted in Alaska, yet they adhere to the same tradition and convey the same truth. There's a central core of Orthodoxy that remains the same in every land, even when expressed in local forms. New elements that impede that mission won't last.

Speaking of the stamps of different cultures, it's interesting to think about what Orthodoxy will look like once it takes root in America. Some adaptations are easy to imagine; we can supply American settings for hymns, and in my own parish (Holy Cross Antiochian Orthodox Church, in Linthicum, Maryland) we sing one hymn to a melody that recalls the folk song "Shenandoah." When we held our equivalent of a "Greek Fest," we served barbecue and blueberry pie. (Somehow we didn't attract Greek Fest–sized crowds, though.)

An American way of doing iconography will surely emerge as well. We've just finished filling the interior walls of Holy Cross with icons, and the images, by iconographer Seraphim O'Keefe, show a full range of colors, figures that are a bit less stylized, and a characteristic tenderness and humility in the saints' faces. (They recall the icons painted in Paris by the Russian priest Fr. Gregory Krug, 1908–1969.) There's an appealing and approachable quality overall, and in some respects these icons remind me of premodern European art. Perhaps Western iconography will find itself developing along such lines.

What people from Orthodox lands find perplexing about American inquirers, though, is our determinedly head-driven approach to the faith. We want to read books and talk about theology. We want to study the church fathers and learn about the decisions of the ecumenical councils. We want to talk and talk about what we're reading, and ask lots of questions. All that can seem odd to Christians from historically Orthodox lands.

Fr. Roman Braga, a modern-day elder from Romania (who endured years of torture in Communist prison), reflected in a conversation with a Romanian interviewer on how *different* Americans seem. "They are not simple people," he said. "The seed of faith does not grow directly in their hearts without first passing through their minds."

Americans just approach things differently, too. "I want to give you an example," Fr. Roman said. "We have in our monastery an American nun. She likes to know in advance what will be happening each day, to plan ahead. For us, it is easy to say, 'We will see; it depends on who comes and who goes.' She finds it hard to live in a disorganized way. She wants to be told what needs to be done; and when she finishes something, she wants to be told what should be done next."

Life in Romanian monasteries can include some flexibility, he said, like the rule in the monastic handbook that reads, "If you are tired, you can miss Small Compline [the last service of the day], or read it in your cell, or do whatever your elder tells you to do." Such a rule wouldn't work in America.

"I believe that God has, as a plan for America, a new form of Orthodoxy," Fr. Roman said. "It must be American, just as Orthodoxy in Russia, Romania, or Bulgaria is not exactly the same. It is Orthodoxy, but it is molded to each country's own ethnic culture. Why should we deny the American people the right to develop their own Orthodoxy?"[15]

Orthodoxy blooms in diverse cultures all over the world. Yet, when you come down to it, there's only one kind of Orthodox spirituality. (It's found so consistently around the world that there's no need even for the concept of "spirituality.") Early in my time in this church someone told me that Orthodox devotional writing all sounds alike, no matter which century or ethnic flavor you sample. Amazingly enough, I've found this to be true.

This similarity among Orthodox persists even across a schism that occurred fifteen hundred years ago. The churches that are now called "Oriental Orthodox"—the Coptic (Egyptian), Ethiopian, Eritrean, Syriac, Malankara Syrian (of Southern India), and Armenian Orthodox Churches—are in communion with each other, but not with the Eastern Orthodox Church (the subject of this book). This schism followed the decision of the Council of Chalcedon (AD 451), which declared that Christ is one person in two natures, human and divine. The Oriental Orthodox Churches disagreed, holding instead that Christ has one nature, a nature that preserves both a human and a divine character.

As you would guess, the language is extremely vexed, and didn't always translate well, or even adequately. Conversations between the churches in the twentieth century have invited both sides to consider that the actual differences are less extreme than had been thought. Full reunion of the churches may occur one day, though we must keep in mind that Orthodox do not do anything quickly.

My point, though, had to do with the great length of time this separation has been in place. It's fifteen hundred years—three times longer than Protestants have been separated from Catholics. And yet Eastern and Oriental Orthodoxy look like sisters. Even after all this time, it's the same "spirituality." So much is alike—the reverence toward God, the humility, the warmth of faith, the yearning for beauty—that I feel right at home among Oriental Orthodox Christians. Both their church and mine go back to a common root, and it shows.

In the West we're used to having many different types of Christian devotion to choose from—Franciscan, Quaker, Pentecostal, Baptist,

and dozens more. Multiple flavors can be available within a denomination, too, and even within a congregation. But in Orthodoxy
there's only one, the *same* one, all over the world, from the earliest
centuries till now.

The mystery is why Orthodox people put up with this. Why don't
they demand something fresh and new? Why don't they feel a need
to keep up with the times?

I think it's because Orthodoxy is expected to *do* something. It's not
just a matter of having the right theology, or the right ecclesiastical
institution (though I believe it does have those things). It's that
there is an innate *dynamism*. This faith is expected to accomplish
something—to enable a person to grow in union with God. And
it does this, in visible ways. It keeps on doing what it promises, so
there isn't a restless desire to tinker with it.

The Eastern Christian Way includes the elements we'd associate
with any spiritual path—prayer, fasting, almsgiving, and so
forth—and they fit together organically, like the parts of a diet-
and-exercise program. Somebody who doesn't actually do the work
and put it into practice won't see any benefit (another way it's like
a diet-and-exercise program). But for those who do, transformation
takes place. It happens in ways that are notable and recognizable,
and even, in some cases, miraculous.

This single Way is somehow able to do this within every kind of
person there is, old and young, rich and poor, from every land and
century. Wherever the faith is taken, this Way takes root and bears
fruit. It seems that it addresses something basic to our common
humanity, something shared by all people everywhere. There is a
distinct inner unity to the Orthodox faith, like the deep note of a
bell, that resonates through the ages.

So people don't worry about making it timely. It is timeless.

Since the Orthodox Way is continuously being tested and proved,
people go on practicing it and passing it on to new generations.
It doesn't frustrate, doesn't overwhelm, doesn't disappoint, doesn't
bore. It works. Let's explore this further in the next chapter.

6

"Partakers of the Divine Nature"
(2 PET. 1:4)

Theosis, Saints, Skepticism, Miracles

 he goal of this healing path is union with God. This is called *theosis*, which is usually translated "deification" or "divinization." Those terms are misleading, if not alarming, since it could sound like we expect to become junior gods, each an independent owner-operator of a personal divinity franchise. Fortunately for everyone, that is not the case. We can dismantle the Greek word and see that it is composed of *theos*, which means "God," and the suffix *-osis*, which indicates a process. As red dye saturates a white cloth by the process of osmosis, so humans can be saturated with God's presence by the process of theosis.

This was God's plan from the beginning; we were created in his image and likeness (Gen. 1:26), able to choose, in obedience and love, to be increasingly filled with his glory. When sin and death enslaved us, Christ came to heal our broken human nature and restore the way to union. "He was made man so that we might be made god," in the words of St. Athanasius (AD 296–373).[16]

We can see this transformation in the Gospel story of Christ's Transfiguration. He took Peter, James, and John aside and led them up a high mountain. "And he was transfigured before them, and his face shone like the sun, and his garments became as white as light. . . . A bright cloud overshadowed them, and a voice from the cloud said, 'This is my beloved Son, with whom I am well pleased; listen to him.' When the disciples heard this, they fell on their faces, and were filled with awe. But Jesus came and touched them, saying, 'Rise and have no fear'" (Matt. 17:1–8).

This was not a change in Jesus; he had always been filled with glory. It was a change in the disciples' ability to perceive. (Something similar happened to the two disciples who met Jesus on the road to Emmaus, but did not recognize him until he broke the bread at dinner [Lk. 24:13–35]). The Orthodox hymn for the Transfiguration says that Christ revealed his glory "as far as they [the disciples] could bear it."

Understandably, this made a big impression upon the three witnesses, two of whom later wrote about their time with Jesus. In his second epistle, Peter retells the story, giving the assurance that "we were eyewitnesses of his majesty" (2 Pet. 1:16). Yet he appears to view it not only as something that happened to Jesus, but also as the destiny of all believers. He tells his hearers that they are, even now, "partakers of the divine nature" (2 Pet. 1:4), and that they should pay attention to the mountaintop testimony of Christ's divinity "until the day dawns and the morning star rises in your hearts" (2 Pet. 1:19).

John, one of Peter's companions that day, begins his intricately woven first letter with a similar claim of being an eyewitness of Christ: "That which was from the beginning, which we have heard, which we have seen with our eyes, which we have looked upon and touched with our hands" (1 John 1:1). Perhaps he has the astounding Transfiguration light in mind when he continues, "This is the message we have heard from him and proclaim to you, that God is light and in him is no darkness at all" (1 John 1:5). Later, John connects Christ's glory with our destiny: "It does not yet appear what we shall be, but we know that when he appears we shall be like him" (1 John 3:2).

Christ himself tells us that the glory he shares with the Father will be ours as well:

- "The glory you have given me I have given to them, that they may be one, even as we are one" (John 17:22).
- "Then the righteous will shine like the sun in the kingdom of their Father" (Matt. 13:43).
- "Is it not written in your law, 'I said, you are gods'?" (John 10:34).

St. Paul confirms that our destiny is participation in Christ's glory:

- "We all, with unveiled face, beholding the glory of the Lord, are being changed into his likeness from one degree of glory to another" (2 Cor. 3:18).
- "If children, then heirs, heirs of God and fellow heirs with Christ, provided we suffer with him in order that we may also be glorified with him" (Rom. 8:17).

The light of the Transfiguration is not ordinary earthly light, but the light of God's glory, the light that was before the universe was made, called the "Uncreated Light" in Orthodoxy. God made us like himself (in his "image and likeness") so that we could take on this light as a lump of coal takes on fire. This is the destiny we were created for: participation in the light and glory of God. This expectation is the catalyst of Orthodox spirituality.

How does this work, though? How can poor human clay take on the overwhelming presence of God? St. Cyril of Alexandria (AD 376–444) gives an analogy to the way fire acts upon metal. He wrote, "When iron is brought into contact with fire, it becomes full of its activity"—that is, it takes on the properties, the heat and light, of fire. "While it is by nature iron, it exerts the power of fire."[17]

St. John of Damascus (AD 676–749) likewise wrote that saints "are truly called 'gods' not by nature but by participation, just as red-hot iron is called 'fire' ['fiery'] not by nature but by participation in the fire's action."[18] We remain by nature human, but "participate" in the energy and power of God. This is the destiny Christ reopened to us, by his victory over sin and death.

The miracle of human clay bearing divine fire is foreshadowed in the burning bush (Exod. 3:1–6). God's presence wholly irradiates a dry desert shrub, but does not destroy it. Miraculously, the bush remains intact, remains itself. God's presence doesn't obliterate or replace us, but helps us to become ourselves—each of us the real self he has always intended us to be.

Another image of God's power to fill and yet preserve his creation is the Virgin Mary's pregnancy. How could her womb hold the Lord of All, who exceeds the bounds of the universe? One of the Orthodox hymns to the Virgin says, "He made your body more spacious than the heavens." The kind of icon known as "The Virgin of the Sign" depicts her with her hands raised in prayer, and shows, on her torso, the unborn Christ in her womb. All the dark-blue space around him is filled with stars. He whose glory "fill[s] heaven and earth" (Jer. 23:24) fills us as well, yet with care and precision, and such patient regard for our frailty.

Theosis isn't particularly about morality. If better moral behavior were the only thing needful, Jesus would have told us to imitate the Pharisees. While this transformation will surely give you more victory over temptation, it's not done by trying to be *like* Jesus ("What Would Jesus Do?"). As sincere and well-meaning as that is, human nature is simply too weak to get us very far. Nor does it amount to making guesses at what God would want, and then trying to figure out how to do it. An awful lot of energy and resources get wasted that way.

Theosis is not something we achieve by trying really hard. We require a more radical kind of surgery; in fact, we must die. As we die to self and get out of the way, Christ's life can fill us. "You have died, and your life is hid with Christ in God" (Col. 3:3).

In this light, some Scriptures that might have been heard in a poetic way now make sense simply and directly. Jesus said:

- "I am in my Father, and you in me, and I in you" (John 14:20).
- He prayed, "As you, Father, are in me, and I am in you, may they

also be in us. . . . That the love with which you have loved me may be in them, and I in them" (John 17:21, 26, NRSV).

- "I am the vine, you are the branches. He who abides in me, and I in him, he it is that bears much fruit" (John 15:5).
- "The kingdom of God is within you" (Lk. 17:21).[19]

St. Paul echoed this theme:

- "If anyone is in Christ, he is a new creation" (2 Cor. 5:17).
- "The peace of God . . . will keep your hearts and minds in Christ Jesus" (Phil. 4:7).
- "For me to live is Christ" (Phil. 1:21).
- "It is no longer I who live, but Christ who lives in me" (Gal. 2:20).
- "Christ in you, the hope of glory" (Col. 1:27).
- "And we all, with unveiled face, beholding the glory of the Lord, are being changed into his likeness from one degree of glory to another" (2 Cor. 3:18).

We can say it another way, borrowing St. Peter's term—that we *partake* of Christ. The Bible says we are partakers of "grace," "the promise," "the Holy Spirit," "the glory that is to be revealed," and "the divine nature" (Phil. 1:7; Eph. 3:6; Heb. 6:4; 1 Pet. 5:1; 2 Pet. 1:4). You'll find in Orthodox thought the idea that, while fallen humanity has retained the image of God (that's *eikon* in Greek, "icon"), we have lost the "likeness" (*omoiosis*—there's that *-osis* ending again, indicating a process, in this case a process of "likening" or "becoming-like"). To use a term only marginally less alarming than *theosis*, we are undergoing a process of assimilation.

Is it even possible to talk about such things? Words fail when it comes to experiences of God, for the good reason that such experiences are beyond words. One approach is to dismiss the whole thing, saying that these claimed experiences are generated by human emotion, and the biblical language was never intended to be taken literally. These verses of Scripture, someone might say, were intended only to bring to the hearer the consolation of God's love and power.

If we insist that we *do* mean a literal experience of God, we're confronted by a circus of images of people from all ages who claimed to have had such an encounter—some images entertaining, some pitiful, and some frightening. Even leaving aside the liars and manipulators, people who sincerely believed God had spoken to them have been responsible for all sorts of regrettable moments in history. It would seem that claims of direct experience are too subjective to talk about.

Yet the solution can't be to say that all such claims are merely bursts of overemotionalism. When a person says, "I have experienced performing heart surgery," we are inclined to believe her. It shows little confidence in our Christian faith to preemptively concede that "I have experienced the presence of God" is nothing but moonbeams and wishful thinking.

We should listen to what people report of their experiences of Christ the way we'd listen to the experiences of a roomful of heart surgeons. Some of the experiences they'd report would be common to all of them, some would have happened to half, some to only a few. The more people we manage to hear from the better, because large numbers of reports will give us more detailed and reliable information.

This is true whether we're talking about heart surgery or sensing God's presence in prayer. (In the latter case, collecting the widest range of stories will also make it easier to pick out those reports that are truly cockeyed.) In the Orthodox tradition, where guidance by a spiritual mother or father is the rule, the degree of knowledge assembled over the centuries can fairly be called a science.

Isn't the purpose of every religion to enable contact with God? Christians do lots of other things—give aid to the poor, for example—but many a secular agency could say they do the same, maybe more efficiently. But always and everywhere people have looked up from the mud and seen the stars, and hoped that something or Someone was there.

We Christians *know* Someone is there. We know that he loves us and has promised he will never leave us (Matt. 28:20). Orthodox Christians would add: he wants us to be in direct communion with him. Not just the clergy, not just monastics, but every human being. The path to this union is challenging—it will challenge your pride in particular—but it is open to one and all.

If you're thinking about entering a spiritual tradition that is expected to produce deep changes, you're likely to want to know what those changes would be. We can generate a list of traits: more loving, more humble, more simple, more gentle, and so forth. But a list of terms doesn't convey very much. What we really need is to look at someone who has *done* it. If we can see a transformed person—or better yet, thousands of them, so the whole range of personalities shines forth—we'll have a better idea of where we're going.

Once I gave a talk about theosis at a theological school, and afterward a student came up, pen and paper at the ready. He asked me, "Are there any case histories?" I couldn't figure out what he meant, so he said, "Has anyone ever actually tried to *do* this?"

It hit me how difficult this is to visualize, if you don't have an example of how it works out *in practice.* It's the saints who are our "case histories." They give us an opportunity to see how a multitude of people, from all backgrounds, ages, and stations of life, "did it." We put their icons in our homes like a boy who dreams of being a baseball player and puts up posters of his heroes. We gaze at the saints so we can learn how to do what they did.

Being a saint is not a private attainment, a kind of spiritual mountain-climbing. Its goal is not simply to accumulate more spiritual experiences. As spirituality has gained popularity in recent years, I've sometimes felt that there's an unpleasantly narcissistic edge to it, as if it's a spiritual makeover project. The real mark of a saint is, instead, that his transformed life overflows for others. The Christ-filled person acquires nothing for himself; he dies to self. In that dying he receives life, and gives it to all.

How to summarize what that looks like? I could describe dozens of different saints, trying to render all the shadings. Instead I'll give you the description Fr. Vasileios Gontikakis, abbot of Iveron Monastery, gave of a prayerful man he knew. I think it's a good snapshot of the typical changes we might see in someone who has spent many years practicing the Orthodox Way.

> [He is] at peace in himself in such a way as to *be* peace for [others]. . . . He pours out strength and comfort. In his presence one feels boundless peace and security. Near him everything is filled with light. Uncertainties vanish; one begins to love Christ, and to love life. . . . He has a treasure of inexpressible joy hidden in an earthen vessel. . . . He moves untroubled in the midst of all things. . . . Wherever he places his foot he finds a rock, because everywhere he has humbled himself and let the other pass over him. In all his words he speaks clearly, he finds the image he desires, because he has never mocked anyone, has wounded no one, and never hurt any creature. . . . His whole body, as it were, forms a laugh of silent joy. Gentleness and radiance flow from him. . . . This light . . . helps everyone to find his own true self. It helps everyone to love his own life, leading him forward in the light which knows no evening.[20]

Yes, I'd say that description includes characteristics you would see in many Orthodox saints. It calls to mind a saying from St. Seraphim of Sarov (AD 1759–1833): "Acquire the Spirit of Peace, and thousands around you will be saved." Some Christians worry a great deal about evangelism—how to present Christianity so that it will attract nonbelievers. But one person who dies to self this thoroughly can bring thousands to salvation just by the light of Christ that shines through her. Someone who is filled with the living presence of Christ will love as he loved, and minister to others as he did, sometimes even in miraculous ways.

You may quite reasonably be wondering *how* such an assimilation can take place. We can say that it is like the unborn Christ dwelling within Mary's womb; but pointing to that mystery doesn't really make it more comprehensible. Orthodox theology can go a little further to describe, though never explain, this mystery. The key terms are "essence" (*ousia* in Greek) and "energies" (*energeia*). All human beings share a common *ousia*, a common human nature, characterized by traits like reason, memory, imagination, and will. This human "essence" is what links us with each other and distinguishes us, as a group, from other creatures (who have their own *ousia*).

However, each human is a distinct person (a *hypostasis*, in case you just can't get enough of those Greek terms), employing his allotment of our common traits in a wholly unique way. We can't know Jim as he knows himself inside, but we can know him in a person-to-person encounter, experiencing his "energies"—the unique ways he expresses this *ousia* all humans share.

Likewise we can say that Father, Son, and Spirit share a common *ousia*, one eternally beyond human comprehension; there is an inner life of the Trinity that we will never comprehend. Yet each member of the Trinity is a distinct person, and bears that common essence in a unique way. We cannot know God in his essence, but can experience and know him by his "energies," his life and presence overflowing in this world.

This process of transformation is what God intended for Adam and Eve, and they were brought into Eden able to grow in union with him as they voluntarily chose to love him. But their fall broke something in our common nature, and we have been born ever since with damaged hearts, weak before sin. We don't trust God, but put our own interests first in a fearful and greedy way. Because we fear death, we sin; because we sin, we are bound over to death. It's the most vicious of cycles. We are lost, helpless, and can do nothing to save ourselves.

So Christ assumed our human nature and followed our common path into the realm of Death. "Since therefore the children share in flesh and blood, he himself likewise partook of the same nature, that through death he might destroy him who has the power of death, that is, the devil, and deliver all those who through fear of death were subject to lifelong bondage" (Heb. 2:14–15).

As Adam and Eve were in the beginning, so we are again because of Christ's work. We can choose—or refuse—to receive God's indwelling Spirit and be assimilated to his life. We can learn how to be engaged continuously with his presence, praying "at all times in the Spirit . . . alert with all perseverance" (Eph. 6:18). Independence from God, on the other hand, is not freedom, but death. God is Love, Life, Light, he is the Way and the Truth, and we are our true, living selves only when we abide in him.

When people first hear of theosis it might sound dreamy, theoretical, insubstantial, perhaps a little New Agey. But in practice it's very grounded. Not merely in the sense that progressing in this path will make you more stable and tranquil, more patient with others and able to love them. It does that, but it's grounded in a more literal sense, too. For God is present with us not only in a spiritual sense, but in the material dimension as well. He lives in us just as the life of a vine flows through its branches (John 15:1–16).

The Eucharist is an experience of this. When we partake of Communion we really do receive the body of Christ. It is, inexplicably, a joining of our awkward and misused, overindulged bodies with the body of its Creator and source of its life. Impossible, really, but the voice of the one who said, "Let there be Light," says, "This is my body"—and so it is. We can't understand it, but fortunately, we don't have to. What we receive each Sunday in dumb incomprehension is what we are receiving, through prayer, in a lifetime of submission to God's will and his leading. We are gradually being healed, restored, "deified," enabled to bear the presence of God, just as we receive that presence in a material way in Communion.

If God is present within both us and the created world, anything is possible. Those who progress far on this path sometimes show visible signs of this transformation. As these men and women get better at discerning his presence, their intercessions become more accurate, more in tune with what God intends to do. Those intercessions are then followed by healings and miracles. As they cooperate with God's power, they become participants in his work in the physical world. This should be no surprise: "Truly, truly, I say to you, he who believes in me will also do the works that I do; and greater works than these will he do, because I go to the Father" (John 14:12).

Some Christians are uncomfortable with the idea of miracles, though. Maybe it's the memory of medieval charlatans or modern-day television preachers defrauding the simple. But the existence of fake miracles doesn't prove there are no real ones. If anything, it suggests the reverse; people make fake diamonds *because* there are real ones.

I gained an insight about skepticism some years ago from Fr. George Calciu (1925–2006), who was my spiritual father (that is, I went to him for confession and he counseled and prayed for me). Like Fr. Roman Braga, he was a survivor of Communist persecution and torture in his native Romania, a true Christian hero. Fr. George was well read; before entering the priesthood he had taught French literature, and could readily drop an allusion to Proust. But once, he was giving a retreat at my church during the Nativity Fast (called Advent in the West), and mentioned a naive folk story about Christ's Nativity—I don't remember what it was, but it was something akin to the Western Christian legend that animals can talk on Christmas Eve. It took me by surprise, and in my heart I judged him, thinking, how could someone so literate and spiritually experienced believe such a thing?

In his next sentence he said something that smashed all my preconceptions, and I only wish I remembered the words he used so I could quote him exactly. But what I gathered from it was this challenge: If you believe a simple story like that, what do you lose? If you go to heaven and find out that it didn't happen that way, what did it cost you? Isn't there sweetness to such trusting, childlike faith, and doesn't it enable greater openness to the Lord? On the other hand—if you scrutinize and object to such things, what do you gain? And what, in fact, might you lose?

Of course, I can't force myself to believe in something that, deep inside, I just don't think could have happened. Nobody can. But, just as my reflexive modern skepticism keeps credulity in check, I can follow up with a check to my skepticism. Hasn't God done more extraordinary things than this? Didn't he raise Christ from the dead? Why should I balk at this whimsical story? "Omnipotence" means God can do anything—even this, if he wanted to.

I don't win a prize for scoffing at it. If I restrain my scoffing and leave the possibility open (for I'm not required to make any decision about it, one way or the other), I can take a small step back toward the childlike trust that Christ praised so highly. "Truly, I say to you, whoever does not receive the kingdom of God like a child shall not enter it" (Lk. 18:17).

If miracles are ever possible, then unilateral rejection of them must "grieve the Holy Spirit" (Eph. 4:30). Wrongly ascribing a miraculous event to evil deception could even approach the "blasphemy against the Spirit"—no minor risk, since Christ said that this is the only sin that "will not be forgiven" (Matt. 12:31).

On the other hand, openness to miracles prepares us to see miracles. Once you've seen them, your beliefs about miracles are based on experience. As the beloved contemporary monk Elder Paisios (1924–1994) said, "Little by little [the prayerful person] will experience small and great divine events, and become more faithful, living the divine mysteries up close. Then he becomes a theologian,* for he did not grasp the divine mysteries with his mind, but lived them in reality."[21]

It might seem odd to jump from talk of theosis to the subject of miracles and healings. It leaps across our ideas of sophisticated and

---

* In Orthodox usage, a "theologian" is not a person who writes about theology, but a person who has experienced God's presence directly in prayer, perhaps even seen his Light, the Uncreated Light that existed before the world was made. "If you pray truly, you are a theologian," said Evagrius Ponticus, AD 345–399 (*Treatise on Prayer*, 61).

unsophisticated faith traditions, and across our concepts of prayer as self-focused or other-focused. The connection, for those on the path of theosis, is love. The most telling of spiritual disciplines is how we relate to other people. It's a marvelously handy spiritual discipline, too, because other people are just about everywhere you look. God puts others in our lives not only for our joy and comfort but also to irritate and provoke us, so that our flaws rise to the surface where we can recognize and deal with them. Love is not easy. If you think you love everybody, you're probably not letting them get close enough.

People have different ideas of what "love" should look like, so what onlookers see a holy person doing might not always fit their definition of the word. But it will indisputably look like humility.

Let's talk about that. As much as we've discussed transformation in Christ, it might not have occurred to you that the ways the Lord will change you will not necessarily make you more popular. Some people have high expectations about that; they'll say they don't like to talk about faith in Christ, but instead expect that others will be so impressed by their Christ-filled lives that they will want to be like them. (I've heard that approach called "evangelism by narcissism.")

But picture a holy person like the one Abbot Vasileios describes; imagine him moving through your day and doing the things you do. Frankly, a lot of people are not going to understand him. Those exposed to him long-term will sense that there is something powerful and delicately beautiful here, but that doesn't mean they'll like it.

Whom *do* we admire these days? Our time loves stories about getting even. It wants a completely evil bad guy to hate and condemn, unimpeded by the complexity such judgmentalism runs into in real life. They want victims that they can identify with, so they can enjoy taking vengeance. Putting people down, mocking their appearance, silencing them with a vicious one-liner—those things are popular. I'm surprised at how many bumper stickers presume a preexisting combative relationship with the whole world. But those themes and attitudes aren't characteristic of Christian life.

The characteristics that *will* occur, however, like gentleness and simplicity, are not much valued. They may either go unnoticed or be found irritating (think of how people roll their eyes at the *Simpsons'* TV character Ned Flanders, though he's the most consistently kind and generous person on the show.) "If the world hates you, know that it has hated me before it hated you. If you were of the world, the world would love its own; but because you are not of the world, but I chose you out of the world, therefore the world hates you" (John 15:18–19).

The idea is to love the world, even though it hates you. That is what Christ did, and what he can do in you. Progress in the spiritual life is literally growth in communion and union with Christ, and he has loved every human being in the whole history of the world.

St. Nikolai Velimirovi (1924–1994) wrote, "If ninety-nine of us are good and saintly but one of our brothers is far from our solace and support, in sin and darkness, be sure God is not among us ninety-nine, but he has gone to find our brother whom we have lost and forgotten."[22]

As the saints grow in prayer, they get better at sensing God's will, and their intercessions are followed by healings and miracles. As they cooperate with God's power, they become participants in his work, in this physical world. Here are some ways that might work out in practice.

Sometimes friends of these saints discover that they are not bound by the laws of space and time. Even those who withdraw from the world, "wandering over deserts and mountains, and in dens and caves of the earth" (Heb. 11:38), may be given grace to see the whole of suffering humanity in prayer, and intercede in power. I know someone who was protected in a building collapse by a man she didn't know. Recognizing him in a photo years later, she learned that he had never left his monastery in Greece. Even those who live in the far wilderness, unseen by any other human being, can by God's mercy see the whole world, and pray.

Sometimes people discover that such saints have an unusual rapport with animals. These stories often involve bears or lions. Two

nuns who went to visit St. Seraphim of Sarov (1754–1833) in his
forest hermitage were terrified when a bear lumbered toward them.
St. Seraphim addressed the bear, "Misha [Mikey], why do you
frighten my poor children? Better go bring some kind of sustenance,
since I have nothing to give them." The bear returned two hours
later, bearing a honeycomb wrapped in leaves.

These men and women may be "soul-readers," able in loving prayer
to see a person's history and entire inner world. This trait sounds
intimidating, but in experience it can be quite liberating, bringing the
things we don't want to talk about into the healing light. A holy elder
may do this by referring obliquely to someone else's problems, and it's
not till you're on the way home that you realize he was talking about
you. One person wrote that, when she visited a monastery, a monk
she was talking with solved a problem that had plagued her family
for twenty years. But she didn't realize it immediately, because he'd
framed it as if talking about someone else.

Abbot Vasileios writes of his holy friend,

> Gently and without tumult, he allows the splendor which
> dwells in him to soften and illumine, to console and gladden,
> the man who is his brother. . . . He discerns where things are
> leading. . . . He is a surgeon. He exposes your difficulties one
> by one, in the most natural way. You do not suffer from the
> operation you are undergoing. Another has suffered for you
> first, the Lord Jesus. And now you can find yourself in this
> place of peace which His sufferings have created for you.

He goes on,

> You perceive that he is helping you discreetly. He does not inter-
> fere harshly. He does not impose himself in some magical way.
> He shows you how your true self should function according to
> its nature. He leaves you free. And you find yourself a prisoner
> of the truth, of freedom, of reality itself. And you go away con-
> soled, liberated from darkness, at peace, strengthened.[23]

It's true that people can get into deep trouble when they go exploring in the realm of miracles, prophecy, and other phenomena. Two
things make this safer in Orthodoxy. The first is accountability: each
person has a spiritual mother or spiritual father to counsel and guide
them, and each of them has their own elder, and so on.† Each
person continues to lay his spiritual life before a more-experienced
guide, and benefits from his or her discernment.

The second factor is experience—two thousand years of experience in discernment and "test[ing] the spirits" (1 John 4:1). Orthodox
writings about the path of theosis have accumulated into a library's
worth over the centuries, and those works are full of down-to-earth
advice and practical psychology.

A last element I should mention is that at the height of the
experience of theosis, union with God, some have a vision of the
"Uncreated Light" (sometimes "Uncreated Energy"), the light that
was God's before the universe was made.

Abbot Vasileios writes of its effect on his friend: "He is weak, like
a spider's web. . . . He receives such a deluge of grace that his house
of clay is overwhelmed. His feeble body can no longer endure; he
overflows, is set on fire, and all within him and round him becomes
light."[24] It is said that, in comparison with this Light, our earthly light
seems like darkness; St. Ambrose (AD 340–397) said that "material
light pours out a dark mist, so that the light of true glory is not seen."[25]

But you cannot aim for these sorts of experiences. You have to
aim for Christ. To aim instead for the gifts would be a short trip
to demonic confusion. In this regard, the American work-hard-
get-results mind-set can be perplexing to Eastern Christians.
Fr. Roman Braga (whom I mentioned earlier, discussing what
Americans inquirers are like) said that a clergyman from a Western
denomination came to him "asking how many times he should say

---

†   An elder is a *geronda* or *gerondissa* in Greek, *starets* or *staritsa* in Russian.

the Jesus Prayer in order to see the Uncreated Energy." Fr. Roman told him, "Do not say the prayer anymore."[26]

In some ways, theosis doesn't fit our concept of "spirituality," because it's not a solitary achievement. One of those things that I didn't notice for years is that Orthodox don't refer to the people who have advanced on this path as "mystics." Mystics are as solo mountain climbers, whose descriptions of the heights inspire our awe. But Orthodox saints of this type would instead be called "wonderworkers". We know them as people who do things that benefit others, for they are people in relationship. Christ is in them not for their own private enjoyment, but to reach and bless others.

Not all who go to see a holy monastic are respectful. Some want to witness a miracle, others are skeptics hoping to expose a fraud, and some come just to have fun provoking him. When young visitors pressed Elder Paisios to perform a miracle, he went into his hut and came back out with a knife. He told them to stand up, saying, "I will cut your heads off and then I will miraculously glue them back to their place." He warned them not to stand too close together, in case he got the heads mixed up. The young men hurriedly assured him that they weren't looking for that kind of miracle.[27]

Though we've taken some time to explore the concept of theosis, you'll find that it isn't something Orthodox talk about all the time. It's a personal thing, not the stuff of everyday conversation. It would be pointless, and dangerous, to try to evaluate how far you had advanced toward theosis. In every situation, humility is the best course.

7

"Christ and Him Crucified"
(1 COR. 2:2)

Icon of the Crucifixion, Models of Atonement, The Light of God, Lamentations for the Crucified Christ

ear us, behind the chanters' stand, we can see a large icon of the Crucifixion. The Virgin Mary and St. John stand on either side of the cross, Mary looking up at her Son, while the other women disciples gather around and hold her; touchingly, she is smaller than they are, this heartbroken little old woman. She is on the left and St. John on the right, and he is looking down, resting his cheek against his palm, bewildered and sad. Behind him stands the centurion, St. Longinus, who lifts his arm to gesture toward Christ: "Truly this was the Son of God!" (Matt. 27:54).

But you might notice something different about Christ himself. He doesn't look as if he is *suffering* on the cross. Instead, he is victorious. Rather than sagging from the nails in his hands, he stands strong, as if he is holding the cross upright. He ascended the cross voluntarily, and turned it into a throne. His arms are spread and hands lifted as in prayer, like worshipers in the book of Psalms, and in frescoes in the Roman catacombs. His expression is composed—resolute, even. "It is finished" (John 19:30).

When the movie *The Passion of the Christ* (2004) came out, its bloody violence sparked a lot of discussion. Many news stories explained that, in the early church, depictions of the Crucifixion were restrained; but with the coming of the Plague, in the fourteenth century, depiction became more graphic. It was said that people were seeing so much suffering in that terrible time that they began showing the brutality of the Cross more realistically.

After that change began, artistic treatment of the Crucifixion continued to develop in the West, till by now it's been presented in almost every way imaginable. (I saw, in a gift shop, a purple teddy bear with the Crucifixion embroidered on his tummy.) But in the East it didn't change; Christ is still depicted on the cross as noble and strong.

It wouldn't be accurate, though, to think that this is because the early Christians didn't see death in terrible forms, like people of the Plague did. Crucifixion was only one of the ways Romans thought up to execute people, and Christians saw, and suffered, death in cruel and grotesque ways. When persecuted early believers looked at Christ, they didn't need to see more suffering. What they needed to see was victory.

In the Roman catacombs there are many frescoes that show biblical characters who were condemned to death, like Daniel in the lions' den, and the three young men in the fiery furnace. Icon scholar Leonid Ouspensky notes that these paintings do not show the terrible moment of sacrifice, but rather how the faithful person responds in such circumstances. "That which could calm, strengthen, and teach was portrayed, and not that which could possibly repel or frighten."[28]

No doubt more-graphic representations of the Crucifixion began to appear in Europe because of the inescapable sights and smells of the Black Death, and also due to a general trend toward increased naturalism in art. (Some artists actually used corpses as models.) But I think another reason was that a new theory emerged about the meaning of the Cross—about *how* Christ saves us, and what he saves us from.

The earliest understanding, as we saw in the icon of the Resurrection, was that Christ went into the depths of Hades, following the path of all human life; but once there he destroyed its power and set us free. Sin is a corruption of the soul, an illness that feeds on itself and leads ultimately to death. Death is an inevitable consequence of Adam and Eve choosing to separate themselves from God; he is life, so separation from him is death. It is not a punishment God inflicts. A mother who says, "If you keep climbing up there, you're going to fall and break your leg," and is proved right, has not inflicted the broken leg to punish the child's disobedience.

Salvation means that we are being healed in soul and restored to God's image and likeness; for the departed, it also means being rescued from the realm of Death, just as the children of Israel were freed in the Red Sea.

But a shift in thinking took place later on in Western European Christianity. It was St. Anselm, archbishop of Canterbury (AD 1033–1109), who first clearly formulated a line of thought that had been present in seed form in Western theology for centuries.[29] God cannot simply forgive our sins without punishment, he said, for that would leave sin uncorrected; nothing in God's kingdom could be left uncorrected. Furthermore, it would mean that God treats sinful and sinless people alike. That would be unjust.

St. Anselm reasoned that some restitution (or, to use the old term, satisfaction) had to be made to God in return for the great offense that our sin presents to his honor. This echoes the feudal system of his time, which laid great emphasis on preservation of honor. A feudal lord was not free to forgive a slight—not even if the offender had taken responsibility, apologized, and was truly sorry. Penitence was not enough. A lord was obligated, for the sake of the social order, to require satisfaction.

Since God's honor was infinitely greater than that of any earthly ruler, it would be impossible for humans to render the satisfaction required. By dying on the cross, Christ offered to the Father a gift he did not owe. "One who could freely offer so great a gift to God clearly ought not to be without reward," Anselm wrote: the Son ought to receive some reward from the Father. "If the Son chose to make over the claim he had on God to man, could the Father justly forbid him doing so?"[30]

From this point on, a shift takes place in Western theology. For the early church, Christ's work is aimed at Death; he defeats it and sets us free. "The reason the Son of God appeared was to destroy the works of the devil" (1 Jn. 3:8). But now Christ's work is seen as being aimed, not at Death, but at the Father; now, he is paying our debt so we could be forgiven. Originally, salvation was a victory, like the Exodus through the Red Sea; now, it becomes a transaction.

The idea that we needed to be saved from a malevolent enemy begins to diminish. The idea that we needed to be saved from just retribution begins to grow. Of course there is more subtlety than that—a great deal of thought went into these matters—but speaking broadly, the understanding of salvation began to change.

St. Anselm understood the Cross as providing "satisfaction" for God's injured honor (so it's called the "satisfaction atonement" theory). But before long, other theologians, who judged this view too legalistic, proposed that Christ came instead to teach, inspire, and provide us with a good example (the "moral influence" theory). In this other view, Christ's self-sacrificing death draws the Father and the human race into loving reconciliation.

A variation we hear today holds that Christ was in fact not God, but merely a great teacher who provided an example for us to follow. St. Augustine responded to an ancient variation on this theory by saying that, if imitation of a righteous man were all we needed, we wouldn't speak of "Adam and Christ" but "Adam and Abel." Adam's virtuous son supplied us with a fine example. We needed more than that.[31]

While Anselm proposed that God sent his Son so he would not have to punish us for our sins, others proposed that the Cross *was* the punishment for our sins ("penal substitutionary atonement theory"). In that case, Christ absorbed that punishment in our place (his suffering accomplished the "expiation" for our sins). Or perhaps the Father was consumed with wrath for sinners, and only the sight of Christ's death could soothe his anger (his suffering accomplished the "propitiation" of the Father). Some said that God has chosen whom he will call to salvation before our lives begin ("predestination"). Others carried it further, saying that God creates some people for salvation, and just as deliberately creates others for damnation ("double predestination").

Another idea was that Christ had supplied on the cross much more "satisfaction" than was necessary, since a single drop of his blood would have sufficed. The sinless Virgin Mary and other saints, by their holy lives, also contributed to the satisfaction of God's honor, so that there is now an overabundance of merits, far exceeding the debt. This "treasury of grace," administered by the Catholic Church, can be applied in the form of "indulgences" to lighten the temporal punishment for sinners. (In the Roman Catholic understanding, Christ pays the eternal debt for our sins, but we ourselves must pay the temporal debt, either in this life or the next.)[32]

This is only a hop and a skip over some of the variations, and if you wanted to explore further you could go on reading for years. For their part, lifelong Orthodox are often astonished to learn that anyone believes something had to happen before the Father could forgive us. They assume that he simply forgives us, as the father of the Prodigal forgave his son (Lk. 15:11–32).

So, as we look again at this large icon of the Crucifixion in St. Felicity's nave, let's think about the different ways the scene can be depicted. If you believe that Christ's suffering pays the sin-debt we owe to the Father, then it might be fitting that it look like a brutally violent event. Our sins are overwhelmingly evil and numerous, and we would be helpless before such debt. We gaze upon the awful extent of Christ's suffering, and realize the awful extent of our sin.

But in this icon of the Crucifixion, Christ isn't depicted in terrible suffering. Instead, he looks serene and majestic—heroic, even in death. He looks like a victorious champion.

How do we usually depict heroes? Imagine that a police officer risks his life to rescue some foolish teens who had strayed into the wrong part of town and been kidnapped by drug dealers. He manages to locate the kidnappers' lair and breaks down the door, shielding the kids as they all run free.

But at the last moment he himself is captured. The evil ones pull him back inside and torture him. He accomplished a great rescue, but it cost him much suffering. That pack of foolish and disobedient teens got themselves into a bad situation, and were helpless to rescue themselves. It was only by the courageous self-giving of the officer that they were saved.

The officer's sacrifice would make a big impression on the townspeople, and they might decide to put up a statue in his honor. It touches them deeply that he endured torture and humiliation to set their children free. But would they want the statue to show him undergoing that torture, broken and bleeding? No, of course not. It is his *victory* they want to proclaim. The pain he endured increases their gratitude all the more, and they might even say, "He bought their freedom with his blood." But it would seem disrespectful to pry into the details. They honor his dignity by drawing a curtain over that hideous scene.

Now imagine a movie director comes to town, and says he wants to make a film about that brave officer. To the townspeople that sounds like a great idea. But then he explains that most of the film will focus on the officer being tortured. That's more interesting than the rescue itself. He wants to show the officer's debasement and humiliation, with plenty of gore. I think the townspeople would find that repulsive, and insulting to the hero they admire.

During Holy Week, the Orthodox Church honors Christ's suffering and death with a service called the Twelve Passion Gospels. (This falls on the evening of Great and Holy Thursday, called Maundy Thursday in the West.) In the course of the service the priest and deacon read through the Passion narrative in all four Gospels, beginning with Christ's final talk with the apostles (John 13:31–18:1) and concluding with Pilate's setting a guard at the tomb (Matt. 27:62–66). It's an Orthodox custom to kneel during these Gospel readings, and between them we stand to offer hymns and prayers. The service takes about three hours (the first reading alone is twenty minutes) and lays to rest any concerns that Orthodox do not sufficiently engage with the Scriptures.

When we come to the point of the Crucifixion, we sing:

> The one who robes himself in light stands naked before the judge;
> He receives a blow on the cheek from hands he himself formed;
> The law-breakers nail the King of Glory to the Cross.
> Now the veil of the temple is torn in two and the sun is darkened,
> Because it could not bear to see God abused,
> The only God, before whom all Creation stands in holy fear. . . .
> All Creation trembled, O Christ, to look upon your Crucifixion.
> The foundations of the earth shook before your fearsome power;
> The sun and moon turned away, and the temple veil was torn in two,
> The mountains quaked, the rocks were split.
> With the faithful thief we cry out,
> "O Savior, remember us."

All creation was shaken with fear and astonishment at seeing their Creator's self-emptying, his humiliation "unto death, even death on a cross" (Phil. 2:8). Icons sometimes include, in the sky behind the cross, the sun and moon turning away, and distraught angels covering their eyes. When a hero is being broken by evil, we turn our eyes away.

Like artists in every form of media, the writers who crafted the Gospels had some choices available when it came to describing the Crucifixion. The four authors wrote their Gospels in different styles and emphasized different aspects of Christ's life—but when it came to the Crucifixion scene, they all made the same choice. They depicted it with great restraint, and as briefly as possible. "They crucified him," say Matthew, Mark, Luke, and John (Matt. 27:35; Mk. 15:24; Lk. 23:33; John 19:18), and present no further details.

Surely that wasn't because they were unfamiliar with death in terrible forms; the Romans loved to crucify people. Nor were they embarrassed that the Lord had died the death allotted to criminals. St. Paul proclaimed, indeed, that he would glory in nothing but the Cross (Gal. 6:14). Nor did they avoid the gory details because of a general inclination toward daintiness; Judas's death is described in graphic terms (Acts 1:18).

So why this restraint? I think it might have to do with those different understandings of salvation. Which do you think is most important, the suffering or the victory? An artwork that focuses on the pain and blood presumes that we can empathize with Christ's suffering; we can know what it felt like. A work that draws back in awe assumes that we can have *no idea* how it felt; we could not begin to comprehend it. When God comes to suffer and die, all we can do is fall down before him in awe.

Some would call the more-graphic presentation "realistic." But what was reality on that Good Friday? A bloody depiction could only show the reality that was visible to human onlookers, presenting what it looked like to those who mocked Christ as much as those who mourned him. The icon shows a deeper reality, perceptible only to those who have eyes to see. On the cross, our Lord and God was triumphant. He was winning for us a victory over our ancient enemy, Death.

Are we able to see that deeper "reality"? Much of the work in spiritual growth is along that line; we are always trying to adjust our perception so we can see the "real" reality, trying to crash through our habitual assumption that we are alone in this world, that God is too busy to notice what we're doing, and that if he's watching at all, it's "From a Distance."*

The kind of "realism" icons bring helps correct our perception, bringing it into accord with the presence of God throughout all creation, mightier than the forces that heave up mountains, and closer than a sigh. We need to see victorious images of the Crucifixion—in fact, need to see Christ's victory in every icon—precisely because our grasp of reality is so intermittent and weak.

---

* I wonder if that song is so popular because some people would actually *prefer* a God who stayed at a distance, and didn't take an active interest in their daily lives.

Speaking of God's presence with us, let's get a closer look at the chandelier; it hangs in the center of the nave, to represent the presence of Christ the Light in our midst. This is a large and imposing creation, descending in multiple tiers of brass with light-bulb candles encircling each level. At the very bottom there is a small brass hand, the fingers arranged as if giving a blessing.

This is a liturgical chandelier. During Matins on the great feasts of the church year, when we're singing Psalm 134/135 and 135/136—the *Polyeleos*, or "Many Mercies" hymn—a member of the congregation will take this chandelier by its brass hand and start it swinging in a circle. The enormous, heavy structure will go swooping around, tracing big circles in the air, creaking, throwing light in all directions. When it starts to slow down, someone standing nearby will give it another swing. The sight is imposing and impressive, and a little bit scary—which is the way we should feel about God, I suppose. The custom arose on Mount Athos, the peninsula in northern Greece that is populated entirely by monks and regarded as the center of Orthodox spirituality. When a chandelier is fitted with flaming candles, and the spinning light is glancing off golden icons and mosaics, the effect is awesome indeed.

Let's think for a minute about the properties of light, since we tend to miss an aspect of its meaning in the Scriptures. Until modern times the only source of light was fire, whether an oil lamp, a cooking fire, or the blazing midday sun. When you see a reference to *light* in any ancient text, keep in mind that the author expected you would picture *fire*. So when the Bible says, "God is light" (1 John 1:15), we shouldn't picture a table lamp. St. John had something more dangerous in mind.

Through most of history, respect for fire was one of the first lessons children learned. Used wisely, fire is a blessing; it gives light and warmth, cooks food, cheers the soul. But misuse can be catastrophic, leading to searing pain, destruction, and death. Fire will not change its nature, but we will be changed by fire, to our good or loss, depending on how we approach it. "Our God is a consuming fire" (Deut. 4:24; Heb. 12:29). So be wise. "The fear [reverent awe] of the LORD is the beginning of wisdom" (Ps. 111:10).

Reflecting on the nature of fire helps us understand how the presence of God could be joy to some and pain to others. In the next life we will all be in the presence of God. We are in his presence now, but it is veiled by creation, and in the next life the veil is taken away. What will that unveiled presence be like? Someone who loves God will find that all-pervading light to be overflowing with life and joy, and fully comprehend what it means to say "God is love" (1 John 4:8, 16). But one who "love[s] darkness rather than light" (John 3:19) will find the inescapable light misery and destruction; for her, this light will be paradoxical darkness, an "outer darkness [where] people will weep and gnash their teeth" (Matt. 8:12; 22:13; 25:30).

But if God is offering us his love, some ask, how could it feel like pain? A friend told me the story of how, as a child, he went with his mother to give a Christmas gift to an estranged aunt. The mother opened a gift the aunt offered, and found something insultingly cheap. She thanked her, and offered her own gift. When the aunt had unwrapped it just enough to see she'd been given something lovely and valuable, she exploded in rage; she shouted, "You did that on purpose!"

Even in this life, for some people, love burns. And God is always love. He is always light. He is always fire. People can experience that presence in very different ways, depending on whether they welcome or try to defy him.

St. Isaac the Syrian (d. AD 700) describes the pain of love in another way:

> Those who are punished in Gehenna are scourged by the scourge of love. . . . I mean that those who have become conscious that they have sinned against love suffer greater torment from this than from any fear of punishment. For the sorrow caused in the heart by sin against love is sharper than

any torment that can be. . . . This is the torment of Gehenna: bitter regret. But love inebriates the souls of the children of Heaven by its delectability.[33]

As we look up into the dome, past the chandelier, we can see that there is an icon of Christ at the top, looking down and blessing us. No matter how many icons are in a church, the highest one should always be of our Lord. The dome is supported by four large columns, and the transition from circular dome to square floor plan is smoothed by four long triangles (called *pendentives*). These triangles, reaching down from the dome to the tops of the columns, are filled with icons of the four Evangelists. Their work in writing the Gospel is a kind of transition, too, for it brought the knowledge of Christ and his saving work into the world.

Passing under the dome, we now move toward the front of the church, nearer the iconostasis. You'll notice there is no pulpit. St. Felicity's priest, Fr. John, just stands in front of the iconostasis when he preaches, though some other Orthodox churches do have pulpits. You'll notice, near the iconostasis on the right, a wooden armchair with elaborately carved arms and back; this is the bishop's chair, which he uses when he visits, and which, when he's not here, reminds us of his covering prayers.

There is an unfamiliar item of furniture in the corner, and it looks something like a double-decker wooden table, with fancy carving all around. This is the church's bier, which is used once a year on the evening of Great and Holy Friday (called Good Friday in the West), as we enact Christ's funeral procession. Earlier that day, at noon on Holy Friday, the bier is set in front of the iconostasis, and children of the parish, guided by a few adults, cover it with flowers.

Now, look up at the large needlework icon framed and hanging above the bier. It's called the *epitaphion*, and depicts the Lord lying on a slab of stone, while his mother cradles his head and St. Nicodemus and St. Joseph of Arimathea bow at his feet. Around the four sides of the image are embroidered the words of the troparion to St. Joseph of Arimathea.

> Noble Joseph brought your pure body down from the tree,
> And wrapped it in fine linen;
> He anointed it with precious ointment,
> Arrayed it, and laid it in his own new tomb.

After the bier is decorated there is an afternoon Vespers service in which the epitaphion is laid upon the bier, as St. Joseph and St. Nicodemus laid Christ's body. Then, at the evening service, we sing funeral hymns (the Lamentations) around this bier, the children alternating verses with adults. Then the bier is shouldered by four parishioners who lead the congregation outside in a candlelit procession, and around the exterior of the church. When the four bearing the bier arrive back at the church door, they lift it high, and each worshiper bows to enter the church by passing below it, representing our humble acceptance of Christ's death on our behalf.

After the close of the service, volunteers take turns keeping vigil by the bier all night long. They stand at the chanters' stand and read the Gospels aloud from the end of the Lamentations service until the beginning of the Divine Liturgy on Holy Saturday morning.

Before the Friday-evening service ends, a chanter sings this ancient hymn, attributed to St. Epiphanius (AD 310–403):

> When Joseph saw that the sun had hidden its light,
> And the Temple veil had been torn in two at the Savior's death,
> He came to Pilate and pleaded with him, crying out:
> Give me this stranger, who from his youth has wandered homeless, like a stranger.
> Give me this stranger, whom his own relatives have killed like a hated stranger.
> Give me this stranger, who appears, strange wonder, as a guest in the house of death.
> Give me this stranger, for he gives shelter to the poor and strangers.

Give me this stranger, whom his own kinsmen have estranged
  from the world in their envy.
Give me this stranger, that I may entomb him who, like a
  stranger, had no place to lay his head.
Give me this stranger, whose mother looked upon his lifeless
  body and cried out:
"O my Son and my God!
As I behold you dead all my inward parts are wounded and my
  heart is in flames;
And yet I trust in your Resurrection, and I magnify you."
With such words honorable Joseph pleaded with Pilate.
Then he took the Savior's body and, with holy fear,
Shrouded it in linen with fine ointments.
In his own new tomb he laid you, O Christ,
You who give to all everlasting life and great mercy.

8

"Image of the Invisible God"
(COL. 1:15)

Iconoclasm, The Iconostasis, Images of Christ, Images of the Theotokos, The Image Behind the Image

n the 1920s, archaeologists began to uncover a significant find: a garrison city that had been built on the banks of the Euphrates, at the eastern edge of the Roman Empire (today it's in Syria). When the Persians attacked, around AD 256, Roman soldiers strengthened their defenses by packing earth and sand into several of the buildings that stood along the inside of the city wall. But the Persians conquered that city nevertheless, then abandoned it. This beleaguered city, known as Dura-Europos, then enjoyed a little posthumous good fortune: nothing was ever built on top of its ruins. When scientists began removing the centuries of sand, they found it perfectly preserved.

One of the buildings that had been preserved was a Christian house church—the earliest yet found. Its walls were decorated with paintings, and show many biblical scenes: Christ and St. Peter walking on the water, the healing of the paralytic, and the women coming to Christ's tomb to anoint his body (Orthodox call them the "myrrh-bearing women"). Archaeologists also found scrolls bearing Eucharistic prayers in Hebrew. (They resemble the Eucharistic prayers in the *Didache*, an important early Christian text, written about AD 80, when the Gospels were being written).

This was clearly a church building. An Orthodox church built today, or at any point in history, could look much the same, with walls covered in icons (as at St. Felicity).

But something else was found in the ruins of that city. Another of the preserved buildings was a synagogue—and it, too, was covered with paintings of biblical scenes. Abraham and Isaac, Pharaoh's daughter finding baby Moses, Ezekiel's visions, narrative scenes, portraits of Bible characters—about a hundred images when the building was complete, of which fifty-eight remain. These paintings resemble the ones in the house church nearby. They look like icons.

Both Christians and Jews of Dura-Europos filled their worship spaces with images drawn from the Scriptures, and did not think this was idolatry. Greco-Roman homes had long been decorated with wall paintings and mosaics, and the custom may have passed over to religious buildings without a lot of debate.

But in the seventh century something happened that provoked a *great deal* of debate. The Muslim faith arose and swept through the region, and three of the Pentarchy cities—Jerusalem, Antioch, and Alexandria—as well as many other Christian communities fell to the sword. Islam forbade the use of images, and some Christians wondered if God were permitting this destruction as punishment for idolatry.

Backed by the command of the Roman emperor in Constantinople, the iconoclasts (it means "icon smashers") began destroying every icon in reach. Images were burned, crushed, hacked, thrown in the sea, and covered with paint or plaster. This is why so few early icons remain; the ones with a chance to survive were in remote locations, like the Roman catacombs, the St. Catherine Monastery on Mt. Sinai, or the buried church of Dura-Europos.

No doubt there had been excesses among those who loved icons, and it was right for the church to spend some time thinking through the question. What is an icon, and what is an idol? Does an image of a person relate or connect to that person in any real way? Does how we treat an image pass through it, so to speak, to the person himself?

You might think, "Of course not. That's superstition." But remember some years ago when the singer Sinéad O'Connor tore up a photo of the pope on live television? There was immediate and widespread outrage, and not only among those who liked the pope. It struck people as appallingly rude, and seriously damaged the singer's career. But someone could well say, "Why all the fuss? She only tore up paper and ink. It didn't actually hurt him."

Yet we sense somehow that a photo is more than paper and ink; it connects with the person in some way. Think about how people react when a flag is burned, or how crowds rejoiced when a statue of Stalin or Saddam Hussein was pulled down. The honor or dishonor shown to an image is passed on to its prototype; that's something we grasp instinctively.

A monk called St. Stephen the New (he was "New" in the eighth century) showed the iconoclast emperor Constantine that he himself knew this. St. Stephen was challenged to trample on an icon of Christ, to prove he agreed that it was merely wood and paint, and that such an action gave no disrespect to the Lord. Instead, he placed on the ground a coin bearing the emperor's image. He then set his foot upon it—and was immediately executed.

The Syrian monk St. John of Damascus (AD 676–749) deserves credit for much of the theological labor that established what icons are and how they should be handled.* He used the example of the emperor's statue: we know it's appropriate to treat the statue with respect, even though we also know it does not embody the emperor but is a mute object, made of wood and paint.[34]

That example reveals something else we already know: that we can honor the emperor without treating him like a god. There are gradations of respect. To God alone we give worship, and to the

---

* He lived in Muslim-held lands (Damascus and Jerusalem) and, ironically, was able to write in defense of icons because that put him out of the emperor's reach. St. John also wrote the first Christian critique of Islam. He had close exposure to that faith, as his father was secretary to the caliph in Damascus.

"friends and servants" of God, the saints and prophets (as well as earthly leaders), we accord honor of a lesser degree.[35] Worship of God contains and exceeds all the lesser forms of veneration, like a state contains a city.

Iconoclasts often covered up icons with images of the cross, but St. John pointed out that this was merely to swap one image for another. A cross displayed in a church is not *the* cross, but a copy of it. If we can honor an image or replica of the cross, why not the image of the Crucified One, who gave the cross its meaning? We don't honor the wood for its own sake, St. John said, but because of what it represents. If the two beams of a wooden cross were separated, he said, he would not hesitate to use them for kindling.[36]

St. John affirmed that we must not make images of the unseen God, and cannot depict mysteries God has not shown us. But when Christ took on flesh, he deliberately made God visible, in the form and to the extent that he himself chose. He became "the image of the invisible God" (Col. 1:15), choosing to reveal something that was formerly invisible. ("He who has seen me has seen the Father," John 14:9). What God has made visible we can likewise depict in visible ways; what remains unseen we will not depict.[†]

St. John cited the Council of Trullo (AD 692), which addressed the custom of depicting Christ as a lamb (for example, depicting St. John the Forerunner pointing toward a lamb and saying, "Behold the Lamb of God," John 1:29, 36). The council noted that this representation was an ancient custom, a "symbol of grace," but that it was better to present to the people "that which is perfect . . . Christ our God . . . in his human form." Henceforth Christ was to be shown in the form he had chosen for himself, as a human being, and not as an imaginary lamb.[37]

"Of old, God the incorporeal and uncircumscribed was never depicted," St. John wrote, adding:

[†] That rule would exclude some of the Christian art I've seen, such as Christ embracing a new arrival in heaven.

Now that God has been seen clothed in flesh and conversing with humankind, I make an image of the God whom I see. I do not venerate matter, I venerate the fashioner of matter, who became matter for my sake, and deigned to dwell in matter, who worked out my salvation through matter. I will not cease from venerating that matter which works my salvation.[38]

St. John pointed out that God instructed Moses to make the ark of fine wood and gild it outside and in, so that the people who gazed upon it would be moved to love and worship God. Sight is "the noblest sense,"[39] and we sanctify it when we look upon those things that remind us of God's faithfulness and his works in history. St. John wrote that, when he comes into church "strangled with thoughts, as if with thorns," and beholds a beautiful image, it "delights my sight like a meadow and imperceptibly introduces my soul to the glory of God." For the illiterate, images are even more essential: "What a book is to the literate, that an image is to the illiterate."[‡]

In AD 787 the empress Irene convened the seventh ecumenical council to settle the controversy. The council ruled that images of Christ and his saints could be painted, woven as fabric, and made as mosaics. These images should be displayed in churches, homes, and elsewhere, so that those seeing them would be moved to remember and love the persons depicted. The council wrote, "The veneration accorded to an icon is in effect transmitted to the prototype; he who venerates the icon, venerates in it the reality for which it stands."[40][§]

---

‡   I understood this long before I became Orthodox. When my son was a toddler I bought a plaque that showed Jesus with a group of children, embracing them. I would show it to him at bedtime, and tell him Jesus loved him, and we would both kiss it.

§   You might be wondering why Orthodox churches have flat-panel depictions and low-relief carvings, but not statuary. There's actually no rule against statues, but for some reason they haven't been much used. Perhaps it's because the art forms affect the viewer differently. The figure you see in a flat icon might be anywhere, might be any size; but a statue shares room space with you, and you can walk all the way around it. Statues may have been more common in the earliest years; St. Eusebius says that the woman healed of a flow of blood (Mk. 5:25–34) made a statue depicting this miracle, and it was still visible in Caesarea Philippi in his day (Church History 8:18).

An important point had to do with a distinction between two Greek words, which English, unfortunately, cannot convey. The council declared that icons should be given the sort of honor called *proskynesis*, but not *latreia*. The first term, *proskynesis*, means the physical act of veneration, of bowing or bending the knee. We might bow this way before God, and also before a king or an icon; it is a common gesture of respect. But *latreia* is worship, which we give to God alone. Christ uses these terms in his rebuke to Satan: "You shall *proskyneseis* the Lord your God, and him only shall you *latreuseis*" (Matt. 4:10).

The seventh ecumenical council wasn't the end of the story, for iconoclasm soon reasserted itself. Another empress, this one named Theodora, convened a council that proclaimed a final vindication of icons. On the first Sunday of Lent, AD 843, she and all the royal family made a grand procession, with the city's clergy and monastics, carrying recovered icons back and restoring them to their places. This event is called the Triumph of Orthodoxy, and is observed on the first Sunday of Lent in Orthodox churches everywhere, with worshipers bearing icons in procession. The congregation proclaims these words, drawn from the acclamations of the seventh ecumenical council:

As the Prophets foresaw,
As the Apostles instructed,
As the Church received,
As the Teachers defined,
As the Universe confirmed,
As Grace illuminated,
As the Truth made clear,
As falsehood was thrown down,
As Wisdom was revealed,
As Christ has appointed,
Thus we announce,
Thus we assert,
Thus we proclaim Christ as our true God,

And also honor his saints,
In spoken words,
In written words,
In thoughts,
In offerings,
In church buildings,
In holy icons.
On the one hand, worshipping and honoring Christ as Lord
and God,
And, on the other hand, reverencing and venerating his Saints
As true servants of the same Lord.
This is the Faith of the Apostles.
This is the Faith of the Fathers.
This is the Faith of the Orthodox.
This is the Faith which has established the universe.

We've looked at several icons already, but now let's look at the iconostasis itself. You'll notice that it's a wooden screen standing between the nave and the altar area, about ten feet high. The side facing us displays a row of large icons side by side. In the center there is a waist-high door in two panels; these are called the "Royal Doors" or the "Holy Doors," and only clergy may pass through them. In many Orthodox churches a curtain hangs behind the Royal Doors, and it is opened and closed at certain points in the liturgy.

The Royal Doors bear an icon of the Annunciation, the moment the angel Gabriel appeared to the Virgin Mary to tell her she would have a son (Lk. 1:26–38). On the left panel the angel Gabriel is striding toward Mary, who, on the right panel, is gracefully holding a skein of red wool, and just now looking up toward him. This is the moment when everything begins.

To the right of these doors, on the iconostasis itself, is an icon of Christ, and it is imposing. Many icons depict Christ at various moments in his earthly life—at his baptism, transfiguration, or crucifixion. But the icon placed to the right of the Royal Doors will always show Christ as *Pantocrator*, "Ruler of All." His right hand is raised in blessing, and in his left he holds a large book inscribed, "I am the way, and the truth, and the life" (John 14:6). The inscription can vary, but it is always one of Jesus' sayings from the Gospel. Sometimes the book is shown closed, and the cover is elaborately decorated and fitted with jewels. This represents the Gospel book, the book that contains the Gospel passages read during services, which is kept upon the altar.

Notice something about Christ's halo. Three sets of parallel lines are inscribed on it, making the form of a cross. Within those lines, at the top, there is what looks like the letter *O*, and on the sides *W* and *N*. These three Greek letters (omicron, omega, and nu) are found in the Septuagint at Exodus 3:14, when Moses asks God what he should say when the people of Israel ask who sent him. The Lord replies "I am *O WN*"—a nearly untranslatable term that means "the one having existence" or "the one who is." (It's masculine rather than neuter, and so refers to a person, not the abstract concept of existence.) So these letters in Christ's halo tell us that he is the same God who spoke to Moses. The Orthodox belief, in fact, is that all the Old Testament appearances of God are manifestations of Christ.

To the left and right of Christ's head there are other letters, *I C* and *X C*. These are the first and last letters of "Jesus" and "Christ" in Greek. All icons of Christ will have these initials, and icons of his mother will have *M P* and *Θ Y*, the first and last letters of the Greek words that mean "Mother" (*Meter*) and "of God" (*tou Theou*). Icons of saints will have their names inscribed near their heads, and icons that show biblical events will be likewise labeled. Inscribing the name is the last step in making an icon; it is what makes it an icon, and not just a religious picture. A friend of mine silk-screened some saints' images on T-shirts, but made sure she removed those identifying letters. It would have been awkward if you were wearing one of those T-shirts and someone decided to venerate it.

You might notice that the eventual decision in favor of icons came about with the help of two women leaders, the empresses Irene and Theodora. This tells us something about how Orthodoxy views the role of women; we see that devout women can rule an empire, holding authority over both men and women, and even call a council of the worldwide church. These two ruled as regents for their minor-aged sons, but rule they did, and won important victories. In other Orthodox lands women reigned in their own right, like St. Tamar of Georgia (AD 1160–1213), still honored by her people as "Tamar the Great."

As we said earlier, the way to learn the Orthodox Church's view of something is to look at its prayers, hymns, and icons, and note what it praises in the lives of the saints. A glance at history reveals that a woman saint might be a political leader like St. Irene or St. Theodora; or she might be an evangelist like St. Mary Magdalene, St. Photini (the "woman at the well" of John 4), or St. Paul's companion St. Thekla, all of whom bear the title "Equal to the Apostles." A woman saint might be a teacher, a preacher, a spiritual mother, a miracle-worker, a healer, an iconographer, a theologian, a hymnographer, a counselor, a debater, a writer of prayers and theology, a martyr, or a fool for Christ.

Of course, men can be all those things, too. In other words, there aren't a lot of ministries that absolutely require a clergy collar. Ordination deserves great honor, for the work of the visible church and the gift of the Holy Mysteries (sacraments) have no earthly equal. But God has plenty of work for laypeople to do. We exaggerate only a little to say that you could draw a circle six or seven feet around an altar, and grant to lay men and women the whole rest of the world. That's where most of God's work gets done.

My husband and I were supporters of women's ordination in our previous denomination, and we recognized that, when we became Orthodox, the all-male priesthood was part of the package. We assumed that in time we'd learn the Church's reason for this.

Time passed, and we never did learn the reason. It turned out that this has never been controversial, and since theology is done on a "need to know" basis, the reasoning has never been explicitly formulated. (It seems significant that no previous generation of Orthodox Christians has been troubled by the all-male priesthood. Apparently something was obvious to them that is no longer obvious in our time.) Orthodox can't just adopt the explanations other churches give, in this or other matters; we need to think it through in the context of our own history and theology. Maybe the time has come to undertake that theological labor.

The icon that balances Christ Pantocrator, to the left of the Royal Doors, is of a woman: St. Mary the Theotokos, holding the infant Christ. You will always find her here, at Christ's right hand, for "on your right hand stands the queen" (Ps. 44/45:9).

In the West this image is called simply "Madonna and Child," but in the East there are a few more distinctions. If the Christ child is shown embracing his mother, his cheek pressed to hers and his arm around her neck, it is an *Eleousa* icon, which means "Tenderness." The best-known icon of the Virgin Mary, the "Virgin of Vladimir" (twelfth century), is an Eleousa.¶

Another way of depicting them is with the child sitting up on her lap, while she gestures toward him, showing the way to salvation. This kind of icon is called a *Hodigetria* ("Directress" or "She Who Shows the Way"). It's said that the original Hodigetria was painted by the Evangelist Luke, who interviewed the Virgin Mary in her old age while researching his Gospel.** The earliest Madonna-and-Child image yet found is in the catacomb of Priscilla in Rome, and dates to about AD 250. It's a fresh, naturalistic image, captured in a few allusive strokes: Mary is nursing her baby, but as we approach they both look up at us.

¶ The three stars on her shoulders and forehead signify her virginity before, during, and after Christ's birth.

** St. Luke's Gospel is the only one that tells us things Mary alone would know, such as the story of the Annunciation.

A third kind of icon of the Theotokos is the Virgin of the Sign, which shows a pregnant Mary standing with her hands raised in prayer, and her unborn Child visible in her womb. At St. Felicity, as at many Orthodox churches, the Virgin of the Sign fills the apse that rises behind the altar.

As we look at the arrangement of icons here, we see another example of how Orthodox tradition can be stretchy in some ways but not in others. On an iconostasis, the icon of Christ will always be on the right and Mary on the left.[††] Yet, as Mary holds her child, she might hold him in either her right or left arm; it doesn't matter, and that detail would go unnoticed. However, the icon of Mary on an iconostasis will almost invariably be one of these that show her holding the child in her arms, and not a standing Virgin of the Sign; if there's one of those (there doesn't have to be), it would be in the apse behind the altar.

I am calling this an icon of the Virgin Mary, but it is equally an icon of Christ, who in this case is being held in his mother's arms. This icon shows Christ at his first Advent, when he came to earth as a baby, while the Pantocrator to the right shows him at his second coming, when he will appear as Judge and Ruler of All. These two images flank the Royal Doors of the iconostasis, and through them we see the altar, where Christ comes to us in the present moment, in the Holy Gifts of his body and blood.

To the right of Christ, on this iconostasis, we see an icon of St. John the Forerunner (so called because he went before the Lord to proclaim his coming. "Behold, I send my messenger to prepare the way before me," Mal. 3:1). He is often shown turned toward Christ and making an imploring gesture, beseeching him in prayer. You might be surprised that St. John has large, multicolored wings;

†† In fact, anywhere icons of Christ and the Virgin are placed, they should be arranged that way, right and left; if more icons are added, these two hold the center.

this is to represent his role as a messenger. The Greek word *angelos*, "angel," means "messenger," and St. John is sometimes called "the Angel of the Desert."

To the left of the Theotokos there is an icon of St. Felicity, the patron saint of this parish. The icon of a parish's patron holds this spot, so you should always be able to tell the name of a church by looking at its iconostasis.[‡‡] Of course, we don't know exactly what she looked like, but icons aren't supposed to be historical records anyway. They aim to reveal instead the spiritual reality of the events and characters they depict. An icon of St. Felicity should show us how she looked when the light of Christ was shining through her. Every icon is really an icon of Christ.

While we don't know what St. Felicity looked like, in the case of some saints we do—a likeness may have been made while the saint was alive, such as the mosaic of St. Ambrose in his cathedral in Milan, or a fragment of a description may have come down, like the one about St. Paul's receding hairline or St. Andrew's wild gray locks. For a great many saints nothing is known besides gender and ethnicity. But we already know what people look like from the outside. What we need is some idea of where we're going; we need to gaze upon the image of a person transfigured in Christ.

The advent of photography complicated the visual arts in many ways, and that's true of iconography, too. Irina Yazykova writes in her book *Hidden and Triumphant*, about iconography in the Soviet era, that when depicting a contemporary saint an iconographer may make the mistake of replicating a photograph *too* exactly. Such icons are

> not quite iconographic—but more like portraits. The viewer has no feeling of an encounter with the saint's essence as it exists in the kingdom of heaven and finds no evidence of the miracle of transformation. In other cases, we notice a different extreme: in an effort to create generalization of the image the artist falls

---

‡‡ Now that I think about it, it's not clear when this skill would be useful. If you regularly wake up in a church and don't know where you are, you have bigger things to worry about.

into abstractionism. The saint's well-known face is distorted to the point that it is no longer even recognizable. The holy countenance has been transformed into a mask.

Whether the likeness is too exact or too vague, the icon cannot serve as a window into the kingdom of heaven:

> The viewer fails to feel an inner connection with such an icon, and it fails as an aid to prayer because no connection is made with the true prototype. Somehow the iconographer must find his or her way through these contradictory temptations in order to create an authentic new icon. [41]

The emphasis on Christ alone behind the life of every saint is one reason icons rarely depict the Virgin Mary by herself. Almost always, she is shown with her child. The intention is not so much to elevate the status of Mary as to ground the reality of Christ—to show that he was God from the beginning, from the moment he was conceived.

Though this iconostasis has only the one row of saints, they are sometimes built higher, sometimes in many tiers reaching to the ceiling. There might be a tier of biblical prophets, one of the twelve Great Feasts, or one showing saints standing in lines to the left and right, facing Christ in the center and lifting their hands in prayer. That arrangement, showing saints interceding in a row, is called a *deesis*. The two figures in the center, each facing Christ, are always Mary and John the Forerunner.[§§]

On this iconostasis there are doors on either side of St. Felicity and St. John, and an icon of St. Michael is installed on the left door and St. Gabriel on the right. These are called the "Angel Doors."[¶¶] Only clergy use the Royal Doors, but these are for

---

§§ This has a Western parallel in the medieval chancel screen or rood screen, a partition between the nave and chancel; these often displayed statues of St. Mary and St. John the Evangelist on either side of a crucifix.

¶¶ There's a variation: sometimes sainted deacons, like St. Stephen and St. Philip, are depicted instead. In that case they're called "Deacons' Doors."

others who have a liturgical reason, or the priest's blessing, to go behind the iconostasis.*** The altar area is off-limits except for those who have duties there; even dusting and vacuuming is done by the priest or by someone he appoints.

In front of each of the icons of Christ, the Theotokos, St. John, and St. Felicity is a hanging red glass lamp. This is called a *lampada*, and it is filled with oil (usually regular olive oil) and has a wick floating on top. As with the candles, these originally had the practical purpose of illumination, and in some churches have been replaced by electric lights.

Standing on the floor in front of the iconostasis are two large brass candlesticks, each supporting several circular tiers of candles. When worshipers enter the church, after venerating the icon next to the narthex door, they will come forward and venerate the icon of Christ, and then that of the Theotokos. It's like arriving at a dinner party and greeting first the host and then his mother. People pause to pray in front of the icons, and may leave a candle in the adjacent stand. There are also large vases of flowers on the floor in front of the icons of Christ and his mother. (No flowers on the altar; only a few items may be on the altar, as we will see.)

You might notice that the iconostasis, and in fact the entire altar area, is raised up a step from the rest of the floor of the nave. This platform is called the *bema*. The part of the bema that provides a walkway in front of the iconostasis is called the *solea*, while the little half-circular projection directly in front of the Royal Doors is called the *ambon*. This is where a deacon leads intercessions, and at St. Felicity the Scriptures are read here, too.

Let's step onto the solea and take a look through the Royal Doors.

*** When asking permission to do something, Orthodox ask for a "blessing" to do it.

9

"Your Body Is a Temple"
(1 COR. 6:19)

Icons in the Apse, The Altar, Divine Energies, Relics

tanding on the solea, we can look over the waist-high Royal Doors and view the area behind the iconostasis. Orthodox Christians refer to this part of the church as "the sanctuary." (Confusingly enough, in many Western churches that term refers to the entire worship space.) The whole area behind the iconostasis may also be called "the altar"; that term can mean both the Holy Table itself, and the entire area behind the iconostasis. It's good to know that, because you'll hear clergy refer to being "on the altar" or "in the altar," which would otherwise be a startling image.

Now, too, we can see the icons that fill the back wall of the apse— yes, there are icons here, too. If you're not used to it, a kind of visual overload might reasonably set in. But let's stick with it; you can learn a lot about Orthodoxy from icons.

Directly behind the altar, at floor level below the apse, there is a depiction of the Communion of the Apostles. Christ stands in the center, robed as a high priest, and stretches out his arms to offer the Bread and Cup (Orthodox call these the Holy Gifts) to his disciples. St. Peter, on the left, and St. Paul, on the right, are the first to receive, and behind each of them five other apostles wait their turn, bowing in reverence.

This icon doesn't depict the historic event of the Last Supper; St. Paul wasn't there that night. You do sometimes see that event depicted in icons, and it shows the more-familiar scene of the apostles arrayed around a table with Christ in the center. In that case the icon is called the "Mystical Supper." It would show on the right extension of the table—that is, on Christ's left hand—one disciple leaning forward, reaching into a serving bowl for a piece of bread. That's Judas, for Jesus said that his betrayer would be "he who has dipped his hand in the dish with me" (Matt. 26:23). Among the apostles Judas alone is shown in profile; in an icon, a half-hidden face indicates evil.

But this icon is called "the Communion of the Apostles," and depicts the Lord giving Communion to the apostles in a heavenly setting. Above this icon stands the Theotokos, rising into the curved ceiling of the apse, with her hands lifted in prayer. This is the Virgin of the Sign that we mentioned in the previous chapter; it is a very early way to depict the Virgin, and appears several times in the Roman catacombs. This stance is called the *orans* position (Latin for "praying"); many psalms speak of prayer with lifted hands, as in "I lift up my hands toward your most holy sanctuary" (Ps. 27/28:2, NRSV). The Theotokos is, in a way, our worship leader, showing us how to pray.

The name "the Virgin of the Sign" comes from the prophecy: "The Lord himself shall give you a sign; Behold, a virgin* shall conceive, and bear a son" (Isa. 7:14, quoted in Matt. 1:23). So this is an icon of the pregnant Virgin Mary, and we see, depicted in a disk on her torso, Christ in her womb, surrounded with stars.

This icon is also called the "Platytera," from a Greek word meaning "more spacious." It's a reference to a hymn in honor of the Virgin (called a *Theotokion*) from the Liturgy of St. Basil the Great (AD 329–379).

All Creation rejoices in you, O Mary, full of grace,
Both the angels and all humankind;
For you are a temple hallowed and set apart,
The glory of the company of virgins,

---

* You no doubt remember this verse as "a virgin shall conceive," but if you check your Bible it will probably say, "a young woman shall conceive." As we noted in chapter 3, the Greek Old Testament (the Septuagint or LXX), produced about 250 BC, has "virgin," while the Hebrew Old Testament (the Masoretic text or MT), produced about a thousand years later, has "young woman."

And in you God took on flesh and became a little child,
Though he is our eternal God.
He made your womb to be his throne;
He made your body more spacious than the heavens.
All Creation rejoices in you, O Mary, full of grace;
Glory to you.

The altar table itself (also called the "Holy Table") is in the center of this space, and that might be a surprise if you picture traditional liturgical churches having a high altar set against the back wall. Even in ancient Orthodox churches the altar was set forward; an apse provides a curved back wall, so a wall altar wouldn't fit. Also, sometimes the priest circles the altar swinging incense, or chants a series of prayers from all four of its sides in sequence, so there needs to be a way to walk around it. (The priest never stands behind the altar to lead prayers while facing the congregation, though.) When someone needs to cross from one side of the sanctuary to the other, he passes behind the altar, not in front.

In some ancient churches you may see behind the altar, lining the apse, semicircular ranks of stone benches that rise like steps or seats in an amphitheater. This is called a *synthronon* (the "common throne"), and in the most ancient churches it provided a place for clergy to sit during services. The topmost center seat was the bishop's throne. There's a story about St. Peter, the patriarch of Alexandria (d. AD 311), who would never sit on his throne or even on the steps below it. The faithful complained about this—they wanted to see their bishop in his majestic "High Place"—but he explained, "Whenever I approach the throne, I see a heavenly light and power upon it, and that is why I do not dare climb and sit on it." St. Peter is called "the Seal of the Martyrs" because he was the last patriarch of Alexandria to die for his faith.

St. Felicity's altar is a wooden table, about three feet square by three feet tall, and topped with a white damask cloth. Historically, altars have been made of stone, chiefly marble, but in some lands it is hard to get quarried stone. St. Innocent Veniaminov (1797–1879), a Russian bishop who came to the Aleutian Islands as a missionary, designed an altar that could be built anywhere out of local wood. So this altar, following that design, has four legs and a low cross-brace, just above floor level, joining them in an X. A wooden cross stands upright at the center of the X, below the table. When the table was made, a hole was drilled down through the top of this cross.

When the bishop came to consecrate St. Felicity Church, he brought three small packets of saints' relics, each one mixed with beeswax and wrapped in aluminum foil. During the service the bishop placed two of these into the opening in the upright cross beneath the altar, the relics of St. Cosmas Aitolos (executed by Ottoman Muslims in 1779) and St. Elizabeth the New Martyr (executed by Bolsheviks in 1918). He placed as well a scroll of paper listing the names of all the members of the church, then sealed the opening with molten wax. (The book of Revelation mentions martyrs' relics below an altar; we'll look at that Scripture soon.)

The third relic was of St. Juvenaly Hovorukhin (AD 1761–1796), one of the first American saints. When Russian merchants began trading with the Native Alaskans, there was a call for missionaries to bring the gospel to the new land. St. Juvenaly was one of a small band that journeyed all the way from the Russian border of Finland—eight thousand miles—to answer the call. This third relic was sewn to a golden cloth called the *antimens*, which is kept on the altar. We'll take a closer look at the antimens in the next chapter; for now, let's talk a little more about relics.

To many Christians the honoring of relics seems weird, primitive, a sick sort of magical fetishism. It sounds incompatible with Christian faith, not only because skeletons are creepy, but also because the human body, in fact the entire material world, is inherently suspect. If "God is spirit" (John 4:24), the world of matter must be at best illusory, at worst fatally deceitful, in its seductive allure.

Though this is widely assumed to be a tenet of Christian faith, it's actually a misunderstanding. In ancient Christianity, as in classic

Judaism, God does not stand apart from his creation and require us to choose. Instead, he permeates and fills it. "'Do I not fill heaven and earth?', says the LORD" (Jer. 23:24), and Isaiah heard the angels cry, "The whole earth is full of his glory" (Isa. 6:3). An often-used Orthodox prayer to the Holy Spirit says that he is "everywhere present and filling all things." As the Psalmist says:

> Whither shall I go from your Spirit?
>> Or whither shall I flee from your presence?
> If I ascend to heaven, you are there!
>> If I make my bed in Sheol, you are there!
> If I take the wings of the morning
>> and dwell in the uttermost parts of the sea,
> Even there your hand shall lead me,
>> and your right hand shall hold me.
> If I say, "Let only darkness cover me,
>> and the light about me be night,"
> Even the darkness is not dark to you,
>> the night is bright as day;
>> for darkness is as light with you. (Ps. 139:7–12)

Ancient Judaism recognized God as present throughout his creation. Not in a merely analogical sense—"If God made this, he must be like that"—but actually permeating and pervading it. This isn't pantheism; the idea is not that the material world contains God, as an animist might think that there's a god inside a tree. Instead, God simultaneously fills his creation and infinitely exceeds it. We don't have to puzzle over the question of whether God is immanent (present in this world) or transcendent (vastly beyond it). He's both.

St. Paul expressed this idea several ways:

- "In [Christ] all things hold together" (Col. 1:17).
- "Through [Christ] are all things and through [him] we exist" (1 Cor. 8:6).
- God the Father "is above all and through all and in all" (Eph. 4:6).

- To the Athenians he quoted the poet Epimenides of Knossos: "In [God] we live and move and have our being" (Acts 17:28).
- "Ever since the creation of the world his invisible nature, namely, his eternal power and deity, has been clearly perceived in the things that have been made" (Rom. 1:20).

Earlier I said that, when I was newly Orthodox, I felt like some unidentifiable thing was really *different* about it, compared with all the other sorts of Christian faith I'd known. When I came upon the little word "energy," I felt I'd found one of the clues. You'll probably be surprised to learn that *energeia* and its relatives occur dozens of times in the New Testament—surprised because we don't see "energy" in our English translations.† Most New Testament uses of *energeia* occur in St. Paul, for he often speaks of God "energizing" within us:

- "God is energizing in you, both to will and to energize for his good pleasure" (Phil. 2:13).
- "The word of God . . . is energizing in you believers" (1 Thess. 2:13).
- St. Paul sometimes combines it with *dynamis*, "power": "For this I toil, striving according to the energy of him energizing in me with *dynamis*" (Col. 1:29).
- The coming of the evil one will be "according to the energy of Satan . . . with all *dynamis* and with signs and false wonders" (2 Thess. 2:9).

If you could read the Bible with those energy words leaping out at you, it would be easier to grasp how God is present within this physical world. He is present in a supernatural way, energizing people and producing miracles; he is also present in a natural way, for he animates all creation ("I am . . . the life," John 11:25; 14:6). He even manifests himself at times in his Uncreated Light, as at the burning bush (Exod. 3) and Christ's Transfiguration (Mk. 9:2–8) There is an essence to

---

† Students of philosophy will recognize the term from Aristotle, but its meaning is a little different in the everyday Greek of the Bible.

God, an *ousia*, that we can never grasp, but his energies surround and fill us in natural and supernatural ways.

This term *energy* should not be taken to mean that God is present only when things get noticeably lively, but rather that he is the life that underlies everything in existence. His energy is what gives us bodies and breath, and also makes us *more* than bodies and breath: it gives us awareness and individuality, and enables us to see others and love them. "In him was life, and the life was the light of all people" (John 1:4, NRSV).

So why don't we see those energy words in our English Bibles? Because when St. Jerome (AD 331–420) was translating the Bible from Greek into Latin, there wasn't a good equivalent. "Energy" wasn't a Latin concept. An earlier Latin translator had just transliterated *energeia*, and it might have been adopted into Latin that way. But St. Jerome chose instead to use the term *operatio*, which means "operation" or "work."

We have the word *energy* in English now, of course, and it could be popped right into place when new translations are made. But we've read the Bible for too many centuries with the assumption that God "works" and "operates" instead. Yes, "working" and "energizing" are somewhat similar, but the energy words have a different feeling, don't they? If God is "energizing" in his creation, his life is coursing through every molecule. If, on the other hand, he is "working" in it, he can set it up and walk away, like the watchmaker in the Enlightenment-era analogy who put his masterwork together and then left it to run on its own.

In the last century quantum physics has made discoveries that disrupt our sense of matter as stolid and inert. We learn that within each atom there is ceaseless motion, that matter and energy are somehow equivalent, and that the apparent solidity of the visible world is an illusion. Everything we can see is, in a sense, alive, vibrant—as if God were continuously calling it into existence.

It's worth repeating that God's energies, by which we experience him in this world, are not all there is to God. In his essence, his unknowable inner reality, God is beyond anything we could sense or think. He is beyond existence, and also beyond anything we might imagine "nonexistence" to mean; he is beyond "being" and "nonbeing," beyond any pair of opposites you could name. It is true that "God is love" (1 Jn. 4:8), and yet we could also say that God is *not* love, because what we mean when we say the word "love" is utterly inadequate. Whatever we think or picture when we say "love" is too shallow to describe the reality.

One reason we get mixed up about materiality, and the human body in particular, is that St. Paul makes an emphatic distinction between "flesh" and "spirit." He says, for example, "the desires of the flesh are against the Spirit, and the desires of the Spirit are against the flesh; for these are opposed to each other" (Gal. 5:17). St. Paul often uses the term "flesh" in a negative way, but here's where we get confused: the opposite of "the flesh" is not bodilessness. It is a good and holy body. St. Paul chastised the Corinthians,

> The body is not meant for immorality, but for the Lord. . . .
> Do you not know that your bodies are members of Christ? . . .
> Do you not know that your body is a temple of the Holy Spirit
> within you? . . . Glorify God in your body." (1 Cor. 6:13, 15,
> 19–20)

There's a popular impression that Christians believe death will free us from these gross corporeal bodies, and at last we will enter an ideal ethereal state. But that's actually a variation of the heresy called Gnosticism. We aren't composed of a spirit operating a body, like a person driving a car; God created us to be embodied beings, both in this present life and for eternity. When body and soul are separated at death, it ruptures this unity. We won't experience the fullness of heaven until body and soul are reunited again at the Resurrection on the Last Day (1 Cor. 15:35–41). Transformation in Christ does not mean escape from our bodies, but right and holy embodiment.

So having a physical body is not the problem; an unrestrained and distorted appetite is the problem. God designed all creatures with bodily desires that sustain and pass on life; among our fellow animals we humans can observe many lessons in how to handle them in a well-proportioned way. Moderation doesn't come easily to humans, though, and misuse of our bodies injures both body and soul. We are prey to imperious desires that command our obedience (called "passions" in Orthodox writing).‡

Those who persevere in the Way find that the passions can gradually be healed (in rare instances, not gradually but suddenly and miraculously). The Lord will "give you the desires of your heart" (Ps. 37:4), give you the desires themselves, so that you are no longer in bondage to compulsions you hate. The passions are not annihilated, but redirected; anger, for example, can be turned into the strength and energy to live a holy life. Just as spiritual disciplines strengthen our ability to guide the body, bodily disciplines, like fasting, bring about healing in the soul. Orthodox frequently use the term *ascetic* when speaking of habits of prayer, fasting, and so on. Unfortunately, that term has come to mean, in common use, "ascetic in an extreme and unhealthy way." It comes from *asketes*, and means someone training to learn a professional skill or win an athletic contest.

An athlete would not intentionally injure himself, and you rarely find in the Christian East the medieval European theme of physical self-punishing called "mortification of the flesh." This is a subtle distinction, because just denying yourself ice cream can feel like self-punishing. Ascetic disciplines have to be challenging, or they'd be ineffectual. But the goal is increased self-control, rather than pain or punishment. The disciplines look forward at the contest ahead, rather than backward at paying for bad deeds. (It's still useful to understand past failures, because it helps us recognize and resist our weaknesses; that's like a football team studying videos of their past mistakes.)

In Western medieval spirituality the idea developed that one can prayerfully offer to endure suffering in return for alleviating the

---

‡   The Greek word is *pathos*, "suffering," and is the same word used for Christ's suffering, his Passion, on the cross. The term shares a root with "passive," as the violence of the passions is something we suffer and endure.

suffering of someone else. This isn't an idea found in Orthodoxy, nor in the Scriptures, I believe. A person can always endure suffering in a way that turns it to the good; but suffering is not in itself a good thing. God is not required to maintain a certain level of suffering in the world at all times, so that one person can feel better if another offers to feel worse. We can pray for someone's suffering to be relieved, without thinking another person has to shoulder the weight.

Transformation is a challenging process, and was so even for St. Paul, who compared it to an athlete's training. "Every athlete exercises self-control in all things. They do it to receive a perishable wreath, but we an imperishable [one]. . . . [So] I pommel my body and subdue it" (1 Cor. 9:25, 27). "I press on toward the goal for the prize of the upward call of God in Christ Jesus" (Phil. 3:13–14). He challenged himself, and turns the same challenge on us: "Present your bodies as a living sacrifice" (Rom. 12:1).

Far from urging his spiritual children to despise the body, St. Paul calls us rather to use it rightly, and offer it to God for our transformation. And, far from condemning sex, he singles out the one-flesh union of husband and wife for highest praise: "This mystery is a profound one, and I am saying that it refers to Christ and the church" (Eph. 5:32).

God made this world beautiful and pleasurable—"behold, it was very good" (Gen 1:31)—and made our good bodies participant in it, so that they continually feed from the earth and then return to it. Though God is incalculably more immense than creation and exceeds it beyond our capacity to grasp, he is also intimately present throughout it, as near as a prayer, a breath. "Your Father knows what you need before you ask him" (Matt. 6:8), because he is already here, within us, every moment of our lives.

But the Greco-Roman world in which Christian faith first appeared had markedly different ideas. A person of Platonist or Gnostic bent would consider the claim that God became incarnate, coming to earth in a human body, both revolting and hilarious. In his *On the Incarnation* (written about AD 320), young St. Athanasius defied "Greek wisdom and the philosophers' noisy talk." He wrote,

> Some may then ask, "Why did [God] not appear by means of
> other and nobler parts of creation, and use some nobler instru-
> ment, such as the sun, or moon, or stars, or fire, or air, instead of
> mere man?" The answer is this: the Lord did not come to make
> a display. He came to heal and to teach suffering humanity.[42]

It's interesting that, in the New Testament, miraculous healings so
often include a physical element—the touch of a hand, often, but
other forms of matter as well. Jesus sometimes healed people by
applying some material (such as, mud to the blind man's eyes, John
9), and a woman was healed by touching Jesus' garment, without
even asking for his prayers (Mk. 5). He could certainly heal by prayer
alone, but often chose to use a physical medium as well.

St. James asks, "Is any among you sick? Let him call for the elders
of the church, and let them pray over him, anointing him with oil in
the name of the Lord; and the prayer of faith will save the sick man.
. . . The prayer of a righteous man has great power in its effects" (Jas.
5:14–16). St. James says that the sick person should ask the church
elders to come pray at his bedside—and not only pray, but anoint
him with oil as well. The physical presence of those praying must
bring some additional element, as does the vial of oil.

The book of Acts tells us that St. Paul and St. Peter were used by
God for healing through their physical presence alone, even without
reference to their prayers. In Jerusalem "they even carried out the sick
into the streets, and laid them on beds and pallets, that as Peter came
by at least his shadow might fall on some of them" (Acts 5:15). "God
did extraordinary miracles by the hands of Paul, so that handkerchiefs
or aprons were carried away from his body to the sick, and diseases
left them and the evil spirits came out of them" (Acts 19:11–12). This
same Paul, whose contact with ordinary items of cloth imbued them
with God's healing power, whose prayers brought about healings and
raised the dead, teaches us that the body is a temple of the Holy
Spirit.

The Church didn't begin honoring relics for theoretical reasons, but
because people kept running into situations where contact with the

body of a holy person, alive or dead, worked miracles. Astonishingly enough, there's an example of this in the Old Testament. "As a man was being buried, lo, a marauding band was seen and the man was cast into the grave of Elisha; and as soon as the man touched the bones of Elisha, he revived, and stood on his feet" (2 Kgs. 13:21).[§]

We've been slowly circling back to the concept of relics here. If God permeates all creation, that includes our bodies; they set forth his glory as much as an oak tree or a waterfall. But there's also an element of *increase*; just as our souls can be increasingly filled with the light of Christ, just as our hearts can increase in his love and our minds in his light, our bodies can be increasingly submitted to him and experience increasing transformation.

How can mere mortal flesh bear the presence of God? As we said in our previous discussion of theosis, our model is Christ's human body transfigured with divine light. We see it again in the burning bush, and in the Virgin Mary's pregnancy. When God chooses, ordinary matter can bear his presence, and not be consumed by the fire of his glory.

When a holy man or woman dies, the soul and body are torn apart, but the body (just like the soul) continues to bear the effects of its lifetime experience with God's presence; "death no longer has dominion" (Rom. 6:9) over those united with Christ. Perhaps a holy woman's touch accompanied her prayers with healing power. Even after death, her dry bones could continue to transmit God's life-giving power. "For the gifts and the call of God are irrevocable" (Rom. 11:29).

In the early centuries martyrs were killed in hideous and humiliating ways, and their fellow Christians risked their own lives

§   The passage ends there, but I've always wondered what happened next. I can picture that man, newly returned to life, opening his eyes—and the first thing he would see was a marauding band sweeping down on him. Hopefully, they'd be so spooked by a dead man leaping to his feet that they'd flee back the way they'd come.

to recover their ruined bodies and give them honorable burial. A martyr's tomb would become an important focal point for the community, and a place of prayer. Enclosing martyrs' relics in an altar has been the custom ever since.

I mentioned earlier that this appears in the book of Revelation. St. John was "in the Spirit on the Lord's day" (Rev. 1:10), at worship on a Sunday, when he heard voices crying out from beneath the altar. "I saw under the altar the souls of those who had been slain for the word of God and for the witness [*martyrian*] they had borne; they cried out with a loud voice, 'O Sovereign Lord, holy and true, how long until you will judge and avenge our blood on those who dwell upon the earth?'" (Rev. 6:9–10).

When missionaries went out to carry the gospel to new lands, there wouldn't be any existing martyrs' tombs (not until those missionaries were killed, perhaps). A tiny bit of a relic—even a few chips of bone mixed with beeswax—could be taken along for the founding of a new altar and a new church.

I've heard it said that "the whole purpose of the Orthodox Church is to produce relics." It's a shocking way to put it, but what it means is that the church exists for *people*. The church exists to help men and women come "out of darkness into his marvelous light" (1 Pet. 2:9). As our Lord says, "The sabbath was made for man" (Mk. 2:27). Anything else the church does—and it may have very important work to do—is temporary, because this fleeting world is temporary. What lasts forever is people.

Those who are filled with Christ in this life experience this transformation, not only spiritually, but in their bodies as well, because God permeates all of nature. Those effects can linger even after the body and soul are separated to await the Last Day. The purpose of the Church is to produce people who are so transformed by Christ that even their relinquished bodies retain the brilliance of his presence.

10
"Into the Sanctuary"
(Ps. 72/73:17)

The Antimens, A Valid Eucharist, Liturgical Implements,
Various Crosses

ow, as we continue looking through the Royal Doors, let's talk about the altar. The first thing we notice on top of it is a square of white cloth spread out over something book-shaped—the Gospel book, as it turns out. This large book with a golden cover contains all of the Gospel passages read in worship over the course of the church year. A book of the Epistle readings, the *Apostolos*, is kept on a nearby table.*

Underneath the Gospel book is where we'd find the antimens, which I mentioned in the last chapter. It is a rectangular piece of heavy gold silk, the size of a large scarf. It's imprinted with an icon, the same image as that on the epitaphion, with "Noble Joseph" of Arimathea and Nicodemus preparing Christ's body for burial.

A church's antimens is a document, signed and dated by the bishop, authorizing the Divine Liturgy to be celebrated for this community. This document is printed on fabric for durability, so it can be folded, carried, and unfolded as needed. It is kept on top

---

* Curiously, the book of Revelation isn't included in that volume. It was one of the last books accepted into the Bible, and by that time the common cycle of readings, the *lectionary*, had already been set.

of the altar inside a larger protective cloth, and opened every time the Divine Liturgy is celebrated. The relic of St. Juvenaly in its foil packet was sewn to the back of the antimens under a patch of white cloth. The bishop instructed that this should be done either by the priest or by his wife, while seated beside the iconostasis.

The antimens documents the bishop's authorization of the Eucharist in this community. We see in St. Paul's letters that there is already a concern for the right order of the church, under a bishop's authority. Even then, there was danger from false shepherds, and false sheep, too. One of the earliest church fathers, St. Ignatius of Antioch (AD 35–108), wrote, "Let no one do anything that pertains to the Church without the bishop. Let that Eucharist alone be deemed valid which is celebrated either by the bishop or by the one to whom he has entrusted it."[43] As early as AD 108 we already find the concept of a "valid" Eucharist, under a bishop's authority.

The Eucharist cannot be celebrated without an antimens. With it, the Eucharist can be celebrated anywhere. "Antimens" comes from the Greek *antimension*, which means "instead of the table." If necessary, St. Felicity's pastor could celebrate the Divine Liturgy where there is no altar table—a home, hospital room, or campground—by bringing the antimens with him.

On the back corners of the altar, left and right, are pillar candles in heavy brass candlesticks. Centered between them is a tall brass box shaped like a church. This is the tabernacle (or *artophorion*, "bread-carrier"), where a portion of the consecrated bread and wine of the Eucharist is kept; the priest or deacon can take it from here to the sick or those unable to attend worship. Some liturgical Western churches have the same custom (they would call this the reserved sacrament), and you would know that the body of Christ was present in the tabernacle if there was a light burning before it. If you look up above the altar here, you'll see hanging from a chain an ever-burning glass oil lamp, called the Unsleeping Lamp.

The Orthodox tradition concerning the bread in the tabernacle is a bit different from that of the West. For one thing, there is no white, full-moon wafer to display, for we use leavened bread. This was a great controversy in the eleventh century, when Western and Eastern Churches separated. The West used unleavened bread because it was the kind that would have been on the table at Passover, during the Last Supper. The East used leavened bread, associating the rising of the bread with the action of the Holy Spirit throughout the church, as in Christ's parable of the leaven (Matt. 13:33).

Both churches, over time, faced the practical problem that when Communion was being given to worshipers the elements might be spilled, dropped, or—even worse—hidden and carried away to be used in attempted magic. The West began to distribute only the consecrated bread, not the wine, and the flat, unleavened host left no crumbs. In the East, the bread is mixed with the wine and administered by a spoon. Worshipers who wish to receive Communion form a line and, one at a time, stand in front of the priest or deacon who is administering the sacrament and open their mouths wide. Altar boys hold a red cloth open beneath their chins to catch anything that might fall.

At St. Felicity Church, the bread-baking assignment rotates every week among parishioners. Several round loaves, called *prosphora* ("offerings"; the singular is *prosphoron*), are prepared. They are stamped with a seal that has at its center a square that contains a cross, and in the four corners of the cross there are these Greek initials: IC ("Jesus"), XC ("Christ"), NI and KA ("conquers"). In a preparation service at the beginning of Sunday worship (one that comes before Matins and the Divine Liturgy), the priest will cut one of the prosphora along this square, separating out a cube of bread from the center of the loaf. This is called "the Lamb," and is the portion that will later be consecrated.

On the morning of Great and Holy Thursday, at the Divine Liturgy that commemorates the Last Supper, the priest consecrates *two* Lambs. One is distributed that day, while the other is set aside. Wine is poured upon it three times, and then it is allowed to dry out; after that, it is finely sliced and placed in the tabernacle. Throughout the coming year, the priest or deacon will take bits of it to those who can't come to church.

Although this consecrated bread is kept in the tabernacle on the altar, Orthodox don't have the custom, popular in some Western liturgical churches, of holding devotions before the reserved sacrament, or of displaying the consecrated bread for adoration. In the West, a custom grew up of lifting certain elements out of the hubbub of ordinary parish life and worship, and making time to contemplate them devotionally.[†] It's a habit that can be puzzling to Eastern Christians. When I was newly Orthodox I read an essay by an Orthodox priest expressing surprise at the Roman Catholic devotion to the Sacred Heart of Jesus. He asked, how could you divide Christ up into pieces, and pray to his heart alone?

Lying on the altar next to the covered Gospel book is a silver cross about a foot long. The top of it, with the crossbar, takes the shape of a diamond in an elaborate knotted design, and a smaller diamond is at the bottom. Though you might think first of Celtic knotwork, this cross comes from Ethiopia. Interlace patterns were popular throughout the ancient world, and are still characteristic of Ethiopian liturgical items.

This is a hand cross, which the priest uses to make the sign of the cross and bless the worshipers at certain points during the liturgy. The church has a few other hand crosses—one of carved and inlaid wood from the republic of Georgia, a wooden one with an image of the Crucifixion painted on the front surface, and one of incised golden metal from Greece. This last is called a "budded" cross, because the ends of the four beams bear rounded extensions like the buds on a branch.

You might be puzzled by the old, very worn hand cross that has three crossbars. This is a Russian cross, made of bronze. The top bar represents the sign above Christ's head, which read "Jesus of Nazareth,

---

† This custom does shake up our ideas of linear time. The French nun St. Thérèse of Lisieux devoted herself to adoration of Christ during his child-hood. In a church in Rome I saw a painting of St. Thomas Aquinas presenting a recently reposed cardinal to the Virgin Mary, during the Annunciation.

the King of the Jews" in three languages (John 19:19–20). His hands were nailed to the middle bar and feet to the bottom bar. This bottom bar is depicted at a slant, up on the left and down on the right, and the usual explanation is that it points up toward the good thief, on Christ's right hand, and down toward the bad thief, on his left.

At the end of the service Fr. John stands in front of the Royal Doors holding one of these crosses, and the worshipers line up, as at Communion, to kiss it and then his hand. This is the Christianity of lands where kissing is a more common social gesture than we're used to here, but it can still seem like a terribly obsequious gesture. We might think it dangerously tempting for the priest, as well, inviting him to an inflated sense of importance. The intention is rather the reverse, that with this kiss we honor the office of the priesthood, and remind the priest how much he has to live up to.

The most important thing in Orthodoxy is holiness—the indwelling of Jesus Christ transforming our daily lives. It's *not* assumed that the people with the most prestige in the church are the holiest. Sometimes they are, and it's great when that happens. But even bad leaders can't harm the church's treasure, the ancient accumulated wisdom about how to be transformed in Christ. In the case of disappointing leaders, if you have to, you can just wait them out. God has a mandatory retirement plan in mind for everybody, sooner or later.

Also, holiness is not confined to the ranks of clergy, monks, and nuns, but can bloom anywhere. One of the ancient stories tells of two monks who were pleased with their own spiritual progress. An angel appeared, and told them that he would show them someone far more advanced than they. He then took them to a nearby village and showed them a farmer's wife—an ordinary woman, living in the world with her husband and children, not subject to their rigorous fasting or celibacy.‡ So holiness can be found in any walk of life; clergy don't automatically get an extra helping.

---

‡ St. Juliana of Lazarevo (1530–1604), also called Juliana the Housewife, was a Russian wife and mother of seven. She ran the household for her husband's family, gave her food to the poor, and nursed the sick during an epidemic. She's a popular saint, and an example in comparatively recent times of holiness in an "ordinary" life.

In Orthodoxy there's less of a division between clergy and laity than there has historically been in the West, I think partly because most parish priests are married. It's hard to picture the priest as dwelling in some higher realm when you know he was up all night, cleaning up after a kid with a stomach virus.

The majority of Orthodox priests are married, and nearly all of those who pastor churches. But he must be married before he's ordained; an Orthodox priest (or deacon) can't *get* married. It would be strange for a priest to be hearing the confessions of women in his parish while also dating them. Some seminary grads put off ordination for a while, hoping to meet the right girl. Bishops are not married, but are chosen from the ranks of the unmarried priests, whether they were never married or are widowers.

Also, it helps that the Orthodox missionary approach has always been to offer worship in the language people use every day. When clergy instead serve the liturgy in a language they alone understand, it makes them seem like exalted beings, standing between God and ordinary people. Worshiping in the vernacular does run into a practical problem, however. In some Orthodox lands the language that was commonly used a thousand years ago has changed, and is difficult for today's worshipers to understand. This is not a problem the Church knows readily how to solve.

A few more things should be noted in the sanctuary. There is a large brass lamp stand with seven branches behind the altar, right in front of the Communion of the Apostles icon. This is a *menorah*, the kind of lamp stand that stood in the Jerusalem temple, and that Christians continued using in their worship. If this church had a curved-bench synthronon lining the apse, as ancient churches did, with the bishop's throne in the center, this lamp would be standing before it. St. John saw a menorah burning before the throne in his vision of heavenly worship: "Before the throne burn seven torches of fire, which are the seven spirits of God" (Rev. 4:5).

Against the wall on either side of the apse are two tall processional candles, and two banners bearing icons. There is also a processional cross with an icon of the Crucifixion on one side, and on the other the empty cross, with Joseph of Arimathea's ladder leaning against it. But there's another pair of processional items that aren't immediately identifiable: two long poles that have at the top something that looks like a golden sunburst, with an angel's face in the middle. These are liturgical fans and originally served the practical purpose of driving small insects away from the bread and wine. (When intended for such use they were probably made of lighter materials—cloth or feathers.) Deacons no longer fan the gifts to keep the insects away, but these fans, with their images of seraphim, still remain in the altar and join in a procession.

Against the wall on the right there is a small stand with a hook, and hanging from the hook is an incense pot, known as a censer. This is a covered golden bowl, the lid pierced thoroughly with holes, designed to hold burning incense. The altar boy who prepares the censer will first put in a disk of charcoal and light it, then sprinkle on top some nuggets of incense. Incense in pellet form, as distinct from incense sticks and cones, is made by rolling the resin of certain trees with various herbs or essential oils. Incense can be purchased in many different fragrances, and the priest may choose a particular scent to suit the feast or season at hand (roses, for example, on a feast of the Theotokos). The censer hangs from long chains, which bear twelve bells for the apostles. During a procession the priest or deacon will walk through the church, swinging the censer toward icons and also toward worshipers, for they too are icons of Christ.

To the right of the apse is an icon of the Resurrection of Christ, and a small table beneath it holds a number of icons. These belong to members of the church, and were brought to the priest to be placed within the sanctuary for forty days, to bless them. (A priest can also bless an icon by praying over it and sprinkling it with holy water.) Nearby there are shelves bearing service books, small scissors (used in tonsuring—snipping a few hairs from someone who has just been baptized or chrismated), rose water (sprinkled around the church during the Lamentations service mentioned earlier), anointing oil, a traveling Communion kit, extra candles and lighters, and all the odds and ends a priest might find useful. If you look at the back of the iconostasis you'll see hooks for hanging vestments and cassocks when not in use. (Brocade vestments take up too much room to store here, and are kept in an adjoining room called the *sacristy*.)

To the left of the apse there is an icon of the Nativity of Christ, and beneath it there is the *Prothesis* table. Here are the various things necessary for Communion: wine and water, spoon and "spear" (an implement with a triangular blade, used for cutting the prosphoron), chalice and *diskos* (a golden dish on a pedestal).

On a Sunday morning Fr. John arrives early and begins by praying several brief services. First he walks through the empty church, saying entrance prayers and venerating the altar and the icons; this service is called the *Kairon*. Next, he puts on his vestments, reciting a verse of Scripture or prayer over each piece; this is the *Vesting* service.

Then he comes to the table here for the *Proskomedia* ("Preparation") service. Taking up the spear, he cuts into the prosphoron (Communion loaf) along the lines of the square embossed on top, removes the Lamb, and places it in the center of the diskos. He mixes water and wine and pours it into the chalice. He cuts small pieces from other prosphora loaves and places them around the Lamb; these represent angels, saints, or people for whom the congregation is praying. He accompanies each symbolic action with a verse of Scripture or a prayer.

When he has finished all this, he sets over the Lamb a golden frame in the shape of an X (this is called the *asterisk,* which means "star"), and says, "And the star came and stood over the place where the young child was" (Matt. 2:9). He covers the chalice and diskos with a square of brocade known as the *aer.* The Proskomedia service concludes with a censing of the entire church. At this point people are starting to filter in, and Fr. John will cense them along with the icons, the altar, and everything else.

The last thing to notice behind the altar is the large standing cross to the right of the apse. It is made of wood, and an icon of the crucified Christ, cut out in the shape of his body (this is called a *corpus*), is attached to it with nails. On Great and Holy Thursday, during the service of the Twelve Passion Gospels, this cross is set up in the nave of the church with the corpus removed. Early in the evening we sing:

> Why, Judas, did you betray the Savior?
> Did he shut you out from the company of the disciples?
> Did he keep from you the gift of healing?
> Did he sit at table with the rest, but send you away?
> Did he wash the feet of the others, but pass you by?
> How much kindness you have forgotten!
> The unworthiness of your mind is now exposed,
> As is Christ's boundless, patient loving-kindness, which we praise.

The fifth Gospel reading tells of the Crucifixion. Then, while everyone kneels with their faces to the floor, Fr. John processes through the church bearing this icon of Christ's body high. He brings it to the cross and affixes it with the nails.

After censing it, he bows to the floor three times and then venerates the icon, kneeling to kiss the feet of Christ. All the worshipers gather behind him and do the same, bowing, crossing themselves, and kneeling at Christ's feet. Meanwhile, a chanter is singing:

> Today he who hung the world upon the waters is hung upon a tree.
> He who is King of the Angels is crowned with thorns.
> He who robes the sky with clouds is robed in purple mockery.
> He who set Adam free in Jordan's waters is slapped on the face.
> He who calls the Church his Bride is nailed to the Cross.
> He who is born of the Virgin is pierced with a spear.

We worship your passion, O Christ.
We worship your passion, O Christ.
We worship your passion, O Christ.
Show us also the glory of your Resurrection.

PART

INSIDE THE
LITURGY

*Now we shift from an empty church to a full one. Part 2
leads us through the two services offered most frequently,
Great Vespers and the Divine Liturgy, and a number
of practical and theological considerations will pop up
along the way. We'll talk about sacramental confession,
repentance, the need for spiritual direction, and the reality
of spiritual warfare. We'll talk about some other practical matters, such as the church calendar.*

*Part 2 will also cover some big concepts such as the
fall of Adam and Eve, free will, and synergy. We'll
resume our discussion of the nature of sin and salvation.
We'll also reflect on the wonder of God's love, and the
need for Christians to live their faith from the heart.*

11
"Reconciling the World"
(2 COR. 5:19)

*Immaculate Conception, Original Sin, Sin as Sickness,
Salvation as Healing, Christ the Champion*

Great Vespers, December 8—
Eve of the Conception of the Theotokos

*E*verybody agrees: the best service to bring someone to,
if they're visiting an Orthodox church for the first time,
is Vespers. This is an evening service ("Vespers" comes
from the Greek word for "evening," *hespera*) and it's not too long—
anywhere from thirty minutes to an hour. But the main attraction is
that it doesn't include any scary stuff. Low-church Protestants will
not be making a dash for the parking lot, knees and elbows pump-
ing. Vespers is composed mostly of chanted Scriptures (the Psalms
in particular) and intercessory prayers, that is, prayers for the needs
of others. The priest's role is minimal; he worships along with the
congregation, while the choir or chanters lead the way. It's a quiet
service, tranquil and softly lit.

At St. Felicity it's the choir that leads Great Vespers, though at
most churches this is a chanter's service. But in this parish they
found that the best time for choir practice was immediately before
Great Vespers on Saturday night, so the choir members are all here
anyway. Vespers is offered at St. Felicity on a few weeknights, too,
and those services of daily Vespers are briefer, led by a chanter or

two. The night before a Divine Liturgy, however, there is always a full-length Great Vespers. The church follows the ancient Jewish custom of starting a new day at sunset, so Vespers is the first service of the day. Tonight's hymns will offer clues about which saint or feast will be our focus tomorrow morning.

As we come through the doors from the narthex we see that the choir's corner at the back of the church is full, and choir members are arranging their music, paper-clipping pieces together, or reading over the evening's newer pieces. Most of the Great Vespers service is the same from week to week, but there will be a few pieces that occur only around this time of year, or only on this day. Hank, the choir director, faces them, and, as usual, he looks tense. He always wants the worship to be perfect, but it never is.

We turn to venerate the icon here, on the "Today's Special" stand just inside the door from the narthex. It is not the familiar one of St. Felicity, but instead one that shows an elderly couple embracing, the wife rising on her toes to throw her arm around her husband's neck. Behind them is a bed; apparently, the scene is taking place in their bedroom. A length of fabric, like a scarf, trails across the tops of the towers behind them, a convention that lets us know when a scene is transpiring indoors. (There are no ceilings in icons; God sees right through every ceiling.)

Tomorrow is December 9, the Feast of the Conception of the Virgin Mary. In the West this feast is observed a day earlier, on December 8, and is called the Feast of the Immaculate Conception. Some people are confused by that term, and think it refers to Christ being born of a Virgin. No, this feast has rather to do with the conception of the Virgin Mary in the womb of *her* mother, St. Anna.

In the teaching of the Roman Catholic Church, this conception was "immaculate" because Mary was "preserved free from all stain of Original Sin" (*macula* is the Latin word for "stain").[44] The concept of original sin was developed by St. Augustine of Hippo (AD 354–430);

he proposed that, because Adam and Eve fell into sin (called "the Fall"), every person is born with a broken human nature that inclines us to sin.

That's not a view unique to St. Augustine, of course; it's common Christian belief just about everywhere. Even those who take Adam and Eve as symbolic characters regard this story as conveying something true about our human condition.

But St. Augustine developed a corollary to this theory. He said that we also inherit the *guilt* for our ancestors' trespass. We are born already guilty of sin, because we all share in responsibility for the Fall of Adam and Eve.

In Roman Catholic teaching, God exempted the Virgin Mary from this tragic condition, because he intended her to be the mother of Christ. That's what the term "Immaculate Conception" means: when St. Anna conceived her daughter, Mary, the child bore neither the sinful nature of humankind nor guilt for the Fall. The Feast of the Immaculate Conception has been celebrated in the West for some centuries, though the Catholic Church did not proclaim it official dogma until 1854.

The Immaculate Conception is not an Orthodox doctrine; we believe that Mary was born with the same broken human nature as the rest of us. So was Jesus, in fact. As St. Gregory of Nazianzus (AD 329–389) said, "That which he has not assumed he has not healed."[45] Christ was a real human being, not an exceptional hybrid. He was not immune to temptation; he was "in every respect . . . tempted as we are, yet without sin" (Heb. 4:15). So Orthodox believe that both Mary and Jesus were crafted of the same human clay as we are, and like us were exposed to temptation.

But there's that other matter, the question of guilt. St. Augustine taught that every human being is born, not just disposed to sin, but already *guilty* of sin, because we all share in Adam's guilt. The test case was newborns who die before they are baptized. St. Augustine had the courage of his convictions, and said yes, such children were condemned and excluded from heaven, although he believed they would experience "the mildest condemnation of all."[46]

(The theologian Abelard [AD 1079–1142] proposed that these children abide in "Limbo," where they know neither the sufferings of hell nor the joys of heaven. This view was taught in the Roman Catholic Church for centuries, but a recent document approved by Pope Benedict XVI pulls back from that conclusion and says that there are "reasons for prayerful hope" that unbaptized babies are saved.[47])

Eastern Christians have never believed that we are born guilty of the sin of Adam and Eve, so where did this idea come from? It's one of those strange footnotes of history: St. Augustine derived it from a Scripture verse that, as he read it in Latin translation, contained an ambiguous preposition.* The verse is Romans 5:12, and in the Greek original St. Paul says, "Sin came into the world through one man, and death through sin; and so death spread to all men, because all men sinned." The syntax is a bit convoluted, but in short: sin came into the world through Adam; sin produces death; death has now spread to everyone, because everyone sins.

But in his Latin version, instead of *"because* all men sinned," St. Augustine read, *"in whom* [that is, in Adam] all men sinned." If all members of the human race participate in Adam's sin, he reasoned, we also share in his guilt. As *The New England Primer* of 1690 put it, "In Adam's Fall we sinned all."

Orthodox value St. Augustine's devotional writings, but are more selective when it comes to his theology. We recognize that every person, in fact all creation, has been damaged by the Fall. (We don't call this by St. Augustine's term, "original sin," since that theory includes "original guilt," but instead speak of the "ancestral sin.") Yet we hold that everyone is born in innocence. We don't bear guilt for our sins until we are mature enough to take responsibility for our moral decisions. Children eventually begin going to confession along with their parents, but the church doesn't assign an expiration date for childhood innocence.† The Orthodox Church doesn't presume to say who does or doesn't get into heaven at all; that's God's business.

---

* Brilliant as he was, St. Augustine didn't read Greek well. As a child he had a mean Greek teacher, and it spoiled him for life.

† In the West, a child has been traditionally considered capable of telling right from wrong at age seven, and at that age becomes responsible for his sins. A mom reported that she heard her little girl telling her older brother on his seventh birthday, "Congratulations, Timmy! Now you can go to hell!"

So as we meet for Vespers on this Saturday evening in December, we are celebrating simply the conception of the Virgin Mary. It was like the conception of any other child, for she was really one of us. In the drama of salvation, Mary is the gift contributed by the human race. At Vespers on Christmas evening we will sing:

> What can we offer you, O Christ, when you come to earth as one of us, for our sake? Every living thing takes existence from you, and offers thanks:
> The angels give songs of praise, the heavens give a star,
> Wise men give costly presents, while shepherds give their simple awe,
> The earth gives a cave, and the cave gives a manger.
> And we give you a mother, a virgin mother.
> You who are God from all eternity, have mercy on us![48]

We learn from that early-church "prequel," the *Protevangelium of James,* that Mary was conceived in the usual way, by an elderly couple named Joachim and Anna. According to the story, Anna and Joachim were wealthy but childless. After Joachim was openly mocked for this in the temple, they parted to spend fervent time in prayer, and both received word that they would conceive. Some icons show them meeting in great joy at the city gate; others show them embracing in their bedroom.‡

There seems to have been no doubt in the early church that life begins at conception. Not only do we celebrate Mary's conception on December 9, but also John the Forerunner's on September 23, and the conception of Christ on March 25, the Feast of the Annunciation, exactly nine months before Christmas.

---

‡ The icon for the Feast of the Birth of the Virgin Mary, September 8, depicts the same bedroom: as Anna reclines, bustling women attend to her and bathe the baby, and Joachim peeks in shyly at the door.

One more thing, before we leave the concept of the ancestral sin. Though East and West have historically disagreed on whether all humanity inherits Adam's guilt, we agree that we receive and pass on a brokenness that inclines us to sin, and through sin to death. But did you ever wonder *how* it is passed on?

St. Augustine, considering the problem with some literalness, thought that it was transmitted in the act of reproduction, as evidenced by lust.[49] "Insofar as [Christians] are the children of God, they do not beget in a carnal manner. . . . [Christians who do] become parents, beget children because they have not yet put off the entirety of their old nature." He could not have foreseen children conceived *in vitro*, without sex, but their passionless conception probably does not render them incapable of sin.

There hasn't been a sense of urgency among Orthodox to specify the mechanism by which this susceptibility to sin and death is passed on, but rather a general perception that we share some things simply because we are all part of the same human family. We are one in a common life. The disease of sin runs through us all. When Adam and Eve broke God's law, they simultaneously broke his creation, and that condition rolls on from one generation to the next.

But you know what's odd about that, to me? That we have never gotten used to this. Everybody knows *something is wrong*. Every religion recognizes that something is wrecked in the world, and in our lives. You don't have to be a professional philosopher to notice this; a shepherd on a hillside could compose a psalm that expresses its poignancy well.

Yet we don't just accept it, as we do so many other regrettables in life. Some days it's going to rain, some little league teams are going to lose. I have to stand on a kitchen chair to reach the top shelf, but I don't really *grieve* over being five foot one. We don't wage futile, tearful battle in our thoughts over the injustice of not being able to fly, or to leap about in time, or to turn into a graceful giraffe. We accept the great majority of limiting or uncomfortable conditions we find within and around us. But the sickness of sin, which causes evil people to do heinous things, and even the less evil to gravely damage themselves and other people—that is something we never quite get used to.

Once after I'd given a talk on Orthodox spirituality, an audience member asked me why Christians put so much emphasis on sin and repentance. Why not, as she'd learned at a Buddhist retreat, simply accept that this is the way we are? Why not drop the word *sin* and practice "radical acceptance"?

In reply, I didn't have to say, "Because sin offends God." It's more than sufficient to note that sin offends *us*. We couldn't *bear* to simply accept the evil in the world. We somehow know we were made with something else in mind. It's like we're born with a memory of something we've never seen. We yearn to return to a place we've never been. We mourn that loss and seek it every day, no matter what our religion, or none.

How do we inherit this fallen human nature? It comes to us simply because we are human, and our life is continuous with all our fallen ancestors.

But here's an Orthodox idea that was quite new to me. This oneness of human life permits the reverse to happen as well. When Christ entered the human race, he set an opposite force in motion, a strain of healing from sin that spreads outward, just as sin-sickness spread from Adam and Eve.

That's a startling thought, if you're used to thinking of sin and salvation as external events. If sin were just a bad deed, an infraction of the law, it could be paid by a third party, as a speeding ticket might be. But in the Orthodox understanding, sin is infection, not infraction. Christ comes, not just to pay a debt, but to heal us. To treat sin as something external, superficial, that could be resolved by paying a fine, just doesn't take it seriously enough. Sin isn't a string of bad deeds. It's an inward-spreading condition, a sickness of the soul.

God could not bear to see his beloved, whom he created and destined for glory (Eph. 1:12), sick and in chains. Seeing us afflicted and in pain, in his great compassion, Christ came to deliver us—not just from the penalty for sin, but from *sin itself* (John 1:29). And he began that process in an elegantly simple way, by stepping into the flow of human life. With his Incarnation, his healing power began to stream into the life that we all share.

When I was newly Orthodox, I kept asking people what early-church writings I should read to understand the Orthodox view of the Atonement. People kept telling me to read *On the Incarnation* by St. Athanasius (AD 296–373). I would say, "No, I'm not asking about the Incarnation; I'm trying to find out about the Atonement." (It took me awhile longer to notice that Orthodox don't even use the word *atonement*. They just call it salvation.) But as I read St. Athanasius's marvelously inviting treatise, I saw what they meant. It caused the concept of salvation to expand for me on every side. Salvation is so much more than the moment of the Cross. It's the *whole story*.

Christ did not come just to enable our forgiveness, but to restore the "image [and] likeness" of God (Gen. 1:26) that was damaged by Adam and Eve. It is like when a king visits a city, St. Athanasius wrote; his residing in a single house brings honor to the whole city. "So it is with the King of all. . . . He has come to our realm, dwelling in one body among the many, and as a result the conspiracy of the enemy against mankind is checked, and the corruption of death is abolished." When the Son of God clothed his incorruptible nature with our human nature, "we were all surely clothed with incorruption, by the promise of the resurrection."[50]

What's unexpected in this view of salvation is the idea that life in Christ will change us, not in an external way, as a legal fiction (being "imputed" righteous), and not in some vague spiritual sense, but objectively, ontologically—a change in our very being. This happens because Christ literally shares in our nature; we are united with him in the way we are united with every other human being. The victory he won flows to us as well. Now we are being restored to God's "image and likeness" just as a damaged portrait could be restored, when the person depicted brings it back to the artist and sits for it once again (another of St. Athanasius's analogies). We are being healed of the wounds we bear from our own sins and those of others, and turned into the person God had in mind before we were formed in the womb (Jer. 1:5).

The initiation and completion of this project come entirely from God; we were helpless to save ourselves. Our rescue began when

Christ entered the human race, joining in our pitiable condition. Though sinless, he accepted the consequence of sin, following the whole of the human race into the grave. And there, as God, he arose and destroyed it. "Since therefore the children share in flesh and blood, he himself likewise partook of the same nature, that through death he might destroy him who has the power of death, that is, the devil" (Heb. 2:14). He rose, and "raised us up with him" (Eph. 2:6). "[He] was put to death for our trespasses and raised for our justification" (Rom. 4:25).

A hundred years before St. Athanasius, St. Irenaeus (AD 115–202) explored a related line of thought, and presented Christ as summing up and completing all that was in Adam. "He has, in his work of recapitulation, summed up all things [*recapitulans recapitulatus est*], waging war against our enemy, and crushing him who had at the beginning led us away captives in Adam."[51] Adam and Eve failed to resist the evil one when temptation struck, leaving the human race chained to the cycle of sin and death. Christ came in human form to retrace their steps, so to speak, and "recapitulate" the battle. (Irenaeus's view is sometimes called the "recapitulation" theory. Orthodox don't use that term; it's just an aspect of salvation.)

In this sense, we can say that the Orthodox faith teaches a "substitutionary" theology of salvation (though, again, you wouldn't encounter that term). Christ substitutes for us, represents us, in the battle with the evil one, as David represented the entire Hebrew people in single combat against Goliath (1 Sam. 17). Christ substitutes for us, not to satisfy our debt or to receive our punishment, but as our champion, taking our place in a battle we could never win.

God did not choose to defeat the evil one simply by means of his overwhelming power, but instead "emptied himself, taking the form of a servant" (Phil. 2:7). St. Irenaeus continues,

> For indeed the enemy would not have been fairly vanquished, unless it had been a man born of a woman who conquered him. . . . And therefore does the Lord profess Himself to be the Son of man, comprising in himself that original man . . . in order that, as our species went down to death through a vanquished man, so we may ascend to life again through a victorious one; and as through a man death received the palm [of victory] against us, so again by a man we may receive the palm against death.

St. Paul expressed it simply and directly: "For as in Adam all die, so also in Christ shall all be made alive" (1 Cor. 15:22). A Scripture we cited earlier also bears repeating here: "Since therefore the children share in flesh and blood, he himself likewise partook of the same nature, that through death he might destroy him who has the power of death, that is, the devil, and deliver all those who through fear of death were subject to lifelong bondage" (Heb. 2:14–15).

In the Christian West there are many different theories of the atonement; we looked at some of them in chapter 7, and compared them with the Orthodox view, just called "salvation." But notice something here. Salvation points in at least three directions:

1. We humans are restored to a right relationship with God. This is expressed in words like *mercy, forgiveness, righteousness,* and *justification.*
2. The evil one is defeated and his captives set free. Here we encounter terms like *redeem, ransom, deliver,* and *save.*
3. The Father accepts his Son's self-offering. Now we find terms like *sacrifice, offering,* and *gift.*

"Salvation" can be viewed from these three vantage points and, no doubt, more. We'll keep going over this ground and seeing how the pieces fit together in the next chapter, then resume the Vespers service in chapter 13.

12

"Not Counting Their Trespasses"

(2 Cor. 5:19)

Love's Offering, The Meaning of Ransom, Pressing the Metaphor, Take the Earliest View

s embodied creatures, our physicality is part of both our falling and our rising. We inherit our share in death and sin through our membership in the human race, and we received an infusion of life and healing when Christ entered the human race. "Who will deliver me from this body of death? Thanks be to God through Jesus Christ our Lord!" (Rom. 7:24–25). We rely only on the power of Jesus Christ, who has defeated death and opened the door to eternal life. The Resurrection troparion of St. John of Damascus (AD 676–749), sung hundreds of times in the season of Pascha, proclaims:

> Christ is risen from the dead,
> Trampling down death by death,
> And upon those in the tomb bestowing life!

In this understanding of salvation, Christ is not only our healer but our rescuer as well. We are held captive by sin and death, and he enters human life in order to go the way of all flesh and enter the realm of Hades. "The last enemy to be destroyed is death" (1 Cor. 15:26), and when death is vanquished, we are truly free.

Christ is also a sacrificial offering to the Father. The author of Hebrews tells how Christ's sacrifice completed and replaced the temple sacrifices of bulls and goats. The earlier covenant, between God and his people under Moses, was "ratified" by an offering of blood. Moses sprinkled the tent, the worship implements, and the people with "the blood of the covenant which God commanded you" (Heb. 9:20). The author of Hebrews goes on, "Under the law almost everything is purified with blood, and without the shedding of blood there is no forgiveness" (Heb. 9:22).

But, he continues, this was not effective, and never could be: "It is impossible that the blood of bulls and goats should take away sins" (Heb. 10:4). Then he ascribes to Christ the words in Psalm 39/40:6–8:

> Sacrifices and offerings you have not desired,
> But a body you have prepared for me;
> In burnt offerings and sin offerings you have taken no pleasure.
> Then I said, "See, God, I have come to do your will, O God
> (in the scroll of the book it is written of me)." (NRSV)*

When Christ enters the body his Father prepared for him, the futile, repetitive shedding of animal blood is brought to an end. "We have been sanctified through the offering of the body of Jesus Christ once for all" (Heb. 10:10).

Christ's death on the cross was an offering to the Father—but it wasn't a payment. This is a distinction we don't usually catch, because we don't make sacrifices anymore. But it was never the case that the Father needed animal blood before he could forgive his people. Rather, the people needed to *offer* it.

---

* "A body you have prepared for me" is an eloquent foreshadowing of Christ's incarnation; it appears in some copies of the Septuagint (including, apparently, the copy used by the author of Hebrews). The Hebrew text is quite different: "Ears you have dug for me." English translations based on the Hebrew render this as something like, "You have given me an open ear."

Sinners needed to make a costly gift as evidence to themselves and everyone that they were sincere; they really were sorry for their sin, and truly desired to renounce it. The offered blood "ratified" the covenant; it demonstrated the human partners' commitment to that covenant. It was a gift, the kind given to heal a relationship.

Whenever people forge a covenant, it is appropriate for them to give gifts, in fact very costly gifts if the covenant is a significant one. These gifts don't buy the other person's compliance with the covenant; they have no power to coerce. But, as emblems of trust, they serve to seal or ratify the covenant, giving evidence of sincerity and commitment on both sides.

This can be rather a new thought, if we have been used to thinking of salvation as a transaction: a big debt on this side, and a big payment on that side, and now we're in the clear. But our relationship with God doesn't have a legal or financial character. It is a relationship of love. And love functions under different rules than law and finance do. For example, love "does not keep account of wrongdoing." (That's how 1 Cor. 13:5c would be literally translated.) Love doesn't keep track of how many sins there are, and sit back with arms folded until it is paid off. Love doesn't worry about who owes what. When it starts fretting about being cheated or not getting a fair shake, it has stopped being love.

Yet love does give gifts, sometimes very costly gifts, as a seal and proof of commitment. Picture a man who gives his fiancée an engagement ring. The ring does not have the character of a contract or legal obligation; he isn't buying the girl from her family, or bribing her away from them. The size of the diamond has no literal correspondence to the size of his love. Yet it is appropriate that the ring be costly in proportion to his resources; it is right that it be something of a sacrifice, because it is evidence of his love, to her and to all the world. Love wants the world to know.

I think where we make a mistake is in thinking the Old Testament sacrifices were akin to the offerings under the old Greco-Roman religion, which were aimed at paying off debts to the gods, or bargaining for divine favors. That's a rather crass idea, and unworthy of attribution to the God-guided Jewish people. No, they gave gifts to God on all sorts of occasions: freewill offerings, peace offerings, thank offerings, and gifts in fulfillment of vows, in addition to offerings for sin.

We can tell that these were not understood as payments for sin, since, if they were, each sin would have its own set cost, no matter who committed it. Instead, the payment amount depended on what a person could afford. The law says that a person must give a lamb as a sin offering, "but if he cannot afford a lamb, then he shall bring, as his guilt offering to the LORD for the sin which he has committed, two turtledoves or two young pigeons" (Lev. 5:7). The same sins can be acquitted with different-sized sacrifices; what matters is that the giver feel it to be a sacrifice. You need to give something that represents a sacrifice *to you*.

That kind of flexibility does not constitute justice. If a poor man and a rich one commit the same sin, the poor man's sin is as grievous as the rich man's; the debt to God is objectively the same. But the law prescribed that each one bring the sacrifice she could afford. The whole point was in the *giving*. It's giving that heals a relationship, and the face value of the gift isn't the point.

Gift-giving is what you do when you love someone; and when you come to a new depth of relationship, or forge a new commitment, it feels right to mark it with a gift. It ought to be a gift that really costs you something. Christ offered himself to the Father as the representative of the whole human race, marking our entry into the new covenant. God gave us a costly gift as well—forgiveness of all our sins. On both sides, human and divine, the exchange was of a gift, not a transaction or payment.

These gifts seal the reconciliation of God with humanity: "In Christ God was reconciling the world to himself, not counting their trespasses against them" (2 Cor. 5:19). Note that St. Paul says "*not* counting their trespasses"; he does not say God counted the trespasses, weighed the Cross, and considered the debt justly paid.

It's notable, in the Old Testament Scriptures, how little interest God has in the sacrifices themselves. He's interested in the relationship. Making a sacrifice gives evidence of how deeply you value that relationship; making a sacrifice in the wake of sin shows how deeply you repent of that sin. But making the sacrifice without repentance is not only useless, but also insulting. God has contempt for such empty gestures:

> I hate, I despise your feasts. . . .
> Even though you offer me your burnt offerings and cereal
>   offerings,
> I will not accept them. (Amos 5:21–22)

Imagine a faithless husband who keeps cheating on his wife, and every time she finds out he tries to smooth things over with a gift of expensive jewelry. The day will come when she will throw it in his face. A gift that expresses deep repentance is a beautiful thing, but a gift that is insincere and manipulative is insulting, regardless of its cost.

The further absurdity of such attempted bribery is that God already owns everything. He even gave us the Christ that we offer back to him. So an insincere offering is like that callous husband, instead of buying his wife something new, taking a bracelet out of her jewelry box and wrapping it in new gift paper. To sin and then try to buy God off with something he already owns—something you can get your hands on only because he put it in your keeping—is as infuriating as it is ludicrous.

> For you have no delight in sacrifice;
>   Were I to give a burnt offering, you would not be pleased;
> The sacrifice acceptable to God is a broken spirit;
>   A broken and contrite heart, O God, you will not despise.
>   (Ps. 50/51:16–17)

A sincere and penitent heart, even if it can give no gift, is sufficient. Penitence with a gift, a costly gift, is a lovely and fitting thing. But a gift without penitence is garbage.

Let's try to picture Christ's self-offering as a gift, not a payment, to the Father. Remember my story about the brave police officer? Maybe I can stretch it a little further. Imagine that the frightened parents contacted the police, and the chief of police gathered his officers together and laid out his plan. He said that he needed a volunteer to break down the door, then hold back the captors till all the kids have run free. But, he warns, there's a risk that the rescuer himself might not escape, in the end.

The heroic police officer might stand and say, "I will go and accomplish your plan. And if it costs my life, then I offer it as a testament to your leadership, and in your honor." (I admit, my story isn't built to stretch this far.)

Obviously, the officer is not giving this sacrifice to the chief in order to persuade the chief to set the kids free. He's not trying to get the chief to do anything. The chief and the officer are on the same team. But within their bond of mutual love, it is fitting and beautiful that the young man give, and the chief receive, this costly offering, on the occasion of the young man's victory.

I sometimes hear people say that we should use *all* of the theories of the Atonement, because each one supplies something essential to our understanding. I can't agree completely, because the early-church belief that God forgives freely isn't compatible with the later theory that he had to be paid first (whether for the sake of his honor, or to achieve justice, or for some other reason). But there is much beauty to explore in the scriptural language of *offering*, once it's liberated from the overtones of a one-for-one transaction.

Salvation is the free forgiveness we receive from God, and also a rescue action whereby we were redeemed from the captivity of death. There remains this third aspect, threaded through Scripture in the language of offerings and sacrifices, where we see that the Son offers himself and the Father receives the offering—and yet it was always the Father who sent his Son into the world (John 3:16), as he provided the ram for Abraham's sacrifice (Gen. 22:8).

The solemnity and rigor of the system of sacrifices was set before God's people to teach what gifts mean within a relationship of love, and how very great love can make possible the greatest of gifts: "Greater love has no man than this, that a man lay down his life for his friends" (John 15:13).

One more detail to clear up. What about the word *ransom?* "The Son of Man came . . . to give his life as a ransom for many" (Matt. 20:28; Mk. 10:45).

This term *ransom* is sometimes understood as Christ paying the sin-debt to the Father. But when there is a kidnapping, the ransom wouldn't go to the chief of police. The ransom would go to the kidnapper. Christ's life is the ransom that sets us free, redeems us, from Death—not from the Father.

When we hear the word *ransom* we picture a big bag of money with a dollar sign on it, the kind that well-appointed bank robbers carry in cartoons. But the term used to mean simply setting someone free. You could "ransom," "redeem," or "deliver" someone in a number of ways. You could do it by meeting the kidnapper's demands, or paying the slave owner's price; or you could offer to take the person's place (as some saints freed slaves by taking their place); or you could just help him escape.

God took that third course; by his power, he opened a way of escape. He "redeemed [Israel] . . . out of Egypt with a mighty hand" (Deut. 9:26). He didn't pay any ransom money; he didn't give Pharaoh anything (or refuse to act until *he* had received something). He just set them free by his "mighty hand."

In our story, the brave young officer "ransomed" the teens out of captivity simply by breaking down the door, so they could run free. He "ransomed them by his blood," because he stayed to make sure the last had escaped, even though it was then too late to save himself.

Someone who didn't understand English very well might say, "Who did he pay?" Did he trade the kidnappers a little vial of blood in return for the kids' freedom? Or did he give his blood to the police chief? (And how would that free the kids?) No, we'd explain, it's a figure of speech. Nobody actually *received* any blood. It was a courageous, self-giving act, but not a transaction.

This most ancient view of salvation, that Christ rescues us from Death, is usually called the "ransom" theory by Western theologians, setting it alongside the "satisfaction" and "moral influence" and other theories that emerged after the East-West split. (They are rooted, as I said before, in differing interpretations of Scripture; people's choice of one theory or another depends on who they think has the most accurate Bible interpretation.) But I think *ransom* is a misleading term, since that word's meaning has become restricted to paying for someone's release, rather than setting them free by a mighty act; we picture that bag of money. So I call this the "rescue" theory, since that recalls the Old Testament event that most clearly foreshadows Christ's victory on the cross, the deliverance in the Red Sea. (As I've said before, Orthodox don't call it "the rescue theory" or give it any other label; it's just "salvation.")

The understanding of salvation as a rescue action was reintroduced to the West in the last century by the Swedish Lutheran archbishop Gustaf Aulén (1879–1977). He called this view *Christus Victor*,[52] which was also the title of his widely read book. Aulén makes the point that, although we call this the "ransom" (or "rescue") or *Christus Victor* theory, it isn't a fully worked-out theory; it doesn't attempt to answer all the questions. The earliest Christians were sure that that Christ's resurrection freed us from Death, but didn't venture to say exactly how it worked. Yet they went confidently, willingly to their deaths in the Roman persecution, armed with this belief alone—not even a full-fledged "theory" but simply an "idea" of the Atonement, in Aulén's view.

In some of the early Fathers' writings you hear a theme that, by becoming incarnate and dying, Christ *tricked* the devil; Hades gulped down his human body, and then was exploded by his divinity. The Syrian hymnographer St. Romanos the Melodist (AD 475–518) wrote a hymn-sermon depicting an argument between the evil one and gluttonous Hades, who has devoured all the dead from the beginning. In this somewhat-humorous dialogue they gaze upon the cross, and the evil one keeps boasting, "Look at that Cross! It's my greatest triumph." But Hades isn't sure he agrees; his stomach doesn't feel so good.

The evil one deceived by Christ's human disguise is a theme some early authors enjoyed; the devil was tricked like a fish swallowing a baited hook (St. Gregory of Nyssa[53]) or like a mouse taking the bait in a trap (St. Augustine[54]). In that sense Christ could be seen as offering to the evil one a *decoy* ransom, like that money-bag with counterfeit bills and a dye pack inside. No church father proposed that the devil received a *genuine* ransom in return for our freedom. The devil didn't deserve such payment, and in any case Christ would have taken it back when he rose from the dead.

We can bring in the concept of justice again here, not in the earlier sense of paying the Father our sin-debt, but in recognizing that God acted fairly toward the devil in winning our freedom. He could have swept away the consequences of sin, the suffering and death that all humans face, simply by an act of power. But, respecting death as the natural consequence of sin, he sent his Son to undergo our common experience of human life and death. The devil took the bait, seizing not a sinful man but a sinless one, and losing everything as a result.

God beat the devil fair and square. Christ's work fulfills eternal justice in that sense, rather than in the sense of a payment to balance sin.

To anyone who interpreted "ransom" as a literal payment, St. Gregory of Nazianzus (AD 330–339) warned that the analogy cannot be pressed. "To whom was that blood offered, that was shed for us? Since a ransom belongs only to him who holds in bondage, I ask to whom this was offered?"

To the devil, perhaps? But it would be outrageous for the evil one to receive "ransom not only from God, but ransom which consists of God himself." The devil, a murderer and liar from the beginning (John 8:44), had no right to payment. "But if [the payment is] to the Father, first I ask how? For it was not by him that we were being oppressed. And second, why should the blood of the Only-Begotten delight the Father, who would not receive even Isaac when he was being offered by his father as a sacrifice?" If God would not receive the offered blood of Isaac, why would he be pleased with the blood of his beloved Son?

St. Gregory sums up: the Father accepts Christ's sacrifice without having demanded it; the Son offers it to honor him; the defeat of the evil one is the result. "This is as much as we shall say of Christ; the greater portion shall be reverenced with silence."[55]

In the end, there is little we can comprehend about these things. This was a battle fought over the children's heads. All we need to know is that we have been rescued; we are free, safe, and loved.

And with that we should join everyone for Vespers—at least the ones who are here. The service is about to begin, but at St. Felicity there's a persistent problem with worshipers arriving late.

13

"The Lord Is King"

(Ps. 9:37/10:16)

*Tardy Worshipers, Confession, New Calendar, God's Love,
Repentance, Hymns for the Theotokos*

hough the choir is here in full force, worshipers continue to straggle in over the next ten minutes or so. On
Sunday mornings, they may be even later. This is one of
Orthodox worshipers' less-flattering traits. They may have an excuse
on Sunday mornings, since there is a series of short and long services
before the main event, so no matter what time you arrive worship is
already going on. No such excuse exists on Saturday night; there is, in
fact, a quiet time of waiting between the end of choir practice and the
beginning of Vespers. Perhaps it is one more sign of the Orthodox
commitment to tradition that they come late to Vespers, all the same.

Not everyone is late, of course. A young woman is kneeling, bent
almost to the floor, half-hidden behind the chanters' stand; her eyes are
closed, and there is a look of intense concentration on her face. A silver-
haired man stands in the nave facing Christ on the iconostasis, gazing at
him with an alert and watchful expression and a trace of a smile.

A couple with three small children chooses a spot in the middle of
the nave, and spends the remaining minutes before the service in an
endless loop of looking toward the altar and settling themselves for
prayer, then having to bend down and say something to the kids.

When another dad comes in with his two little ones, the five small friends sit on the floor together, not completely silent but at least less apt to wander.

A father comes in with a teenager who expresses in every impatient gesture that he doesn't want to be there. Two younger sons dash to the sacristy to get their altar-boy robes. An elderly woman with a bent back comes in using a cane and takes a seat up front; after eighty years of Orthodox worship, there will be no more standing for her.

In a seat at the back, a young man sits and looks over a list on an index card, occasionally making corrections. He plans to make his confession after Vespers, and like some Orthodox he writes out a list, because it makes things easier to say—and harder to omit, should he get cold feet.

At St. Felicity, parishioners make a confession at least quarterly, during the four fasting seasons, or "Lents," of the year.* It's early December now, during Nativity Fast, and Father John will be kept at church for an hour or more after Vespers, hearing confessions. He will stand with this young man in front of the icon of Christ on the iconostasis and say:

> Look, my child, here Christ stands invisibly to receive your confession. Do not be ashamed or afraid, and do not conceal anything, but confess all so that you may receive forgiveness from the Lord Jesus Christ. Here his holy image is before us, and I am only a witness, to bear testimony to all you say. But if you conceal anything, you will instead have the greater sin. So take heed: you have come to the physician, do not depart unhealed.

---

* By "fasting" Orthodox mean abstaining from meat, fish, and dairy—more or less a vegan diet—though fasting before Communion means abstaining from all food and drink. We'll explore fasting more deeply in chapter 19.

Confession is made to Christ, not to the priest; the priest is a witness. But, psychologically, it really does help to have a witness. Sins that are confessed only to the bedroom ceiling have a way of coming back and taunting you. So the young man will talk about the items on his list, and maybe add some he rationalized into leaving off that list, and Father John will give advice about developing the strength to resist. He may recommend a book to be read, or particular prayers to be said.

Such an assignment is not punishment for sin, but resembles advice a coach might give to help an athlete grow stronger. It's forward-looking, toward gaining spiritual strength, rather than backward-looking, toward punishment. But in the case of someone who persists in a sin, and uses the sacrament of confession as a car wash, the pastor may need to use stronger measures. In serious cases, a person may be told to refrain from coming to Communion until his life is in order.

I once asked my husband, a priest, whether it was discouraging to hear such a litany of sins over and over again. He said no, that it was rather the reverse; that it awed him to witness the great love people have for God, and how willing they are to confront their sins and struggle against them. He added that people also should know that, after a priest has been hearing confessions a few years, there is nothing you can say that will shock him. He's heard it all before.

I asked, too, if the majority of sins were sexual; he said no, the majority are sins of pride and anger. Battling anger is a persistent theme throughout Orthodox spiritual writing, both because our first calling is to love one other, and also because anger is very often a clue to pride.

We are now in the lead-up to Christmas, and non-Orthodox are usually aware that Orthodox observe some feasts on different days than the West does—they've heard of "Greek Easter" or "Russian Christmas." Most Orthodox in America follow the same calendar as the West—we call it the "New Calendar"—and celebrate Christmas and other feasts on the same date (with the exception of Pascha, that is, Easter). But some, including most Orthodox overseas, follow what's called the "Old Calendar."

What's the difference? The Old Calendar is off by eleven minutes a year. That doesn't sound like much but, compounding over the centuries, the error now amounts to thirteen days. What that means is that, though Old-Calendar Orthodox celebrate Christmas on December 25 like everyone else, they don't get to December 25 until the rest of us have moved on to January 7.

Early in the twentieth century some of the Orthodox churches adopted the New Calendar to remedy the discrepancy, while some kept the Old Calendar. But *all* Orthodox still celebrate Pascha together—and they observe it according to the Old Calendar.

Unlike Christmas on December 25, Pascha does not fall on a particular date each year. How can we know when Pascha should be observed? There was a lot of local variation in the early church, and communities celebrated Pascha at different times. Standardizing this was one of the goals of the First Council of Nicaea (AD 325, the same council that wrote the Nicene Creed). The council decreed that henceforth Pascha would be observed on the first Sunday after the first full moon that appeared on or after the vernal equinox.

That sounds complicated, but we can take it apart. First find the vernal equinox. That's the day in spring in which day and night are the same length (equinox means "equal-night"); sunrise and sunset are exactly twelve hours apart. The vernal equinox isn't hard to find; it usually falls on March 20. (The autumnal equinox, on the other end of the year, comes around September 22.)

So find March 20 on a calendar. Now, when will the first full moon occur, on or after that date? The city of Alexandria was renowned for its astronomers, so the church there was given the honor of declaring when this full moon would occur.

Now you know when the first full moon after the spring equinox will be. So, last of all, identify the first Sunday on or after that full moon. That's Pascha.

And actually nothing has changed; Pascha, or Easter, has been calculated in this way throughout church history, since the fourth century. So why do West and East celebrate the feast on different days? It's because, under the Old Calendar, there's that slip of thirteen days. Just as Old-Calendar Christmas, December 25, falls on New-Calendar January 7, the vernal equinox that occurs on March 20 isn't observed on the Old Calendar until everyone else has moved on to April 3. Depending on when the next full moon appears, Pascha and Western Easter can fall on the same date, or be as much as five weeks apart.

The delay in celebrating the Feast gives this advantage: you can buy Easter candy half price. Old-Calendar Orthodox enjoy a similar savings thanks to their Christmas-in-January, and are also grateful that the Feast of Christ's Nativity is not swamped by the wild commercialism that surrounds New-Calendar December 25.

As the minutes tick down to 6:00 PM, more worshipers come in. Most are carrying a candle or two they picked up in the narthex. Each worshiper venerates the icon of the Conception of the Virgin, just inside the door, then goes up to the iconostasis and stands before the icon of Christ. They make the sign of the cross and follow it with a bow (or bow first and then cross themselves), stretching the right hand to the floor, a gesture called "making a *metania*."

The more complete way to bow before the Lord is to kneel and, putting the palms of your hands on the floor, touch your forehead to the floor. That is called "making a prostration," and it is what you should picture when the Scriptures say, "They fell on their faces."† It's a way of expressing respect and awe, and that is seen from one end of the Bible to the other (Lev. 9:24, Jdg. 13:20, 1 Kgs. 18:39, Matt. 17:6, Rev. 7:11, and elsewhere). Today we associate it with

---

† It's actually more ergonomic to aim to let your palms hit the floor first, then the knees. Monks and nuns who do many metanias in a row do it that way, and push off from their hands to return again to their feet.

Muslims, but they got it from their Christian ancestors, who inherited it from Judaism. Making a prostration takes some room, and some agility; a metania is a more compact substitute.

Each person makes two metanias before the icon of Christ, prays, and then venerates it with a kiss. Some light a candle and leave it in the adjacent stand, while others continue to carry theirs. When they step away from the icon, they face it and make one more metania.

Next, each worshiper moves toward the icon of the Theotokos, to their left. They step down from the solea to the nave floor and, as they cross in front of the altar, pause and make a metania. They then come up to the Theotokos icon and repeat the process they went through before: two metanias, prayer, kiss. Those who have held on to their candle till now will light it and leave it in the candle stand here. Stepping to the side, they make one more metania toward the icon of the Theotokos, and then join the congregation, or go to pray before other icons in the nave. In some churches there may be icons that have a relic of the depicted saint embedded at the bottom of the image, or a collection of relics in a case. These, too, attract those who want to stop and pray.

A little girl, accompanying her mother, has brought a pink rose in a small bottle to leave before the Virgin. Both the little girl and her mother are wearing head coverings—long scarves that have been wrapped loosely over their heads and around their necks (this helps keep them from coming loose while bowing). A few of the women and girls at St. Felicity wear head coverings, but most do not; it's a matter of choice. One of the older ladies favors large hats, and the tiny, elderly Ethiopian parishioner comes to church swathed in yards of white gauze, and worships barefoot.

Head coverings are used more consistently in traditionally Orthodox countries than they are here, but on a visit to a monastery you may discover that they are de rigueur. Both men's and women's monasteries may have rules about this and other items of clothing; they may require that sleeveless shirts and shorts be covered up, for the sake of modesty, and that women wear skirts. Usually monasteries that have such rules are prepared to help you meet them, and offer boxes or bins of scarves, large-size shirts, wraparound skirts, and other items that you can layer on top during your visit. Before you visit a monastery, it's a good idea to look at their website and see what they prefer. Sometimes you'll come to a gatehouse at the monastery entrance, where a monk or nun is assigned to look over pilgrims and assist in wardrobe corrections.

By the way, in the Orthodox Church there aren't religious orders, as in the West—Franciscan, Benedictine, Jesuit. Monasteries may differ in their daily schedules and labors, but the spiritual path itself is the same all over the world. Both men's and women's communities are called monasteries, though you sometimes hear the term *convent*. Occasionally a monastery is home to both men and women, who live in separate houses but worship together. That's called a "double monastery."

As we draw closer to 6:00 PM, the number of worshipers increases, and a loose line extends back from the icon of Christ to about the middle of the nave. The church bell begins to toll, and the line disperses.[‡]

Now the pastor, Fr. John, and Deacon Andrew stand before the altar and make three metanias.[§] They turn around and, with arms crossed over their chests, bow to the congregation. This is an unspoken request for the forgiveness of their sins, and the worshipers bow to them in return. Fr. John will make this gesture during the Divine Liturgy tomorrow morning, too, and at that time say, "Forgive, brothers and sisters. For those who love us and for those who hate us."

Fr. John is still a young man, and has been a parish priest only five years. He understands better each day that only God's grace can

---

[‡] If you run out of time to venerate the icons, it's okay. Some will dart up to make these prayers during the early part of the service, but it's not required.

[§] The Orthodox custom is to call clergy by their title and first name, "Father John"; the custom in liturgical churches in the West is instead to use their title and last name, "Father Brown."

enable him to be a pastor to this congregation. So many members are older than he is, and going through troubles he's never had to face. The merry, family-centered Christmas season is especially hard on the lonely, and he keeps those of his spiritual children particularly in prayer.

Entering the sanctuary he reverences the altar, then intones, "Blessed is our God, always, now and ever, and unto ages of ages." The choir and people respond, "Amen," and then sing,

> Come, let us worship and fall down before God our King.
> Come, let us worship and fall down before Christ, our King and our God.
> Come, let us worship and fall down before the true Christ, our King and our God.

With each line, everyone makes a metania, enacting the words "fall down." The choir and congregation then begin to chant Psalm 103/104, a favorite psalm to many because of its rich descriptions of the natural world.

> You are clothed with honor and majesty,
> Covering yourself with light as with a garment,
> Stretching out the heavens like a curtain.
> He lays the beams of his chambers in the waters;
> He makes the clouds his chariot;
> He walks upon the wings of the wind. . . .
> He laid the foundations of the earth, that it should never be moved.

The psalm continues to explore the beauties of the earth: that by God's command it brings forth food for every creature, "wine that gladdens human hearts, oil to make their faces shine, and bread to strengthen their hearts." It provides trees for the birds to nest in, mountain crags for the wild goats, and dens for the lions. The ocean, too, is full of innumerable and unknown creatures. The cycle of life and death is in the hand of God.

When you open your hand, they are all filled with good;
When you hide your face, they are troubled.
When you take away their breath, they die and return to the
    dust.
When you send forth your spirit they are created,
And you renew the face of the earth.

This is an appropriate psalm to read when we reach sunset, and look back over the cycle of our day and our lives. While the worshipers are chanting this psalm, Fr. John is at the altar, quietly saying the seven prayers at the Lighting of the Lamps.

You only are God, O Lord, and among all the gods there is none like you. You are powerful in mercy, and you are compassionate in your power. You strengthen and save everyone who calls on your holy name. . . . Enlighten our understanding and enable us to know your truth. Grant that this day, and all our lives, will be tranquil and without sin. . . . Fulfill, O Lord, all our prayers that are for our salvation. May we love you with holy fear, and always do your will. . . . We give thanks for your immeasurable patience. You do not punish us as we deserve, but abound in mercy and compassion. . . . For you are a good God and you love mankind; we ascribe glory to you, to the Father and to the Son and to the Holy Spirit, now and ever, and unto ages of ages. Amen.

When I was newly Orthodox, I noticed how often prayers end with this reference to God's goodness and unending love. It seems the right balance for a faith that puts very great emphasis on repentance. Sometimes a prayer concludes, "For you alone love mankind." A startling way to put it, but true: every human love is feeble, every human love can fail. The only love that is worthy of the name is God's love for us.

Why is repentance so important? This emphasis may call to mind a long-standing argument between Catholics and Protestants, as to whether we must do or contribute something in order to gain salvation. (This old argument is often described as "grace versus works.") The Roman Catholic teaching is that the "eternal punishment" for our sins was remitted on the cross, but there remains a "temporal punishment" that sinners themselves must experience "either here on earth, or after death in a state called Purgatory."[56] Churches of the Reformation insisted instead that Christ's death on the cross paid the whole penalty for our sin, and there is nothing left over for us to bear.

The Orthodox view is not like either the Protestant or the Catholic one. We start with a whole different premise. There's no concern about paying the price of our sins, because the Father forgives freely, without needing to be paid. Salvation is a rescue, rather than a transaction. But we are continually called to repentance because we have a powerful yearning to return to sin, and the contagion of death it brings.

Repentance is not an easy road. I like to say, "Everybody wants to be transformed, but nobody wants to change." Transformation *means* change. And change means admitting that you need to change; it means identifying what your habitual sins are, and doing your best, God working in you, to break your slavery to them.

In a way, repentance is just another word for honesty—taking an honest look at yourself and recognizing what binds you to death. You can see this in the word *repentance* itself. In Greek it's *metanoia*, which is a compound made from the prefix *meta* and *nous*. (*Nous* means the mind's ability to understand or comprehend; we'll talk more about the *nous* later on.) "Meta-morphosis" is the transformation of the *morphe*, the shape; "meta-noia" is the transformation of the *nous*. "Be transformed by the renewal of your *nous*," says St. Paul (Rom. 12:2).

Repentance is rethinking: it means recognizing our patterns of sin instead of denying them. We seek to understand the complicated ways the passions work in and confuse us; above all, we desire to be healed. *The Shepherd*, a Christian text from about AD 140, says, "Repentance is great understanding."[57] The process of healing takes a long time, as we continue to repent and understand ourselves better as the years go by. With practice, we can learn how better to cooperate with God's power, and overcome temptations. As we continue in humility, we can gain victory from one sin after another.

This is a complex therapeutic process, and it is going to happen in the order that God knows best, which might not be the order we expect or prefer. Sins form an interlocking substructure within our frail and foolish selves, and that framework has to be dismantled in the right order. A sin we especially long to cast off might be held in place by a different sin, one that has to be removed first, even if we don't grasp the connection and consider it less important.

Or, to change the metaphor, the process is like carefully removing the layers of an onion. You have to deal with the next one that presents itself, even if you'd prefer to jump ahead.¶ "I have yet many things to say to you, but you cannot bear them now" (John 16:12).

Fortunately, God is in charge, and already within you, deeper in you than you are in yourself. If you continue to follow the spiritual exercises you've pledged yourself to, like an athlete continuing his exercises, and cling above all to humility, you will be amazed at what God can do with you—and in such a natural way that each step feels quite obvious, and never more than you are able to bear. God is the doctor and we are the patients, but we have a choice about whether we are going to be a *cooperative* patient. We'll investigate the topic of free will a little more later on.

The last of the tardy worshipers, Fr. John's wife, Beth, at last slips in the door. She was stopped in the parking lot by an older parishioner who wanted to complain that Father's sermons are too long; can't she make him stop?

¶ A wise elder is of immense help in this process. The Holy Spirit will ensure that your pastor and confessor has everything needed to guide you well, but if you want to talk about deep levels of prayer, a good place to look for an elder is at an Orthodox monastery. A truly gifted elder will probably deny that he or she is one, but word still gets around.

A *Presbytera* is a regular target of such comments. Though an Orthodox priest is called "Father," as in some Western churches, there is no English equivalent for his wife's title. The Greek version, "Presbytera," is perhaps the most commonly used, but in a church with a Russian ethnic background she may be called "Matushka," in a Romanian church "Preotesa," in a Ukrainian church "Panimatka," in an Arab church "Khouria," in a Finnish one "Ruustinna," in a Serbian one "Popadija," in an Indian one "Kochamma," in an Albanian one "Prifteresha," in an Armenian one "Yeretzgin," in an Egyptian (Coptic) one "Tasoni"—you get the idea. The title either means "Mother," parallel to "Father" for the priest, or it is the word for "priest" with a feminine suffix. It indicates her share in her husband's pastoral ministry, and she is honored as the spiritual mother of the parish. Presbytera Beth is pregnant with their first child, and nothing endears a clergy couple to a parish like a new baby.

When the Psalm and the seven prayers are finished, Dn. Andrew leads the congregation in an *ektenia*, that is, a series of intercessory prayers (also called a litany). He is a retired military officer, trim and gray, and his posture is exemplary. The Greek word *diakonos* means "servant," and the deacon's main role is to assist the priest.

Dn. Andrew stands on the solea, facing the icon of Christ, and lifts the end of his stole (his *orarion*) with his right hand. He begins chanting petitions, and each time the people sing the response, "Lord, have mercy." He sings, "For the peace from above, and for the salvation of our souls, let us pray to the Lord," then "For the peace of the whole world; for the good standing of the holy churches of God, and for the unity of all, let us pray to the Lord." There are about a dozen of these petitions, and the response each time is the same.

After chanting an abbreviated version of Psalms 1–3 ("Blessed is the man who walks not in the counsel of the wicked"), followed by a brief ektenia, the choir chants Psalm 140/141, "Lord, I call upon you, hear me," then Psalm 141/142, "I cried to the Lord with my voice." They sing this (and the whole service) a cappella—voices alone, no accompaniment. Choir director Hank gives the pitches for each part, singing "La, la, la" in descending notes, before almost every hymn.

(A young lady who visited my church, Holy Cross, was asked afterward how she liked the service, and replied that it would be better if "that annoying lady"—our choir director—didn't sing "La, la, la" before every hymn.)

As the choir leads this hymn, the worshipers join in to varying extents. One person sings along boldly, another just hums; one is silent, another sings only the *ends* of the phrases. I found it pretty confusing at first. It reflects, I think, the unself-consciousness that C. S. Lewis noticed when he described worshipers kneeling, sitting, or standing, doing whatever they preferred. (One distinctive choice is to chant or hum the *ison*, a single, low note that undergirds the melody.)

I confess that when I first began attending Orthodox services it bothered me that *everyone* wasn't singing. It looked to me as if many members of the congregation were just standing there (when do we get to sit down?) and not really participating. With time I came to see that the silent worshipers may be praying with the most intensity. Everything doesn't have to show on the surface. The important thing is that we are united as a community, doing the work of worship. The freedom to engage with that worship however you like allows room for some to choose silence.

When they reach the line "Let my prayer be set forth before you as incense," Dn. Andrew, now standing within the Royal Doors of the iconostasis and facing the altar, lifts up the censer. He then begins the Great Censing. He walks around the altar, stopping at each of its four sides and swinging the censer toward it. He censes the Prothesis table and the High Place, then comes through the north door of the iconostasis (the one with an icon of the archangel Michael on it), and censes the icons on the front of the iconostasis. Then he walks through the entire church, swinging billows of gray-white smoke as he goes. As he circles the interior of the church, he censes all the icons, and also the worshipers, who bow to him in return.

As he passes by, one of the little boys leaps to his feet and gawks openly. The Great Censing is the most fascinating thing he sees all week. His dad made him a pretend censer out of a plastic bowl and some lengths of twine, and he likes to march around the living room swinging it. Playing church is a lot of fun, for little boys especially, it seems. If clergy aren't striding through a room swinging a blazingly-hot metal bowl, trailed by clouds of smoke, they're sprinkling everyone with water, smearing oil on their foreheads, throwing leaves into the air, or just shouting; yes, the rubrics (liturgical instructions) sometimes specify "In a loud voice." At regular intervals, deacons get to shout that everybody should pay attention, a gratifying aspiration for little boys.**

As Dn. Andrew circles past the choir, one soprano claps a hand over her ear; the chiming of the bells on the chains is making it hard for her to find her note. The choir is endeavoring to learn how to sing these psalms each Saturday night in the Byzantine Tone appointed for the week, and it takes some getting used to.

Earlier we noted that there are eight troparia of the Resurrection, and a different one is sung each Sunday, in order. Since Sunday begins on Saturday night, the first time we hear the week's troparion is at Saturday Vespers, and it sets the melody, or Tone, used for these Vespers psalms. Since the words of the psalms stay the same, but the music (Tone) changes, those words fall in different melody-places every week. Tonight we sing the psalms in Tone 3, because the third troparion of the Resurrection is the one appointed for this week. We'll sing the troparion itself at the end of the service.

As the choir comes to the last verses of Psalm 141, they begin to chant in unison, and continue through Psalm 129/130, "Out of the depths," and Psalm 116/117, "Praise the Lord, all you nations."

** Children can memorize and replicate a surprising amount of the liturgy, but they are stumped when it's time to read the Gospel. The little son of a friend simply read from the volume of a different text that he knew by heart, *Where the Wild Things Are.*

However, now they don't chant the psalms straight through, but pause at the end of each verse for a solo chanter to insert a short one- or two-line hymn. These short inserted hymns are called *stichera* (singular, *sticheron*), and they differ every week; some differ every day of the year. So if you have been doing your best to follow along in the worship book, this is where you will give up. Not only are there eight different multipage settings for this hymn (since it is sung each week in a different Tone), but the stichera verses for the day's saint or feast aren't in the book at all. The only people with a copy are the two choir members who were assigned to chant them tonight.

At Great Vespers the first few stichera are always about the Resurrection. You can see, below, how the stichera intersect the psalm:

> *Choir and people, Psalm 141:8a*: Bring my soul out of prison, that I may praise your name.
>
> *Chanter*: O Christ our Savior, you broke the might of death by the power of your Cross, and you exposed the lies of the evil one. Through faith in you the human race has escaped his malice, and we are saved.
>
> *Choir and people, Psalm 141:8b*: The righteous shall wait for me, until you recompense me.
>
> *Chanter*: O Lord our God, the glory of your Resurrection illuminated all of Creation, and opened Paradise for us once more. For this reason, we offer you our praise and worship forever.

After that come the stichera about the saint or feast of the day. Today they are about the Feast of the Conception of the Theotokos.

> *Choir and people, Psalm 129:6*: From the morning watch until night, from the morning watch, let Israel trust in the Lord.
>
> *Chanter*: Anna, who wept for her childlessness, now dances with joy, for the Virgin Mary is conceived, and Mary

in time will conceive the Incarnate Word. Anna cries out in a loud voice, "Rejoice with me, all you tribes of Israel! I have conceived by the will of God, my Savior, for he has heard my prayers and taken away my sorrow. He has healed the pains of my heart through the pains of childbirth, as he promised."

In the *Protevangelium* St. Anna comes across as a very likeable person, vigorous and down to earth.

Choir and people, Psalm 116:1: Praise the Lord, all you nations, praise him, all you peoples.

Chanter: The God who made water flow from a barren rock has caused your barren womb to bear Mary, the Ever-Virgin, and she in time will bear the Living Water. You are delivered from shame, O Anna; you are no longer fruitless, but will bear the rich farmland who will bear the Wheat of Life. By God's will all humanity will be delivered from shame, because our Lord takes on human form to rescue us, through his great mercy.

Icons of St. Anna usually depict her holding her infant daughter, resembling icons that show Mary holding the child Christ. But traditional images of St. Anna in the West show her teaching the young St. Mary, while holding an open book (the Scriptures, no doubt). That makes a good point: Mary's wise and courageous character, which prepared her to say, "Let it be to me according to your word" (Lk. 1:38) as soon as she grasped what God was asking, was formed in childhood by *somebody*. Who else but her mother?[††]

[††] Here's an appealing tradition that developed in Western Christianity: woodworkers and cabinetmakers took St. Anna as their patron, because they had the honor of crafting the wooden tabernacles used in churches to house the silver or gold vessels that, in turn, held the consecrated Eucharistic bread. In like manner, Anna's womb contained the Virgin Mary, who was to hold Christ in her womb.

In Orthodox worship there is a custom that, after a series of brief hymns, the last one will be about the Virgin Mary. This kind of hymn is called a *Theotokion*.

> O most honorable Lady, we can but wonder at your giving birth to the incarnate God. For you, the all-pure one, gave birth to a Son without a father, who from eternity was begotten of the Father without a mother; and yet the essence of each remained intact. O Virgin Mother, pray to your Son, our Lord, that he will save us, for with faith we call you truly the Theotokos.

There's a good bit of theology packed into those lines—the newborn Son who is without a father, yet from eternity is the Son without a mother. That would be something any worshiper, even an illiterate peasant, could meditate on all week (and setting it to music gave memory a helping hand).

The hymn calls Mary "all-pure," but, as we saw in chapter 11, that doesn't refer to exemption from the effects of the ancestral sin. The Eastern Church believes that the Virgin Mary experienced temptation and was knowledgeable about sin, yet resisted it all her life. She did this using the same tools we have: prayer and fasting and great love of God. "A stranger to any fall into sin, she was not a stranger to sinful temptations," wrote St. Ambrose (AD 340–397).[58] This is why she is hailed in some hymns as our best example of heroism in the battle against sin, our "Captain, Queen of War" and "Champion Leader."

14

"Lord, Have Mercy"

(MATT. 20:31)

*Mercy, Forgiveness, The Love and Compassion
of God, The Nature of Sin*

As these psalms and verses end, the deacon, priest, and two altar boys leave the altar by the St. Michael door, the one to our left, process a short way into the nave, and then circle around and line up again facing the Royal Doors. Dn. Andrew, standing in front, lifts the censer high and calls out, "Wisdom! Let us attend." At that, everyone begins to sing one of the oldest hymns known to Christian faith, the *Phos Hilaron*, or "Joyous Light."

> O joyous light of the holy glory
> Of the immortal Father,
> O heavenly, holy, blessed Jesus Christ!
> Now as we come to sunset, as we see the evening light,
> We praise the Father, Son and Holy Spirit, one God.
> It is right to praise you at all times with joyful voices,
> O Son of God, Giver of Life,
> Therefore the whole world glorifies you.

From ancient times—no one knows how long—this hymn has been offered at the end of the day, when lamps are lit to dispel oncoming darkness. St. Basil the Great (AD 329–379) notes that "it seemed fitting to our fathers not to receive the gift of the light at eventide in silence, but, on its appearing, immediately to give thanks" by chanting this hymn. He continues, "Who was the author of these words of thanksgiving at the lighting of the lamps, we are not able to say. The people, however, still utter the ancient form."[59] By the middle of the fourth century this hymn was already viewed as ancient, and the name of its author was long lost.

It's interesting to note that this hymn gives honor to the Trinity, Father, Son, and Holy Spirit. The doctrine of the Trinity is not fully spelled out in the New Testament, but was part of the bedrock of the faith by the time of this very early hymn.

For most of history this hymn was accompanied by the lighting of oil lamps and candles, but tonight one of the men in the choir steps over and turns up the dimmer switch, brightening the lights that shine on the iconostasis. As we sing, Dn. Andrew censes the icons of Christ and the Theotokos, and when we reach the line, "Now we come," he and Fr. John process back to the altar through the Royal Doors. The altar boys continue to the right and go through the St. Gabriel door.

Dn. Andrew calls out, "The evening prokeimenon!" A *prokeimenon* is a hymn of a few short Scripture verses, sung by a chanter and the congregation responsively (that is, taking turns). There is a different prokeimenon at Vespers for each night of the week, and on Saturday evening the chanter sings, "The Lord is King, he has clothed himself with majesty" (Ps. 92/93).

Everyone repeats that line after him, like the chorus of a song. Then the chanter sings the next line of the psalm, "The Lord is clothed and has girded himself with strength." We repeat "The Lord is King . . ." and continue to sing it each time, as the chanter goes through the successive verses of the psalm. At the end we all join in a final repetition of that first verse.

This is likely the earliest way of getting people to sing along in worship. We noted above that Pliny had learned from the Christians he interrogated in AD 112 that they "sing responsively a hymn to Christ as to a god." With responsive singing a congregation can join in, even if there are no hymnbooks, even if they couldn't read anyway. You could still sing a simple line to them, and they could sing it back. They could keep repeating that line while you chant the verses in between.

This kind of "call-and-response" singing is a little different from *antiphonal* singing. In that case, two people, or two groups of people, divide a song into short portions and take turns singing them. The men and the women might alternate verses, or the choir alternate with the congregation. With antiphonal singing, both groups need an ability to read and access to the words (unless they all have the hymn memorized). Responsive (or responsorial) singing probably came first, and antiphonal singing later. The latter may have seemed a suspicious innovation at first. St. Basil, writing about AD 375, appears to be defending the practice when he says that it "strengthens [the singers'] recitation of the words, and at the same time controls their attention and keeps their hearts from distraction."[60]

Dn. Andrew leads us in another *ektenia* (litany) of intercession, this time for all the ranks of clergy, monastics, and laity, "for those who bear good fruit and do good works in this holy and all-venerable temple, for those who serve and those who sing, and for all the people here present, who await your great and rich mercy." This is the ektenia "of fervent supplication," and the response is tripled: "Lord, have mercy; Lord, have mercy; Lord, have mercy."

The parishioners are learning to sing this response in some of the languages represented among the congregation, and a cheat sheet giving pronunciation is clipped to a tenor's music stand.

English: Lord, have mercy
Greek: Kyrie eleison
Arabic: Yaa rabbu-r am
Slavonic: Hospodi pomiloi
Romanian: Doamne miluyeshte
Albanian: Musheer o zot

Indonesian: Toohancasi hanila
Tagalog: Pagninoon maawaka
Armenian: Dehr vohrmyga
Korean: Chuyo pulsahi yokisoso
Georgian: Upalo shehgvitskalen
Spanish: Señor ten piedad
French: Seigneur aie pitié
Ge'ez: Egzi-o tasahal
Amharic: Abetu marenhe Christos
Swahili: Bwana udu mea
Gaelic: A hear-na djane tro-care-eh
Hebrew: Adon ra em na
Urdu: Tu reham kar khuda
Cambodian: Priah aw-tho hai

Slavonic is the ancient liturgical language of Russia, as Ge'ez is of Ethiopia. Amharic is Ethiopia's official language, and Tagalog is the Philippines'. The assortment reflects in some cases the birthplace of parishioners, and in others their more-distant ethnic background; it also represents lands where this parish is supporting missionaries. At St. Felicity, the concept of "multicultural" keeps expanding on all sides.

"Grant, O Lord, that we may keep this night without sin," everyone prays, and then there is another ektenia. This one begins with the response of "Lord, have mercy," then changes to "Grant this, O Lord." We pray for "an angel of peace, a faithful guide, a guardian of our souls and bodies," for remission of sins, and for "a Christian ending to our life, painless, blameless, and peaceful."

Fr. John chants, "Let us bow our heads unto the Lord." As everyone stands with heads bowed, he prays:

O Lord our God, you bent the heavens and came down for the salvation of all. Look now upon your servants, for we are your inheritance. We bow our heads and bend our necks in submission to you, for you are the awful Judge, and yet you love mankind. We do not seek help from any human power, but we call upon your mercy, looking confidently for your salvation.

What does "looking confidently" mean, when it comes to salvation? For many Protestants, "assurance of salvation" is a central doctrine. Some go so far as to say "Once saved, always saved": once you have accepted Christ as Savior there is *nothing* you can do to lose your salvation, even if you tried.

Orthodox seek instead to balance two truths. It is sobering to recall that we will one day die and face the judgment, and every sin will be revealed before the "awful Judge." On the other hand, he "loves mankind" and has already accomplished everything necessary for our salvation. But, on yet another hypothetical hand, though he is always faithful, we are not. If Judas could betray him, even after walking beside Jesus for years, how dare we be complacent?

As St. Paul says, "Let anyone who thinks that he stands take heed lest he fall" (1 Cor. 10:12). The Desert Father Abba Xanthias said, "The Thief on the cross was justified by a single word; while Judas, who was counted in the number of the apostles, lost all his labor in one single night, falling from heaven to hell. Therefore let no one boast of his works, for all who trust in themselves fall."

I've heard Orthodox people say "Salvation is a process." That's not quite right, because you wouldn't be deprived of salvation if you died soon after you became a Christian and hadn't had time to make much progress. Salvation isn't a process; salvation is a gift. But *life* is a process. We have to keep on making the decision to belong to Christ, over and over again, day by day, and even minute by minute.

Mercy is a word that comes up frequently in Orthodox prayer, and newcomers can find that unsettling. Why do we have to keep begging God to be merciful? Is he really that bad-tempered? To us, a plea for mercy sounds like a criminal begging a judge for a lighter sentence.

But lots of people in the Gospels asked Jesus for mercy, and none of them were seeking leniency. What they sought was Jesus' compassion.

- The Syro-Phoenecian woman begged for her daughter to be freed from a demon, saying, "Have mercy on me, O Lord!" (Matt. 15:22).
- The ten lepers cried, "Jesus, Master, have mercy on us!" (Lk. 17:13).
- Blind Bartimaeus shouted, "Jesus, Son of David, have mercy on me!" (Mk. 10:47), even though everyone was telling him to be quiet.

The petitioners weren't begging to get off easy. They were people who knew their need, and cast all their hopes on Jesus.

We, too, say "Lord, have mercy," reminding ourselves that he is merciful and all-powerful, and that he will readily hear us just as he heard them. In Greek *Kyrie eleison*, "Lord, have mercy," resonates with the word for olive oil, *elaion*, the medium for healing balm. (The good Samaritan cared for the beaten man's wounds, "pouring on *elaion* and wine," Lk. 10:34.)

"Lord, have mercy" contains all those meanings, yet there's a strain of penitence, too. It is appropriate, when we ask for Christ's help, to recognize how poorly we reciprocate his kindness. Every day we contribute our share of garbage and confusion to the world's dysfunction. The tax collector in Christ's parable "would not even lift his eyes to heaven but beat his breast, saying, 'God, be merciful to me a sinner!'" (Lk. 18:13)

The many repetitions in Orthodox worship of "Lord, have mercy," the many references to sin and repentance, are designed to keep us from trusting in ourselves. They train us in self-skepticism. But they also continually remind us that God *is* merciful, and faithful in his love. We are striving always to hold two things in balance: sorrow over our weakness before sin, and joy at God's all-transcending love.

St. John Climacus (AD 525–606) coined a word for it: *charmolypi*, a combination of two Greek words, meaning "joy-making sorrow," penitence that produces joy. That's not just metaphoric: as you advance along the way of prayer you find that deep repentance really does produce a deep joy, mixed with gratitude and a great sense of freedom.

There's a pattern often seen among the great saints, East and West, that those who ascend the highest seem to be most conscious of their sin. They see themselves as worse sinners than anyone else; even St. Paul said, "I am the foremost of sinners" (1 Tim. 1:15, a line Orthodox repeat in a prayer before receiving communion.) Perhaps this is because the closer you get to the light, the darker you see your shadow. But I think something else is going on, as well.

When you become *utterly* convinced of God's love, you're convinced that his love precedes and follows and surrounds every moment of your life, past, present, and future. There is nothing that he can't forgive—nothing that, in terms of your eternal salvation, he hasn't already forgiven. If you're deeply convinced of that, when a guilty memory surfaces, you don't panic, blame self, blame others, spiral downward. The memory arises into a place completely surrounded by God's love. You think, "You loved me then, too. You were forgiving then, too."

There is simultaneously a sting of regret—"How ungrateful, how selfish I was, when God loves me this much"—and a flood of gratitude. You realize God's love is even greater than you knew before. One at a time your bad memories have their teeth pulled in this way. Finding repentance is like finding a vein of gold in a mountain, and following it into ever-deepening joy.

When asked, "Are you saved?" a popular Orthodox response is, "I have been saved [by Christ's death on the cross]; I am being saved [by the indwelling Holy Spirit]; I shall be saved [by God's mercy on the Last Day]."

God will always love us. He chose to create us and to become our Father, and his love will continue no matter what we do. He *wants* to save us; he "desires all men to be saved and to come to the knowledge of the truth" (1 Tim. 2:4). God will always be faithful—but we can't be so sure of ourselves.

So we maintain an honest, practical humility, much like that of an addict who struggles to resist a bottle or a pill. No matter how much

love there is on one side of a relationship, it is possible for one on
the other side to destroy it single-handedly. Love may continue, but
it is no longer a relationship.

While we have complete assurance of God's love and his desire to
save us, we remain wary of our own fickle hearts. We keep asking
for mercy because we keep needing it. Staying balanced on this
point between penitence and joy creates a condition of dynamism
and energy that is a distinguishing mark of Orthodoxy; you'll meet
it over and over again.

But let's admit: it can be hard to stay on a balance point. We
go through cycles of feeling anxious, feeling guilty, feeling resentment, feeling rebellious, and then feeling relief when we identify a
worse sinner than ourselves. We're unstable, I think, because it is
so hard to grasp how absolute God's side of the relationship is. He
loves us, even while we are sinners, and nothing can halt or deflect
the force of his love. He *is* love, and his love fills the universe. It
comes entirely from him, and knows no limits. It takes no notice
of whether we are loveable or not, whether we want him to love us
or not. He will love us no matter what, and nothing can stop him.

That's not only hard to believe, but also somewhat uncomfortable
to believe, because we can't imagine what it would be like to feel
that degree of love for someone else. The love we give is often
impetuous, beguiled by superficial things, and if those things alter,
it can fail. Mere familiarity can exhaust our enthusiasm. The bride
who adores every inch of her groom on the day of their wedding
will three years later be going shopping on Sunday afternoons so
she doesn't have to listen to the way he clears his throat. So we
might suspect that God loves us this expansively only because he
doesn't know us very well. One day this inexplicable love might
encounter what we are really like, and end.

Add to that another quirk of our psychology: we don't like to feel
indebted. When we receive a gift and can give nothing in return, it

makes us uneasy. That doesn't change when the giver is God. We'd almost *rather* have a sin-debt that could be calculated exactly, and find a way to pay it back. With his vast and unreasonable love God is calling us into a recklessly self-giving relationship, nothing held back. There are a number of all-too-human reasons we'd prefer a formal agreement with clear obligations on both sides.

The early Christians understood God's forgiveness to be absolutely free, and that view continued for a thousand years (and on till today, in the East). In chapter 7 we talked about St. Anselm (eleventh century), who thought that God *couldn't* forgive us until the sin debt was paid—that even God must bow to justice, and there could be no forgiveness without restitution. St. Anselm's solution was that Christ's death on the cross satisfied the demands of God's injured honor, and made forgiveness possible.

This was an immensely satisfying idea—a "satisfaction" theory of the Atonement in another sense of the word. It was more in line with the way humans treat each other, and on that level made more sense. It was easier to grasp than God's daunting, unreasonable love. It relieved the stress of being loved and forgiven for reasons we can't control—reasons wholly within God himself.

The problem is, if anything had to be repaid before God could forgive us, then it wouldn't *be* forgiveness. Here's what I mean. Imagine that at the end of a restaurant meal the manager tells you, "No charge! Your debt is forgiven." On the other hand he might say, "No charge! The guy over at that table paid your debt." That's the difference between forgiveness and third-party payment. God does the first; he actually *forgives* us. Forgiveness must be free, if it is to be forgiveness at all.

That's not to deny that we owe God a great debt for our sin. But he does not require payment. No matter how large or small the debt, he just forgives us. "A certain creditor had two debtors; one owed five hundred denarii, and the other fifty. When they could not pay, he forgave them both" (Lk. 7:41–42).

That's how we are supposed to forgive each other, isn't it? If someone injures us, we are supposed to forgive them without demanding restitution, or even requiring them to say they're sorry. St. Paul says, "As the Lord has forgiven you, so you also must forgive" (Col. 3:13).

This is one of Christ's most difficult teachings, and one of the least likely to be actually put into practice, but we can't say it's complicated. Even when restitution is appropriate or necessary, even when trust can't yet be restored, we are still supposed to give preemptive, unilateral forgiveness.*

But there's a problem. If you and I forgive each other in this way, without repayment, we do the very thing that troubled St. Anselm: we treat sinner and sinless alike, we leave sin uncorrected, and we set the scales of justice out of balance. If the Father had to submit to the demands of justice, wouldn't the same be true for us? We *couldn't* forgive a serious injury unless there was punishment and restitution; to waive repayment would undermine eternal justice.

No nonserious injuries either, if we're going to be consistent. Even the smallest wrong puts justice out of whack. If we were strangers on the subway and you stepped on my foot, we'd have to figure out what it was worth (A quarter? How hard did you step?), and you would have to pay me before I could forgive you and we could get on with our day. If I said, "It's okay, don't worry about it" and left this wrong unpunished and unpaid, I would be wreaking injustice, and treating you the same as the innocent billions who never stepped on my foot.

Now, St. Anselm would have thought the solution to this dilemma was obvious: God's honor is infinite, but mine isn't. I learned from James Bowman's book *Honor: A History* that in traditional societies no one "would suggest that the low-born and ill-bred were as capable of honor as the nobility."[61] People in the lower classes don't even *have* honor. It belongs to the wealthy and powerful alone, and they are obligated to preserve it. So I can forgive freely, but God's hands are tied.

---

*   That doesn't mean putting yourself at risk, for example, in an abusive relationship. Forgiveness addresses something in the past, while trust concerns the present and future. You can forgive past deeds, while reserving present and future trust until you see evidence that you will be safe.

In *Lord, Have Mercy*, Scott Hahn presents this point of view in the context of sacramental confession (now called reconciliation) in the Roman Catholic Church. Our offenses against God are vastly more serious than those we commit against each other, he says. It is like the penalty you'd receive for punching the president of the United States, compared with the penalty you'd get for punching your neighbor.[62]

But these days we're not shocked when a powerful person forgives freely, are we? When Pope John Paul II was shot, in 1981, he immediately forgave the gunman. He didn't withhold forgiveness till his honor was restored—even though he held the post of highest honor in the Catholic Church. And this free forgiveness didn't astound people. People didn't complain that, by forgiving the gunman freely, he damaged eternal justice, or undermined the honor of the papacy.

Apparently free forgiveness made sense in Christ's time, as shown in the parable of the prodigal son; it also makes sense to us today. But in Anselm's time, this was a problem. He worked out the theology to solve that problem, and it took lasting hold.

The need to require fitting restitution for bad deeds appears, at first glance, absolutely essential. But on reflection it falls apart. If God demands restitution, and we are supposed to forgive the way he does, we would have to do the same. And if we had to do that—receive satisfaction before granting forgiveness—we could hardly get through a day for all the confusion and aggravation it would cause. It is right for us simply to forgive some things, and not demand that everything be made fair and square. Forgiveness does not count the cost. Forgiveness is free.

St. Isaac of Syria, a seventh-century bishop of Nineveh, points out that we can't call God just, in human terms, since he pays the laborers who worked only one hour as much as those who worked all day, and the father of the prodigal embraces his son with no demand for restitution. "Do not call God just," St. Isaac says, "for his justice is not manifest in the things regarding you."[63]

✛ ✛ ✛

What kind of love does God have for us? When we're trying to understand God's love, it's best to think about how a parent can love a child, even an angry, rejecting child. Ezekiel gives us this heartbroken cry: "As I live, says the Lord GOD, I have no pleasure in the death of the wicked, but that the wicked turn from his way and live; turn back, turn back from your evil ways; for why will you die, O house of Israel?" (Ezek. 33:11).

Christ taught us to call God "Our Father," and gave us a story to demonstrate what a father's love is like. When it begins, the younger son in the family is already a vortex of resentment and disdain. He asks his father to give him his share of the estate, that which he would normally have received upon his father's death. It was the equivalent of saying, "You are dead to me." Then the son turned on his heel and left, and he didn't go off a few blocks to pout. He immediately set out for "a far country," putting as much space as possible between him and his father.

This father no doubt knew his son well. This was probably not the first angry outburst. As the son packed his goods and headed off, the father watched him go. In that desert, treeless land, he could follow this angry son with his eyes, watching as the figure got smaller and smaller in the distance, till it finally disappeared. The father watched for a long time. The next day he brought out a chair, and he watched some more. He kept watching. Day after day went by. One day he saw a tiny figure, far away on the horizon. It was his son, coming home.

"While he was yet at a distance, his father saw him and had compassion, and ran and embraced him and kissed him" (Lk. 15:20). This father isn't concerned for his honor, or even his dignity. Though his son had given him a deadly insult, he runs to him and catches him up in an embrace. The son doesn't even get a chance to make his little "I was wrong" speech. The father is already giving orders for the welcome-home feast.

In another version of the story, the father might have said, "I'd love to take you home, son, but who's going to pay this Visa bill?

Somebody's got to pay the debt first." Or he might have said, "I'd love to take you home, but I can't have people thinking I would overlook such an insult. I'm going to have to punish you, for the sake of the social order."

Or he might have said, "I'm so full of wrath I can't see straight. Even if I killed you it wouldn't be enough. You're not worth killing. You're garbage. But your older brother, who has never offended me—he is innocent. I'll kill him, and the sight of his blood will soothe my wrath." (This last was never a mainstream view in Western Christianity, but was sometimes put forward to help worshipers grasp the seriousness of sin.)

The older brother doesn't always get a fair shake when people talk about this parable. He has a legitimate protest: the younger son has already spent his half of the estate, and now he'll have to live off the remainder, which was to be the "good" brother's share. It *isn't* fair, to tell the truth. When the father welcomes back the prodigal without requiring repayment, it's injustice, in earthly terms. But the father invites the elder son to sacrifice his legitimate claim, and join him in a love that doesn't count the cost.

The relationship between Christ's sacrifice on the cross and the forgiveness of our sins has been understood in many different ways over the last millennium. I think the most straightforward is the one we see in this parable, this very memorable parable that touches all hearers deeply. We see the wandering son and we see the Father's joy, and we see the elder brother invited to give up his claim to justice and join in. Their reconciliation will be marked by a joyful gathering. The costly gift is the fatted calf, the centerpiece of the meal that publicly marks this reunion. It is the father who provides the calf.

Another reason we keep asking for mercy is because our Orthodox definition of "sin" is a little different. In the history of the Roman Catholic Church, for example, much thought has gone into defining *when* someone becomes guilty of a sin—what, exactly, constitutes (these are technical terms) "culpability," and when a sin is "imputed."

In that church, a sin is classed as *mortal* only if it fulfills three criteria: it must involve a "grave matter," the person must have had "full understanding" of the wrongness of the act, and he or she must have done it with "deliberate consent." If one or more of those factors are missing, the deed might be classed as a lesser, *venial* sin, or possibly not involve culpability at all. "Unintentional ignorance can diminish or even remove the imputability of a grave offense," says the Catholic Catechism.[64]

This concept of sin goes well with the idea of atonement we considered earlier, that a sin amounts to breaking the law, and justice, or God's honor, must be satisfied before forgiveness can be bestowed. Sins are seen as distinct, wholly intentional, objectively wrong actions, which could theoretically be repaid by a third party.

For Orthodox, sin is the vast condition of brokenness and corruption pervading creation. We suffer from it as we do from breathing polluted air. We perpetuate it with the fearful, selfish things we do and say and think. Our sin doesn't hurt only those near us, but contributes to the wrecked, off-balance condition of all creation.

The radio humorist Garrison Keillor told a story that illustrates our interconnection. It concerns a man who is tempted to commit adultery, but on reflection sees how one act of betrayal can unbalance an entire community.

> I saw that we all depend on each other. I saw that although I thought my sins could be secret, that they would be no more secret than an earthquake. All these houses and all these families, my infidelity will somehow shake them. It will pollute the drinking water. It will make noxious gases come out of the ventilators in the elementary school. When we scream in senseless anger, blocks away a little girl we do not know spills a bowl of gravy all over a white tablecloth.[65]

We would be helpless in this mess, without the help of Christ. Orthodox believe that he came, not just to pay the debt for sin, but to begin our healing, the refashioning of the human race. We were intended to bear the image and likeness of God, and when it was damaged in the Fall, he came to restore it. As we are assimilated to his life in the process of theosis, we are increasingly healed, and become sources of healing for others—lights in the darkness.

There's something else about sin, though. We can contribute to the world's burden of sin *unintentionally*. Perhaps you once said something in a conversation that you later learned had hurt one of the hearers very much. You would deeply regret the pain you caused. Even though you didn't mean to, even if it was only in a small and transient way, you nevertheless contributed to the world's burden of darkness and grief.

This, too, is sin. It's inevitable that we will do such things, and right that we are sorry for them, even if, under the above conditions, we would not technically be "culpable."

And what about all the times you hurt someone, and *didn't* find out? How often we hurt people by not noticing them, or not remembering them, when we intend no hurt at all. The hurt is exactly that: they weren't important enough for us to remember. And let's not get started on the times that, in some sneaky corner of our hearts, malice *was* mixed up in what we "unintentionally" did or didn't do.

The Lord knows all about it when I flounder in such sins, even when I manage to keep my own awareness vague. He knows me well, and the evil one does, too, and my closest family and friends all have a front-row seat. The only one left out of this information loop—the only one with a sunny impression of my all-around niceness—is me.

All of that jumble of pain is sin. Whenever we contribute to this deadly smog, we participate in sin, even if we didn't intend to do it, or didn't know it was a sin. In a prayer before receiving Communion, Orthodox say, "Have mercy upon me and forgive my transgressions, both voluntary and involuntary, of word and of deed, of knowledge and of ignorance."

It sounds strange to ask forgiveness for sins that were involuntary, or even unknown; by the definition above, we would not be culpable for unintentional deeds. But if you caused a friend some hurt or pain without meaning to, of course you would be sorry. Of course you would ask him to forgive you, once you knew what you'd done. You'd also be sorry that you had added *any* more pain to the weight of this weary old world. Culpability is not the point. You wouldn't say of a friend you'd unintentionally wounded, "He might be hurt, but that doesn't concern me. I didn't do it on purpose."

With a friend, it's all about keeping a relationship in good repair. It's the same way with God.

Once I was invited to give an evening talk at an Orthodox church, and during the service beforehand the priest inserted a petition for me in the ektenia: "For the Khouria Frederica. . . . " I was expecting a prayer that God would guide my words, that the evening would be a blessing for those attending, something along those lines. Instead, he prayed "that our good God will forgive all her sins, voluntary and involuntary, of word and of deed, of knowledge and of ignorance, let us ask of the Lord," and all the people responded, "Lord, have mercy." I was caught by surprise at this intimate prayer, but had to acknowledge its accuracy.

You might think that, given this much broader definition of sin, it would be impossible to bear the weight. But it actually sets us free—free to be powerless, and cling to nothing but the cross. We are enmeshed in sin simply because we "bear flesh and live in the world," as a Holy Week prayer says. We can't escape it, and our hearts are crooked enough to perpetuate it in ways that don't even rise to awareness.

Christ "takes away the sins of the world" (John 1:29); not just the penalty for sin, but the sins themselves. We come to him like the sick and blind who begged for healing. And so we keep asking for mercy.

A morning prayer says:

> O Lord Jesus Christ, my God, the all-merciful, you came
> down to earth and took on flesh in order to save all, because
> of your boundless love. O my Savior, save me by your grace,
> I beg of you. For if you saved me for my good works it would

be not grace but an obligation, O my Lord, you who are all-compassionate and infinite in mercy.

For you said, O my Christ, "Whoever believes in me shall live and never see death." If faith in you saves the desperate, then save me, for you alone are my Creator and my God. Let it be faith that you see in me and not good works, O my God, for you could not find any works that would justify me. Let my faith suffice instead of any works, may it speak for me and acquit me, that I may become a partaker of your everlasting glory. Do not let the evil one snatch me away from your fold. O Christ my Savior, whether I desire it or not, save me. Come to me quickly, quickly, for I am perishing. You alone are my God from my mother's arms. Help me, Lord, to love you more than I once loved sin, and to work for you more diligently than I worked for the evil one. For I will work for you above all, my Lord and my God, Jesus Christ, all the days of my life, both now and ever, and unto ages of ages. Amen.

I love that phrase, "whether I desire it or not, save me." Come, Lord Jesus!

15

"Awake, Sleeper"

(EPH. 5:14)

Satan, The Nous, Watchful Prayer,
God's Presence in the Heart

he daily transition from light to darkness, and the long journey of the night, can give opportunity to miserable and afflicting thoughts. As we bow our heads near the end of the Vespers service, the priest prays for our protection: "Guard them through this evening and all through the night, from all enemies, from the malignant power of the devil, from despairing thoughts and evil imaginings."

I had been Orthodox for some years when I noticed that there was something missing from the usual round of theological topics— something big. Western Christianity has had to do a great deal of painful struggling with the "problem of evil," the question of why there is suffering in the world. It could fairly be said that that is the single most significant, and most unsolvable, religious issue there is, and atheists certainly love to bash religious believers with it. They ask: How can God let an innocent person suffer? We draw a blank, and that lack of an answer points in the chilly direction of doubting the goodness of God.

But at some point I noticed that this question just wasn't coming up in Orthodoxy; people weren't tormented by it like we are in the West. They suffer as much as people anywhere, of course, and recognize the great tragedy of suffering. But they don't compound that pain with worries about God's goodness or power. Apparently, they thought of this as a question that has an answer.

One part of the answer is to think, when we see suffering, "I did this." Because all human life is one, because we all swim in a common sea, I helped cause this, with my heedless, selfish sins. I helped pollute the world and make it the kind of place where this can happen. Of *course* my sins are going to hurt the innocent. Like air pollution, the fog of sin hurts everyone who breathes.

But there is another part to that answer: "An enemy has done this" (Matt. 13:28). There is a malevolent agency that savors and exploits the evil we do.

The devil has largely disappeared from Western Christian theology. I think this was one unanticipated effect of St. Anselm's theory; it presents salvation primarily as an interaction between the Father and the Son, and the devil has no practical role. Of course, people did not immediately eliminate the devil from their understanding of the world, but in time he began to fade. He became an extra standing at the edge of the stage with a tail and pitchfork, while the Father and the Son got all the lines. Even among conservative Christians, many don't believe in the devil anymore, or they consider him irrelevant. Unfortunately, that doesn't make him go away.

Some people are simply incredulous that Orthodox Christians still believe in the existence of the devil; it's a concept that seems naive and outdated. But this belief is based on a great deal of direct experience, and goes back a very long time. Spiritual warfare is a major theme in the New Testament, and exorcism was a regular part of Jesus' healing ministry.

It would be too narrow to think only of exorcism, though. We're talking about the presence of evil all through the world, in all its many guises. Orthodox would say that there is not only evil resulting from the brokenness of creation, but also the deliberate, malicious work of demons, intelligent beings that hate the human race.

This belief is not unique to Christianity; most people, in most times and places, have believed in the existence of evil spirits (a belief likewise based on experience). Even those who dismiss such ideas can usually recall a time they felt a mysterious unease, and sensed a disturbing quality hanging about a place, or even a person. We might be receiving such spiritual perceptions pretty regularly (positive ones, too, of course), but we don't note them consciously, because we think we don't believe in that stuff. That stuff could be real, all the same. It doesn't care whether you believe in it or not.

The evil one loves to see the good and innocent suffer. It's a twofer: he gets to enjoy the spectacle of suffering in those who least should bear it, and he gets to enjoy the anguish this causes to the less-innocent ones who are looking on. The fact that such events grieve and trouble us delights him all the more, since there's a chance he can destroy our faith. One of the ways we bear the burden of our sins is in the wrenching pain of watching the innocent suffer, and knowing that we helped make this a world where that can happen.

I shouldn't have to say this, but the evil one is really *evil*. Don't just picture him trying to tempt a fat lady to eat more chocolate. Picture the most hideous story you've heard of torture or child abuse. In the very worst of it there is a flash of glee. That's his fingerprint.

Anything that causes you pain satisfies his purposes—he loves suffering. But his larger goal always is to alienate you from the Lord. It doesn't matter whether the temptation is toward pleasure or toward fear and despair; he'll use anything, if it can draw you away from the side of Christ. He is always working to disrupt our sense of reality.

What reality would that be? Earlier we talked about how an icon of the Crucifixion shows us the ultimate reality of that event, the truth a news photograph could not have captured. We are trying to keep our thoughts always allied to this great victory, always present to the Lord, who never leaves our side. We are trying to form the habit of staying in reality. (The Orthodox Way has exercises to strengthen this ability; we'll get to them soon.)

The Scriptures call us to wake up and pay attention. "Awake, O sleeper, and arise from the dead, and Christ shall give you light" (Eph. 5:14; a line, it appears, from the earliest Christian hymn). God is here, in this present moment. Dispel your futile and wandering thoughts. Focus on him instead.

The professional demon in C. S. Lewis's *The Screwtape Letters* is able to distract an atheist, briefly tempted toward faith, by showing him a city bus and a boy selling newspapers. The implication is that thinking about the great questions guides the mind to God, while life's ordinary sensations drag it away.

It's true that, when we're suffocated by the world's distractions, it can be easy to avoid God. But we're also quite capable of spending our time pondering the great questions *instead of* dealing with God. Thinking and talking about God is not communion with God. Only prayer is prayer. Both worldly distractions and theoretical cogitating can be used to avoid the challenge that ultimately faces each of us: that we are called to enter a direct, personal relationship with God, one where he will be God and we won't be.

When we are in such a relationship, the world God made is not necessarily an *alternative* to communion with him, but potentially a *medium* of that communion. In the Scriptures, the natural world is not a distraction or temptation, but the footstool of God. When we attend to it, we find it filled with his presence.

Reality is God's home address. The city bus and the boy selling newspapers, or whatever you see when you go out today, are part of that present reality. So we endeavor to keep standing there, alongside our Lord, in watchful prayer: "Continue steadfastly in prayer, being watchful in it with thanksgiving" (Col. 4:2).*

When we look at the way the Scriptures understand thinking and the mind, we meet a number of surprises. For one thing, the Bible doesn't share our culture's high regard for human reason. Our ability to reason is just as damaged as the rest of creation. We're quite as likely to use that rational capacity for plotting and scheming for our own advantage as for meditating on truth and beauty.

So the Scriptures do not heap high praise on human reason. In fact, a recurring theme is that the mind (often the Greek word is

* In Western spirituality, there are forms of prayer (often termed "meditation") that make use of the imagination, for example, picturing yourself in a Bible story. Orthodox spirituality strongly opposes this. God is fully present to us *in reality*, and that's where we need to train ourselves to stay. The mind that is captivated by mental images is vulnerable to confusion and even delusion. As above, watching inner movies about God is not prayer. Only prayer is prayer.

dianoia, which means the reasoning faculty) is full of trickery and self-deception:

- "The imagination [*dianoia*] of man's heart is evil from his youth" (Gen. 8:21).
- "The LORD saw . . . that every inclination of the thoughts of their hearts was only evil continually" (Gen. 6:5, NRSV).
- "He has scattered the proud in the imagination [*dianoia*] of their hearts" (Lk. 1:51).
- "Out of the heart come evil thoughts" (Matt. 15:19).

You might have noticed another surprise in those verses: the Bible authors assume that thinking takes place in the *heart*, not the head. Despite our settled assumption that "mind" equals "head," in the Bible your "thinker" is physically located in your heart.

- "Mary kept all these things, pondering them in her heart" (Lk. 2:19).
- "The word of God . . . [pierces] to . . . the thoughts and intentions of the heart" (Heb. 4:12).
- "Take heed lest there be a base thought in your heart" (Deut. 15:9).
- "Preserve me from violent men, who plan evil things in their heart" (Ps. 140:1–2).

In fact the heart, *kardia* in Greek, is the center of the entire person. It's the seat of our awareness, the place we abide within ourselves and look out at the world, It's "home base."

Here comes another surprise: within the heart, the Scriptures see no distinction between reason and emotion. This is such a staple of our culture—we're so convinced that reason and emotion are opposites—that the omission of this assumption in the Bible is hard even to grasp. But I've come to think that, really, the Bible has the more accurate view of how humans are made.

Emotions and reason are not, in reality, two separate things, but two aspects of the same inner process. Our emotions are always caused by thoughts; whenever you're feeling an emotion, it's because of something you're thinking (possibly something quite rational). And everyone knows how our reasoning can be influenced by our emotions. These aren't two equal-and-opposite functions, but a single integrated process.

That's an idea that takes some getting used to, but it has great significance our witness to Christ. There's a widespread cultural assumption that you can't experience God with your mind, which leaves only one alternative: if you experience God at all, it's with your emotions. The assumption that humans are composed solely of "head" or "heart" compels agreement with the assertion that, if a person claims to have experienced the presence of God, it was just a case of emotional projection.

As we said above, that's a false dichotomy; reason and emotion aren't alternate states but function in tandem. And they're not the only equipment we have. We possess many other overlapping and cofunctioning abilities—thoughts, memories, fantasies, will—which bubble together in the cauldron of the heart. They are integrated aspects of the whole person.

Here's one more surprise. When we ask the question: How do we experience God? the scriptural view would be that we *do* encounter him by means of our mind. Not by our ability to reason, though; we do this by means of the *listening* mind.

As the old saying goes, "The Greeks had a name for it." In this case, they had a name for a function of the mind that is usually unnamed and, for us English speakers, goes mostly unnoticed.

If you think about it, the mind has two "gears," forward and reverse. Forward gear is when you are thinking something through, following a line of thought, reasoning in a logical way—the *dianoia*, above. In English today, when we speak of "the mind" we mean those active ways of thinking (usually setting them opposite to the "the heart" or emotions).

But the mind also has a "reverse gear": it can *receive* information. This is our ability to understand, comprehend, discern, or perceive. In biblical Greek it is called the *nous*, pronounced "noose." (As with *energeia*, the word doesn't mean in Scripture exactly what it does in Aristotle and Plato.)

We use the nous all the time; it's the faculty that enables us to take in information of any sort. If we listen to a story, watch a movie, or just pay attention to what someone is saying, we absorb that content by means of the nous. Broadly speaking, it is our capacity to encounter life firsthand, our receptive awareness.

If you open the door and perceive that it is raining, you make that deduction from all the messages your senses bring in: you hear, see, touch, and even smell the rain. All that incoming data would be worthless, though, if there weren't a center of operations—a place where the "you" of you receives and processes all this information (while sitting in a nice leather executive chair, as I picture it). An Orthodox post-Communion prayer asks, "Enlighten the simple unity of my five senses." The nous unites the five senses, along with its other work.

If God were to interact with us, it would be by means of the nous, not through our emotions or our reasoning ability. When God spoke to a prophet, he communicated by means of the prophet's mind—his receptive, listening mind. He wasn't limited only to the prophet's emotional "heart" or logical "head," for he had created him with many other capacities, including, obviously, an ability to take in information. God speaks to a prophet by means of his mind, and if he chose, he could do the same with us.[†]

Here's an example of how the word *nous* is used in Scripture. When Christ appeared to his disciples after his resurrection, he "opened their nous to understand the Scriptures" (Lk. 24:45). Since English translations say that he opened their "mind," you might have thought he made them intellectually sharper, better equipped to defend the Scriptures. No, he enabled the disciples to *perceive* something; he enabled them to see the prophecies of his life and work woven through the Old Testament like a silver thread. It had

---

† Of course, you might well have some thoughts and emotions after such an encounter! But those are reactions to the experience, not causes of it. If you open the door and it's raining, you might have some practical thoughts and disappointed feelings; but those reactions were provoked by a direct and authentic encounter with rain.

been there all along, but they had been unable to see it. When Christ opened their nous it was like a grimy window being opened, and they suddenly could see these prophecies everywhere.

You may have had an experience like theirs, though for a far less exalted reason. Can you remember what it's like when you're watching a movie, and you come to a surprise ending? Your mind receives this "revelation," and, flashing backward through all the previous scenes, discerns different meanings in all that went before. That might echo, in a small way, what this astounding insight was like for the disciples.

St. Paul uses the word *nous* some eighteen times in the New Testament. For example:

- He says of nonbelievers, "Their very *nous* . . . is corrupted" (Titus 1:15).
- Nonbelievers live "in the futility of their *nous*" (Eph. 4:17).
- Christians "have the *nous* of Christ" (1 Cor. 2:16).
- He told the Ephesians, "Be renewed in the spirit of your *nous*" (Eph. 4:23).
- To the Romans he said, "Be transformed by the renewal of your *nous*" (Rom. 12:2).
- "The peace of God which passes all understanding" is actually "The peace of God which surpasses the *nous*" (Phil. 4:7).

I had a dramatic conversion to Christianity; I was a young college grad and calling myself a Hindu when, as a hitchhiking tourist in Dublin, I went in a church and stopped to look at a statue of Jesus. I suddenly heard a voice inside, speaking to me, saying, "I am your life." (It wasn't a voice I heard with my ears, but resonated inside, filling my awareness.) When I tried to describe this to others later on, I would say that it was like there was a little radio in my heart that I had never known was there. Suddenly it snapped on and I could hear a voice inside, speaking to me. I had no doubt who it was, for our Lord speaks "with authority" (Lk. 4:32).

When I ran across this little word, *nous*, many years later, I realized that it was the "little radio" I had been trying to describe. Everyone is born with this little radio; everyone is capable of hearing the voice of God. It doesn't matter whether you're a rational or an emotional sort of person. God will speak to you, in any case, through your mind—your receptive, listening mind.

In the West we usually think of an experience of God as being quite subjective. It is something that happens privately, to you alone; it happens *inside* you, rather than visibly in the outside world; it concerns your emotions, and maybe was generated by your emotions; it's a personal experience, one you cannot claim happened in the objective world we all share.

I am saying the opposite of that. What the disciples saw at Christ's Transfiguration happened in the real world. The glory of God had always been present in Jesus, but only at that moment were their eyes opened to perceive it. Likewise, the disciples on the road to Emmaus were walking with Jesus the whole time; it was only when he broke the bread that their eyes recognized him.

Here's a memorable story along those lines, from the Old Testament:

> When an attendant of the man of God rose early in the morning and went out, an army with horses and chariots was all around the city. His servant said, "Alas, master! What shall we do?" [Elisha] said, "Do not be afraid, for there are more with us than there are with them." Then Elisha prayed, "O LORD, please open his eyes that he may see." So the LORD opened the eyes of the servant, and he saw; the mountain was full of horses and chariots of fire all around Elisha. (2 Kgs. 6:15–17, NRSV)

Such events don't necessarily happen only to two or three people. The entire company of the Israelites witnessed this manifestation of God's presence:

> On the morning of the third day there were thunders and lightnings, and a thick cloud upon the mountain, and a very loud trumpet blast, so that all the people who were in the

camp trembled. Then Moses brought the people out of the camp to meet God; and they took their stand at the foot of the mountain. And Mount Sinai was wrapped in smoke, because the LORD descended upon it in fire; and the smoke of it went up like the smoke of a kiln, and the whole mountain quaked greatly. And as the sound of the trumpet grew louder and louder, Moses spoke, and God answered him in thunder. (Exod. 19:16–19)

None of these events were private, interior, immaterial, subjective, or emotionally produced. All took place in the objective world, and were visible to others. These people became able to see something that was already there; they'd just needed to have their "eyes opened." Or, as Jesus said repeatedly, "He who has ears to hear, let him hear" (Mt. 11:15; Mk. 4:9, 23; Lk. 8:8; 14:35).

If this is the case, why *don't* we hear God's voice? Because the nous is broken. Like everything else in creation, it sustained damage as a result of the Fall. The darkened nous doesn't much *want* to hear the voice of God. It is hungry and craves input, wanting to be always filled with sounds and sights and entertaining thoughts. It would rather avoid God—hiding, as Adam and Eve did when they heard his footsteps in the garden (Gen. 3:8).

Because the nous is damaged, we perceive this world wrongly often enough, and misunderstand situations and other people. Much of our misery is rooted simply in not being able to understand. A lifetime of misperceptions bends and dents the mind, so that we don't comprehend God, or anyone else, very accurately.

What's going on in our minds most of the day doesn't really deserve to be called "thinking." Our thoughts go drifting aimlessly, reacting to random blurts of memory, desire, fear, aggravation. We stare entranced at the pictures in our head, and tag along behind wherever they lead.

That internal parade of images is something Orthodox spirituality has always cautioned against; it disrupts prayer and dazzles and
confuses the mind. But we today must live in the most unreality-
saturated generation in history, with movies, videogames, and
superhero mythology pressing in on us from every side. Glamorous
unreality makes present reality look dowdy. It will take some time
and effort, some growth in self-control, to detox the nous.

Since it is by the nous that we encounter life firsthand, its distor-
tion affects all our relationships and choices. We urgently need it
to be healed. The nous is sometimes called "the eye of the heart,"
because its function is receptive, like that of an eye, and its healing
is described as an inflow of light. We can see that in these passages:

- "When your eye is sound, your whole body is full of light" (Lk.
  11:34).
- St. Paul spoke to the Ephesians of "having the eyes of your
  hearts enlightened" (Eph. 1:18).
- "Recall the former days when, after you were enlightened, you
  endured a hard struggle with sufferings" (Heb. 10:32).

The early Christians called baptism "Enlightenment." St. Justin
the Martyr (AD 100–165) wrote of baptism, "This washing is called
illumination, because they who learn these things are illuminated in
their understanding."[66]

The enemy of our communion with God is the evil one, who
"comes only to steal and kill and destroy" (John 10:10). He aims
at our thoughts, because that's where everything begins. Sin starts
with a tempting thought, one that finds receptivity and a willingness to go on thinking about it. "Each person is tempted when he
is lured and enticed by his own desire. Then desire when it has
conceived gives birth to sin; and sin when it is full-grown brings
forth death" (Jas. 1:14–15). Our communion with God is fractured
long before we take action on a sinful impulse—it begins to crumble
as soon as we start entertaining the thought.‡

---

‡ This is why rage is the equivalent of murder (Matt. 5:22), and lustful thoughts
the equivalent of adultery (Matt. 5:28).

202 ▛   WELCOME TO THE ORTHODOX CHURCH

Perseverance in prayer, cultivating a mental habit of being attentive to God's presence, gradually creates a steady place inside. It is a place where we can stand beside the Lord and see all that comes and goes. We become able to recognize harmful thoughts when they are approaching and deflect them, instead of collapsing and letting them carry us away.

You already have some ability to do this; there is a part of your mind that *watches your mind* and evaluates your ideas. (Saying, for example, "That's a stupid idea.") What happens, in prayer, is that that island of thought-observation gets bigger. It gets more stable and more reliable. As you grow in confidence, getting more attuned to the Lord's presence and guidance, you can become quite dexterous in deflecting the thoughts that come to wound you.

(Don't be afraid of them or feel guilty about them, by the way. They'll continue to show up all your life, inflicted by the evil one or your unhealed self. You're not at fault for such thoughts; you have no choice about when they appear or what they say. But you do have a choice about whether to invite them to come in, sit down, and chat awhile. A common monastic saying is, "The birds fly overhead, but you don't have to let them nest in your hair.")

If you're used to thinking of sin in terms of "culpability," as specific and deliberate deeds, then focusing on thoughts can seem impossibly small. But if you think in terms of soul-sickness, of sin as a systemic corruption that marches on to death, then it makes sense to go to the root. That's what a surgeon would do. We might wish that our faith would instead keep us happy and comfortable, but it's when the surgeon says, "All we can do is keep her comfortable" that you're really in trouble.

Granted, this takes some effort; it's an exercise in mental self-control. You'll encounter real inward resistance because the broken nous prefers to prowl about uncontrolled. It does this motivated not only by pleasure, but by fear and loneliness as well. Not all tempting thoughts are attractive; they could be self-hating, fearful, or disgusting instead. We end up flapping around after loose thoughts all day like a spooked chicken.

One day after another passes in this way, and a whole life can be squandered in aimless wandering. People take up this admittedly difficult spiritual path when they become convinced that it is worth it. They become convinced that being able to abide steadily in God's presence will not only transform their own life, but also enable them to pray with increased clarity and effectiveness for those they love. In that light, the challenge that lies ahead is worth accepting. "Take every thought captive to obey Christ" (2 Cor. 10:5).

Watchfulness was a theme our Lord emphasized in his teaching. He exhorted his disciples, "Watch and pray that you may not enter into temptation" (Matt. 26:41). We're to be always ready, like the virgins who had filled their lamps (Matt. 25:2), like the householder wary that a thief might come (Matt. 24:40). "I say to you what I say to all: Watch" (Mk. 13:37).

St. Paul kept urging his hearers to watchful, constant prayer:

- "Continue steadfastly in prayer, being watchful in it with thanksgiving" (Col. 4:2).
- "Pray at all times. . . . Keep alert with all perseverance" (Eph. 6:18).
- "Take every thought captive to obey Christ" (2 Cor. 10:5).
- "Be constant in prayer" (Rom. 12:12).
- "Pray constantly" (1 Thess. 5:17).

This can sound so tense that it might be surprising to hear that our goal is actually learning how to *rest*. We learn to cultivate inner stillness by turning ourselves away from the clamor of the mind's random, pointless wandering. This stillness is called *hesychasm*, a Greek word that means "silence" and "rest." (A person practicing it would be called a hesychast, or a hesychast elder, but it would be laughably prideful to apply the term to yourself.) In terms of prayer, hesychasm means the waiting, listening stillness in which we hear God's voice: "Be still, and know that I am God" (Ps. 46:10). God spoke to Elijah not in wind or fire but in a "still small voice" (1 Kgs. 19:12).

You can't *compel* God to speak, of course, but you can practice listening, and that's why hesychasm aims at quieting the self, holding the nous open and attentive. "When you pray, go into your room and shut the door" (Matt. 6:6), the inner door that shuts out the world's agitation and prepares a place for Christ.

Quiet or stillness is not the same thing as vacancy. It's dangerous to try to make your mind blank. The Lord said that when an evil spirit has been driven out of a man, if it returns and finds him empty, "he goes and brings with him seven other spirits more evil than himself, . . . and the last state of that man becomes worse than the first" (Matt. 12:43–45). Hesychast stillness is not emptiness but attentiveness, alert and expectant, as you would wait and look for the One who is the source of all love.

Orthodox writings on prayer often speak of "drawing the mind down into the heart" or "praying with the mind in the heart." Our mind, habitually drawn to aimless wandering, must find its true home in the *kardia*, the heart, which is the center of our being. There the nous can stand beside the Lord and look out with courage and love at all of life. The heart is "the place in man at which God bears witness to himself,"[67] and the heart is good at recognizing that witness, and hearing the ring of truth.

I expect I've said this enough already, but "drawing the mind into the heart" doesn't mean becoming less logical and more emotional. (Though that's what I thought it meant, years ago, when a monk told me that I needed to live less in my mind, more in my heart. I thought, "My husband is going to be surprised to hear this.") Bringing the mind into the heart means disciplining your mental attention, which habitually hungers to be entertained or distracted (that kind of activity does feel, somehow, like it's hovering around your eyes or forehead), and training it to rest in the heart.

This language isn't wholly metaphoric. Even without praying, you can try on different thoughts and see how those that are idle and dispersed (imagine overhearing news about a celebrity who doesn't interest you) or united and strong (recall something you have firm convictions about) seem to lodge at, or emerge from, different places in the head or chest. As your ability to pray with attention increases, you'll notice that more of your inward self is focused on prayer, making it ever more honest and undistracted; you're likely to find as well that it is progressing physically toward the heart.[§] The word *authentic* is overused, but it would be a good fit here.

Bringing the mind into the heart isn't something you can force to happen—it comes as a gift of the Holy Spirit—but as you keep practicing watchful prayer you'll find that you are being led forward. Praying teaches you *how* to pray, and keeps showing you, step-by-step, what it means to pray with the mind in the heart.

Awhile back I mentioned the Desert Fathers and Desert Mothers, men and women who went into the wilderness of Egypt and Palestine to devote themselves entirely to prayer, beginning as early as the second century. When other people came to live near these elders and learn how to pray, the first monasteries were formed. The collected sayings and stories of the Desert Elders is one of the treasures of early Christian spirituality.

Over the years a great deal of knowledge grew up about this path of transformation in Christ, the goal of which is theosis. The church exists to support and enable that process of transformation. Monks and nuns are the explorers who devote themselves to it full-time, and bring back guidance for all. Over the centuries the human psyche has been closely mapped by these explorers, and its tricks and self-deceptions brought to light.[¶]

These Desert Elders sought a way to "pray constantly" (1 Thess. 5:17), as St. Paul said, and continuously practice the presence of God. They found, of course, that a persistent problem is the mind's tendency to wander. One minute you're focused on God, the next you're wondering what's for dinner. So they tried to corral

---

§ Orthodox spiritual direction emphasizes: do not allow the mind to descend any further than the upper chest or, if God wills, the heart. A known risk in some religions is a form of psychosis that accompanies more-extensive body awakening.

¶ One of the foremost works is *The Ladder of Divine Ascent* by St. John Climacus, the sixth-century abbot of the monastery on Mt. Sinai. I was advised to read only a page a day, because it needs time to sink in. That's good advice.

the attention by repeating short prayers or lines from Scripture. A number of different versions were tried, and the one that proved most useful was, "Lord Jesus Christ, Son of God, have mercy on me." This is called the "Jesus Prayer."

The idea is to acquire the habit of praying it continuously at the back of your mind, holding your attention in the presence of the Lord throughout the day. Many Orthodox Christians carry (or wear around the wrist) a prayer rope, a length of black yarn tied with a series of elaborate knots, to keep track of repetitions of the prayer. Giving the hands something to do helps keep the mind from wandering. With practice the prayer becomes automatic, like background music, holding the mind in the presence of Christ.

Along the way you become aware that there is a physical component to this process. When you pray you can feel your mind becoming more gathered together, more focused, and more settled down inside. You sense that it is no longer buzzing around your hairline, working in scattered and partial ways, but is becoming more like something you mean "with all your heart."

In your heart is hidden, from the time of your baptism, the Holy Spirit himself. His prayer is within you: "We do not know how to pray as we ought, but the Spirit himself intercedes for us with sighs too deep for words" (Rom. 8:26). The mind descends into the heart and finds that the Lord is already there. We begin to become who we were eternally intended to be. St. Theophan the Recluse (AD 1815–1894) said, "When the mind is in the heart, this is in fact . . . the reintegration of our spiritual organism."[68]

You would think the heart would be a small, intimate space, but perseverance in prayer reveals that, like Mary's womb, a small place can contain infinity. "The kingdom of God is within you" (Lk. 17:21), our Lord said.

The Desert Father St. Macarius (AD 300–391) wrote:

> The heart itself is but a small vessel, yet there also are dragons and there are lions; there are poisonous beasts and all the treasures of evil. And there are rough and uneven roads; there

are precipices. But there is also God, also the angels, the life and the kingdom, the light and the apostles, the treasures of grace—there are all things.⁶⁹

It wasn't the end of the story when the prodigal came home. He needed fresh clothes right away, and probably needed a bath, too. He was no doubt malnourished, weak from his long journey on foot, prey to illness, infection, and parasites.

But those sorts of things would be the easiest to heal. The prodigal didn't come home because he'd had a personality transplant, but because he was desperate and had nowhere else to go. He may be just as angry as he was before, and now his pride is stung by having to accept charity. He might resent his goody-goody older brother, who resents him in return. He might be embarrassed in front of the servants, who saw him at a point of great humiliation. He's come home, but his journey is not over.**

As we progress in prayer our eyes are opened again and again to how much healing we need, so much more than we expected. Our Father, in his tender pity, and with his precise knowledge of how we are made, doesn't reveal the entire makeover plan at once. "I have yet many things to say to you, but you cannot bear them now" (John 16:12). C. S. Lewis wrote that we think at first God is going to turn us into a "decent little cottage," but as deep, wrenching change continues we realize that he is building a palace. "He intends to come and live in it himself."⁷⁰

This is the core of Orthodox spirituality: guarding the mind, because the mind underlies the body, emotions, and everything else. Guard it and hold it steadfast in the presence of God. All the resources of the church—liturgical, theological, sacramental, pastoral—have the purpose of nourishing and expanding that inner

---

** We call this story "The Prodigal Son," but Jesus began it with, "There was a man who had two sons" (Lk. 15:11). It didn't start, "There was a son." The point of the story is the father's love rather than the Prodigal's actions.

communion. Taken together, they represent the science of oneness with God, what the book of Acts calls "the Way."

The Vespers service is now winding down. Having finished the prayer for our protection from evil thoughts, we sing a series of hymns praising the Resurrection and Christ's Davidic lineage. We then sing the hymn of St. Simeon, the one who held the infant Jesus in his arms. "Lord, now let your servant depart in peace, according to your word" (Lk. 2:29–32). This restful hymn is treasured by Christians in many denominations.

We next say the series of prayers known as the "Trisagion prayers"; these occur at nearly every occasion of Orthodox worship. "Trisagion" means "thrice holy," and the prayer itself is:

> Holy God, Holy Mighty, Holy Immortal, have mercy on us.
> Holy God, Holy Mighty, Holy Immortal, have mercy on us.
> Holy God, Holy Mighty, Holy Immortal, have mercy on us.

The story behind this ancient prayer is that, in AD 434, there was an earthquake in Constantinople, and the clergy and people fled to the fields outside the city to pray. They offered litanies: the clergy chanted petitions, and the people responded, "Lord, have mercy."

Somehow in the midst of the tumult and shaking of the ground a little boy was tossed up into the sky, into heaven. When he fell to earth again he reported that he had heard angels singing, "Holy God, Holy Mighty, Holy Immortal." The people immediately began chanting this hymn themselves, adding as a refrain, "Have mercy on us!"

I was attending a mainline seminary in the 1970s when some liturgical reformers recommended using the Trisagion in worship, explaining that it had been used in the early church. "You're kidding!" I thought. "They still know what some of the early church's prayers were? Why haven't we been using them all along?"

The set of Trisagion prayers includes a few others and wraps up with the Lord's Prayer. Then we sing the Resurrection troparion, and the one appointed for this week is Tone 3:

> Let the heavens exult! Let the earth rejoice!
> For our Lord has done great deeds with his mighty arm.
> He has trampled down death by death,
> And has come forth as the firstborn of the dead.
> He has freed us from the abyss of Hades,
> And bestowed on the world his great mercy.

If translators are being precise, you'll see references to "Hades" rather than "hell," because, technically, hell—the "lake of fire" (Rev. 19–20)—doesn't exist yet. When we come to the end of our earthly lives, death rips body and soul apart. The friends of God then dwell in Paradise ("Today you will be with me in Paradise," Lk. 23:43), and those who "loved darkness rather than light" (John 3:19) dwell in Hades. But we were created as embodied beings, so our sojourn in Paradise or Hades is temporary. At the Final Judgment there will be a resurrection of all human life, and we will be restored to our bodies in some unimaginable form. Those who love God will henceforth be with him in heaven, and those who reject him will experience hell.

Such terms are utterly inadequate, for none of them are places in a geographic or even spatial sense. Yet we who know no other form of existence can't talk about the matter for long without using the preposition *in*, and envisioning separate locales. All these terms actually point toward the same all-encompassing thing: the fire of God's love, in his unveiled presence.

Next comes the troparion of St. Anna, since tonight we are celebrating her conception of the Virgin Mary. We rejoice with St. Anna because of her role in the lineage that culminates in Christ:

Today the chains of barrenness are broken,[††]
For God has attended to the prayers of Joachim and Anna,
And promised them, though it was beyond all hope,
That they would give birth to a holy girl child.
From her the Infinite One will be born in mortal form,
When he commands his Angel to cry out to her,
"Hail, O full of grace, the Lord is with you."

Hymns to the saints persistently draw our attention back to Christ. Just as every icon is really an icon of Christ, hymns about saints proclaim his glory in their lives.

The Resurrection troparion is followed by a Theotokion. When we sing about the Virgin Mary, we usually focus on her pregnancy and birth-giving rather than other periods in her life. We never stop exploring the incomprehensible role she was given to play in the story of salvation.

O Theotokos, through you was revealed to those on earth
The mystery unknown by the angels, hidden from all eternity,
That, by his own good will, God would become man,
Uniting human and divine natures without confusion,
And accepting the Cross for our sake.
By it he raised to life again the first-created of the human race,
And delivered our souls from death.

Again, there's a lot of theology packed in there: "God would become man, uniting both natures without confusion." Christ was both fully human and fully divine, a point that was worked out painfully in the fifth century amid a flourishing array of alternatives. Some said Jesus was a human being whom God adopted as his Son at his baptism. Some said he only *appeared* to be human, but was really entirely divine. Some said he was both, but the divinity overwhelmed the humanity like the ocean absorbing a droplet. Or perhaps Christ had both a human and a divine nature, which remained separate in him

---

[††] Hymns are often set in the present tense. In the timeless time of worship, great events of salvation always take place "Today."

(picture a bicycle built for two). In that case, the Virgin Mary gave birth only to his *human* nature. The consensus that emerged was that Christ was fully God from eternity, and became fully human as well; from the moment of conception he was both God and man. That's why we call Mary "Theotokos," declaring by that title that she is the "Birthgiver of God."

Christian writers in the West have sometimes suspected the Orthodox Church of being "anti-intellectual" (though the work of the ecumenical councils suggests some competence in that area). The charge reflects the zeal for refining theological and philosophical concepts that has been evident in the West throughout the last millennium—from St. Thomas Aquinas and twelfth-century scholasticism, through the sixteenth-century Reformation, through the seventeenth-and-eighteenth-century Enlightenment, and up through the last century.

In the process, the ability to reason was regrettably detached from the ability to commune with God. Theologizing and praying were sent to separate corners. Under those circumstances the two could no longer act as correctives on each other. Wider extremes appeared of ungoverned, self-indulgent emotionalism, and ungoverned, self-indulgent intellectualizing.

The dangers of the latter are not often perceived, but they arise from the false assumption that it is possible to talk about God behind his back. We can't stand outside God and examine him under laboratory conditions; we can't even begin to comprehend him. All we have to work with are these pitiful human brains—and they're limited.

The limitations show when you consider how vigorously philosophers and theologians have disagreed with each other down the centuries. Great minds have applied themselves to the same great questions over and over, but rarely arrive at the same conclusions. It seems the human mind is less capacious than it thinks it is.

Fr. Thomas Hopko, the dean emeritus of St. Vladimir's Orthodox Seminary in New York, was asked at an academic conference about the use of philosophy in writing and talking about theology. He replied, "I don't think there *is* such a thing as philosophy or theology. There are *people*—who think, who act, who interact."

That may sound surprising, especially coming from a seminary dean. But it captures an important truth. Whenever cogitation is going on, it's going on inside a person. It's going on inside a mind that is damaged, like the rest of creation, by the Fall. Such a person is not an infallible reasoning machine, but an eternal being designed to bear the light of Christ, and growing daily either toward or away from that destiny.

The church fathers, Fr. Hopko went on, used the concepts of their time to communicate with contemporaries, but they regarded philosophy's achievements with some skepticism. St. Gregory of Nyssa (AD 335–395) wrote that secular education is "always in labor but never gives birth,"[71] and St. Gregory of Nazianzus (AD 330–390) said, "We theologize in the manner of the Apostles, not that of Aristotle."[72] Orthodox hymnography regularly contrasts the mentally darkened philosophers with the wise fishermen.

(On the other hand, wherever there is truth, it is God's truth. St. Justin the Martyr said that when philosophers and wise elders of other faiths speak the truth, it is because they have had some share in the "seed of the word [*logos*]." Wherever truth appears, it was given by our Lord Jesus Christ. "Whatever things were rightly said, among all people, are the property of us Christians," he wrote.[73])

Fr. Hopko continued, "There is no 'reason alone' that you can appeal to," no autonomous reasoning ability that would enable any person, even an atheist, to do theology accurately.‡‡

"What is autonomy but the nous?" he asked. "The *ratio*, human reason, is fallen too! There is no 'reason alone.' . . . People are filled with hang-ups and passions and prejudices, even when they're philosophers. As you may have noticed."

Fr. Hopko continued, "The mind is fallen. . . . The image of God cannot be totally obliterated, but it is fallen, it is screwed up, and

---

‡‡ I know it sounds funny, but that's the lingo: you "do" theology.

unless it is illumined and saved by the Lord it cannot function properly. If you're not following a holy *praxis*,§§ your mind's not going to work right."[74]

I quote Fr. Hopko at length because this line of thinking is so unexpected. His emphasis on a holy praxis is particularly important. Philosophers and theologians don't work in a vacuum but in a social environment where, as in any profession, there are prizes to win or lose. There are temptations to judgmentalism, anger, stung pride, ridicule, and all-around anxiety. A pattern develops of searching others' work for flaws, and seeking ways to put one's own original ideas in view. Spiritual dangers abound, so spiritual disciplines are vital.

In *Aristotle East and West: Metaphysics and the Division of Christendom*, David Bradshaw notes that Orthodoxy did not produce original theologians like Augustine or Aquinas. Instead of prizing original thinking, "[the Byzantines] valued fidelity to the existing tradition. What one finds in the East is not a series of towering geniuses, but a kind of symphonic movement, in which the role of a great thinker is to pull together and integrate what others before him have said in a more piecemeal way." [75]

It seems to me that the mood in Orthodoxy is more collaborative than competitive, not because Orthodox Christians are less argumentative by nature, but because theological writing has retained a connection with worship and prayer. The Orthodox faith has a practical and even measurable goal: enabling union with God. We can try various prayer and spiritual practices and see, over long centuries, what works best. Participants are contributing to a shared store of knowledge, working together on something to benefit all. They have a common goal.

Elder Paisios (1924–1994) warns, "It is a great evil when we theologize cold-heartedly with our mind. This . . . gives birth to

---

§§ *Praxis* means a process or a practice. In this case, it means the full practice of the Christian life: communion, confession, prayer, fasting, almsgiving, and so forth.

Babel (confusion). On the other hand, in theology¶¶ there are many tongues (many gifts) but all tongues are in agreement because they have one Master, the Holy Spirit of Pentecost, and the tongues are of fire."

He went on, "The word of the mind does not bring change to souls, for it is flesh. The word of God that is born of the Holy Spirit has divine energy and changes souls."[76] Long experience shows that intellectualizing about God does not increase communion with God; it may even hinder it. There's a practical reason for that. The mind, with its two gears, has this limitation: it can only use one gear at a time. You can receive something into your mind, or you can use it to produce ideas, but you can't do both at the same time.

As St. Maximos the Confessor (AD 580–662) wrote,

> We cannot use our intelligence to think about God at the same time as we experience him, or have an intellection about him while we are perceiving him directly. . . . By "perceiving him directly" I mean experiencing divine or supernatural realities through participation. What we have said is confirmed by the fact that, in general, our experience of a thing puts a stop to our thinking about it, and our direct perception of it supersedes our intellection of it.[77]

Curiously enough, the premier Western theologian, St. Thomas Aquinas, had an experience at the end of his life that radically changed how he saw his own work, and that echoes St. Maximos's thought. While at worship on the Feast of St. Nicholas, December 6, 1273, he had an encounter with Christ. It seems it was fairly overwhelming, but he never described it to anyone.

After that, he stopped writing. His assistant begged him to resume his widely acclaimed work, but he refused. He said, "I cannot, because all that I have written seems like straw to me."

Sometimes it is necessary for the Church to do some hard analytical labor; sometimes confusion sweeps in like a tornado, and it is

---

¶¶ That is, theology in the Orthodox sense of immersion in Christ.

necessary to state the truth explicitly and in detail. But the fact that you have to do this work is itself a sign that you've lost the thread. It's like a husband and wife who start arguing over what "I love you" means; they have lost touch with the experience of love itself. You can't experience something and scrutinize it at the same time. So we thank God for his guidance whenever such theological labor is necessary: "The Spirit of truth . . . will guide you into all the truth" (John 16:13). But when we have to pull over and look at the road map, we're no longer rolling toward the goal.

With the closing prayers complete, Fr. John now stands in front of the Royal Doors holding the Greek hand cross, and the worshipers line up to come forward and, one at a time, kiss it and then kiss Fr. John's hand.

The congregation forms itself into a straggling line, and little ones hop and fidget till it's their turn. Most people exit the church after venerating the cross, but a few take seats on the chairs on the left side of the nave, toward the back. Fr. John will be hearing confessions while standing in front of the icon of Christ on the right side of the iconostasis, and waiting on the left confers a little privacy. A choir member stays behind to chant the pre-Communion prayers for tomorrow, which gives a bit of audio cover.

The young man who was working on his list in the previous chapter keeps to his seat in the very back. He takes out the card and looks it over again, with a furrowed brow. Now it's only a matter of time.

16

"Time for the Lord to Act"
(Ps. 118/119:126)

Kairos Time, Doctrinal Development,
Chanting the Scriptures, Mercy

February 17—Sunday of the Publican and Pharisee

eacon Andrew, standing beside the altar, says to Fr. John:
"It is time for the Lord to act." Those ancient words
mark the beginning of the Divine Liturgy, the service
in which bread and wine become the body and blood of Christ. This
challenging phrase is taken from Psalm 118/119, in which the psalmist exhorts the Lord to rise up and defend his holy law:

> It is time for the Lord to act,
> > for your law has been broken. (v. 126)

This is not just a call to worship; it is a call to battle.

We participate in the Lord's battle, for we are his body, but who
are we fighting? That sort of language, once common in Christian
worship, is mostly avoided these days, when bloodshed among
adherents of different religions is all too often in the headlines.
Orthodox worship is based on ancient texts, though, so old-
fashioned "fightin' words" sometimes come up. We should take a
few minutes to understand who or what our opponent is.

First of all, it is not other people. The Orthodox Church, like all true Christian churches, loves and welcomes adherents of other faiths. Christ came in love, and he came for everybody, not just already-Christians: "I have other sheep, that are not of this fold; I must bring them also, and they will heed my voice. So there shall be one flock, one shepherd" (John 10:16). Christ extends his welcome even to those who hate or mock Christianity, and those who perse-cute Christians. No one is excluded.

So who are we fighting, then? As we saw earlier, the enemy we are fighting is the devil, the evil one. Salvation is a victory over forces that seek to enslave us, and it was foreshadowed on the banks of the Red Sea. Christ's incarnation, death, and resurrection revealed his victory over evil and death. In the Divine Liturgy that work continues. Today the Lord will enter his temple "invisibly borne by hosts of angels," and then enter the temple of our bodies by means of the Eucharist. In this way the boundaries of the kingdom of God are always being expanded, driving back the forces of evil.

"It is time for the Lord to act," time to redeem his world from the forces that have broken his law and despised his rule. In Greek the word used here for "time" is *kairos*, the right time, the appointed time. There's another Greek word for time, *chronos*, which refers to orderly, ordinary clock time, but kairos time is momentous, and any time the Divine Liturgy begins we are there. The sequence of familiar earthly events is broken, and we are brought into the throne room of God. There, worship never ceases, as angels and saints of all ages continually sing his praise. When the time comes for the Lord to act, we are swept up into that community and add our wavering voices to theirs.

For all their theological drama, these words are spoken to the priest quietly, while worshipers are singing the closing hymns of Matins, the service (about an hour long) that precedes the Divine Liturgy.* The words are not part of the congregational worship but

---

*   *Matins* comes from a Latin word that means "of the morning." Orthodox also call this service *Orthros*, which means "daybreak."

are spoken by the deacon to the priest alone; it's the equivalent of "Let's roll." One of the deacon's duties is to serve as a prompter. The Divine Liturgy includes lines for the deacon that include telling the priest what he should say or do next, as well as instructions for the congregation: stand up straight, bow your heads, pay attention.

When this final Matins hymn ends, the first words of the Divine Liturgy the congregation will hear are Dn. Andrew's "Father, give the blessing," and Fr. John proclaiming, "Blessed is the Kingdom, of the Father and of the Son, and of the Holy Spirit, now and ever and unto ages of ages, Amen."

As we observed at Vespers, the church is not yet full, and people will continue to trickle in through the early part of the service. Today's worship actually began when Fr. John and Dn. Andrew arrived about 7:00 AM. They offered the three short services I mentioned in chapter 10: the Kairon (prayers on entering the church, with veneration of icons), the Vesting prayers (prayer and Scripture as each liturgical garment is put on), and the Proskomedia (prayers as the bread and wine are prepared for the liturgy). By the time they'd finished, a few chanters had arrived, who took over responsibility for Matins.

At some churches these opening services are overlapped, with the clergy saying their preparatory prayers quietly while Matins is chanted. At other parishes Matins is not offered on Sunday morning at all, but a modified version is added to the end of Vespers on Saturday night, resulting in a service called "Vigil" or "All-Night Vigil." (It doesn't actually last all night—two or three hours, usually—and worshipers may come for only part of the service.) A church that offers Matins on Saturday evening as part of Vigil won't repeat it on Sunday morning. Instead they may have a fifteen- or twenty-minute service called "Hours."

Matins is a beautiful service, an offering of psalms and other hymns, but it's also the most unpredictable of Orthodox services, because the choice of hymns is governed by an extremely complex set of rules. I've heard it said that the Matins you hear on any given day might not be repeated exactly that way again in your lifetime.

Matins on the Feast of the Annunciation could, in theory, be done—are you ready for this?—seventy-six different ways, depending on what other feasts or saints' days surround it.

This would be the hardest service for a newcomer to try to follow in a book. So just listen, pray, absorb, and, if you want to, join in the singing. Key prayers are repeated, and complex ideas are expressed poetically and set to catchy (it is hoped) melodies.

When Matins is over, the Divine Liturgy begins immediately, with no break between the services, so the "9:30" on the sign outside is only an approximation. Whenever you show up, it's like stepping into a flowing river. Some people are here before Matins begins, while others arrive after the Divine Liturgy is underway. (They face this deadline: those who come too late to hear the Gospel reading should not go up to receive Communion.)

Unlike Western churches, at an Orthodox church there is only one Eucharist on a Sunday (or any day, for that matter); you can't choose an earlier or later service. A congregation is a family, and there is one table, one meal.

After the opening proclamation, Dn. Andrew stands in front of the Royal Doors of the iconostasis and, lifting high the end of his long, narrow stole, intones a series of petitions. "For the peace from above and for the salvation of our souls, let us pray to the Lord," he chants. "Lord, have mercy," the congregation responds. He prays in this way for "the peace of the whole world," for bishops and earthly rulers, for healthful seasons, for those who are sick and suffering or held captive.

During this prayer no one is facing the congregation. Fr. John is standing before the altar, facing the church's eastern wall; Dn. Andrew is standing in front of the Royal Doors, facing the same way; the entire congregation, filling the nave, follows suit. When a worship leader faces a congregation, it creates a circular, communal feeling that is very effective for some purposes (such as teaching, or preaching a sermon). But when we are worshiping, we're united, moving forward as one. We are not focused on each other, or even on worship, but focused on Christ the Light, the Morning Star, who will come as lightning flashing from east to west (Matt. 24:27). Our attention flows together, flows forward, in a dynamic way.

After the last petition of this litany, Dn. Andrew says, "Calling to remembrance our most holy, most pure, most blessed, glorious Lady Theotokos and Ever-Virgin Mary, with all the saints, let us commit ourselves and one another and all our life unto Christ our God." There's an example of the piling-up-more-words impulse: not the language of a lawyer but that of a child, who can't find enough ways to say how wonderful her mother is.

But it also shows a characteristic way of relating to the Virgin. We are addressing the Lord, but remember that all his friends are here, too, including his mother, our dear friend and best prayer partner. When we are with him we are with all who love him, and might sometimes address one of his earthly or heavenly friends.

Next come three short hymns known as the "Antiphons." In the earliest centuries, these hymns were sung by people as they were on their way to worship, or waiting outside church for the official entrance of the clergy. The hymns (which, despite the name, aren't necessarily sung antiphonally) are composed of verses from the Psalms or Beatitudes, or offer brief prayers of intercession (such as, "Save us, O Son of God, who rose from the dead"). After the second antiphon we sing a hymn attributed to the emperor Justinian (AD 483–565).

O Only-begotten Son and immortal Word of God,
Who for our salvation willed to become incarnate
Of the holy Theotokos and ever-virgin Mary,
Who without change became man and was crucified,
Who is one of the Holy Trinity,
Glorified with the Father and the Holy Spirit,
O Christ our God, trampling down death by death,
Save us!

As we saw before, theological controversies in Christianity tend to circle back to the person of Jesus himself. How can he be God and human at the same time? Wouldn't the divinity overwhelm the humanity? Was the humanity an illusion, like a mask God put on? Today, the most prevalent challenge to classic Christianity is that Jesus was not God at all, but a human being who attained a very high level of spiritual insight; in this view, the most important thing about Jesus is his teachings.[†]

The "Only Begotten" hymn aims to settle things once and for all, putting the Orthodox view in short, emphatic, and singable lines. It's so crammed and compact that you might think it unlikely that you could retain anything useful, but recall how much of the Divine Liturgy stays the same from week to week. You would sing this hymn every Sunday, year after year, and it would take root.

This hymn wasn't added to the liturgy until the sixth century, which brings to mind our earlier discussion of what it means for a church to be "unchanged." The Orthodox faith certainly does *accumulate*—like a snowball rolling down a mountain. It never occurs to anyone that less might be more; more is always, gloriously, more. The centuries pass and the worship is continually elaborated, increasingly adorned. But the new must match the old. New additions that don't support transformation in Christ are shed, sooner or later (like those Western-style icons we saw in chapter 5).

This way of doing things, in which we keep accumulating more of the same, is different from two other approaches that allow for more variation. The first is the idea that our theological understanding is always increasing, so our way of expressing the faith is continuously evolving and becoming more precise. The second is that, though the faith remains unchanged, we must find new ways of expressing it for each generation.

The first idea, that the faith is always being expressed more explicitly and in greater detail, might seem like common sense at first. But if "theology" is not just abstract discussion but literally "the knowledge of God," is there any evidence that we today know God better than any previous generation? If theological knowledge had been steadily and uninterruptedly *increasing* all these centuries, we'd all be walking on water.

[†] A common corollary is that all his closest followers have gotten his teachings all wrong.

Conversely, this would also mean that the earliest Christians had the *least* accurate understanding of their faith. Compared to us, they must have had the barest sliver of the knowledge of God—even though we trust them to have written the New Testament and chosen which books to include in it, even though they died for their faith with a courage we'd find hard to match. That doesn't sound likely, either. While it's true that each generation of scholars wrestles with the theology they receive (or, at least, they wrestle with each other), it's not evident that the result is always progress.

The second approach is to say that we must keep reframing eternal truths for a changing culture, presenting the Lord in new ways. But we're not smart enough to do that. We're so immersed in our own culture that we can't view it clearly enough to make accurate alterations.

There's also a danger of mixing up, with this noble impulse, a desire to please popular opinion and make Christianity look more contemporary, more cool. That project inevitably bears a self-defeating air of desperation. Studying what the culture approves, then copying it, guarantees that you will always be a step behind. There's a saying, "If you can see a bandwagon, it's too late to get on it."

We just don't have sufficient perspective to take this great mystery, this Lord whom we love more than life, and say anything both cool enough and true enough to be persuasive to the contemptuous or uninterested. Instead of straddling two worlds, we can keep our focus entirely on the Lord, and let the fire of our faith express what we have found.

So there's something to be said for old-fashioned "unchanging." If we attract people to Christian faith by means of clever wording, we aren't being fair to them. They have a right to know that this path includes a cross; anything else is false advertising. Bearing our own crosses well, in humility and kindness, is more eloquent than the coolest ad campaign.

During the singing of the third antiphon, Fr. John takes up the Gospel book that rests on the altar. He gives it to Dn. Andrew, and they go out through the St. Michael door, with two small altar boys bearing candles in front, and a larger one with a processional cross following. Dn. Andrew holds the Gospel book up before his face, showing that it is Christ himself who enters into the midst of our worship.

This procession is called "the Little Entrance" (there is a grander and more thorough "Great Entrance" coming up). After leaving through the left-hand door of the iconostasis they immediately circle to the center and line up again facing the Royal Doors. In ancient times this was the beginning point of the liturgy, with the clergy forming a line to lead the congregation into church.

Once they are standing in place Fr. John prays quietly, "Master, our Lord and God, you have established the orders of angels and archangels to serve your glory. As we enter, let an entrance of holy angels accompany us, to serve with us and glorify your goodness." The presence of angels in our worship is frequently brought to our attention in the prayers of the liturgy, and sometimes confirmed by young children.

There are a number of prayers in the liturgy which bear a note, in the written text, that the priest should say them "in a low voice." Usually these prayers are spoken quietly while another prayer or hymn is going on. They're not *secret* prayers; it is all right to overhear them, or read them in a prayer book. Perhaps this custom originated as a way to double up on the long service by doing some things simultaneously, or maybe it was a measure taken, in those premicrophone days, to conserve the priest's voice for the most important parts. It's no doubt a blessing for clergy to have a chance to pray privately for a moment, and speak to their Lord without an audience.

As the third antiphon ends, the altar party is still standing in place, facing the Royal Doors. Dn. Andrew cries out, "Wisdom! Let us attend!" The choir leads the congregation in singing,

Come, let us worship and fall down before Christ!
O Son of God, risen from the dead,
Save those who sing to you:
Alleluia, Alleluia, Alleluia.

At "fall down," worshipers make a metania, crossing themselves and bowing, reaching toward the floor with the fingertips of their right hand (the more limber among them actually reach it). While they are singing, the priest and deacon go through the Royal Doors, where Dn. Andrew gives the Gospel book to Fr. John, who returns it to its place on the altar. The altar boys complete their procession by going through the St. Gabriel door, on the right side of the iconostasis.

A small collection of hymns follows. The first is the Resurrection hymn, and as we noted before, there are eight of these troparia, sung in rotation from one Sunday to the next. Today the Resurrection troparion is Tone 5.

We the faithful praise and worship the Word,
He who is coeternal with the Father and the Spirit,
And was born of the Virgin for our salvation.
He willed to ascend the Cross in the flesh,
And to suffer death, so he could raise the dead
By the glory of his Resurrection.

Today is the Sunday of the publican and Pharisee, so among the following hymns we sing the kontakion of the day.

Let us flee the haughtiness of the Pharisee's talk!
Let us embrace the majesty of the publican's tears!
Let us cry to the Savior, "Have mercy on us,
For you are the only merciful One!"

Longtime Orthodox in attendance may do a double take if they haven't been keeping up with the liturgical calendar. When the publican and Pharisee appear on a Sunday it means that Great Lent is coming. Those seven weeks of fasting (that is, keeping a largely vegan diet) which end with Pascha, are preceded by three Sundays of preparation, each with its appointed Gospel reading. The one about the publican and Pharisee (Lk. 18:10–14) is the first.

Many Orthodox Christians say they actually look forward to Lent each year, as a fresh challenge. But make no mistake, it *is* a challenge. Lent comes toward us on the calendar like a marathon we'd promised to run.

Next we sing the ancient Trisagion hymn three times, in English, Greek, and Arabic.

> Holy God, Holy Mighty, Holy Immortal, have mercy on us.
> Agios O Theos, Agios Iskiros, Agios Athanatos, eleison imas.
> Qudduson Allah, Qudduson Alqawee, Qudduson Allahthee,
>   layamoot irhamna.

After the third repetition, Dn. Andrew turns toward the congregation and says, "Dynamis!" That Greek word is the source for "dynamite," and in this instance means "This time, sing it louder!" We sail into the last repetition of the hymn vigorously.

In some churches the exhortation to sing more loudly is given in English, "With strength!" or it might not be spoken at all. At one church they were not used to hearing this line, and when their new pastor called out "Dynamis!" the choir, then the congregation, went absolutely silent. The choir director thought he must have done something terribly wrong to make the priest shout his name: "Dennis!"

During the Trisagion, the two little altar boys come stand on the solea holding processional candles, and face each other on either side of the Royal Doors. Dave, a young dad in the congregation, gives up the toddler he was holding and takes the silver-covered Epistle book from the chanters' stand. He goes up to stand between the candle-bearers, facing the altar. When the last notes die away, Dn. Andrew proclaims, "Let us attend!" and Dave chants the prokeimenon (the biblical verse that precedes a reading). Today it is: "Make a vow unto the Lord our God and keep it. In Judah God is known; his name is great in Israel."

Some people take a seat for the reading of the epistle, and you should feel free to join them if an open chair is handy. It is *always* all right to stand during Orthodox worship. When in doubt, stand. But if everyone else is sitting, you might want to take your stand toward the back of the church. I tend to go up front when visiting another church—as a pastor's wife, I know how much the clergy wish people would come forward—but there have been times when I happened to glance around and realized I was the only person standing.

Again Dn. Andrew says, "Let us attend!" and Dave turns around to face the congregation. He chants from a letter St. Paul wrote to his young friend St. Timothy, encouraging the young man to persevere through persecution (2 Tim. 3:10–15). At St. Felicity it's the custom to chant the epistle in the eighth Tone; the classic *Grove's Dictionary of Music* notes that Martin Luther also recommended the eighth Tone for the Epistle reading. (I don't know whether his eight Tones corresponded to the Byzantine Tones, though.‡)[78]

It may sound surprising, but one reason Orthodox chant rather than read the Scriptures during worship is so the reader *won't* deliver it with expression. The idea is that the congregation should be allowed to encounter the text directly, not filtered through someone else's dramatic interpretation. Dave has taken a few months' chanting classes from the choir director, and so he experiments with some melisma as he goes along, but when the toddler starts to squawk for daddy he opts instead for brisk efficiency.

As Dave returns to the congregation, the choir leads the congregation in a couple of repetitions of a threefold Alleluia, with a soloist supplying verses in between: "O Come, let us sing with joy unto the Lord. Let us come before his presence with thanksgiving."

---

‡ My musically knowledgeable friend assures me that Luther would have known the same eighth Tone as Christians in the East because "Tone 8 in both East and West is in the Hypomixolydian mode." Glad we cleared that up.

A triple "Alleluia" before the Gospel reading is one of the most ancient of worship traditions.

Dn. Andrew then comes out from the altar with the Gospel book and proclaims, "Wisdom! Let us attend! Let us listen to the holy Gospel!" With everyone standing, he chants the story of the prideful Pharisee and the tax collector in a strong, clear voice. Tax collectors have never been popular, but in ancient Israel they were especially hated as collaborators, for the money they collected went to their conquerors, the Roman Empire. Tax collectors were further despised because they were cheats; they earned their wealth by overcharging their neighbors and skimming the proceeds.

In this story Jesus calls us to admire the oppressor and despise the oppressed. We are called to emulate the humility of a wealthy and powerful traitor, while rejecting the complacency of a faithful, generous, and self-denying victim of injustice.

This is shocking when you stop to think about it. It shows how literally Christ meant it when he said "my kingship is not of this world" (John 18:36). Political power is so irrelevant to Christian life that you can't win points even for *not* having it, and being poor and oppressed. The only thing that counts with God is humility. This is a good reading to hear as we head into Great Lent, reminding us not to judge how others do or don't keep the fast.

There's an interesting word in this Gospel passage. In the Greek text, when the tax collector cries, "God be merciful to me a sinner!" he doesn't use the most common word for mercy, the one in "Kyrie, eleison." Instead, he says *"hilastheti me,"* using the verb *hilaskomai,* which appears in many forms throughout the Scriptures. (It appears in exactly the same form in Psalm 78/79:9, which may be an echo Christ intended his hearers to catch: "O God . . . *hilastheti* [forgive] our sins.") It's notable that Jewish scholars who translated the Septuagint, around 250 BC, used the verbal cousin *hilasterios* for the "mercy seat" in the temple (Exod. 25:17–22). The mercy seat is the place where God resides, where his people receive mercy.

I guess I need to defend my assertion that this is interesting. Here's what I'm getting at: this word means "mercy" when the publican uses it, and "mercy seat" in the Jewish-Greek Old Testament. But when English translators come to members of this word-family (*hilaskomai, hilasterios, hilasmos*) in the New Testament Epistles, instead of using synonyms of forgiveness or mercy, they use "propitiation" (which is an offering meant to appease a god) or "expiation" (which is an offering meant to repay a debt). This reflects the second-millennium view that a payment was necessary for the Father to forgive us, rather than the early Christian view that the Father simply forgives us—no charge. It's another example of how our assumptions can color what we think—and what translators think—the Bible says.[§]

Those who came to Matins today heard the troparion that trumpets the coming of Great Lent.

> Open to me the gates of repentance, O Giver of Life,
> For early in the morning my spirit comes to your holy temple,
> Bearing the temple of my body, all defiled.
> But in your compassion purify me,
> For the sake of your loving-kindness and mercy.

[§] That, of course, is why there are such vehement arguments over Bible translation. A Jewish man once e-mailed me to ask: Jewish kids learn Hebrew and Muslim kids learn Arabic, so why don't Christians teach their children biblical Greek? If they love the Bible as much as they say, why are they satisfied with reading it in translation? It's a good question.

17

"Choose This Day"

(JOSH. 24:15)

Love and Forgiveness, Processing with the Gifts,
Free Will, Synergy, The Power of Choice

s Fr. John comes forward to preach his sermon, worshipers find chairs or sit on the floor. A toddler takes the opportunity to break into a run toward the far corner of the nave, but another parishioner intercepts him and sends him back the way he came. There's something to be said for pews, in terms of kid-control, because they provide mini-corrals and divide the congregation into smaller units. The drawback is that they divide the congregation. Without them worshipers merge and morph like a giant, prayerful amoeba.

Fr. John tries to keep his sermons brief, fifteen or twenty minutes, though he doesn't always succeed. It's not that deeper exploration of the Scriptures is unimportant, but that Sunday morning is not the time for it. We are now focused on engaging God directly, worshiping him, rather than learning about him intellectually. At St. Felicity there are study groups on Tuesday morning and Wednesday night, and the men's fellowship gathers for breakfast and study of a Bible commentary once a month. So after a simple but clear explication of what this Gospel requires of us, Fr. John returns to the altar.

As the congregation stands up again, a handful of worshipers make their way toward the front of the church, where they gather in front of the icon of Christ. There's a young couple with two small children, an older woman, and a tall teenaged boy. These are the catechumens, who are preparing to be received into the church. Their sponsors, or godparents, come and stand behind them.

Dn. Andrew stands nearby on the solea and sings out, "Pray to the Lord, you catechumens." He chants an ektenia asking that the Lord will "teach them the word of truth" and "reveal to them the gospel of righteousness." Instead of chanting "Lord, have mercy" after each petition, the choir quietly sings a flowing, murmuring repetition of that phrase in the background. When Dn. Andrew says, "Bow your heads to the Lord, you catechumens," they do, and Fr. John prays, "Look down upon these your servants, the catechumens, as they bow their necks to you. In due time make them worthy of the laver of regeneration" (that is, baptism), and membership in Christ's body, the Church.

As the catechumens and their sponsors filter back into the congregation, you might glimpse a small table in front of the icon of Christ, and on it a platter of something white, molded like a hill, with a taper candle on top. The whiteness you see is packed powdered sugar, and if you were closer you'd notice also a decoration of white Jordan almonds in the form of a cross. This dish is called *koliva*, and was placed here during Matins by a member of the congregation, Esther, who lost her father two years ago.

The koliva will remain here throughout the service, and afterward be carried to the parish hall, where it will be served out in small cups, in honor of Ernest's memory. Koliva is composed mostly of boiled wheat berries, which have a nutty, crunchy quality, mixed with honey, chopped nuts, and dried fruit. The recipe varies based on ethnic tradition, availability of ingredients, and personal taste, but at its most basic, koliva means kernels of wheat and sweetness. "Truly, truly, I say to you, unless a grain of wheat falls into the earth and dies, it remains alone; but if it dies, it bears much fruit" (John 12:24).

This dish is prepared to accompany a memorial service, which in this case does not mean a full-length funeral but a brief set of commemorative prayers; such a memorial service will be offered for Ernest at the end of the Divine Liturgy. When members of the congregation want to commemorate a loved one, they ask Fr. John if he could add a memorial service to the liturgy on a Sunday close to the date that the person reposed. On that day family members bring a dish of koliva to the liturgy and place it on a small table before the icon of Christ.

The Orthodox tradition is to keep revisiting the loss of a loved one and offering prayers on a regular basis, which may be a bit of ancient wisdom about the cyclical nature of grieving. Departed loved ones are commemorated on the third day after death, the ninth day, the fortieth day, and on the anniversary of the death every year thereafter. When ancient Roman Christians gathered to pray in the catacombs, it was likely for memorial services like these.

Next comes the Cherubic Hymn, which marks the point at which the two ancient services were joined, the service of prayers and readings with the Eucharist, to compose the Divine Liturgy. We sing the first part of the hymn before the Great Entrance.

> Let us who mystically represent* the cherubim,
> And who sing the thrice-holy hymn to the life-creating Trinity,
> Now lay aside all earthly cares.

The "thrice-holy hymn" is "Holy, Holy, Holy, Lord God of Sabaoth, Heaven and earth are full of your glory." When we sing it during the Eucharistic prayers we will "represent the cherubim" and all the angels, for Isaiah heard the seraphim singing this in his vision of the heavenly temple (Isa. 6:3). "Now lay aside all earthly cares" is a reminder; the Divine Liturgy is sprinkled with such exhortations to pay attention to the work at hand.

We sing this slowly and repeatedly, for Fr. John has a lot to do in the meantime.

---

* In Greek, "represent" here is "icon-ize"; we serve as icons of the cherubim as we sing their hymn.

He prays quietly at the altar for himself and for us, that the "Good Lord who loves mankind" will cleanse us and enable us to approach the Eucharist without condemnation. He prays for himself, admitting his unworthiness to handle the Holy Gifts. "Nevertheless, through your boundless and indescribable love for us, you became man," he says, as well as becoming our High Priest.

In a circling pattern, this quiet prayer keeps restating the goodness of God and his love for us, and the priest's unworthiness before these awesome mysteries. "I come near to you and bow my neck, and I pray: Do not turn your face away from me, do not cast me out from among your children, but accept these gifts which are offered to you by me, your sinful and unworthy servant. You are he who offers and is offered, who accepts and is received, O Christ our God."

The service of ordination to the priesthood is marked by similar fear and trembling, though it is surprisingly brief, inserting an extra ten or fifteen minutes into a usual Divine Liturgy. At the middle of that service, before the Eucharistic prayers begin, the deacon who will be made a priest is brought out of the midst of the congregation by two priests, who are his sponsors. One stands on each side, holding him by the arms, and as they approach the altar they bow him to the ground three times, calling out each time to the bishop, "Command!"

Yet when the priest-to-be kneels at the altar, now probably at a peak of nervous tension, the first words the bishop speaks are appropriately comforting: "The Divine Grace, which always heals that which is infirm, and completes that which is lacking, elevates [Name], the most devout Deacon, to be a Priest."

Then the new priest stands in the Royal Doors facing the people. The bishop removes the deacon's stole from his shoulders and takes up the items in a priest's set of vestments, one at a time. There are cuffs that lace around the wrists, a belt, an *epitrachelion* (a stole), and a *phelonion* (similar to a Western chasuble, but cut high in front to free his arms to hold the chalice). As the bishop lifts each piece, he blesses it and loudly proclaims, "He is worthy!" All the people shout in reply, "He is worthy!" Then the congregation sings slowly, "He is worthy, he is worthy, he is worthy," while the bishop clothes the new priest in each vestment.[†]

Considering the intimidating responsibility of the priesthood, it seems like good psychology to start him off with a reminder that the Holy Spirit will complete in him anything that is lacking, and that the bishop and people are so confident of his calling that they will shout and sing, "He is worthy!"

As we continue singing the Cherubic Hymn, Fr. John repeats more prayers and then recites Psalm 50/51. (It's an Orthodox custom to repeat this psalm during daily devotions, and we soon get it memorized.) He then walks around the altar, pausing at each of the four sides to swing the censer, dispersing clouds of fragrant smoke.

Once during this part of the service I was holding my grand-daughter Ruthie, then about two and a half. We were standing directly in front of the Royal Doors, with a full view of the altar, and Ruthie was instructing her dolly in the proceedings.

But when my husband began to cense around the altar she was suddenly struck with wonder. She stared wide-eyed at the scene, and began laughing with amazement and delight. With shining eyes she exclaimed over and over: "At the same time! At the same time!"

It still gives me chills. All I could see was my husband going around the altar, like he always does. But she could see something else, something happening "at the same time," and it must have echoed his movements in a glorious way. Ruthie would pause and grasp for other words to describe what she was seeing, then return to the only ones her toddler-sized vocabulary could supply: "At the same time!"[‡]

Fr. John then comes out onto the solea to cense the iconostasis and the people. Returning to the altar, he and Dn. Andrew venerate

---

[†] They may sing this in other languages, like "Axios!" in Greek and "Moustahiq!" in Arabic.

[‡] Her dad's suggestion that she meant, "Look, Papa can swing a censer and walk at the same time!" was disregarded.

it, saying, "O God, be gracious to me a sinner, and have mercy on me." They ask each other's forgiveness, and then Fr. John stands in the Royal Doors and bows to the congregation, saying, "Forgive me, my brothers and sisters. For those who love us and those who hate us." The people bow to him, offering their forgiveness and joining in this prayer.

These acts of repentance and forgiveness are brief glimpses of a yearly event, coming up in just three weeks. On that Sunday night there will be the Vespers service that marks the beginning of Great Lent, and after it comes the Rite of Forgiveness. The congregation will form two lines in the nave of the church, facing each other in pairs. One of each pair will make a metania, honoring the presence of Christ in his fellow parishioner. Then he will ask the person for forgiveness, putting it in his own words: "My sister, forgive me for any way I have offended you," "Please forgive me for all my sins against you."

That person assures him of forgiveness, then makes a metania and says in return, "And please forgive me," again putting it in her own words. The two embrace, and then each of them takes a step to the right, and faces a new partner. (When you get to the end of the line, change sides to the other line.) It takes an hour or so for every member of the church to ask forgiveness from, and offer forgiveness to, every other.

Children forgive their parents. Brothers forgive sisters. Parishioners who have been at odds must look each other in the eye and ask to be forgiven. No one may brush the request aside, saying, "Oh, but you haven't done anything!" You don't know; maybe this person had judgmental thoughts about you. Even when I am aware of no offense, I can always ask people to forgive me for not praying for them enough, for ignoring them, for irritating them, and for contributing my own share of sin-pollution to the world they have to live in.

This event, called Forgiveness Vespers, marks the beginning of Lent. (We don't have Ash Wednesday; the custom of marking the head with ashes may go back as far as Pope St. Gregory the Great in the sixth century, but it was not known in the East.) It's the most explicit time all year that these parishioners demonstrate their love for each other, in some cases love of enemies. Though it begins with some trepidation and self-consciousness, by the end the room is full of tender joy.

Forgiveness, compassion, humility, and refusing to judge are recurrent themes in Orthodoxy. An Old Testament scene that comes up regularly has to do with Noah who, after returning to dry land and planting a vineyard, got drunk one day and lay disheveled in his tent. His son Ham saw this and told his brothers about it, apparently thinking it was funny. But "Shem and Japheth took a garment, laid it upon both their shoulders, and walked backward and covered the nakedness of their father" (Gen. 9:23). Thus we should cover each other's sins.

"He is a man; do not rejoice in his fall," writes St. Nikolai Velimirovich (1880–1956), a survivor of Auschwitz who knew the evil men can do. "He is your brother; let not your heart leap for joy when he stumbles. God created him for life, and God does not rejoice in his fall. And you also, do not rejoice at that which grieves God. When a man falls, God loses; do you rejoice in the loss of your Creator, of your Parent? When the angels weep, do you rejoice? . . . When one sheep is lost, should the rest of the flock rejoice? No, they should not. For behold, the shepherd leaves his flock and, being concerned, goes to seek the lost sheep. The shepherd's loss is the flock's loss too. Therefore, do not rejoice when your enemy falls, for your Shepherd and his Shepherd, the Lord Jesus Christ, does not rejoice in his fall."[79]

The evil one hates it when we love each other. When it comes to feats of asceticism, he can surpass the greatest spiritual athletes in nearly every way—he never eats, never sleeps, knows no physical temptations. But he cannot love.

Any talk of the spiritual life is bound to refer to the standard trio of prayer, fasting, and almsgiving. But it occurred to me that something was missing from that list: the very difficult spiritual discipline of loving other people. Granting forgiveness is hard enough, but *asking* for forgiveness is even harder. Orthodox writings continually stress humility, and humility, like pride, has to do with how you see yourself in relation to others. It seemed to me that this fundamental discipline, of loving other people and regarding oneself with humility, had been left out of the threefold summary.

But I think the key is that third word "almsgiving," or "charity." It comes from the Latin *caritas*, which means love (in Greek, *agape*). Giving alms to the poor is one way of showing love, and an important aspect of Christian faith; the exhortation to give to those in need is present already in the letters of St. Paul (Rom. 15:26, 1 Cor. 16:2, and elsewhere). In the years of persecution, Christians did not have to use their imagination to identify with the poor and oppressed, for they *were* the poor and oppressed. The care believers showed for the needy, sick, homeless, travelers, and those in prison did much to draw new members to the faith.

One way this was done locally was for worshipers to give their contributions to the parish's deacon, who would then distribute funds according to need. After the faith was given its freedom, this work could be done more openly, and the First Council of Nicaea called for hospitals to be built in every cathedral town in the empire. For all the hand-wringing over the moral failures of our age, some things have actually gotten better, and one of them is this recognition of the need to care for the poor. The importance of charitable acts and giving is so widely praised today that I don't have to convince you of its significance in Christian life.

But the vocabulary of love is broader than the giving of money. In fact, the love we are supposed to bear for others, like the love our Father gives us, knows no limits. It might sound strange, but we're supposed to love the *rich*, too. We're supposed to love everybody. "Judge not" (Matt. 7:1) rules out judging even those we disagree with politically. We don't get credit for loving our friends and family (and those who share our opinions), because everybody does that, as Jesus said (Matt. 5:43–48). If we are to be like him, we must love our enemies. (In his day, enemies were clearly visible as soldiers of the occupying army. That's who he told his hearers to love.) We can practice love and humility even when we're alone, in our thoughts and prayers for others. Prayer, fasting, and almsgiving are the classic trio of the Christian life, and the larger meaning of almsgiving (charity) is love.§

There's a prayer we say only during Lent, called the Prayer of St. Ephraim the Syrian (d. AD 373). It goes:

> O Lord and Master of my life, take from me the spirit of sloth,
>   despair, love of power, and idle talk;
> But give to your servant instead a spirit of wise prudence, humil-
>   ity, patience, and love.
> Yes, O Lord and King! Grant me to see my own failings and not
>   to judge my brother, for you are blessed unto ages of ages.
> Amen.

At the end of each line, the people make a full prostration, kneeling and touching their foreheads to the floor. This made a big impression on my husband, who visited an Orthodox church for the first time during a Lenten Vespers service. He told me, "That's how we should be before God."

How we are before God includes not judging our brother, and being at peace with all. The evil one has no use for that, and prefers prickly solitude. "In early Christian symbolism the desert was the dwelling place of Satan who, despite all his apparent interest in human affairs, actually preferred to be left alone," writes John Dunlop. "The exodus of the early monks to the desert was a direct challenge to Satan. St. Anthony, the spiritual father of all monks, went directly to dwell in the tombs and challenge Satan in his own kingdom of death."[80]

---

§   I fudge a little there on etymology, because the word for "alms" in the New Testament is not Greek *agape* or Latin *caritas* but the rather longer word from which we get the adjective *eleemosynary*; that word does, in fact, refer specifically to charitable giving. You can see the root word *eleos*, "mercy," hiding in there. Apparently the word *alms* is the result of medieval English speakers attempting to pronounce the Latin word *eleemosyna* and giving up.

Behind the iconostasis the clergy and altar boys are getting ready for the procession called the Great Entrance. Fr. John takes the chalice and paten in his hand, as Dn. Andrew says quietly, "Lift up, Master." Fr. John says, "Lift up your hands to the holy places, and bless the Lord [Ps. 133/134:2]. God has gone up in jubilation, the Lord with the voice of the trumpet [Ps. 46/47:5]."

The reminders spoken by the deacon were written into the liturgy in ancient times, so that the liturgy could be offered the same way everywhere. Spontaneity wasn't something God prioritized when he told Moses how he wanted to be worshiped. The first Christians, basing their worship upon the Jewish model they knew, didn't emphasize being casual, or funny, or emotionally moving. Spontaneity has its limitations; anyone who has participated in open, unplanned worship week after week knows that, when people are regularly required to say or do things off the top of their heads, it tends to become banal. (It also tends to develop a pattern.) Among the early Christians the aim was to worship in common with all churches everywhere, so a priest is expected to read the prayers from a written text and not trust his memory.

One of the sopranos, who has been appointed to keep watch, sees that Fr. John is holding the chalice, and is now ready for the Great Entrance to begin. She signals to Hank, the choir director, and he brings this first part of the Cherubic Hymn to a close. The procession makes its way out from the altar, through the St. Michael door, and into the nave. As they walk Fr. John prays for the bishops and civil authorities, and then for the parishioner Mark and his family. Mark baked the prosphora this week, and left the five round loaves in the sacristy yesterday. He included a list of family and friends, living and departed, whom he wanted Fr. John to pray for during the preparation of the loaves this morning, and during the Great Procession.

While the altar party continues its progress toward the back of the church, Fr. John chants the names on Mark's list, and when he comes to his own name asks prayers for "the unworthy priest John."¶

¶   This is the conventional way for a priest to refer to himself, but he alone uses the term. You don't introduce your pastor as "the unworthy priest John."

He goes on to chant the names that are on the parish prayer list, as well as others that he's been asked to include in these petitions. During the preparation of the loaf earlier this morning, he separated out small crumbs as he prayed for each person by name.

The procession passes along the left side of the nave and when it reaches the back circles around and approaches the altar again through the midst of the congregation. Worshipers step to the side as needed, to create a walkway, and little children are lifted out of the way.

As Fr. John passes by, some worshipers reach out and touch or kiss the border of his vestments. An evangelical pastor once wrote to ask me what in the world was going on during the part of the service where the congregation was "worshiping the priest." They are not worshiping the priest. They are joining in the intercessory prayers the priest chants during the procession, and symbolically attaching their own prayers to "the hem of his garment" as he passes by. I think of it as sticky notes—as the priest goes by, people reach out and attach spiritual sticky notes that bear the names of those they have in mind.

As the procession reenters the altar, the choir sings the ending of the Cherubic Hymn, now at a brisker tempo.

> So that we may receive the King of all,
> Who comes invisibly borne by hosts of angels.
> Alleluia, alleluia, alleluia.

Fr. John places the Holy Gifts on the altar and censes them, while continuing his quiet prayers. He says:

> You were in the tomb with the body and in Hades with the
> soul,
> In paradise with the thief, and on the throne with the Father
> and the Spirit,
> O Christ,
> You who are everywhere present and fill all things.

Dn. Andrew returns to the solea for another litany, to which we respond initially with "Lord, have mercy" and then change to "Grant this, O Lord." The petitions ask for "an angel of peace, a faithful guide, a guardian of our souls and bodies," acknowledging that the Lord gives to each person an angel (*angelos*, "messenger") as his representative and our guide. We ask God's help to "complete the remaining time of our life in peace and repentance," and that in time we will arrive at "a Christian ending to our life, painless, blameless, peaceful, and a good defense before the awesome judgment seat of Christ."

Why might we be concerned about the Final Judgment? As we noted before, Orthodox don't have a doctrine of "assurance of salvation," but it's an extremely popular idea elsewhere; today even nonchurchgoers are quite sure they're going to heaven. Author Christian Smith, in his book on the religious beliefs of American youth, *Soul Searching*, gave the name "Moralistic Therapeutic Deism" (MTD) to a package of popular ideas he'd observed.[81] MTD includes the belief that God made the world and "watches over us," that he wants us to be nice, that the goal of life is being happy and feeling good about oneself, that God is needed only when there is a problem, and that all people who are "good" (by self-evaluation, so pretty much everybody) are going to heaven.

They have a good excuse for holding such beliefs, because it's the version of Christianity that has been most widely taught over the last fifty years. It began as a well-meaning effort to make Christian faith more attractive, more relevant, and more useful, and was in part an embarrassed overreaction to stereotypical preachers of past generations who specialized in "fire and brimstone" (Lk. 17:29; Jesus himself coined the phrase, so perhaps we shouldn't dismiss it too lightly).

If sins are misdeeds, like breaking the speed limit, it would be reasonable under MTD to assume that God will simply forgive and forget. Why would he want to punish us? Doesn't he love us? And didn't he make us with these weaknesses in the first place? If your sins are the list of all the bad things you've ever done, any God worth the name would surely tear it up on Judgment Day.

But if sin is sickness, corruption unto death, it's different. God hates sin like the parents of a leukemia victim hate cancer. He hates whatever hurts humankind, and sin is the miasma of agitation, selfishness, and fear that surrounds us and seeps into us from every direction, in the years of this broken life. But a zealous, challenging God, intent on our transformation, is a hard sell these days, since an up-to-date alternative God, ingratiating and sympathetic, is available on every corner.**

The problem is that, to grow in holiness, we have to change. And we *really* don't like to change. Change might mean giving up habits we enjoy, and when that hits home, people can surprise themselves with how absolutely they refuse. "No man ever hates his own flesh, but nourishes and cherishes it" (Eph. 5:29).

This is why, I think, the people in greatest spiritual danger are those who think they can be their own spiritual directors and manage their own spiritual growth. Continually choosing the things they find appealing, they'll keep on reinforcing their own flaws. Such a person can arrive at the end of her life comfortable, self-satisfied, and proud of her spiritual accomplishments, only to discover that it was all a charade; she was enslaved by delusion, trapped in a hall of mirrors.††

People simply aren't capable of directing their own spiritual lives. We don't have the necessary perspective, and are pitifully ignorant of the hidden manipulations at play in our hearts. The wisest course is to submit yourself to a local gathering of the church, one that has real people in it (some of them irritating people, so your bad traits will rise to the surface, where you can deal with them). We need a spiritual mother or father, someone wiser than we are, whom we can trust to confront us with the truth, and whom we can rely on as an athlete trusts a personal trainer. In the face of a culture that demands autonomy, independence, and freedom from obligations, spiritual growth requires us to accept the limitations of becoming part of something bigger than ourselves—becoming part of our

---

** C. S. Lewis wrote, "We want, in fact, not so much a Father in Heaven as a grandfather in heaven—a senile benevolence who, as they say, 'liked to see young people enjoying themselves.'" (*The Problem of Pain* [New York: Macmillan, 1962], 40.)

†† Orthodox spirituality recognizes delusion as a genuine danger (*plani* in Greek, *prelest* in Russian). The sure sign of someone far gone in delusion is a refusal to consider that she might be wrong.

Lord and his body, the church. An online mutual-interest group is not enough. We need a church manifested in a local face-to-face community, and an elder who can be the healer and guardian and challenger of our inner life.

As we've said before, salvation is a rescue operation, as at the Red Sea. Christ has opened the way for us, and the Father willingly wipes away our debt. But the problem is we *keep returning to slavery*. We do this voluntarily. We cling to our sins. We are tempted to live as on a highway median—glancing backward at our precious sins with longing, calculating that we'll still have time to make a dash for God's side at the end.

Do we have the power to resist sin? This was a controversial question in the fifth century, when a dispute arose between the British monk Pelagius (AD 360–420) and St. Augustine of Hippo (AD 354–430). It's been a controversial question ever since, in fact, wherever sin is understood as a debt we owe to God. The presenting problem is that, if human beings are able to withstand sin by our own efforts, maybe we are paying some of our own sin-debt—which would mean Christ's death on the cross did not pay it all.

Pelagius taught that humans are born free from sin, and able to choose whether or not to sin. (Though only Christ, he taught, had ever *succeeded* in leading a sinless life.) He taught that we fall into sin because we have the example of other sinners before us at all times; we see sin all around us, and then make it habitual in our own lives. Pelagius thought it would be possible to live a sinless life, if we had before our eyes only the example of people who were really, really good.

St. Augustine opposed this, saying that we are born with a corrupted nature, inclined to sin (Orthodox would agree), and also born guilty of Adam's sin (Orthodox would not agree). He also taught that our nature is *entirely* corrupted, and contains no health at all. (Orthodox would, again, not agree. This doctrine is called "total depravity," and was also taught by leaders of the Protestant Reformation.) Because we are completely corrupted, St. Augustine said, we are not able to choose not to sin. We will sin every time, unless God intervenes.

The Church, East and West, condemned Pelagius as a heretic, and regards Augustine as a saint (though no saint is perfect). But Orthodox don't agree with St. Augustine's stand against free will.

Again, the view of salvation makes a difference here. If salvation means paying the Father the debt we owe him for our sins, it would *have* to be entirely Christ's doing. If the cross wasn't enough, we're all in trouble.

But if you look at salvation instead as a rescue action, free will has different implications. You can choose whether or not to *accept* a rescue; and you don't have to do anything to *deserve* a rescue.

Earlier we looked at that New Testament word *energy*, which appears in verses such as "work out your own salvation, for God is energizing in you" (Phil. 2:12). St. Paul also makes use of the word *synergy*—another Greek word taken up into English—to speak of the dynamic interaction when a person cooperates with God or with other people.

- "We are God's *synergoi*" (1 Cor. 3:9)
- Timothy is God's *"synergon* in the gospel of Christ" (1 Thess. 3:2).
- St. James says that, when Abraham offered Isaac on the altar, "Faith *synergei* his works" (Jas. 2:22), his faith synergized with his works.
- St. Mark says that, after Christ's ascension, the apostles "preached everywhere, while the Lord *synergountos* [synergized in them] and confirmed the message" (Mk. 16:20).

This synergy should not be understood in the sense of humans giving God a hand with a tough project; rather, it is the life of God within us, energizing and transforming us to the extent we trust and allow him to do so.

As the scholar David Bradshaw writes, "If one were to summarize the differences between the Eastern and Western traditions in a single word, that word would be 'synergy.'" He goes on,

> For the East the highest form of communion with the divine is not primarily an intellectual act, but a sharing of life and activity. . . . [This view] led to a tendency to think of earthly, bodily existence as capable of being taken up and subsumed within the life of God. Emphasis was placed, not on any sudden transformation at death, but on the ongoing and active appropriation of those aspects of the divine life that are open to participation. . . . The underlying belief in synergy as a form of communion with God remains as clear in Gregory Palamas [AD 1296–1328] as it is in St. Paul.[82]

When we think about God's work in the world as energy rather than remote direction, the idea of his synergizing with us, and the role of free will, opens up. We can't claim that *anything* we do is entirely our own effort. It is all begun, sustained, and completed by God. We could not even breathe, we could not hold our body's molecules together, if he did not do it in us.

And yet we can discern his leading, and choose to resist or respond. If we respond, it is his doing. We would say that it is only his life and energy within us that makes it possible for us to choose, of our own free will, to do his will.

It's perhaps easier to understand this when we remember that the relationship between us and God is not simply one of power, not a question of who is in control, but a relationship of love. And love has a powerful—we might say irresistible—effect. When you feel that someone really loves you, you're strongly drawn toward that person; you feel like a flower opening to the sun. It feels like we choose with our whole hearts to move toward that love.

But what if God made us that way? Maybe we are programmed to respond like that to love, and couldn't resist it if we tried. But if you try to imagine rejecting such love and turning away from it, it feels like you're fighting *against* your free will, your deepest longing.

It's hard to separate that which is our own will from that which is God's will, especially if God is living within us, and not just giving orders from far away. If it is his life within us, giving and receiving that love which is himself, it's hard even to identify what "free will" means.

Of course, the situations we encounter in daily life are much less clear-cut. Many times a day we meet situations where God's love within nudges us toward a certain course, but our selfish will shouts to go the other direction. If we do as God calls us, we give him the credit. If we choose sin instead, we take the responsibility. Then we confess, seek forgiveness, and try to do better next time.

Around the time of the Augustine-Pelagius controversy, St. John Cassian (AD 360–435) and his friend St. Germanus made a pilgrimage through the desert monasteries, talking with the Desert Fathers and recording their answers to difficult questions. This collection of conversations, called *The Conferences*—in Latin, *Collationes*—was appointed to be read at mealtime in Benedictine monasteries. (That's why a light meal came to be called a "collation.")

When St. John Cassian and St. Germanus came to the desert of Scetis in Egypt, they visited a number of hermits and monastic communities. There they met the old abbot Paphnutius, who was called "the Buffalo" because of his silence and ability to endure solitude. When they asked him about the role of free will, Paphnutius pointed to the example of Abraham. God said to him both "leave your country" and "go to the land I will show you" (Gen. 12:1), which shows that he both calls and completes our perfection. Paphnutius said, "'The land I will show you' is not one you can discover by your own efforts, but one which I will show, not only to one who is ignorant of it, but even to one who is not looking for it."[82]

St. Germanus then asked, "Where then is there room for free will, and how is it ascribed to our efforts that we are worthy of praise, if God both begins and ends everything in us which concerns our salvation?"

Paphnutius replied, "This would fairly influence us, if in every work and practice the beginning and ending were everything, and there were no middle in between."

If you could arrange to keel over and die the moment you became a Christian, you'd never have to wrestle with the paradox of free will. But for most of us, there's all this middle-in-between. Every day is packed with it. Moment by moment, we are faced with decisions, shoved this way and that, compelled to make one choice after another whether we want to or not.

Abbot Paphnutius went on, "As we know that God creates opportunities of salvation in various ways, it is in our power to make use of the opportunities granted to us by heaven more or less earnestly." He continued,

> We ought every moment to pray . . . that he who is the unseen ruler of the human heart may vouchsafe to turn that will of ours to the desire of virtue, though it is more readily inclined to vice. . . . The Lord's help is always joined to [our effort], that we may not be altogether destroyed by our free will, [and] when he sees that we have stumbled, he sustains and supports us, as it were by stretching out his hand.

St. Isaac of Syria also uses this image of God stretching out his hand to help us.

> Just as a mother who, in teaching her infant son to walk, steps back from him and calls him, and as he comes toward her on his little feet he begins to tremble and is about to fall by reason of their softness and delicacy, and she runs and catches him in her embrace, so the grace of God also embraces and teaches those who purely and with simplicity have surrendered themselves into the hands of their Creator, and who have renounced the world with their whole heart and follow after Him.[84]

So if salvation is understood as a rescue rather than payment of debt, the role of free will becomes clearer. Picture a child sleeping in a burning building; the fireman will rescue her, though she has done nothing to deserve rescue. She doesn't even know the building is on fire. When the fireman wakes her up, she might even fight hard against him, insisting that she wants to go on sleeping.

Why should we rescue this child if she has done nothing to merit it? Because she's a member of the human race. She's part of us. That's enough. Christ came to rescue us because the human race is his image and likeness, his creation. He permeates it, and his own energies are the source of its life. His motive is to defend and recover his own possession, to stand on his rights as Creator, and not anything we've done to make ourselves worthy.

The world doesn't know it's on fire. Christ comes to rescue us anyway. But, unlike the little girl, who can be picked up and carried to safety no matter how much she protests, we can refuse to be rescued.

That's true in an ultimate sense—we can choose or refuse eternal reconciliation with God—and it's also true in a moment-by-moment sense. If we've been taken captive by sin, and our Lord holds out the possibility of rescue, we can choose whether or not to respond. If we do accept the rescuer's help, it doesn't mean that we have earned the right to be rescued. He wants to rescue us for reasons within himself, because we belong to him. If we don't accept that help, and refuse to be rescued, we must take full responsibility for our continuing captivity.

Sometimes captives just don't *want* to be rescued. They may have become persuaded that their captors' cause is just, or have developed an emotional dependence on them, or even fallen in love.‡‡ We know what this is like, when it comes to favorite sins. We can find it very hard to give up behaviors we enjoy. St. Paul spoke for all of us when he said,

> I do not understand my own actions. For I do not do what I want, but I do the very thing I hate. . . . I can will what is right, but I cannot do it. For I do not do the good I want, but the evil I do not want is what I do. (Rom. 7:15, 18–19)

―――――――――――

‡‡ This is called "Stockholm Syndrome," for the hostages in a 1973 Stockholm bank robbery who, after they were rescued, defended their captors' actions.

Elder Paisios, a contemporary monk of Mt. Athos, said, "When people are tortured by a specific passion, they claim that a certain power prevents them from restraining and being good. They should know that this power, which acts as an obstacle, is rooted inside them."

What is this power? It's *love*. "Since they love their passions, it is natural that they are unable to get rid of them. When you love something, you want it." His advice is: "They must hate their passion, and then find something better to direct and transfer their love to."§§, 85

God is all-powerful, but the one thing over which he's chosen to cede control is what we decide to do. He created us in his image and likeness and surrounded us with bountiful creation, and then lets us choose how we will live. When we are at the end of our life's journey, we will be what we made of ourselves, one decision at a time.

Christ said the Final Judgment will be like separating sheep from goats (Matt. 25), and that's a chore that doesn't require close scrutiny. Over a lifetime our choices turn us into one or the other, and at the end it won't be hard to tell what we chose to become. From Christ's description, Judgment Day will not be so much like judging a criminal trial, but like judging a livestock show.

Making regular trips back to Egypt is a dangerous game. Step by unseen step we could be conditioning ourselves to find God boring, and forging habitual self-indulgence into chains of addiction. We could pass an unmarked point after which we would have neither the motivation nor strength to repent and turn one last time. That's why we receive salvation as a sure and certain gift from God, yet view our traitorous desires with suspicion.

Along with everything else God gives us, we ask him to give us the strength and the will to persevere. It *all* comes from him: our rescue, his forgiveness, and our ability to endure. We are saved entirely by grace, dependent on God even for our ability to love God.

---

§§ A pastor I know says he often has to remind his parishioners, "Your body is a temple—not an amusement park!"

What do you love more than anything else? It was a question St. Herman of Alaska (AD 1756–1837), the hermit of Spruce Island, asked when he was invited to dinner with the captain and officers of a Russian ship in Kodiak Harbor. The men gladly described the things they yearned for: riches, glory, a beautiful wife, a noble ship to command.

St. Herman then asked, "But do you love God?" The men exclaimed, "Of course we love God. How could we not love God?"

St. Herman said, "I, a sinner, have tried to love God for more than forty years, and I cannot say that I perfectly love him. If we love someone then we always think of that one, we strive to please that one; day and night our heart is preoccupied with that object.

"Is it in this way, gentlemen, that you love God? Do you often turn to him, do you always remember him, do you always pray to him and fulfill his holy commandments?" The men had to admit that, by this definition, they did not.

"For our good, for our happiness," St. Herman urged them, "at least let us give a vow to ourselves, that from this day, from this hour, from this minute, we shall strive to love God above all else, and do his holy will."[86]

18

"Where Two or Three Are Gathered"

(MATT. 18:20)

The Kiss of Peace, Love and Communion, The Holy Gifts, Mysteries, Closing Prayers

fter Dn. Andrew chants the last line of the litany, Fr. John turns to face the congregation and says, "Peace be to all." We respond, "And to your spirit." He says, "Let us love one another, that with one accord we may confess—" and we all complete the sentence, singing, "Father, Son, and Holy Spirit, the Trinity, one in essence and undivided." Fr. John then announces, "Christ is in our midst!" and all reply, "He is and ever shall be!"

That is the signal for the Kiss of Peace, which was a widespread custom even in the first century; five of the New Testament Epistles conclude with an instruction to greet one another with a (usually, "holy") kiss. Since these letters were read aloud during worship, perhaps the kiss came at the end of the readings, close to when it is done in the liturgy today.

But there is obvious potential for disruption, with the kiss becoming less a solemn liturgical event and more a sociable one. Some men found the opportunity to greet women overly tempting, as well. So adaptations were made: in some places men and women exchanged the peace only with their own sex (or even stood on different sides of the nave); elsewhere there was no touching, but a bow; among Coptic Orthodox, worshipers kiss their fingertips and touch the fingertips of their neighbor. At most Orthodox churches in America the Kiss of Peace is exchanged only among those at the altar (priests with priests, deacons with deacons), but at some, like St. Felicity, worshipers greet those near them. It is a literal kiss, on the cheek (alternating each side, two or three times; there's some cultural variation),* while repeating that "Christ is in our midst" exchange.

While the people are still exchanging the Kiss of Peace, Dn. Andrew cries out, "The doors! The doors!" This was the signal, in ancient times, for all catechumens and nonmembers to depart and the church doors to be closed behind them.† At these words the community begins reciting the Nicene Creed.

> I believe in one God, the Father Almighty, Maker of heaven and earth, and of all things visible and invisible.
> And in one Lord Jesus Christ, the Son of God, the only-begotten, begotten of the Father before all ages.
> Light of Light; true God of true God; begotten, not made; of one essence with the Father, by whom all things were made;
> Who for us and for our salvation came down from heaven, and was incarnate of the Holy Spirit and the Virgin Mary, and became man.
> And he was crucified for us under Pontius Pilate, and suffered, and was buried.
> And the third day he rose again, according to the Scriptures, and ascended into heaven, and sits at the right hand of the Father.
> And he shall come again with glory to judge the living and the dead, whose Kingdom shall have no end.
> And I believe in the Holy Spirit, the Lord, the Giver of Life, who proceeds from the Father; who with the Father and

---

* Orthodox often greet each other with such a kiss wherever they meet, not only in church.

† A young nephew of mine saw a rock-band bumper sticker that read "The Doors," and exclaimed, "Hey, that guy must be Orthodox!"

the Son together is worshipped and glorified, who spoke
by the prophets.
And I believe in One Holy, Catholic, and Apostolic Church.
I acknowledge one baptism for the remission of sins.
I look for the resurrection of the dead, and the life of the world
to come. Amen.

In the early years of Christian faith, people joining the church
were required, at their baptism, to give a statement of their beliefs;
that's where the idea of a creed (from the Latin *credo*, "I believe")
came from. In time a number of short creeds were in use, expressing
the same points of faith with different wording.

In the early fourth century, though, a great controversy about
Christ's eternal divinity arose (the Arian controversy, originating
with a North African priest named Arius), and in AD 325 the first
ecumenical council met in the town of Nicaea, near Constantinople,
to settle it. That gathering of hierarchs and theologians produced
this creed, up through the phrase "whose kingdom will have no
end." Lingering arguments about the Holy Spirit led to the second
ecumenical council, which met at Constantinople in AD 381, and
there the remainder of the creed was composed.

We recite the creed immediately after we exchange the peace.
You might have missed the connection, but the two things—love
of the brethren, and boldness of faith—go together. Just before we
exchanged the peace, we chanted, "Let us love one another, that
with one accord we may confess . . . the Trinity." The Trinity *is* love,
for the three persons "dwell in one another, in no wise confused but
cleaving together," says St. John of Damascus. "They are made one
not so as to commingle, but so as to cleave to each other, and they
have their being in each other."[87] (This eternally self-giving movement among the three members of the Trinity is called *perichoresis*.)
"I am in the Father and the Father is in me" (John 14:11).

So our ability to say the creed is rooted, somehow, in our love
for each other. There is plenty of evidence for the reverse: theological division and enmity go hand in hand. But how does love
preserve the faith?

On a practical level, mutual love sustains us over periods of doubt. But, more deeply, it may be that mutual love is what ultimately constitutes the Church. "By this all men will know that you are my disciples, if you have love for one another" (John 13:34)—when we love each other it's evidence that we belong to Christ. "Anyone who resolves to do the will of God will know whether the teaching is from God" (John 7:17). When we do God's will by loving one another, we can recognize true teaching, the doctrine that comes from God. Unity of love leads to unity of faith.

Oddly enough, the creed and the peace come at different places in the Western liturgies. There, the creed is recited immediately after the sermon, and the peace exchanged immediately before receiving Communion—variations that equally make sense.

At the conclusion of the creed, Dn. Andrew announces, "Let us stand aright. Let us stand in awe. Let us attend, that we may offer the holy oblation in peace." These words call the congregation to attention, for the Eucharistic prayers are about to begin. (In the ancient *Apostolic Constitutions* the deacon now reminds mothers to take their children by the hand.)

Then a very ancient exchange takes place:

Priest: The grace of our Lord Jesus Christ, and the love of God the
Father, and the communion of the Holy Spirit be with you all.
People: And with your spirit.
Priest: Let us lift up our hearts.
People: We lift them up to the Lord.
Priest: Let us give thanks to the Lord.
People: It is meet and right so to do.

These are the opening words of the sequence of prayers called the *anaphora*, which means "offering up." The same word is used in the Septuagint for the offering the priests of ancient Israel made in the temple.

Fr. John goes on to thank God for our very existence: "You brought us out of nonexistence and gave us being, and when we fell away from you, you raised us up again. You did not rest until you had done everything needful to bring us to Heaven and bestow on us your promised Kingdom." I've always liked that bit about God not resting until he had done everything he could to save us. A parent knows what that is like—the unremitting necessity of doing everything possible to reach and rescue your child.

Fr. John gives thanks that God will receive this offering from his hands, even though "thousands of archangels and ten thousands of angels stand before you, cherubim and seraphim, six-winged, many-eyed, soaring aloft, borne on their wings, singing the hymn of victory, proclaiming, shouting, and crying aloud—" The congregation now joins in, singing the hymn of the angels in Isaiah's vision: "Holy, holy, holy, Lord of Sabaoth! Heaven and earth are full of your glory!" This is the moment we foreshadowed in the Cherubic Hymn, the moment we "represent the cherubim" and "sing the thrice-holy hymn."

Fr. John continues the prayers, telling how, on the night before he died, Christ blessed bread and wine and shared them with his disciples. He repeats Christ's words: "This is my Body" and "This is my Blood," and each time the people say "Amen." In liturgical Western churches these are called the "Words of Institution," and are regarded as the operative moment when the bread and wine become Christ's body and blood. In the East, the transformation is completed a little later.

Fr. John goes on, "As we remember this saving commandment and all that you have done for us—the Cross, the tomb, the third-day Resurrection, the Ascension into glory, the enthronement at the Father's right hand, and the glorious Second Coming—" The congregation joins in, singing, "We praise you, we bless you, we give thanks to you, and we pray to you, O our God." (Worship puts us in a curiously timeless time, where we can "remember" the Second Coming, on an ordinary Sunday in February.)

Everyone has been standing for this very important prayer, but now some worshipers "fall on their faces", dropping to their knees and touching their foreheads to the floor (that is, they make a prostration). Some refrain from doing this because it's too crowded where they're standing, and some because they aren't as limber as they used to be, but some remain standing because there is a very ancient rule that worshipers should not kneel on Sunday. Since Sunday is the day of Resurrection, it is the one day of the week that we should not bow in penitence, but rather stand in gratitude. (Those who *do* prostrate at this point say that they do so as an expression of awe, not penitence.) As usual, it's nobody's business what someone else does.

Meanwhile Fr. John prays that God will send his Holy Spirit upon the bread and wine, and make them Christ's body and blood. This invocation (*epiclesis*) of the Holy Spirit brings to conclusion the transformation of the Holy Gifts into Christ's body and blood, which began early this morning with the Proskomedia (preparation) service.

Though Orthodox believe that the bread and wine truly become Christ's body and blood, they don't use the term *transubstantiation*. That concept means that the "substance" (*ousia*, "essence") of the bread and wine change into the substance of Christ's body and blood, while the "appearance," everything perceptible by the senses, remains as it was. It's characteristic of Western theology to spell things out in increasing detail, but less of a pattern in the East. I expect Orthodox would say that all statements about the Eucharist are likely to be incomplete, because our understanding is incomplete; when the range of what we don't know is unknowably vast, we can let it go without theorizing.

Fr. John prays that all who receive will do so "for healing of the soul, for the forgiveness of sins, for the communion of your Holy Spirit, for the fulfillment of the Kingdom of Heaven, for boldness before you, and not for our judgment or condemnation." One who shares in the Eucharist without the necessary preparation risks "judgment or condemnation"; as St. Paul said, such a one is "guilty of profaning the body and blood of the Lord," and "eats and drinks judgment upon himself" (1 Cor. 11:27, 29).

We give thanks for all those who have "gone before us in faith," offering a hymn in particular to the Virgin Mary; then we pray for the living, for all clergy, monks and nuns, and all our fellow Christians. In the slightly longer Divine Liturgy of St. Basil, which Orthodox use during Lent, we pray as well for "those in deserts and mountains, and living in dens and caves of the earth" (the wording comes from Heb. 11:38). We pray this because there actually are Orthodox Christians who are still doing this—people who choose to live in the desert or wilderness, sustained only by what God provides. This is an extreme kind of spiritual discipline, and Orthodox writings are full of warnings that someone who takes it on prematurely, out of pride, risks insanity. Those who are genuinely called to this life, however, are extraordinary intercessors, and God grants them in deep prayer to see and pray for needs all over the world.

Then Fr. John prays, "Make us worthy, O Lord, that with boldness and without condemnation we may dare to call upon you, the heavenly God, as Father," and we all pray, "Our Father, who art in heaven. . . ."

There are just a few more prayers before Communion, during one of which Fr. John adds warm water to the wine in the chalice. Then it's time for Fr. John and Dn. Andrew to receive Communion, which they do while standing at the altar. While they are receiving we all sing, "Praise the Lord from the heavens! Praise him in the highest!" (That's Psalm 148, one of the rare times when Hebrew and LXX Psalms have the same number.)

Then it's our turn. Dn. Andrew calls out, "With the fear of God, and faith and love, draw near!" He and Fr. John each take up a chalice containing the consecrated wine and bread, and a long-handled golden spoon, and go to stand in the nave on either side of the Royal Doors. They will use the spoon to place a bit of the mixture, now become Christ's body and blood, into the mouths of communicants.

The members of the congregation who will receive Communion group themselves into two lines, stretching back through the nave. As each person moves forward, the altar boys on either side of the chalice lift a red cloth, much like a table napkin, below the communicant's chin.

The person quietly says his or her own name (usually, their "church name," the name of their patron saint). The priest or deacon giving Communion will then say, "The handmaid" (or "The servant") "of God, [Name], receives the precious Body and Blood of our Lord and God and Savior Jesus Christ, to the remission of sins and unto life everlasting." Given the ceaseless stream of faces, it is easy to blank out on a name, so it is helpful for the communicant to quietly supply it first.

How do you get a patron saint? When a person is preparing to join the Orthodox Church, he and his pastor choose a saint to be his patron, a spiritual friend and prayer partner. Some people want to be called by their saint's name, while others keep using their original name (though, when they come to the chalice for Communion, they supply their saint's name). If the catechumen's given name is already the name of a saint, he or she may stick with that.

If your given name is not yet that of a saint (that will be your job), you might think about having a saint who has the same first initial, or one whose feast falls on or near your birthday. But it could be any saint you particularly admire. A woman can choose a male saint, and a man can choose a female, though that doesn't happen often. I know a little girl called "Anna" whose saint is St. John the Forerunner (in Greek, Ioannis), and a man who took the name "Marius" for his patron, St. Mary of Egypt. Some choose, instead of a saint, one of the great feasts of the Church. "Evangeline," which means "good news," is linked to the Feast of the Annunciation. In such a case, the patronal feast day becomes the person's "name day," which is celebrated like a birthday.

A church has a "name day," too, and St. Felicity's feast day was on February 1, a couple of weeks ago. A parish celebrates its patronal feast with a Divine Liturgy, and all the other Orthodox churches in the area are invited to attend; there's usually a reception or potluck supper afterward. Some parishes observe their feast with a liturgy the evening before; some serve a Vespers the evening before, and a Liturgy on the morning of the feast day.

After receiving Communion each person returns to his place, stopping on the way to take a chunk of bread from a basket held by an altar boy. This is the remainder of the loaves Fr. John used during the Proskomedia (preparation) service earlier. After the Lamb was removed and set apart for consecration, and other portions and crumbs set aside for saints, the living, and the departed, the remainder of the bread was cut up and put in a large basket. During the liturgy Fr. John blessed this bread, touching it to the chalice.

As communicants return from the chalice, they will take pieces for themselves and for anyone standing near them who isn't going forward for Communion—those who aren't receiving today, or non-Orthodox visitors. It is called *antidoron*, which means "instead of the gifts"; those who receive this bread instead of the Holy Gifts will still be joining us in partaking of the common loaf. (You'll notice that worshipers handle antidoron respectfully and take care not to drop crumbs; the bread has been blessed.) At churches with a Russian Orthodox heritage, the antidoron may be set out on a small table with cups of warm watered wine. Worshipers take a portion and dip it into the cup, or eat it with a sip of wine.

Not long ago many liturgical churches still practiced "closed Communion": only members of that denomination were allowed to receive Communion. In some churches it meant as well that Communion was given only to members who had reached a certain age, or who had received their first Communion or the sacrament of confirmation. The practice of reserving Communion only to members of the Church has become scandalous of late, though, and many think it abhorrent to exclude anyone from the sacrament. If Communion is all about community, then withholding Communion looks like nothing but rejection.

But is that really the case? Is Communion really all about community? I had always assumed so—that sharing in the Eucharist both celebrated our unity as Christians, and forged it. But that's not the only way Communion can be understood.

There is a series of prayers that Orthodox use in preparation for Communion, and it took me some years of saying them before I noticed something odd: that they don't talk about community. Nor do they speak of Communion as something that unites the communicants with each other. The prayers instead use the first-person-singular, "I" and "me," and focus closely on my encounter with the mystery of the body and blood of Christ.

It is a daunting thing to contemplate. The act of consuming the body of Christ is incomprehensible, unimaginable. Yet, almost as a rebuke to our cherished ability to encompass great things with our minds, this will take place not as a solely spiritual or mystical event but by means of my physical body. These pre-Communion prayers express such fear and trembling about that approaching encounter that, for the moment, my fellow communicants are not in mind. Communion *does* unite us with each other, but when we are preparing to receive it something else takes precedence.

The prayers keep stressing that Jesus Christ is coming to me— to me, personally—and, of all things, will give himself as food. I must find the courage to chew his body, like any food; and like any food it will pass through me and become part of my physical body. (No polite evading of that point; a post-Communion prayer says, "Scorch me not, O my Maker, but pass through me for the right ordering of my joints, my kidneys, and my heart.") If you think about what this means—that God will become one with us in a tangible way, as real as the burning bush—it is genuinely alarming.

Of course, many other churches believe, like the Orthodox, that the bread and wine of the Eucharist truly become Christ's body and blood. But it seems that. Orthodox have also preserved an awareness of how inherently *shocking* this is. That Christ became human is astonishing enough; that he becomes *food* is outrageous, even frightening.

That is how his Jewish hearers reacted when Jesus said, "Unless you eat the flesh of the Son of Man and drink his blood, you have no life in you" (John 6:53). In the course of this passage he says this several ways, repeating for clarity; he speaks of eating his "flesh" rather than his "body" (the word used in the other Gospels), and sometimes uses the graphic word "chew," *trogo*, the word for a cow chewing its cud, instead of "eat," *phago*. Our English translations gloss over that distinction, but our Lord left no room for other interpretations.

A Protestant minister once told me that this couldn't be what Jesus meant, because his Jewish audience would have been offended. They would have heard it as cannibalism, and abandoned him. Well, yes, that's exactly what happened. "When many of his disciples heard it, they said, 'This is a hard saying; who can listen to it?'" (John 6:60). Note that this is not the usual hostile Pharisee contingent, but his *own disciples*; yet they are so repulsed that they refuse to follow him anymore. "After this many of his disciples turned back and no longer walked with him." *Many* of them.

The passage continues, "Jesus said to the twelve, 'Do you also wish to go away?' Simon Peter answered him, 'Lord, to whom shall we go? You have the words of eternal life" (John 6:66–68). Peter's words are hardly enthusiastic; he was bewildered and frightened, no doubt, by the strange things Jesus was saying. But he had followed Jesus so long that he could not turn back. He had to follow, no matter where Jesus was leading.

Orthodox prayers stress the awesome and even dangerous nature of this sacrament. If received carelessly, it can be deadly, as St. Paul warns: "Whoever . . . eats the bread or drinks the cup of the Lord in an unworthy manner will be guilty of profaning the body and blood of the Lord. . . . That is why many of you are weak and ill, and some have died" (1 Cor. 11:27–30). A merely symbolic memorial service would not have such dangerous effects. We preserve a bright awareness of the danger the Holy Gifts can pose to the unprepared.

But what does it mean to prepare? Those wishing to commune must have kept a complete fast from bedtime the night before:

nothing to eat or drink, not even a glass of water.‡ Communicants must also be making confession on a regular basis; some churches expect a communicant to make confession *every* time they receive, immediately before the liturgy. Still other churches require those receiving Communion to prepare by observing a Lenten-type fast (keeping a vegan diet) for the entire preceding week. Some expect that anyone coming forward for Communion has prepared by attending the evening service the night before ("Vigil" or "Vespers"). A person who receives Communion must also be a member of an Orthodox congregation, must affirm all Orthodox theological and moral teachings, and must be under the authority of an Orthodox bishop. One who receives Communion in an Orthodox church is bearing public witness that she is and does all these things.

The priest must guard the safety of every communicant, and see to it that the Holy Gifts are rightly honored as well. This responsibility is driven home in a memorable way during the ordination to the priesthood. During the Divine Liturgy in which he is ordained, there is a moment between the conclusion of the Eucharistic prayers and the distributing of Communion when the bishop places in the hands of the new priest the consecrated Lamb, now become the body of Christ. The bishop tells him, "Receive this pledge, and preserve it whole and unharmed until your last breath, for you will be called to account for it in the second and awesome Coming of our Great Lord, God, and Savior, Jesus Christ."

With those sober words ringing in his ears, the new priest goes to stand behind the altar, facing the congregation. The service continues around him, but he stands there, holding the Lamb in his hands and picturing the years and decades ahead. By the time the bishop calls him back to return the Lamb, so it can be placed in the chalice and distributed to the faithful, he has had ample time to look down the years, and consider all the times he will say the prayers of consecration and give Communion from the chalice. When he is called to account on the Last Day, how will his record appear?

---

‡   An exception is made, of course, if one needs a sip of water to swallow a pill, or if a medical condition requires food or drink. A member of an Orthodox congregation will plan this out with her priest.

So a priest is understandably reluctant to administer Communion to someone he does not know. When a stranger approaches the chalice, he will quietly ask if he or she is Orthodox and eligible to receive.[§] If the person is not Orthodox, the priest may give a blessing instead, making the sign of the cross over him with the chalice.

Two long lines of communicants stretch back through the nave, from the stations where Fr. John on the left and Dn. Andrew on the right are distributing Communion. The first Communion hymn we sing is a prayer from the Divine Liturgy of St. John Chrysostom.

> Receive me today, O Son of God,
> As a partaker of your mystical supper.
> For I will not speak of your mystery to your enemies,
> Nor will I give you a kiss, like Judas.
> But, like the Thief, I will confess you:
> Remember me, O Lord, in your Kingdom.

We glimpse here a moment from the earliest years, when the Eucharist was a secret that Christians would not reveal to the Lord's enemies. Strange rumors circulated about Christians in those days; some said that they practiced incest (because they called each other "brother" and "sister"); some said that they put a baby in a bag of flour, beat it to death, then ate it (a gossip's amalgam of the baby in the manger, the bread of the Eucharist, and Jesus' instructions to eat his body). The martyrs did not dispel such rumors by describing what *did* go on in worship; they protected the inner mystery of the faith, even if they died as a result. When we sing this hymn, we join hands with them.

---

§ It is polite for Orthodox Christians, when traveling, to contact the priest ahead of time and let him know you would like to come for worship, giving your name and that of the parish you attend.

We say that we will not speak of our Lord's "mystery," and should take a moment to examine that word. It's one that St. Paul uses with some frequency (for example, "Great indeed, we confess, is the *mysterion* of our religion," 1 Tim. 3:16), and in the early church that term was adopted to refer to liturgical rites such as baptism and the Eucharist. However, in the Vulgate, the Latin translation of the Bible that became the standard text in the West, *mysterion* is sometimes rendered *sacramentum*; that's the term for a vow with legal significance (for example, the oath a man swore when joining the Roman army). That's how "Holy Mysteries" in the East became "sacraments" in the West.

But in what sense is the Eucharist, or any sacrament, a "Mystery"? "It's a mystery" can sound like the easy way out: "Don't worry about it. You're not supposed to understand. It's a *mystery*." (Make woo-woo eyes and wave your hands around.) But there are different kinds of "mysteries." Some are like puzzles; a solution exists, but some pieces of information are unknown (as in a detective story). Others are cases in which some information is reserved to an inner circle (like the secret rites of a club). But the Holy Mysteries of the Church don't fit either category. Information is not being withheld; it's just beyond our ability to comprehend. We receive the Holy Mysteries in simplicity like children, but we can never fully understand them.

In the West it is commonly held that there are seven sacraments: baptism, confirmation, Eucharist, confession or reconciliation, marriage, ordination, and anointing for healing. Orthodox say that there are *at least* seven sacraments, or Mysteries; we know about the ones listed, but don't know how many other ways God may come to us through the material realm. The whole earth is his, and he can fill it and use it however he wishes. There may be dozens of sacraments, for all we know, but in these seven forms in particular he has pledged to meet us.

When all who were in line have received, Fr. John and Dn. Andrew return to the altar. Fr. John chants, "O God, save your people and bless your inheritance," and we sing, "We have seen the true light. We have received the heavenly Spirit. We have found the true faith, worshiping the undivided Trinity, who has saved us." It is a bold, maybe an offensive, thing to say, that we have found the true faith; but the words should be understood in the Eastern context, where Christians more typically lived alongside non-Christians than beside other sorts of Christians.

After a few more prayers, Fr. John says, "Let us depart in peace."

We say, "In the name of the Lord."
He says, "Let us pray to the Lord."
We say, "Lord, have mercy."

Just when you think you're actually going to depart, it's time to pray again. This time Fr. John's prayer is followed by a short hymn:

Blessed be the name of the Lord,
Blessed be the name of the Lord,
Blessed be the name of the Lord,
Henceforth and forevermore.

When you hear this "Blessed be the name of the Lord" hymn, you can be sure the ending really is in sight. However, this week there will be inserted at this point the memorial service for Esther's father. Ernest reposed two years ago this week.

Esther and her husband, George, make their way forward and stand in front of the large icon of Christ on the iconostasis, near the platter of koliva. Esther's closest friends in the congregation filter forward, too, and stand behind them. A basket full of taper candles lies under the koliva table, and Esther takes up a handful and passes them back, and from there they spread through the congregation. She and George light their candles from the candle stand before the icon, then light the candles of those around them so the flame goes spreading back as well.

The opportunity to hold candles makes a memorial service exciting for children, but when they are packed close among mourners, some of whom have long hair or head scarves, there is a always the possibility that candles will become more exciting than is strictly necessary. So the children are sent to the opposite side of the nave, where Despina, the parish's unofficial grandmother ("Yia Yia"), oversees candle-holding with eagle eyes. We sing:

> With the spirits of the righteous made perfect,
> Give rest to the soul of your servant, O Savior,
> And preserve it in that life of blessedness that is in you,
> For you love mankind.

The prayers of the memorial service ask God to give the reposed two things: rest and forgiveness. Fr. John prays that God will give Ernest rest "in a place of brightness, a place of beauty, a place of repose, where all sickness, sorrow, and sighing have fled away." He then asks God to "pardon every sin which he committed, by word, deed, or thought, for you alone are good, and you love mankind. For there is no one who lives and does not sin, but you alone are without sin, and your righteousness is to all eternity, and your law is truth."

We might well ask what these prayers are asking. Is it possible that God has not yet given Ernest rest, though he's been gone for two years? Has he not forgiven Ernest's sins? We asked for the very same things on this anniversary last year, and at his funeral the year before that. Does God wait until you ask a certain number of times?

Time is the tricky factor here. Christ "always lives to make intercession" for us (Heb. 7:25), but surely his great work is also complete; we expect that each person's death is the moment his ultimate destiny is determined ("It is appointed for mortals to die once, and after that the judgment" [Heb. 9:27, NRSV]), and yet, whenever our departed loved ones come to mind, we cannot help asking God to give them rest, have mercy, and forgive anything that needs forgiving. We don't know what else to say. We love them, and love seeks an outlet. People just *are* going to pray for the dead, no matter what their theological ideas are supposed to be. You can't stop them.

Surely Ernest is now outside of both time and space, in a place (or nonplace) where the cycle of another year is meaningless. But we still live in time, so we have to repeat ourselves. Because Christ "ever lives to make intercession," and we are the body of Christ, we will go on interceding. This doesn't amount to a stack of separate pleadings, but a single intercession that the whole community of believers offers eternally. It is always the part of humans to say, "Lord, have mercy" in every circumstance, no matter how many years tick by. Asking for it reminds us to be grateful for it; gratitude and humility open our hearts. As generation succeeds generation, we participate in this single eternal prayer.

The memorial service concludes with a hymn in which we repeat, "Memory eternal, memory eternal, may his memory be eternal." It is God's memory we are talking about, asking God to always hold this person in his living presence. Again, it's not as if God would forget Ernest if we didn't remind him, but it's our role to continually lift him up and entrust him to God's care.

After this hymn we return to the closing prayers of the liturgy. As Fr. John blesses the congregation, making the sign of the cross with a carved and inlaid wooden cross from the republic of Georgia, everyone sings, "Preserve, O God, him who blesses us, and grant him many years."

Then there is a moment of deflation, when we find ourselves suddenly dropped into the present moment of our ordinary lives. Sunday-school children scramble to the front, for they will be the first to be dismissed. Fr. John makes a couple of announcements about the schedule of services in the coming week, and recommends a retreat that will be held at a church across town. He welcomes the newcomers and invites them to join the congregation for coffee hour downstairs.

Then everyone stands to leave, getting in line once again to kiss the cross in Fr. John's right hand, then kiss his hand. The altar boys begin to chant the post-Communion prayers. Behind the iconostasis, Dn. Andrew is consuming the last of the Holy Gifts and cleaning the Communion vessels. Many who kiss the cross go directly downstairs to coffee hour, but some stay behind until the post-Communion prayers are finished.

After everyone has kissed the cross, Fr. John takes a bottle of blessed oil and invites those remaining to come forward for prayer and anointing for healing, and he anoints each person on the forehead and hands. The crowd dwindles, and eventually Fr. John alone is left behind. He is exhausted. He has been standing in worship for four hours; as one priest put it, "standing in the flame."

PART

Three

INSIDE THE
COMMUNITY

I'd like to give you some feeling for what ordinary life in
the Orthodox Church might be like, so here is a handful
of typical moments: an after-liturgy coffee hour, a late-
night call with a parishioner wrestling with temptation,
and a baptism and chrismation service. We'll also take
a look at a wedding, a house blessing, and a funeral.
Along the way, we'll continue to discuss elements of
Orthodox faith and practice: fasting, doctrinal harmony, and so on.

There's no real storyline here, just some hopefully
useful snapshots. As I said in the introduction, "learning
about" Orthodoxy is different from "learning" it; really
learning it requires immersion. You can't get immersion
from a book, but I'll try to give you a feel for it, and offer
some human details, and that might color and fill out
your understanding.

19

"When You Fast"

(Matt. 6:16)

Keeping the Fast, Expecting to Agree,
Typical Moments from Coffee Hour

Sunday, March 30—Veneration of the Cross, Mid-Lent

We come downstairs into a parish hall that is noisy and crowded. On both sides of the room, tables are lined up in parallel rows, and in the middle is a long buffet that bears a random array of platters and serving bowls. Randomness increases dramatically when you look into their contents. The ethnic range of St. Felicity Church is broad, and the potluck lunch after liturgy is colorful anytime, but Lent brings even more surprises. The Lenten fast means no meat, no dairy, and no fish with backbones; shellfish is permitted, though usually too expensive for a crowd this size. On many days (though not Saturday and Sunday) we fast from alcohol and olive oil as well.

Those ancient fasting guidelines took shape in a Mediterranean context, so it isn't always clear how to interpret them in today's superstore. It is olive oil that is specifically named as restricted, and at St. Felicity they take that rule at face value and permit other oils, as well as margarine. But at other churches it is interpreted to mean no oils at all, and no food cooked in oil—no potato chips, for instance. However, even if margarine makes the cut in regard to oil,

most margarines include dairy products, so there's some close reading of ingredient lists to make sure the margarine in question is truly
nondairy. (The same thing goes for chocolate chips: some brands
include milk products, some do not.) It turns out that "nondairy"
powdered creamer usually includes milk derivatives, so there's
almond milk instead by the coffee pot.

It's an open question how closely an Orthodox Christian should
read those ingredient lists. Some feel that "if you can't see it, it isn't
there," and it's foolish, for example, to reject a loaf of bread because
one of the ingredients is whey. For goodness' sake, you don't eat it
because you have an unbridled craving for whey.

But others say that the added work of scrutinizing labels is part of
the spiritual discipline of Lent. It's *supposed* to be irksome; it's supposed
to disrupt our comfortable routine. Lent is a good time to break up
automatic behaviors and think more closely about what we consume.

This is one of those times when there are "big-*T*" and "small-*t*"
traditions, where we can differentiate between practices that are
universal in the church and those that vary from one nation, or
parish, to the next. The specifics of fasting in Orthodoxy have
long been determined at the parish level, and the saying "When
in Rome, do as the Romans do" had its origin in a question about
fasting. When St. Monica (AD 332–387) moved to Milan with her
son, Augustine, she was puzzled about the fasting customs. At her
previous church they had fasted on Saturday, in commemoration
of our Lord's rest in the tomb; but in Milan, she found, they did
not observe this fast. So St. Augustine, then a catechumen, asked
St. Ambrose, their bishop in Milan, what to do. "When I am here
[in Milan] I do not fast on Saturday; but when I am at Rome I do,"
he answered. "Whatever church you may come to, conform to its
custom, if you would avoid either receiving or giving offense." St.
Augustine calls these different ways of applying a common practice
the "variety in the robe of [Christ's] bride."[88]

So the specifics of what one does or doesn't eat are less important than the discipline of fasting itself; but if we try to make fasting
comfortable, we will miss the point. A non-Orthodox friend laughed

when she heard me say that fasting practices vary from one parish to the next, and exclaimed that, obviously, people would search for the church with the easiest rule. That makes sense if you think of sin as debt, and want to be sure you're making the smallest acceptable payment. But it doesn't make sense if sin is sickness; that would be like searching for the doctor who gives only sugar pills, or the physical therapist who requires the least exercise. Fasting is a voluntary discipline, and if you don't do it, you're the one who loses.

Fasting works pointedly on our craving to "nourish and cherish" (Eph. 5:29) these comfort-loving bodies. And it's a good behavior to focus on, because food-fasting is available to everyone. Other forms of fasting, from entertainment or candy perhaps, might not have significance for one category of people or another; but everybody eats. Gaining control over your desire to eat what you want strengthens your self-control in all areas.

Tertullian, writing early in the third century, refers to this way of fasting as *xerophagy*, "dry eating," since bread and vegetables are cooked and eaten without oil.[89] He likens it to the diet of Daniel and his fellow captives in the Babylonian king's court, who grew stronger when they refused the rich foods from the king's table. Tertullian also points out that we are not rejecting these foods as if they were inherently evil, but only putting them aside temporarily, "abstaining from things which we do not reject, but defer."[90] If steak and ice cream were morally suspect, we wouldn't begin eating them again on the holiest feast days of the year.

Even with local variations, it helps a great deal that everyone is keeping the same fast at the same time. I've surely found that my self-chosen disciplines have a way of getting softened or discarded when they become difficult. Just knowing that others are wrestling with the very same temptations, and counting on you to hold up your end, helps you persevere.

There are a few other common suggestions for having a safe and sane fast. Don't pay any attention to how others are fasting, or not fasting; that only produces judgmentalism. On the other hand, if you are not following the fast closely, don't be obvious about it. Fasting is hard, and we need each other's support. But if you find yourself in a situation where your host is serving nonfasting foods, be flexible; it's better to break the fast than make a show of your spiritual superiority. A friend of mine told me that when he was newly Orthodox he invited his priest over for lunch on a fast day, and served cheeseburgers. The pastor ate the burger, then told him, "From now on. . . ."

If you have health needs that make rigorous fasting unwise, you should talk with your spiritual father and work out an alternative plan. (Pregnant and nursing mothers usually don't fast, and children learn to fast gradually as they grow.) There's a principle in Orthodoxy called *oikonomia*, or "economy," a compound of *oikos*, "house," and *nomos*, "law" or "rules"—literally, "house rules." This principle recognizes the need for flexibility, and that sometimes spiritual progress is better served by amending the rules than by exacting conformity. "The sabbath was made for man, not man for the sabbath" (Mk. 2:27). Wise discernment is needed here because of the temptation to rationalize away whatever you do or don't want to do. That's another reason it's helpful to have a spiritual mother or father, who can help you discern and hold you accountable.

By the way, you might notice people using the terms "Lent" and "Great Lent" interchangeably. Either term can refer to the season of fasting before Pascha, but it is sometimes called "Great" to distinguish it from the three lesser "Lents" of the church year. Dormition Fast (also called Dormition Lent) runs two weeks, from August 1 to the anniversary of the Virgin Mary's repose on August 15. The Nativity Fast (or Nativity Lent) runs six weeks, from November 15 to Christ's Nativity (Christmas) on December 25, and Apostles' Lent runs from the eighth day after Pentecost to the Feast of Sts. Peter and Paul, June 29; that could range from a couple of days to a few weeks.

Orthodox also fast on Wednesday and Friday of almost every week. This is one of the most ancient Christian spiritual disciplines. The *Didache*, a Christian treatise from about AD 80, reminds its hearers that observant Jews fast on Monday and Thursday (as the Pharisee in Jesus' parable says, "I fast twice a week," Lk. 18:12). But, it continues, we Christians don't do that; instead we "fast on the fourth day [Wednesday] and the Preparation [Friday]."⁹¹ The Wednesday fast is said to be in observance of Judas's betrayal, and the Friday fast for the Crucifixion. Altogether, Orthodox are keeping a mostly vegan diet for more than half the days of the year.* Fasting guidelines still leave lots of carbohydrates to choose from, so Orthodox who fast are not necessarily skinny.

There are exceptions and variations that complicate things; there are "wine and oil" days, and "fish, wine, and oil" days, when those normally restricted foods are permitted, and there are a few weeks in the year that we don't fast at all. Since the pattern is not predictable, most Orthodox keep a liturgical calendar on their kitchen wall (or their computer or smartphone) to check the day's specifics.

We pick up a paper plate and head down the buffet table. We come first to a bowl of store-brand powdered-sugar doughnuts; this was probably contributed by someone who doesn't read labels, for they almost certainly contain milk. It's up to each person whether he or she wants to follow St. Ambrose's advice above—to take this as evidence of how fasting is observed in this parish, and "eat what is set before you," as our Lord said (Lk. 10:8)—or to pass them by in order to choose more conventional fasting foods. Don't overthink it.

Next, there's some Louisiana-style red beans and rice, with bottled smoke flavoring to replace the ham hock. (It seems as if most cultures have a rice-and-beans dish, enough that a global tour of such foods could be the theme of a Lenten feast. The Arabic dish *mujaddara* is one of my favorites; tradition holds that this is the "pottage" Jacob offered in exchange for his brother Esau's birthright, Gen. 25:29–34.)

The Ethiopian family has brought a stack of the pancake-like sourdough bread called *injera*, and two kinds of vegetable *wat* (stew) to roll inside it. One good effect of fasting is that, over the years, you get to know the vegan dishes of a great many cultures. There's

---

* Monastics often fast on Mondays as well, and many monks and nuns never eat meat.

a huge bowl of salad with bottles of nondairy dressing, a platter of tater tots, and some peanut butter, jelly, and bread. Next up is a plate of Greek *dolmades*, rice wrapped in grape leaves, which make a tidy and tasty offering on occasions that call for "festive fasting finger foods." (Coffee hour at St. Felicity amounts to a full meal— worshipers skipped breakfast, and they're hungry—but at other churches the offerings may be more modest.)

Finally—there's tofu. Fasters acquire some close familiarity with tofu, though we generally greet it with a sigh. Today there's more enthusiasm, for it appears in the form of some chocolate cream pies, and the recipe is convincing. Cooks learn that family members may eat tofu without objection if they don't know it's there. Hide the wrappers carefully in the trash.

One might dispute the harmoniousness of these flavors, but the harmony of faith among people from so many different ethnicities is both surprising and thought-provoking. In the West, we're used to vigorous disagreement among Christians. Members of the same denomination, living next to each other and alike in almost every way, can disagree vehemently even about something as basic as Jesus' divinity. But Orthodox people who have never met will comfortably agree when it comes to matters of faith, even if that's the only thing they do agree on, even if they come from opposite ends of the globe or, if possible, different centuries.[†]

How does that work? One factor is that the liturgy is the same everywhere you go. It's also a help that it's in the local language, so people can know what the faith *is*. The long-standing tradition in Orthodox missions is to translate the prayers and the Scriptures into the local language, devising a written alphabet first if necessary. If people can understand what's being said in worship, it goes a long way toward teaching them what the faith entails.[‡]

[†] As someone put it, "They might not be speaking to each other, but they can finish each other's sentences."

[‡] St. Innocent Veniaminov (1797–1879), the Russian missionary to Alaska who designed the wooden altar table used at St. Felicity, learned a half-dozen of the languages of the Alaska natives. He then devised an alphabet and used it to translate Scriptures and liturgical texts; many of the original documents are now in the Library of Congress.

But there's another big reason that Orthodox people tend to agree theologically; it's simply that they *expect* to agree. They assume that all Christians share the same faith; there is "one Lord, one faith, one baptism" (Eph. 4:5), so how could they disagree? Jesus promised the Holy Spirit would "guide [his followers] into all the truth" (John 16:13); how could there be more than one truth? Orthodox immigrants have told me they lived in America for many years before learning that Protestants and Catholics believe different things from each other, and from the Orthodox. "I just assumed it was all the same," one told me.

This expectation of harmony tends to generate harmony. In the West, however, we expect Christians will *disagree*. We're used to lots of lively disagreement, when it comes to theology. Lively disagreement can be pleasurable; it's exciting to debate ideas with a nimble opponent, and thrilling if you can defeat him. Presenting and defending new ideas gives bright individuals an opportunity to shine, and many a name is made that way.

But the practical problem is that this opinion-generating machine demands a continuous stream of *new* ideas. The new guy always has to unseat the old guy, and may have to stretch a point to do so. When I was in seminary, a book came out that had a thesis that looked, to me, flatly ridiculous. I asked one of my professors why anyone would publish something so absurd. He explained that every new scholar, if he wants to succeed, has to come up with some original theory—something no one has ever said before. He told me, "After all these centuries, there aren't a lot of sensible ideas left."

In such a setting, old ideas, even if they're only a few years old, look inherently insufficient. This has to be discouraging to those who read Jesus' words to mean that the Holy Spirit is able to lead us into a single, common truth.

If you wanted to prevent this endless convulsing, and to found a church where the members would hold the same beliefs in all times and places, your first thought would probably be to establish strong central leadership. You'd want a ruler who had the power to resolve conflicts and issue binding decisions. Everybody who wanted to be in the church, all over the world, would have to recognize that person as the highest authority, and follow his decrees. Arranging things this way just makes *sense*.

What's funny is that Eastern Christianity doesn't have that at all. The Church is organized the way people naturally group themselves, by "tribe and tongue and people and nation" (Rev. 5:9). So there are Russian Orthodox in Russia, Greek Orthodox in Greece, and hopefully soon a single American Orthodox Church here. There isn't any administrative board above that, and they don't miss it. There's just the common faith, and it holds the Church together from the inside. Surprisingly enough, that's turned out to be sufficient.

This works because of the principle that *everyone* is responsible for passing on the faith just as they received it. That makes it very hard to change things. Someone who tried could succeed only in placing himself outside the community.

Here's an example. In 1893 there was a conference in Chicago that brought together representatives of all the world's religions. An Orthodox priest traveled from Brooklyn to attend the conference, and found an opportunity to share his opinion that all religions are one, and it doesn't matter what name you give to the god you worship. (Needless to say, this is *not* Orthodox doctrine.) When the conference was over he traveled back to Brooklyn, and went to his church. He put his key in the lock—and it wouldn't turn. His parishioners had already changed the locks.[§, 92]

Someone who wanted to revise the faith would find that there's no place to *start*. There's no central office where you could organize a protest. There's no powerful leader you could scheme to replace. You could only show everybody that you'd left the community. The faith itself holds us together, and it belongs to everyone, not only those who have the pleasant advantage of being alive at the present time. The unity stretches back to the beginning. When Orthodox say their church is "apostolic," that's what they mean.

---

§   That's the power of the laity, boy.

Fr. John hasn't made it downstairs yet, so Lauren, the head of the parish council, takes the microphone and asks parishioners at each table to introduce any newcomers or visitors. We are about at the middle of Lent, and she reminds the crowd of two services that have been added to the church's weeknight schedule.

On Wednesday night there's a Presanctified Liturgy (more precisely, a Liturgy of the Presanctified Gifts). Eucharistic liturgies are not served on weekdays during Lent, so this service provides communion from the Holy Gifts that were "presanctified" at today's service. This service is a favorite with many because it is so quiet and intimate. It is said to be the work of Pope St. Gregory the Great (AD 540–604).¶ "Gregorian chant" is named after this pope, because he did so much to encourage and support liturgical chant in the West.

Also, on Friday night there will be the fourth and final portion of the beautiful and poetically complex "Akathist Hymn," written by St. Romanos the Melodist (AD 475–555). The Akathist Hymn addresses the Virgin Mary as the Archangel Gabriel did, "Hail!" (or "Rejoice!," since the Greek word carries both meanings), and repeats that greeting scores of times, with each repetition exploring further the miracle of Christ's incarnation. There's nothing specifically Lenten about the hymn, but the service is offered at this time of year because its theme is the miracle of Christ's conception, and the Feast of the Annunciation (March 25) almost always falls within Great Lent. It's a message from the other side of the year: Christ is coming, to be born in Bethlehem!

Fr. John at last comes downstairs, passing on the way a group of teens headed up to vacuum the narthex, clean kiss marks off icons, and scrape up spilled wax. As tired as he is, he knows that many here have been planning all week to talk to him during coffee hour. Lauren hands him the microphone, and he reads a few items off a list he jotted last night on a sticky note. He announces a collection on behalf of a parishioner who is in his first year at seminary and gives an update on the work of a lone Orthodox missionary priest in Pakistan.

¶ He's called Gregory the Great in the West, and Gregory the Dialogist in the East, for his four-volume *Dialogues*.

He then hands the mic to two college freshmen who are trying to drum up interest in fielding a St. Felicity team to build houses for Project Mexico. They also report that the Orthodox Campus Fellowship chapter has been having good conversations with the Secular Student Alliance; Orthodoxy is a side of Christianity the Seculars had never encountered before.

Dn. Andrew then takes over, and asks for everyone having a birthday, name day, or anniversary that week to stand; when they do, everyone sings to them, "God grant you many years." This is an all-purpose, all-cultures Orthodox song of goodwill, sung whenever someone is being recognized or honored—birthday, baptism, graduation, wedding anniversary, or when their home is blessed.

Next Hank hands out photocopies of sheet music for a new setting of the Cherubic Hymn he'd like to start using. (Orthodox worship music usually has no copyright.) He guides the crowd through the hymn a couple of times, getting increasingly frustrated, for this relaxed, doughnut-happy crowd isn't inclined to concentrate. When it's over, Hank comes over to Fr. John's table.

"I don't see why they can't get that right!" he says. "They're not paying attention!"

"Well, you're right, Hank, this is never a good time to get people to pay attention," says Fr. John. "But they'll learn it in time, by singing it on Sundays. It's all right for it not to be perfect at the start."

Hank draws himself up. "No. It isn't all right. We are here to worship God, and 'good enough' is not good enough. We should do our very best to offer worship that is beautiful."

A red flush comes and goes in Hank's face. Fr. John leans forward to speak to him quietly. "Hey, watch out for your anger. Did you look up what I told you, in the Desert Fathers?" This is old territory for Hank. Anger is something he confesses every time.

"Yes," Hank says, reluctantly changing gears. "Abba Poemen said that the passions work in four stages: the thought appears in your mind, then it shows on your face, then it comes out in your words, then in your deeds. He said that if it comes into your heart, don't show it in your face; if it shows in your face, don't let it come out in words; and if it comes out in your words, at least stop before you put it into action."

"So how do you think you did today?" Fr. John asks softly.

Hank sighs. "I hope I did okay. It must have shown in my face a little, because I could see some people near me starting to look worried. I hope it sounded like urging them to do a good job, and not anger for not doing it right."

Fr. John pats his shoulder, sits back, and says nothing more. Then Hank says abruptly, "I'm going back upstairs." He will sit in the back row with his eyes closed and his jaw set, while the teenagers vacuum around him.

With the announcements over, Fr. John scans the room looking for Dorothea, a classics professor. He spots her and goes to her table. "Hey, Dorothea," he says, "you have a particular attachment to St. Mary of Egypt, don't you?** Could you give a little talk about her after the Presanctified Liturgy, sometime in the next couple of weeks?"

Dorothea has a cool and steady gaze. "Let me think about it," she says. You can almost see the gears in her mind beginning to mesh. "When do you need to know?"

"Any time this week will be fine. By the way, what happened with your friend Bill, who went to the monastery with you?"

Dorothea's sudden smile is broad, but gives nothing away. "You know that he's something of a star in academic circles, and gets top billing at conferences. Well, he talked to the abbess; fortunately, a nun was able to translate. He asked whether the church would have a place for someone of his particular gifts and abilities. Mother told

---

** St. Mary of Egypt (died AD 522) left her parents' home at the age of twelve and pursued sexual adventure insatiably in Alexandria for many years. She followed some young men on a trip to Jerusalem, but when she tried to enter the Church of the Resurrection (known in the West as the Church of the Holy Sepulchre) she found herself unable to pass the threshold. Coming to profound repentance, she crossed the Jordan River to live in the wilderness in constant prayer. Forty-seven years later, a monk spending Lent in the desert encountered her and heard her story. It was put into written form by St. Sophronios of Jerusalem (AD 560–638), and is read in entirety every year at a service in the fifth week of Lent. The fifth Sunday of Great Lent is dedicated to her as well. You'll find her story in my book *First Fruits of Prayer*.

him that she was sure there would be plenty for him to do, and he could start with the breakfast dishes."

Fr. John makes a noise halfway between a guffaw and a gasp. "She *said* that?"

Dorothea says, "He was stung, but on the way home he was saying, 'I guess that's what it used to be like, when people went to visit the Desert Mothers.'"

"The Abbess is really something," Fr. John says, still shaking his head. "Susan went for a retreat last year, and was standing in the back during Vespers, distracted because new shoes were pinching her feet. Suddenly Mother left her place up front and marched over to Susan, looked up and said, 'Think God, not feet!'"

Dorothea nods and says, "Nothing would surprise me. She has a sweet smile, though; it makes it easier to take your medicine."

20

"Each Person Is Tempted"

(JAS. 1:14)

Late-Night Phone Call, Battling Temptation,
Desiring Holiness, Praying for Each Other

Saturday, April 12—Eve of the Feast of St. Mary of Egypt

t was after midnight when Fr. John was awakened by his ringing phone. He picked it up and croaked out, "Hello?"

"Oh, hi, Father," said a timid voice.

"Who is this? Is this Jimmy? Where are you?"

"Hi, Father. Yes, it's me. I'm, um, I'm in my car. I'm out on Pennington Highway. Outside the Chaparral Club."

Fr. John looked over at Beth; she was sleeping with one arm flung over her eyes, and bright-orange earplugs to shield her from his 6:00 AM alarm.

"Jimmy, what are you doing there?," he asked, sitting up. "How did this happen?"

"I don't really know, Father. I just was here, somehow."

"What? You mean, like, you had a blackout?"

"Oh, no. I got in the car and drove here." Jimmy's voice had a catch in it, like a giggle or a hiccup. "I know *that*. I mean, I don't really remember *deciding* to do it. And then here I was!" Fr. John knew Jimmy had a long-term addiction to pornography, but had managed to stop throwing away his money at strip clubs years ago.

Fr. John said, "And yet, Jimmy, you are not *in* the club. You're still outside. And you called me. Tell me what is going on."

"I miss Aileen. Ever since she left me. . . ." The hiccup resolved into tears.

"Jimmy, Aileen did not leave you. You broke up with her. She didn't love you. She made fun of you. She stole cash from your bureau. It was the right thing to do."

"Oh, but Father, I'm so lonely. It's the loneliness that's so hard."

Fr. John was silent. What could he say to a lonely man, when he had his wife and unborn child beside him?

He asked, "We haven't talked since your confession, a few weeks ago. How has Lent been going for you?"

"Oh, I don't know," Jimmy said. "I told you I wasn't going to look at, you know, during Lent. But after awhile it just started happening again."

"Jimmy, come on. Be honest. It didn't 'start happening.' You started doing it." He paused. "Jimmy, do you remember when you first contacted me?"

"Yeah. I was looking for a church. I felt all upside down. I guess that was when Aileen was still with me. So, I guess, it wasn't that great. It wasn't always that great, when she was here."

"No, it wasn't. You said you were struggling with some things. You told me about your problem with pornography and going to clubs like the Chaparral, and how things were with Aileen. You were thinking a church might help."

Jimmy sighed. "I remember. And I'm glad I did, Father. It's not like I question that."

"You said that you loved God and wanted to be near him. I believe you, Jimmy. I believe you love God a lot. And you said you kept making promises, and then you'd fall again. After awhile you felt hopeless about trying again all by yourself. You wanted to know if there was such a thing as support."

"I know. And the church has been a big help to me, really."

"You know, you could find plenty of people who'd say you should stop trying and just enjoy yourself. If that's what you'd rather hear, it wouldn't be hard to find."

"I know. I don't want that, though. I tried that already." He sighed again. "I didn't want to just give up. I wanted to try to make things match up inside, what I believe and what I do."

"Do you think that, when you joined the church, you got what you were looking for?"

Jimmy said, "I don't know. I think what I was looking for was an end to the whole problem. I didn't find that. But it's better than before, sure. I used to not even try to stop myself. Now it seems worth trying. It helps to go to confession, too. Before, when I told God I was sorry, it just felt like I was in a big swamp. It feels realer now."

Fr. John said, "Jimmy, you've come to confession a lot now, and every time you do, everything is forgiven. It's been a long time since you had to confess something like this. What made you want to drive over to the club in the middle of the night?"

Jimmy sighed. "I guess the easy answer is plain old temptation—you know, physical desire. But I don't think that's really it. I know what will happen if I go in the club. And it's something I want. I like it. I wish I didn't, but I do. But it isn't what I *really* want. What I really, really want is someone to love me—like I thought Aileen did." Jimmy heaved another sigh.

This stung Fr. John's heart. The world has become a sexual free-for-all, but even that's no cure for loneliness.

Fr. John asked, "Jimmy, when you visited the monastery last month, and talked with the abbess about temptation, what did she tell you?"

"She said, 'Welcome to the fight.'" Jimmy tried to control his voice. "But, Father," he said, "it's *hard* to fight," and lapsed again into tears.

Fr. John prayed for guidance, asking to know what he should tell Jimmy. It's easy to say, "Keep trying," to someone fighting a long-term battle, but not so easy to be the one who has to do it.

He said, "Jimmy, do you remember the Desert Father St. Conon? It was his job to do the baptisms at his monastery. This was in the days when people were baptized in the nude, and he was always really troubled when he had to baptize a woman. Well, eventually St. Conon got so upset with himself that he decided to give up and leave the monastery. But when he was just about to walk out, St. John the Forerunner appeared to him and said he would help him with his struggle. So he stayed.

"But then a really beautiful woman showed up and wanted to be baptized. The story says she had to wait outside the monastery gate for two days while St. Conon tried to get control of the thoughts that were attacking him. He got so fed up with himself he decided again to leave.

"As he was leaving, St. John appeared to him again, and said the same thing, that he would help him in the struggle. But St. Conon told him, 'You said that before, but you didn't do it.'

"Here's the part I want you to remember, Jimmy. Then St. John made the sign of the cross over St. Conon, and all the thoughts completely disappeared. He never was troubled by those thoughts again. And then St. John said, 'I could have done that earlier, but I thought you wanted the crown.'"

Jimmy was quiet. Fr. John asked, "What are you doing?"

"I'm looking at the sign. It's rainy, and everything else around is dark, but it's bright."

Fr. John paused. "So what have you decided to do?"

A sigh. "I know what will happen if I go in. And that isn't the real thing I want. I want the other side of my life to get stronger. I want to be close to God." A pause. "I want to receive Communion in the morning. I want to be in church tomorrow, and sing along with everybody else."

Fr. John asked again, more gently, "So what are you going to do?"

"I'm going home."

"Good for you." Fr. John listened to the diminishing sniffles. "If you need me again, just call."

"Okay, Father. Thanks."

As Fr. John lay down again he thought about Jimmy's search for love—everyone's search for love. He remembered something an abbot said.

> A scholar attracts by his knowledge, a wealthy man by riches, a handsome man by beauty, an artist by his skill. Only love attracts all human beings. The attraction of love is unlimited. And educated and uneducated, rich or poor, skilled or unskilled, beautiful or ugly, healthy or sick, and young or old—all want to be loved. Christ spread his love on everyone, and lovingly drew all to himself. With his great love he encompassed even the dead, long decomposed and forgotten by men.[93]

Fr. John couldn't get back to sleep. Putting on his bathrobe, he went into the living room, to the icon corner. He lit a candle and looked into the eyes of the icon of Christ. He began to pray for Jimmy.

21

"Make Disciples . . . Baptizing Them"

(MATT. 28:19)

Baptism and Chrismation, Exorcism, Saints' Names,
Anointing Oil, Harrowing Hell

April 26—Holy Saturday

ascha arrives at midnight. The buildup has been intense, starting ten days ago, on the **Friday night before Palm Sunday**, with a service in honor of St. Lazarus ("of the Four Days," as he's sometimes called). (I've put each day of Holy Week in boldface, in case you're looking for a particular one.) Since then there has been a service every night, and a number of daytime services as well; we spend in all about thirty hours in church during Holy Week. It's the most beautiful, rich, and profound series of services in the Orthodox year, and some people set aside a week of vacation time so they can do it all.

Ever since last Sunday, **Palm Sunday**, we have been following Christ on his journey to the Cross. We've gone over the Gospel story prayerfully and in close detail, juxtaposing it with numerous passages in the Old Testament that foreshadow these events. The week began with a series of three services called "Bridegroom Matins," on **Sunday, Monday, and Tuesday night**. (All week we'll see this pattern of Matins services being held the evening before.)

Bridegroom Matins called us to consider the patriarch Joseph of the Old Testament as a type or foreshadowing of Christ, because his brothers believed him dead while he lived, in honor, in Pharaoh's court (Gen. 37:2–50:26). We explored the implications of the parable of the ten virgins, of whom only five were prepared to greet their returning Lord (Matt. 25:1–12), and considered the meaning of the withered fig tree (Matt. 21:19–22). We contrasted the penitent woman, who poured out expensive perfume on Jesus' feet, with Judas, who sold him for a handful of silver (Matt. 26:6–16).

At the third Bridegroom Matins, on **Tuesday** night, Caitlin, who has taken hymnographer St. Cassiane (AD 805–867) for her patron, chanted St. Cassiane's hymn: "The sinful woman spread out her tresses before you, and Judas spread out his hands to the unrighteous. She, to receive forgiveness; he, to receive silver." St. Cassiane gave voice to the penitent woman's wordless act: "Receive the drops of my tears, you who gather the waters of the sea into clouds. . . . I will kiss your feet, at whose sound Eve hid herself for fear."

The icon for Bridegroom Matins shows Christ mocked, wrapped in a robe of royal purple, and crowned with thorns. In an Orthodox wedding the bride and groom are given crowns, so Christ in this icon stands as the Bridegroom of the Church, wearing a crown, not of laurel leaves, but thorns. Each evening we sang,

> I see your bridal chamber beautifully adorned, my Savior,
> But I do not have a wedding garment so that I may worthily enter.
> Give light to the garment of my soul, and save me!

On **Wednesday night** there was a sacramental service of anointing for healing, called Holy Unction. After a series of seven Epistle and Gospel readings about miraculous healing, worshipers clustered at the front of the church while Fr. John held the Gospel book open like a tent over their heads. He prayed, "It is not my sinful hand which is laid upon the heads of these who come for anointing . . . but your hand, strong and mighty, which is in this Holy Gospel."

On **Thursday morning** there was a Divine Liturgy commemorating the Last Supper, and Fr. John washed the worshipers' feet.

On **Thursday night** there was the service of the Twelve Passion Gospels (which I described in chapter 9), and we knelt in the dimly lit church to hear the Passion story, read chronologically from all four Gospels. The large wooden cross had been moved from behind the altar into the nave, and we knelt before it to venerate the feet of the icon of the crucified Christ.

Friday morning there was a service of Scriptures and prayers called the Royal Hours. On **Friday afternoon** there was a Vespers service, in which we remembered the taking down of Christ's body from the cross. The corpus was removed from the large wooden cross standing in the nave and wrapped in a new white sheet and laid on the altar. (In some churches, the next person in the parish to die will be wrapped in this white sheet.) **Friday night** we held the service of Lamentations, and after the epitaphion was placed in the flower-decked bier we made a candlelight procession around the church, singing and carrying Christ to his tomb.

After that, parishioners kept vigil all night long, reading the Gospels aloud from the chanters' stand, right up until the beginning of this liturgy **Saturday morning**. These folks signed up to serve one hour at a time, but some kids from the youth group challenged each other to stay up, praying beside the bier all night long. At this point they are looking rather dazed. As with any morning Eucharist, no one has had food since midnight, nor much of anything to drink. (Readers could take sips of water, if needed.)

The big event is tonight: Pascha (**Saturday night**). Every Christian should experience this at least once. We will gather in the darkened church at 11:30, and sing hymns till midnight. Then Fr. John will turn from the altar to face us, his Paschal candle the only spot of light in the room. He will chant, "Come, take light from the light that is never overtaken by night. Come glorify Christ, who is risen from the dead." He then lights the candles of the worshipers standing nearest him, and from there the light goes rippling back through the congregation.

Fr. John will then lead us in a procession around the church (the "Rush Procession"), stopping outside the closed front doors. As we stand in the cold and dark, with late traffic passing by, we will hear the Good News for the first time. Fr. John will read Mark 16:1–8, and we will learn that the women found Christ's tomb empty, and an angel told them that he has risen.

Then Fr. John will pound a hand cross against the door, as if knocking, and say, "Lift up your heads, O gates! And be exalted, you everlasting doors, that the King of Glory may enter!"

A voice is heard from inside the door: "Who is this King of Glory?" (A skeptical or scoffing tone is appreciated here.)

This exchange is repeated, and at the third repetition Fr. John proclaims, "The Lord of hosts, he is the King of Glory!" (The exchange comes from Ps. 23/24:7–10). Then the doors are flung open, all the lights are turned on, and we return to a nave that is brilliantly lit and overflowing with flowers.

Worship goes on for a while; it's one in the morning, then two. Little children are clustered together on the floor, sleeping in their pajamas. We sing through Matins (this is one of the occasions when we rotate the chandelier) and hear the sermon. It's the same sermon we heard last year; in fact, it's been the same for about fifteen hundred years. The Paschal homily of St. John Chrysostom is brief but electrifying, and just what we need at this point.

> If any one be devout and love God, let him enjoy this fair and radiant triumphal feast.
>
> If any one be a wise servant, let him enter rejoicing into the joy of his Lord.
>
> If any have labored long in fasting, let him now receive his recompense.
>
> If any have wrought from the first hour, let him today receive his just reward.
>
> If any have come at the third hour, let him with thankfulness keep the feast.
>
> If any have arrived at the sixth hour, let him have no misgivings, because he shall in no wise be deprived.

If any have delayed until the ninth hour, let him draw near,
fearing nothing.

If any have tarried even until the eleventh hour, let him also be
not alarmed at his tardiness; for the Lord, who is jealous of his
honor, will accept the last even as the first; he gives rest unto
him who comes at the eleventh hour, even as unto him who
has worked from the first hour.

And He shows mercy upon the last, and cares for the first; and
to the one he gives, and upon the other he bestows gifts.

And he both accepts the deeds, and welcomes the intention,
and honors the acts and praises the offering.

Wherefore, enter all of you into the joy of your Lord, and
receive your reward, both the first and likewise the second.

You rich and poor together, hold high festival. You sober and
you heedless, honor the day.

Rejoice today, both you who have fasted and you who have
disregarded the fast.

The table is fully laden; feast sumptuously. The calf is fatted; let
no one go hungry away.

Enjoy the feast of faith; receive all the riches of loving-kindness.

Let no one bewail his poverty, for the universal kingdom has
been revealed.

Let no one weep for his iniquities, for pardon has shone forth
from the grave.

Let no one fear death, for the Savior's death has set us free: he
that was held prisoner of it has annihilated it.

By descending into hell, he made hell captive. He embittered it
when it tasted of his flesh. And Isaiah, foretelling this, cried:
"Hell was embittered when it encountered you in the lower
regions."

It was embittered, for it was abolished. It was embittered, for it
was mocked.

It was embittered, for it was slain. It was embittered, for it was
overthrown.

It was embittered, for it was fettered in chains.
It took a body, and met God face to face.
It took earth, and encountered heaven.
It took that which was seen, and fell upon the unseen.

O Death, where is your sting? O Hell, where is your victory?
Christ is risen, and you are overthrown.
Christ is risen, and the demons are fallen.
Christ is risen, and the angels rejoice.
Christ is risen, and life reigns.
Christ is risen, and not one dead remains in the grave.
For Christ, being risen from the dead, is become the first-fruits
    of those who have fallen asleep.
To him be glory and dominion unto ages of ages. Amen.

We go seamlessly from Matins into the Divine Liturgy. We sing
the Paschal troparion of St. John of Damascus over and over, in many
languages: "Christ is risen from the dead, trampling down death by
death, and upon those in the tomb bestowing life!"

Fr. John and Dn. Andrew shout, "Christ is risen!" many times in
many languages, and we reply, "Indeed he is risen!" By the time we
receive Communion it's around 2:30 in the morning. The brilliance
of the lights and candles, the incense, the shimmering white and
gold vestments, the processions and chanting, all make things seem
dreamlike.

At the close of the service, when we come up to kiss the cross in Fr.
John's hand, he gives to each person a hardboiled egg dyed red. The
story behind it is that St. Mary Magdalene was arraigned before the
emperor Tiberius and told him of Christ's resurrection. The emperor
scoffed, "A man cannot rise from the dead, any more than one of the
eggs in that basket can turn red." At that St. Mary Magdalene lifted
one of the eggs and showed it to him; it was a brilliant red.

Feasting goes on in the parish hall almost till dawn. (Though experience teaches that, if you haven't had any meat or dairy products
for seven weeks, it's wise not to overdo it.) Many families bring to
the feast a Pascha basket containing some of the foods they missed

during the fast, as well as symbolic foods like grated horseradish, for Christ's bitter suffering. But the sweet is here as well: there's a round loaf of sweet, yeasty bread called *kulich*, accompanied by a rich, creamy spread called *pashka* (Russian), and braided loaves of sweet bread, embedded with red hardboiled eggs, called *tsoureki* (Greek). The Pascha basket is covered with a fancy cloth, often one embroidered with crosses and "Christ is Risen!" At the beginning of the feast the candle in each basket is lit, and Fr. John goes through the hall blessing them with holy water. Then we sing, not for the first or the last time, "Christ is risen from the dead!"*

The Pascha service really is the high point of the year. It's said that for Orthodox, Pascha is the greatest feast; for Western Christians, it's Christmas. Orthodox celebrate Christmas (we call it Nativity) with an extensive service, too (and precede it with a six-week Lent), but Pascha just has a different kind of energy. We're into it heart and soul.

But all that lies ahead; now it is still **Saturday morning**. When we arrive at church we run into a small crowd gathered in the narthex. Today a group of catechumens is going to be baptized and chrismated; *chrismation* means "anointing," and, together with baptism, it is the means by which new members join the Church; it's parallel to the sacrament of confirmation in the West.

This is a most appropriate day, liturgically, for Holy Saturday was the day the ancient church brought new members into the fold. There's Tom and his wife Angie, and their two little ones, Lucy and Paul; Miriam, who is at the end of a long spiritual journey that began with a Jewish childhood; and a lone teenager named Dylan. Tom is the most exuberant of the crowd; he decided years ago that he wanted to be Orthodox, but Angie resisted, finding the church too foreign, too fancy, and too weird.

---

* A short video of Pascha at my church (Holy Cross Orthodox Church in Linthicum, MD) can be viewed at http://tinyurl.com/pascha2014.

This is not an uncommon pattern. I once heard a pastor say if a couple comes to talk with him about Orthodoxy, and one of them is ready to go while the other is reluctant, 80 percent of the time the one who's ready is the husband.† This is a switch on the pattern at many other churches, where the most active segment of the congregation is female, and wives worry about getting their husbands more involved. In the Williams household, it was Tom who placed books and magazines strategically around the house, and kept his laptop tuned to an Orthodox liturgical-music Internet radio station.

In a case like Tom and Angie's, a pastor has to make a judgment call. Sometimes he'll go ahead and chrismate the husband alone, but more often he'll encourage the husband to wait and give his wife time to come around. That can take years. Tom had his first meeting with Fr. John's predecessor, Fr. Daniel, five years ago, when his early exploration of Orthodoxy still involved a lot of theological arguing. Today seems like the final leveling-out stretch of a roller coaster ride.

For Miriam, the ride took even longer. Raised in an Orthodox Jewish home, she followed her generation into spiritual exploration during her college years. A couple of years ago she had a dream about Christ, and it stirred her to try going to church. It was at St. Felicity that she found the kind of worship that most reminded her of her childhood.

Dylan is not quite fifteen and too young to drive, so his mom drops him off at church on Sunday mornings. His parents had never encouraged churchgoing, but Dylan, an avid reader, discovered the ancient church and sought it out. Though he's young, he is intelligent and serious, and Fr. John is satisfied that he understands the faith and accepts all it entails.

One member of the original group of catechumens isn't here. Dale, a self-described spiritual seeker, read every book Fr. John mentioned, and relished discussions of theology, spirituality, and transformative prayer. It took Fr. John awhile to notice that Dale wasn't much

---

† Having been a reluctant wife myself, I empathize. In retrospect I think it's because Orthodoxy's challenging and resolute tone is something that tends to click for men more immediately than it does for women. (Of course, there are exceptions.)

interested in Jesus, though. They met to talk this out, and Fr. John saw that Dale was eager for the Church's spiritual wisdom, but had no intention of becoming a Christian. Fr. John had to tell him that, under those circumstances, he could not make him a member of the Church. Dale wasn't much upset; perhaps he had already settled on a new quest.

Each candidate for chrismation needs a sponsor. Miriam found a natural match in tall, graceful Despina, who takes her faith with similar seriousness. Tom asked Jim and Gena to be his family's sponsors; Jim was his friend, resource, and sparring partner during the half-dozen years of reading and questioning. Fr. John asked Greg to be Dylan's sponsor. Greg and Susan have a small farm with goats and chickens, as well as a houseful of children. Fr. John suspects that intellectual Dylan will gain from some firsthand experience with growing things, balky goats, and manure.

"Chrismation" comes from the Greek word for oil, *chrism*; "Christ" is "the anointed one" (in Hebrew, "Messiah"). Someone who has never been baptized will be both baptized and chrismated, but for a candidate who has been baptized in a different church, chrismation usually suffices.‡

From ancient times, the way into the church included both baptism and chrismation by the local bishop. But as time passed and dioceses grew larger, a bishop was not always available when there were people to baptize. West and East solved this problem in different ways. In the West, baptism can be done by a priest, but chrismation (or confirmation) is still reserved to a bishop, so the two sacraments are often separated in time. A baby can be baptized, but might not be confirmed till early adolescence, when the bishop visits the parish to confirm all who have prepared. The first reception of Holy Communion might fall in the middle of those years, at the age of six or seven, or wait until after confirmation.

---

‡   The exception would be if that previous baptism was not done "In the name of the Father, and of the Son, and of the Holy Spirit," but with some other formula. Some Pentecostal groups baptize in the name of Jesus only, for example, and some mainline churches have begun using new terms like "Creator, Redeemer, and Sustainer."

In the East, baptism and chrismation were kept together, and instead of requiring a bishop for the anointing, a priest performs the chrismation using oil the bishop has blessed. When a baby (or any unbaptized person) joins St. Felicity, she is baptized, then chrismated, and then receives Communion, all during the same service.[§]

Some of today's candidates for chrismation (the Anglican term *chrismands* is handy) have already been baptized—Tom at age twelve, and Dylan as an infant, at his grandparents' insistence. Angie thought she had been baptized as an infant, but the church of her childhood was not able to locate any record of this, so she'll be baptized today just in case. Little Lucy and Paul, and Miriam, will also be baptized. In the Orthodox Church, baptism is by triple immersion; the person is completely covered with water three times. Those who will be baptized are wearing bathing suits and white shorts, covered by a few oversized T-shirts.

The chrismands and their sponsors gather near the baptismal font, the one that was sold as a horse trough; it's been set about in the middle of the nave, filled with warm water, and trimmed with white flounces. All of the chrismands will be anointed on head, hands, and feet, so they are barefoot. Each holds a decorated candle they will have throughout the service, passing it over to their sponsor whenever free hands are required. These candles are not yet lit; that will come at the baptism. Fr. John joins the chrismands beside the font and whispers a few reminders and instructions.

The ceremony begins in a surprising way: Fr. John breathes on each candidate three times, in the form of a cross. He then lays his hand on each head and prays that the Lord will "take far away from them their previous delusion, and bestow on them the faith, hope, and love which are found in you, so that they may know you as the only true God, with your only-begotten Son, our Lord Jesus Christ, and your

---

§   At some churches, though, she wouldn't receive Communion until the next Divine Liturgy is celebrated.

Holy Spirit." When this prayer was composed, the "previous delusion" might have been any of the surrounding religions that would
deny the divinity of Christ.

Then there is an exorcism. Once again Fr. John breathes on each
candidate three times, repeating: "Drive from her every evil spirit
which hides and conceals itself in her heart." When he has marked
each candidate this way, he prays further:

> The spirit of deception, the spirit of trickery, the spirit of
> idolatry and of covetousness, the spirit of falsehood, and
> every corruption that works by the action of the evil one.
> And make him a reason-endowed sheep in the holy flock of
> your Christ.

"Reason-endowed sheep" is an odd term, and even after you eliminate
the mental image of four-legged sheep in mortarboards, it's still a
perplexing idea. In our culture we think of reason and spirituality as
incompatible, maybe even opposites. The Eastern Christian tradition
would instead see Christ as the light, the enlightener, who enables us
to reason well and perceive truth. Most of the time we are walking
around in a fog of memories, cravings, hopes, fears—barely in touch
with our immediate surroundings. It is a kind of insanity. Christ heals
our mind, endowing us with reason, opening our perception to his
Light. (If you want to refresh your memory, we covered this, and the
nous, in chapter 15.)

Now Fr. John asks them, "Do you renounce Satan?" three times, getting the response, "I do." He then asks, "Have you renounced Satan?"
three times, and gets the response, "I have." He says, "Breathe and spit
upon him." All the candidates turn toward the back of the church,
inhale, and then spit (or make a spitting sound) in that direction.

Then they turn again to face toward the altar. Fr. John asks, "Do you
unite yourself to Christ?" (they answer "I do") and "Have you united
yourself to Christ?" ("I have"), repeating each exchange three times.
Fr. John then asks, "Do you believe in him?" The candidates affirm, "I
believe in him as King and God," and recite the Nicene Creed.

Then Fr. John asks three times, "Have you united yourself to Christ?" They answer, "I have." He says, "Bow down before him." All the candidates kneel, though the little children find it hard to keep still in any position. They say, "I bow down before the Father, and the Son, and the Holy Spirit, the Trinity, one in essence and undivided."

"Blessed is God, who desires that all should be saved and come to the knowledge of the truth!" says Fr. John. He goes to cense the altar and iconostasis, then comes back to cense the font. He then prays for the blessing of the baptismal water, making the sign of the cross upon the water's surface three times with the tips of his fingers. He follows this by pouring into the water a little blessed oil, drawing a cross with it three times, while repeating, "Let all hostile powers be crushed beneath the sign of the image of your Cross."

Fr. John then anoints the baptismal candidates with this oil, tracing a cross on their forehead, chest and back, ears, hands, and feet. This is not the chrismation proper, which will come after the baptism, but an anointing with the "Oil of Gladness" that was blessed for this purpose.

Oil is not an easy substance to apply to people, not without making a mess. Fr. John uses a small golden vial that has a glass rod, like a dipstick, in the lid, and with it he can inscribe tiny crosses of blessed oil. (Other priests might use a small paintbrush or cotton swab.) Now the candles are lit, for the time of illumination has come.

Angie goes first, stepping into the font and kneeling down. Fr. John ducks her head under water quickly three times, while scooping handfuls of water over her back and saying, "The handmaid of God Anastasia is baptized, in the Name of the Father, and of the Son, and of the Holy Spirit." Angie took as her patron saint the martyr Anastasia, who was beheaded by the emperor Nero. She will be called by this name from now on in any liturgical setting; at Communion she will hear, "The handmaid of God, Anastasia, receives the Body and Blood of Christ." Paul and Lucy's patron saints are St. Paul and St. Lucia,

Tom chose St. Thomas the Apostle, and Miriam's choice of a patron saint was obvious, for Miriam is the Hebrew name of Jesus' mother.

Angie steps out of the font onto a thick layer of towels, where Gena is ready with a towel to wrap around her. Little Lucy, five years old, steps into the font after her mother, but, feeling nervous, tries to dunk her head faster than Fr. John can do so. When she steps out and into another waiting towel, Fr. John hitches back his phelonion over his shoulders and picks up Paul, who is two years old. Leaning over the font he quickly glides the child through the water three times in a sweeping gesture. Paul is too surprised to cry, but as soon as he's back on his feet and swaddled in a towel he lodges a noisy objection.

Tom grins as he watches his family pass through the baptismal waters, one at a time, and come together again in the household of God. A year ago he couldn't be sure it would ever happen. It wasn't that Angie objected to Orthodoxy—she just didn't get it. She didn't find it attractive in any way. But with time, as she attended services with him, it gradually grew more tolerable, and she eventually felt that any real objections she'd had had been resolved. She's still not enthusiastic, but she came to believe that Tom's fervor had some real and reliable basis. Though she doesn't yet see it herself, she decided to trust his discernment.

Last of all Miriam steps into the font. She kneels, looking very serious, and lets Fr. John dip her forward three times. When she steps out of the font, Despina is ready to wrap her in a white towel and give her a firm hug.

At many churches, the priest now sends the just-baptized to dry off and get dressed; until they return, the choir keeps singing, "Grant to me a shining robe of light, You who clothe yourself with light, O Christ, our most merciful God." But Fr. John prefers to go ahead and complete the chrismation now rather than pause the service, since there isn't much more to go.

The "shining robe of light" the newly baptized will put on is by ancient tradition a white gown. We've all seen lacy white christening gowns for babies, but it's not immediately obvious what the equivalent would be for a fifty-year-old. A parishioner designed a simple white T-shaped garment with a red cross front and back, and made a number of them in various sizes. Two for Angie and Miriam, and two smaller gowns for Lucy and Paul, are folded and resting on the table beside the font. Fr. John now lays a hand on each one, saying, "The servant of God is clothed in the garment of righteousness, in the name of the Father, and of the Son, and of the Holy Spirit."

All the chrismands come up to the iconostasis, where the adults will now receive absolution, the forgiveness of their sins. In the last couple of days Tom, Angie, Miriam, and Dylan have all made their first confession, a "life confession," in which they confessed all the sins of their entire lives, at least all they can remember.

A life confession sounds pretty daunting. But for this as for any subsequent confessions, you don't have to go into the details; it's enough to "file by title" most items. Don't spend your time justifying your actions, or explaining why it was someone else's fault. Confess your own sins, nobody else's.

If there are sins you have forgotten, they're covered. But if there are sins you remember but don't want to talk about, you *need* to talk about them, for your soul's healing. Paradoxically, the sins that cause us shame are the ones that, when confessed, have most transformative power. Almost like a chemical reaction, shame converts into strength to defeat future temptation.

The four adults kneel on the solea, and Fr. John places the end of his stole over each head and prays:

> May God who forgave David through Nathan the Prophet, and the Prodigal Son, and the weeping woman who knelt at his feet, may that same God forgive you all things, through me a sinner, both now and in the world to come, and place you before his Judgment Seat free from all condemnation.

When they stand again it is time for the chrismation itself. The oil, or chrism, used is made and set apart for this purpose alone; Fr. John's bishop provides it, sending more whenever he runs low.

It's handmade by the highest-ranking hierarchs in the world, in an astonishing ceremony that runs for several days. Virgin olive oil is heated in large cauldrons and combined with forty or more fragrant spices and substances, while the Gospels are continuously read aloud. Oil that has been infused with fragrant or medicinal herbs is known as *myron* (pronounced "meer-on"); before Jesus' crucifixion, a woman poured an alabaster flask of "very expensive *myron*" on his head (Matt. 26:7). Chrismation oil is called Holy Myron; you can see the similarity to "myrrh."

The custom began with God's command that Moses make "holy anointing oil" to consecrate the temple implements and priests:

> Take the finest spices: of liquid myrrh five hundred shekels, and of sweet-smelling cinnamon half as much, that is, two hundred and fifty, and of aromatic cane two hundred and fifty, and of cassia five hundred, according to the shekel of the sanctuary, and of olive oil a hin; and you shall make of these a sacred anointing oil blended as by the perfumer; a holy anointing oil it shall be. (Exod. 30:23–25)

In the book of Acts we see that it was the apostles who laid hands on new believers and prayed: "They sent to [the new believers in Samaria] Peter and John. . . . Then they laid hands on them and they received the Holy Spirit" (Acts 8:14, 17). But as the church grew, it was no longer feasible for apostles to visit each new community. Holy Myron developed as a substitute, for apostles could prepare it and then send it in their stead. When new Holy Myron is prepared, some of the old is always mixed in, inviting us to suppose that it is mingled with the original myron prepared by the apostles.

Thinking of the original apostles laying hands on new believers reminds me of "apostolic succession," an important concept in some Western churches. These churches claim an uninterrupted lineage of ordination by the literal laying-on-of-hands (that's why it's called "manual" succession), from the original apostles down to those who serve the Church today.

For some reason this is not a concept that arises much in the Orthodox Church, perhaps because they've had less need historically to assert their authenticity in comparison with other churches. If they thought about it, they'd say that manual succession is a feature of the Orthodox Church as well; but for them the claim of being apostolic more often refers to their holding unchanged the same faith that the apostles preached, "the faith which was once for all delivered to the saints" (Jude 3).

Though the making of Holy Myron takes days, the anointing goes swiftly. The six candidates for chrismation line up facing the iconostasis, with their sponsors standing behind them, holding their candles. Fr. John, on the solea, goes down the line, anointing each person many times, tracing tiny crosses on the forehead, both eyelids, both ears, both nostrils, chest and back, both hands, both feet. With each anointing he proclaims, "The seal of the gift of the Holy Spirit!" and the congregation shouts in reply, "Seal!"

Now sprinkling each of them with holy water, Fr. John says, "You are justified. You are illumined. You are sanctified. You are washed." He then revisits each spot he just anointed and wipes it with a piece of natural sponge, saying, "You are baptized. You are illumined. You have received anointing with Holy Chrism. You are sanctified. You are washed."

Fr. John then prays for the newly chrismated:

> Let your blessing descend upon the heads of your servants. As you blessed David the King by the hand of Samuel the prophet, now bless the head of your servant by the hand of me, a sinner . . . so that as he grows in stature and comes even to ripe old age, he may always glorify you, and see the good things of Jerusalem all the days of his life.

The godparents have brought a cross for each chrismand and now step forward and fasten them around their necks. Traditionally, Orthodox should wear their crosses every day. (These might be unseen, pinned inside the clothing or worn on an inner chain.)

Finally, Fr. John takes a small pair of scissors and cuts little nips of hair from the head of each; this tonsure represents their first self-offering to the Lord. Then the whole group returns to the font and makes a procession around it three times with hands linked, Fr. John leading the way and swinging the censer. As they do, the congregation sings Galatians 3:27, "As many as have been baptized into Christ have put on Christ, Alleluia!"

Now the newly baptized depart to remove wet garments and put on their "robes of light." They and the other newly illumined find places among the congregation, and Fr. John returns to the altar. He intones, "Blessed is the Kingdom, of the Father, and of the Son, and of the Holy Spirit," the signal that the Divine Liturgy is beginning. The service is a bit different today; in Great Lent, we use the Divine Liturgy of St. Basil instead of the usual one by St. John Chrysostom. (They're almost identical, except for some longer Communion prayers in St. Basil's version.)

More notable today, though, is that this is the one liturgy of all the year that we will sing the hymn "Let All Mortal Flesh Keep Silence," in place of the Cherubic Hymn. This is a sober hymn of great awe, and has found its way into some Western hymnals.

All week we have been tracking through the Passion story, but on this Saturday morning we come to a gap in the record. Christ has died, he has been buried, but he has not yet risen, and this in-between time was witnessed by no one on earth. The Scriptures give little detail: St. Peter says that Christ went "in the spirit . . . and preached to the spirits in prison, who formerly did not obey" (1 Pet. 3:18–20), and St. Paul says that Christ "descended into the lower parts of the earth" (Eph. 4:9), a reference to Sheol or Hades. Our Holy Saturday service therefore commemorates a mysterious, unseen event. Christ has gone beyond this earthly existence; he has gone into the realm of Death, and now that dark kingdom is breaking into pieces.

We can't comprehend what that was like, but we know what it means for us. Caitlin stands on the bema and chants today's Epistle reading from the silver-bound Apostolos (Epistle) book:

> We who have been baptized into Christ Jesus were baptized into his death. We were buried therefore with him by baptism into death, so that as Christ was raised from the dead by the glory of the Father, we too might walk in newness of life. . . . For we know that Christ being raised from the dead will never die again; death no longer has dominion over him. . . . So you must consider yourselves dead to sin and alive to God in Christ Jesus our Lord. (Rom. 6:3–11)

After the Epistle reading we expect to hear the threefold "Alleluia" that usually precedes the Gospel reading. But this time we hear instead Fr. John's voice ringing out from behind the altar: "Arise, O God, judge the earth, for to you belong all the nations!" And then a cluster of bay leaves and rose petals bursts into the air. Fr. John walks around the altar throwing leaves and petals as high as he can, while the choir sings Psalm 80/81. Between the verses we all join in the chorus: "Arise, O God, judge the earth, for to you belong all the nations!"

> God has taken his place in the divine council;
> In the midst of the gods he holds judgment:
> "How long will you judge unjustly
> And show partiality to the wicked?
> Give justice to the weak and fatherless;
> Maintain the right of the afflicted and the destitute.
> Rescue the weak and the needy;
> Deliver them from the hand of the wicked."
> They have neither knowledge nor understanding,
> They walk about in darkness;
> All the foundations of the earth are shaken.

I said, "You are gods,
Sons of the Most High, all of you;
Nevertheless, you shall die like men,
And fall like any prince."
Arise, O God, judge the earth,
For to you belong all the nations!

As this hymn is sung Fr. John leaves the altar and walks through the congregation, tossing leaves and petals high; they flutter down on sleeves and shoulders, on children's heads, some landing in the font. After the great mystery of Holy Week, after Christ's mocking and crucifixion, after last night's solemn burial, in the silence of Saturday morning there suddenly comes the advance message: we are free. The poor, weak, and needy of the psalm turn out to be *us*, all of us, the entire human race. We were captured by sin and death, and imprisoned in darkness; but the Lord has broken into the lair of the evil one and overthrown the power of those false "gods." Though we won't see Pascha for another twelve hours, the dark regime is already beginning to fracture, and beams of light are breaking it in pieces.

Fr. John makes a big circle around the room, and petals and leaves rain down, littering every surface. Children stoop down to sweep them into piles, though, strictly speaking, you're supposed to leave them where they lay; they will continue to release their fragrance as they're trampled on in the coming week, Bright Week. Among the newly chrismated only Tom has attended a Holy Saturday service before, and the rest are openly amazed.

For Miriam, the rest of the morning passes like a dream. The newly chrismated go up first for Communion, and she receives it on a spoon, like a baby, with a napkin held under her chin. She knew it would be given this way, but is surprised at how much she feels like a baby at that moment, a baby who is tenderly cared for and safe.

22

"A Great Mystery"

(EPH. 5:31)

Marriage and Remarriage, Betrothal, Crowning,
Marriage in Heaven?, The Best Wine

June 1—Sunday Before Ascension

At 3:00 PM on this Sunday afternoon most of the congregation is back in church for the wedding of Hank, the choir director, and his bride Sophronia. She is also a choir director, and they met at a church music conference last summer. Hank is standing at the back of the church with Fr. John, waiting for Sophronia to arrive, while the choir goes through a collection of festive pieces to fill the time. Hank asked Ann, a member of St. Felicity's choir, to fill in as choir director for this service.

This is a first marriage for Hank, but for Sophronia it comes after a miserable prior marriage that ended in divorce. The Orthodox Church does not automatically permit marriage after divorce. The priest will explore the reasons the previous marriage failed, and if he is convinced this new marriage has more hopeful prospects, he will present the case to the bishop. With the bishop's permission, the wedding can proceed.

An Orthodox wedding service is different in many ways from the ones we're used to. For one thing, there are no vows; in fact, the bride and groom speak no lines to each other at all. The Holy Mystery of matrimony focuses instead on the Lord's action, as he forges a union between the man and woman in the presence of the community.

The wedding service has two parts, which at one time were held on separate occasions. The first is the betrothal, in which the bride and groom exchange rings and are publicly declared to be set apart for each other. The service is, essentially, an official recognition and blessing of their engagement. In ancient times a betrothal was just as binding as a wedding, and breaking an engagement entailed a divorce. Different customs prevail today, so the betrothal ceremony has been moved to a position immediately prior to the wedding ceremony itself, called the crowning.

When Sophronia arrives, tall and statuesque in a simple off-white gown, Fr. John signals to the choir that they are ready to begin, and Ann winds down the last hymn. Hank and Sophronia now stand facing Fr. John at the back of the nave, just inside the narthex doors. Esther and George are standing beside them, as their sponsors. The role of the sponsors in an Orthodox wedding is akin to that of godparents at a baptism: they will pray for the couple and give help and guidance.*

Fr. John begins by asking Hank a question (though not all Orthodox churches include this brief exchange). He asks, "Do you, Henry Romanos, have a good, free, and unconstrained will and a firm intention to take as your wife this woman, Sophronia, whom you see before you?"

"I have, Reverend Father," Hank replies. (St. Romanos, the sixth-century hymnographer, is his patron saint. Sophronia's patron is St. Sophronius of Jerusalem, d. AD 638.)

"Have you promised yourself to any other woman?"

"I have not promised myself, Reverend Father."

Fr. John then asks the same of Sophronia, and receives the same replies (the only time in the service that the bride and groom have lines to speak). The first step today is to make sure that these are the right two people, and that neither one is there unwillingly. It

---

* The Orthodox wedding service doesn't call for bridesmaids and groomsmen, but they can usually be added if the couple desires.

makes you wonder what interesting stories in the distant past caused someone to say, "You know, we really ought to just *ask*, before we do anything else."

Now the betrothal service begins. "Blessed is our God, always, now and ever and unto ages of ages," says Fr. John, the usual opening acclamation of an Orthodox service. Dn. Andrew, standing beside him, turns to face the iconostasis. He lifts his orarion and chants, "In peace let us pray to the Lord," and the people sing, "Lord, have mercy." The Great Ektenia (litany) at a wedding includes additional petitions that the Lord "will send down upon them perfect and peaceful love," that he "will bless them with a blameless life," and that he "will give them an honorable marriage."

At the conclusion of the ektenia Fr. John prays, "O eternal God, who has united those who were separated, and has ordained for them an indissoluble bond of love, who blessed Isaac and Rebecca and made them heirs of your promise, bless these your servants, Henry Romanos and Sophronia, guiding them into every good work." Calling for the congregation to bow their heads, he prays, "O Lord our God, who betrothed the Church as a virgin from among the Gentiles, bless this betrothal and unite your servants in peace and oneness of mind."

Next comes the exchange of rings, and an Orthodox wedding is always a double-ring ceremony. The ancient custom is to wear the ring on the third finger of the right hand, but some Orthodox follow Western practice and wear it on the left hand instead.

Taking Sophronia's wedding ring, Fr. John touches it to Hank's forehead, then to Sophronia's forehead, and then makes the sign of the cross over Hank. He repeats this action three times while saying, "The servant of God Henry Romanos is betrothed to the handmaid of God Sophronia, in the name of the Father, and of the Son, and of the Holy Spirit." He concludes by placing the ring on Hank's ring finger.

Fr. John repeats the process, touching Sophronia's forehead, then Hank's, with the remaining ring, and ends by placing it on her ring finger. He then has Hank and Sophronia exchange rings, sealing their betrothal.

Fr. John prays:

O Lord our God, bless the betrothal of your servants Henry
Romanos and Sophronia, and confirm the word they have spoken. Establish them in the holy union which you ordained. You
made the human race male and female from the beginning, and
created the woman to be partner and helpmate to the man.
Therefore, O Lord our God . . . look now upon your servant
Henry Romanos and your handmaid Sophronia, and establish
their betrothal in faith, in unity of mind, in truth, and love. . . .
Bless this putting-on of rings with your heavenly blessing, and
let your Angel go before them all the days of their life.

The betrothal now concluded, Hank and Sophronia are given lit
candles. (Esther takes charge of Sophronia's bouquet.) Fr. John leads
the bridal party to the front of the church, where there has been prepared a small table bearing the Gospel book, the Georgian hand cross
of carved wood, and a diminutive silver goblet filled with blessed
sweet wine, the "Common Cup" that the couple will later share.

Most notable, however, are the wedding crowns, two wreaths of
artificial ivy sprinkled with white rosebuds. A long white ribbon joins
the two crowns in the back.

As the wedding party processes through the nave to stand before
this table, the choir launches into Psalm 127/128. But the voices aren't
blending right, so Ann signals them to stop. She consults her tuning
fork again, and repeats the "La, la, la" clearly. Everyone knows what
a perfectionist Hank is, and they want to make his special day right.

The choir sings:

> Blessed is the one who fears the Lord, who walks in his ways.
> You shall eat the fruit of the labor of your hands.
> You shall be happy, and it shall be well with you.
> Your wife shall be like a fruitful vine within your house,
> Your children like olive shoots around your table.

Thus shall the man be blessed who fears the Lord!
The Lord bless you from Zion;
May you see the prosperity of Jerusalem all the days of your life;
May you see your children's children.
Peace be upon Israel!

The procession gathers in front of the table, Hank and Sophronia in front, and George and Esther behind them. Fr. John proclaims, "Blessed is the Kingdom of the Father and of the Son and of the Holy Spirit, now and ever and unto ages of ages," marking the start of the crowning ceremony.

Dn. Andrew then leads another litany, asking that the Lord will "bless this marriage as he blessed the wedding in Cana of Galilee" and that he will "give them joy at the sight of sons and daughters." This petition is retained even when the couple appears to be beyond the age of childbearing, acknowledging God's right to have the final word in such matters, given the examples of the foremothers Sarah, Hannah, and Jesus' grandmother, Anna.

Fr. John prays that the Lord will bless them as he blessed Abraham and Sarah, Isaac and Rebecca, Joachim and Anna, Zachariah and Elizabeth. Then, in the First Prayer of Marriage, he prays,

> Preserve them, O Lord, as you preserved Noah in the Ark. Preserve them, O Lord our God, as you preserved the three holy young men from the fire. Let them know the joy that St. Helena had when she found the precious Cross. Remember them, O Lord our God, as you remembered the Forty Holy Martyrs, sending down to them crowns from heaven.

Noah, three young men, Helena, and Forty Martyrs? It sounds like a pretty random collection. But Noah and the young men are there because we are asking God to protect this couple, as Noah was preserved from flood, and the young men were protected from fire. (Those three men were the companions of Daniel who refused to worship the golden statue of King Nebuchadnezzar and were thrown into a furnace to be burned alive, but walked in the fire unharmed.)

We also pray that the couple will know joy, remembering St. Helena who directed an archaeological dig that turned up the cross of Christ's crucifixion. The cross was immediately put to the test, and its power was proved when it was touched to the body of a dead man and he returned to life. Helena's joy at that moment must have been beyond all bounds, and we ask the same for this couple.

The Forty Martyrs of Sebaste were arrested as Christians in AD 320, and condemned to death by freezing: they were herded naked onto a frozen lake one bitterly cold night, and expected to succumb by dawn. One of them found it too much to bear, and took refuge in a warm bathhouse that had been temptingly set up on the shore. But one of the guards saw a heavenly light surrounding the martyrs, and crowns descending from heaven to rest on their heads. He immediately took the place of the prisoner who had lost heart, and so the number of their company remained intact. Like the Forty Martyrs, Hank and Sophronia are about to receive their crowns. Crowns have multiple meanings, which we'll explore in a moment.

Fr. John next prays for the couple's parents (because "the prayers of parents make firm the foundation of houses") and for their sponsors, George and Esther. He asks that the Lord will give Hank and Sophronia "fair children and concord of soul and body; raise them up like the cedars of Lebanon, like a flourishing vine. . . . Let them see their children's children around their table, like a newly planted olive grove, and, possessing your favor, may they shine like the stars of heaven, in you, our Lord and God."

Then, in the Second Prayer of Marriage, Fr. John joins Hank's and Sophronia's right hands, with their matching wedding rings. He lays his hand upon theirs and prays, "Extend your hand from your holy dwelling place and join this your servant Henry Romanos, and this your handmaid Sophronia. . . . Unite them in one mind and one flesh."

Taking up the larger of the two leafy crowns, Fr. John touches it to Hank's forehead and then to Sophronia's forehead, and makes the sign of the cross over Hank. As with the wedding rings he does this three times, repeating, "The servant of God Henry Romanos is crowned unto the handmaid of God Sophronia, in the name of the Father, and of the Son, and of the Holy Spirit." Fr. John places the crown on Hank's head, then takes the remaining crown and repeats the process, touching it first to Sophronia's forehead and then Hank's, and finally placing it upon Sophronia's. Then he lifts both crowns and exchanges them from one head to the other three times, chanting, "O Lord, crown them with glory and with honor." When the crowns are finally settled on the right heads, George and Esther reach up and straighten out the long white ribbon that connects the crowns in back.

This act of crowning is the effective moment of the wedding service; now Hank and Sophronia are husband and wife. The crowns have a double meaning. A new family has been formed, a small kingdom that husband and wife together will rule. But this man and woman are also called to win the crowns of martyrdom, as they die to self daily in service to each other.

Why would martyrs have crowns? St. Paul several times speaks of a Christian being like an athlete, who practices self-discipline for the sake of winning a race or a contest. "Every athlete exercises self-control in all things," he wrote. "They do it to receive a perishable wreath, but we an imperishable" (1 Cor. 9:25). In those ancient contests the winner was crowned with a laurel wreath. (We still speak of "winning your laurels.") As victorious athletes, martyrs have won their crowns.

A marriage is forever. Husbands and wives are separated by death, but only temporarily. Christ taught that no new weddings would occur in heaven—no one will "marry nor [be] given in marriage" since there is no reason to establish new families. When the fiancé of St. Macrina (AD 330–379) died, she refused to take another, believing that he was waiting for her. "It is a sin and a shame if a spouse does not keep faith when the partner goes to distant lands," she said.[94]

St. John Chrysostom (AD 347–407) wrote to a young widow that, if she wished to see her husband again face-to-face ("for this I know is what you especially long for") she should live a life of faith like his. "You will depart one day to join the same company with him, not to dwell with him for five years as you did here, or for twenty or a hundred, or for a thousand years, or twice that number, but for infinite and countless ages." There she will experience a union even more profound than that of earthly marriage, "a union of soul with soul." She will see her beloved "no longer in that corporeal beauty which he had when he departed, but in a luster of another kind, and splendor outshining the rays of the sun."[95]

The purpose of this eternal union is not romantic sentimentality, or simple tidiness—getting everybody lined up two by two, as on the ark. The purpose is not procreation, either; procreation is fine, but hardly needs to be promoted. Bride and groom often come up with the idea all by themselves.

The true purpose of marriage is that these two people support each other on the path to the kingdom. Knowing each other well, knowing their faults and struggles, they can make up, in humility, what is missing, and see in each other the strengths they lack. Accountability shores up resolve. Unity is a bulwark. "And though a man might prevail against one who is alone, two will withstand him. A threefold cord is not quickly broken" (Eccles. 4:12).

In this regard, husband and wife are like two missionaries or monastics who work together on a common cause, and forge a lifelong bond. We can picture such pairs of saints in heaven—the physicians Saints Zenaida and Philonella, the "roving journalists" Saints Sophronius and John Moschus, even Saints Mary and Martha of the Bible—and see how the love they had for each other on earth would only deepen in heaven, and would in no way limit their love for others. In some way, a deep commitment to another person enables *more* love for others; you have twice the resources to draw on, twice the strength, insight, and compassion.†

Perhaps our view of marriage has become too focused on romance, too insistent on the couple alone in a bubble, face-to-face and giddy. As sweet as that is, marriage should always include this component

---

† By the way, if you see the abbreviation "Ss." or "Sts." before some names, it means "Saints."

of growth, increasing in maturity and love for others. The common center of their love gives each partner greater stores of stability, humility, security, and generosity, and flows out from there to the world.

When spouses are praying for each other, encouraging each other, they spur their mates to greater heights. "Let the husband hear of these things [the ways of virtue] from the wife, and the wife from the husband," said St. John Chrysostom. "Let there be a kind of rivalry among all, in endeavoring to gain precedence."[96]

The Scripture readings follow the crowning, preceded as usual by a prokeimenon: the choir sings, "You have set upon their heads, O Lord, crowns of precious stones; they asked life of you, and you gave it to them" (Ps. 20:4–5/Ps.21:3–4), originally written about an earthly king but now pluralized for the husband and wife).

During this hymn Hank's college roommate, Jack, steps forward to read the Epistle. The Scripture readings for a wedding never vary. The epistle is always Ephesians 5:19–33: "Be subject to one another. . . . Wives, be subject to your husbands, as to the Lord. . . . Husbands, love your wives, as Christ loved the church and gave himself up for her."

In many denominations this passage has been quietly shelved, because of that reference to wifely submission. It sounds outrageous these days, and is assumed to be a short hop to wife beating. But such an interpretation doesn't grasp what St. Paul actually says. He begins by saying that both husband and wife should be subject to each other. He ends by saying that the husband must love his wife as Christ loved the church—that is, must be ready to endure torture, humiliation, and death for her, and honor her life above his own. We may take it for granted that a man should die to protect his wife and not the reverse, but it still isn't an ordinary love.

St. Paul concludes the passage with a somewhat cryptic observation that the Scripture which says "the two shall become one flesh"

(Gen. 2:24) actually "refers to Christ and the church." It's shocking, if you think about it; St. Paul is saying that, not just some spiritual or romantic element, but the fleshly aspect of marital union is related to the union of Christ and the Church. "The mystery is a profound one," he says, and does not elaborate further.

In a Christian marriage, sex has some deep and mysterious meaning. St. John Chrysostom explored this in one of his sermons, apparently turning faces red in the congregation. He refers to their discomfort: "You call my words immodest, because I speak of the nature of marriage, which is honorable. . . . By calling my words immodest you condemn God, who is the author of marriage."[97]

He finds one aspect of this mystery in procreation, since two who become one can produce a third, a new person who is made in the image of God. "Not a lifeless image or the image of anything on earth, but of God himself, and after his likeness." The woman receives from the man "the richest part, fused by pleasure, nourishes and cherishes it within and, contributing her own portion, returns it as a child." Alone, we are incomplete, he says. The fact that Eve was made from Adam's side shows that man and woman are "two halves" of a single person; "husband and wife are not two persons, but one."

But, Chrysostom imagines someone asking, what if they do not conceive a child? "Will they not then remain two? No, for their coming together has this effect: it diffuses and commingles their bodies, as [a perfumer] who blends a fragrance into oil has made the whole one."

The Gospel reading is the story of the wedding at Cana (John 2:1–11), at which Christ turned six stone jars of water, each 20–30 gallons, into first-class wine, an oversupply so extravagant that it seems an illustration of St. Paul's saying that God can do "abundantly far more than all we can ask or imagine" (Eph. 3:20, NRSV). Dn. Andrew reads the passage from the Gospel book, and then Fr. John gestures for those who can find chairs to sit down. No chairs for Hank and Sophronia, though, who continue to stand facing him. Fr. John addresses them in his sermon, though he knows from experience that bride and groom often fail to absorb a single word. So he keeps it brief.

Sometimes Fr. John speaks about the point in the story when Mary tells the servants, "Do whatever he tells you." This is what Mary says to each of us—do what the Lord tells you—and being attentive and prayerful is good advice especially for young people beginning a dramatically different kind of life. For Hank and Sophronia, in their late thirties, Fr. John talks instead about the reaction of the steward of the feast to the excellent wine: usually a host pours expensive wine at first, the steward says, and saves the cheaper stuff for when the guests have become less discerning, "but you have kept the good wine until now." For some of us, Fr. John says, God saves the best for last.

After a brief ektenia and the Lord's Prayer, Fr. John gives Hank and Sophronia a drink from the Common Cup, the small chalice of blessed sweet wine. This is not the consecrated wine of Holy Communion, but rather a sharing that represents how they will from now on drink the cup of life together, both its joys and sorrows. Fr. John lifts the cup to Hank three times and then to Sophronia three times, as the choir sings, "I will take the cup of salvation, and call upon the name of the Lord" (Ps. 115/116:13).

Now comes the most memorable moment in an Orthodox wedding, the "Dance of Isaiah." Fr. John joins Hank's hand with Sophronia's and wraps the end of his stole around both; then he leads them around the table three times, as the choir sings:

> O Isaiah, dance with joy! The Virgin is with child and will bear a son, Emmanuel; he is both God and man, and Orient is his name. As we magnify him, we call the Virgin blessed.
>
> O Holy Martyrs, who fought the good fight and have received your crowns: pray to the Lord that he will have mercy on our souls.
>
> Glory to You, O Christ God, the boast of the apostles, the joy of the martyrs! Their preaching witnessed to the consubstantial Trinity.‡

---

‡ The "Dance of Isaiah" is also sung at an ordination, but in that case the newly ordained is led three times around the altar.

Last of all, Fr. John concludes the wedding service with the Removal of the Crowns. He lifts the crown from Hank's head and then holds it out to him to kiss, while chanting, "Be exalted, O bridegroom, like Abraham; and be blessed, like Isaac; and multiply like Jacob, walking in peace, and keeping the commandments of God in righteousness."

Next he removes Sophronia's crown, and likewise holds it for her to kiss, while chanting: "And you, O bride, be exalted like Sarah; and exult like Rebecca; and multiply like Rachel, and rejoice in your husband, fulfilling the conditions of the law, for so it is well-pleasing to God."

He holds both crowns high, and prays:

> O Christ our God, who came to the wedding feast at Cana of Galilee and blessed it, bless these your servants, who are now united in marriage through your providence. Bless their going out and their coming in, and fill their life with good things.

Placing the crowns upon the table, he continues: "Receive their crowns into your Kingdom, preserving them spotless, blameless, and without reproach, unto ages of ages."

For the final blessing Fr. John extends his hand over the bridal pair and prays for "length of days, fair children, prosperity of life, and faith." Last of all, Hank and Sophronia kiss the cross in Fr. John's hand, then turn to face the congregation, while everyone sings, "God grant you many years." Hank begins to relax for the first time in months.

23

"Built His House upon a Rock"
(MATT. 7:24)

House Blessing, Icon Corner, Spontaneous vs. Written Prayers, Meal Blessing

Monday, July 7

n this Sunday evening a couple who are new members of St. Felicity, Paphnutius and Becky, have invited Fr. John and Presbytera Beth for dinner; they also asked Fr. John to bless their new home. As we noted earlier, an Orthodox pastor blesses all the homes in his parish in the weeks after Theophany, but when someone moves into a new home, there is a longer and more complete blessing service. So when Fr. John gets his keys he also grabs his house-blessing kit, a briefcase fitted with pockets and straps to contain the bottles, candles, and other items necessary for this rite.

Paphnutius (he used to be called "Paul") joined the Orthodox Church in college, and hasn't stopped telling people about it ever since, no matter how politely annoyed they become. (Becky was raised in the church.) When you meet someone with an unfamiliar saint-name (Thecla, Euphemia, Barsanuphius) followed by a white-bread American surname, you have probably found an enthusiastic convert, and that's the case with Paphnutius.

When Becky opens the door, Paphnutius comes toward Fr. John with his hands held low, cupped and open. Fr. John makes the sign of the cross over them, then rests his fingertips in Paphnutius's palm as he kisses the back of his hand. Becky does the same; she was taught how to go up and get a priest's blessing when she was two. Paphnutius, then Becky, exchange a "kiss of peace" with Presbytera Beth, a peck at each cheek.

Fr. John's eye is immediately caught by the couple's icon corner, and he and Presbytera Beth cross the room to look at it. Above a bookcase there is a sprawling circle of icons, and at the center a prominent pair. The one on the right is a large reproduction of the famous "Christ of Sinai" icon; the original is at the Monastery of St. Catherine on Mt. Sinai, where it has resided for almost fifteen hundred years.

To the left of the icon of Christ is a smaller, hand-painted icon of the Virgin Mary, and that is how icons are always arranged: Christ on the viewer's right, the Virgin on the left. The icon of the Virgin here is of the sort that is produced in Orthodox countries in large quantities for export. It's not quite the same as (and much less expensive than) a one-of-a-kind icon, but it's still strong and sweet.

Below these two there are icons of the couple's patron saints, Righteous Rebecca and St. Paphnutius of Thebes. The Righteous Rebecca icon has been Becky's since childhood. It's a photocopy of a rather simple image of that ancestor of Christ, laminated to a wooden panel.

Next to Foremother Rebecca (honorific terms for saints are somewhat fluid; she might also be called "St. Rebecca," "Just Rebecca," or "Holy Rebecca") is a large, resplendent icon of St. Paphnutius of Thebes, which was commissioned from the iconography studio of a famed Eastern European monastery. The brushwork is delicate and finely detailed; the saint's face is expressive, yet mysterious: kind, tender, wistful, even sorrowful, but with the faintest smile, like how a heartbroken person might look at a child. It takes all kinds of personalities to make a church, but some of the most interesting faces are like this. The background is a field of dazzling gold. Because the bottommost layer is a coat of white gesso, and the paint, made of egg yolks and ground minerals, is nearly translucent, light striking the icon reflects back through the layers, rendering it luminous.

St. Paphnutius of Thebes was mutilated for his faith by Emperor Maximinus in the early fourth century, but survived to see Christianity legalized by the newly converted Emperor Constantine in AD 313. (Saints like Paphnutius who were tortured, but not killed, for their faith are called "confessors" rather than "martyrs.") He went on to be an important voice at the first ecumenical council, speaking against a theological innovation that would deny Christ's deity. He also spoke persuasively against a proposal that would require priests to be celibate, defending marital love eloquently and successfully, though he himself was a celibate monk.

It is said that Paphnutius was among the tortured saints whom, at the opening of the council, Emperor Constantine venerated, reverently kissing the scars the emperors before him had inflicted. An ancient chronicle says that when St. Constantine came to St. Thomas of Marash, who had been systematically mutilated for twenty-two years (an eye one year, a finger the next), he broke down in tears.

The icon corner is rounded out by some other favorite saints, mostly paper prints and photocopies laminated onto wooden plaques: the youthful martyr St. Panteleimon, who had a gift of healing (d. 305), St. Xenia the Fool for Christ, a homeless widow of St. Petersburg (d. 1803), Abba Moses of Ethiopia, a Desert Father who was formerly the leader of a gang of robbers (d. 405), and a string of others: St. Mitrophan of Beijing (1856–1900), St. Peter the Aleut (d. 1815), and St. John of Shanghai and San Francisco (d. 1966; this popular saint is also called St. John the Wonderworker). A larger icon depicts St. Nino (d. 340), who left her home in Jerusalem at the age of fourteen to bring the gospel to the republic of Georgia. She bears the title "Equal to the Apostles," like St. Mary Magdalene and other evangelist saints.

St. Brigid of Kildare (d. 525) and St. Patrick (d. 460) are here, too; both Western and Eastern Churches honor the saints who lived before the Great Schism of the eleventh century. The faith came early to the British Isles. Tertullian, living in North Africa around AD 200, had heard that the Christian faith had spread even to "the haunts of the Britons," which are "inaccessible to the Romans, but subjugated to

Christ."[98] Just west of London a Roman villa was uncovered that contained a large mosaic image of Christ's face—the earliest depiction of
Christ yet found. The British Isles have an admirable Christian history, and Sts. Patrick and Brigid are only two of scores of indigenous
missionaries and saints.

On the fringes of the icon corner (it's still called that, even when
it isn't in a corner) there are a few images of people who are not yet
officially saints. There is a photo of Mother Alexandra (1909–1991),
whose life concluded in the monastery she founded near Pittsburgh,
but which she began as Princess Ileana of Romania. There is a simple
painting of a small Yupik Alaskan woman, Olga Michael (1916–1979),
a priest's wife whose good deeds have only increased since her repose.[99]

The process of glorification of a saint (in the West, canonization)
is more flexible—some might say less organized—in the Orthodox
Church than it is in other churches. The recognizing of a saint begins
with local veneration; if the people who knew you in your daily life,
who could encounter you at your grumpiest, thought you were a
saint, that's a good sign. If love for such a person continues to spread,
and reports start circulating of miraculous encounters and answers
to prayer, the Church may well declare that a new saint has been
revealed. (The Church doesn't *make* saints; it just recognizes them.
Many millions of saints are known only to God.) Mother Alexandra
and Matushka Olga have not yet had that honor, but those who love
them believe it's just a matter of time.

Last there is a photo of an icon of the Virgin holding the infant
Christ, with shiny streams, like tears of oil, running down from her eyes.
This is a photo of an icon on the iconostasis of St. George Orthodox
Church in the Cicero neighborhood of Chicago. At a Lenten evening
service in 1994, a visiting priest noticed glistening drops on the surface
of this icon. He figured holy water must have been spattered on it at
some service earlier in the day. But then, as he watched, a tear welled
up in the image's lower eyelid and rolled down the face.

In the following weeks, tens of thousands of people came to the
church to pray. The substance—not saline, like human tears, but a
kind of light oil—was gathered and used for anointing, and there were

miracles and healings. (Orthodox call this substance "myrrh"; in some cases, it is intensely fragrant.) Eventually the flow of tears ceased, but the tracks remain, shiny trails that stream down from the Theotokos's eyes, over her red robe and her son's upraised blessing hand.

Copies of this image have found their way into many icon corners, as you might expect. But it's not an isolated case; icons of the Virgin Mary and other saints have streamed myrrh in a number of US states, and around the world. Sometimes it appears, not as a stream of tears, but as an oil that oozes up over the entire surface of the icon. The oil is sometimes very fragrant, and the fragrances differ from one saint to the next.

This icon corner is where Becky and Paphnutius stand and pray together at the end of the day. The top of the bookcase is crowded with books they use during their prayers: a binder of printed-out hymns, a couple of Bible translations, some favorite akathists, and a volume of the lives of the saints. There are a few prayer books, and a small red one looks especially well-used.

Some Christians might think that rather a shame; isn't it restrictive and dry to use written prayers? Why not pray spontaneously?

Of course, people who use a prayer book also pray spontaneously; St. Paul exhorts us to "pray constantly" (1 Thess. 5:17), so most of the day should be taken up with simply worded, or wordless, prayer. Written prayers support that continuous flow of prayer, like a steel frame supports a building.

Actually, when I decided to adopt the habit of stopping for prayer at the traditional times of the day, it turned out to be the single most effective thing I ever did to improve my prayer life. It was effective even though I usually didn't find those prayer times particularly moving. I offered those prayers in a dutiful way, by rote repetition, simply because the time for prayer had rolled around again. The beneficial effect came from the fact that I had to make a stop in the headlong flow of the day, and turn to face the Lord. These interruptions reminded me that God is always present; even when I forgot all about him, he was still here. Sometimes I would check the clock and find it was not yet time to pray, but that moment of checking turned my memory again to God, itself a fleeting prayer.

At first these moments of remembering him were accompanied by a shocked realization of how far from him my mind had strayed over the intervening hours. But that sense of shock gradually lessened, as habitual remembrance of God grew. In time there was no shock at all. Now when I notice it's time to pray I turn toward him with no sense of changing gears; the quiet, all-the-time prayers simply coalesce into specific words. Far from substituting for spontaneous prayer, the discipline of repeating the prayers of the church at their appointed hours made my spontaneous flow of prayer more consistent and continuous.

The prayers of the Church also teach us. "We do not know how to pray as we ought" (Rom. 8:13), and written prayers shape our theology, and move us beyond the trudging list of requests we would generate on our own. Jesus' disciples did not rely on the prayers they themselves thought up, but asked, "Lord, teach us to pray." He did, and gave them the prayer that begins "Our Father" (Lk. 11:1). It's a prayer that we repeat the same way every time, yet it never grows stale.

The *Didache* (AD 80) says that believers should say the Our Father three times a day; that's the earliest example of a Christian "rule of prayer."[100] Of course believers were free to pray spontaneously, too, any time they wanted—preferably all the time, praying "without ceasing." But this nonspontaneous prayer, with its unchanging content, was to be a thrice-daily offering.

There's that aspect of things, too—the making of an offering. It's easy to pray when we're moved and grateful; when we don't have such feelings, but pray anyway, it's a sacrifice, a "sacrifice of praise" (Heb. 13:15). And God honors that; sometimes I think there is more value in our reluctant obedience than our easy cooperation. It's when we don't want to do something, but do it for his sake, that our wills begin to bend.

It's up to us whether what we offer is truly prayer or not. "Saying your prayers" is not the same thing as "praying." Repeating prayers mindlessly is insulting to God, and worthless for you. Elder Paisios (1924–1994) wrote, "Be careful not to squander your valuable strength on superfluous and vain cares, exhaust yourself physically and aimlessly dissipate your intellect and, then, give God your tiredness and yawns at the hour of prayer." That's like "the sacrifice of Cain," he says.[101]

Sometimes we see a custom Christians have continued for centuries, like this daily offering of prayer, and don't immediately understand what good it does. But we can take it up anyway, trusting in the wisdom of our older brothers and sisters in the faith. With time we may come to understand what they knew. A mother feeds her baby nutritious food, but the baby has no idea of that; he only knows that meals keep coming around, and satisfy the pangs of hunger. Yet gradually, imperceptibly, those foods are building him into a strong young man. We don't always understand *why* Christians have carried on a spiritual practice, year after year in cultures around the world. We may even try it and think, "I don't get this." If you stick with it, though, sometimes you might find out what it can do.

The books atop this bookcase fight for space among a host of other things. There is a flowerpot full of sand that serves as a candleholder; beside it are a stack of beeswax tapers and a plastic utility lighter. There's a wooden hand cross, a glass jar of holy water from the Theophany service last January, and a brass incense pot. Beside the censer there is a box of charcoal disks and a plastic bag of little incense pebbles, which nuns at the nearby convent made by rolling fragrant tree resin with essential oils. (What with oil, sand, charcoal, candles, and incense, an icon corner tends to get spattered and dusty.) There's a miniature wooden folding copy of St. Felicity's iconostasis, and a pysanky, an egg that a Ukrainian friend painted with an extremely fine and delicate pattern, a process that is soaked in prayer.

Where do you get all this stuff? Most Orthodox churches have a bookstore, in one form or another. It might be a whole room set aside for the purpose, or a bookcase in the parish hall, with an honor-system box for payments. These stores specialize in Orthodox books and icons, but might also carry prayer ropes, incense, candles, cross jewelry, and other items.

The custom of a church bookstore sprang up originally because these items were so hard to find, and books from the half-dozen Orthodox publishing houses seldom made it into mainstream bookstores. But since the advent of Internet shopping, these sometimes-obscure books and goods have become much more accessible. There's still something to be said, though, for going into a "bricks and mortar" church and talking to real people.

There are two little glass vials, one holding some water from the miraculous spring on Spruce Island, Alaska, home of the beloved missionary St. Herman (1756–1837), and one holding oil from the lampada that hangs above the tomb of St. John the Wonderworker in San Francisco. Both vials were given to them by friends who had made pilgrimages to those sites—a common sort of gift, among Orthodox. (They also give a lot of icons.)

Tucked behind the Christ of Sinai are a couple of palms from the Palm Sunday procession a couple of months ago. Hanging from a hook on the side of the bookcase is a prayer rope with a hundred knots; Paphnutius stands here every morning to pray, and uses it to keep track of repetitions of the Jesus Prayer. (Becky says the Jesus Prayer as she's going to sleep, so she keeps her prayer rope in the drawer of a bedside table. The Jesus Prayer is just right when you wake up in the night and start worrying.)

Among the books on the shelves below is the *Philokalia*, a collection of writings on prayer from dozens of authors, from the fourth through the fourteenth century. The set comprises five volumes (four in English, so far), and is likely too dense and challenging for newcomers to Eastern Christian spirituality. *The Way of a Pilgrim*, an anonymous nineteenth-century Russian narrative, is a more-accessible introduction to the Jesus Prayer.

In addition to the books there is the carved wooden seal Paphnutius and Becky use to imprint the loaves when it is their turn to bake the prosphora (Communion bread). And next to the bookcase a tall wooden plant stand bears, not a plant, but a bulky dictionary-sized volume called *The Great Horologion*; it provides the daily services of the Orthodox Church, along with the names and brief histories of the saints for every day of the year, with their appointed hymns.

Fr. John begins preparing for the house blessing. The apartment is small, so there isn't much ground to cover. He unpacks the kit: a Bible, a bottle of holy water with a sprinkler-top, a jar of olive oil, four glass vigil candles, a hand cross, and a small brass censer with a handle rather than chains. He arranges them all on a table near the icon corner, which Paphnutius has prepared with a white cloth and two candlesticks.

Before he can begin the rite, however, Fr. John has to establish how the home is situated, in terms of the directions of the compass. He goes first to the eastern wall and, in the center of it, marks the sign of the cross with his thumb. He places one of the vigil candles on the floor there. After doing the same at the south, west, and north walls, he calls everyone together in the living room, where they face the icon corner.

The service begins with all praying together the series of Trisagion prayers. Fr. John then asks Becky to read Psalm 90/91, "He who dwells in the secret place of the Most High," a psalm about God's protection. All then sing, to a simple chant melody, a troparion that recalls the time Jesus went to a tax collector's house for dinner.

> As your entrance brought salvation to the house of Zacchaeus,
>   O Christ,
> Now, by the entrance of your sacred ministers, accompanied by
>   your holy angels,
> Give peace to this house and bless it, by your mercy,
> Illumining and saving all who live here.

Fr. John offers prayers that recall houses that were blessed by God, not only that of Zacchaeus, but also Laban's house blessed by the presence of Jacob, Potiphar's by Joseph, and Abinadab's by the ark of the covenant. He prays over the vial of oil, that it will be filled with the grace of the Holy Spirit and expel "every contrary power and satanic snare." A first-time house blessing includes an exorcism.

Fr. John takes up the holy water bottle and asks Becky to go ahead of him, holding one of the candles. They walk through the apartment, followed by Presbytera Beth and Paphnutius, and Fr. John sprinkles holy water on every wall, and also on the computer and the television. He chants continuously, "In the name of the Father, and of the Son, and of the Holy Spirit, by the sprinkling of this holy water, may every evil and demonic action be put to flight." Everyone repeats, "Amen."

Next, he takes the vial of blessed oil and they repeat the procession. He marks a cross in oil at each place where he traced one earlier, praying each time, "This house is blessed through the anointing with holy oil, in the name of the Father, and of the Son, and of the Holy Spirit." Everyone says, "Amen."

After another hymn, Fr. John reads Luke 19:1–10, which tells how Zacchaeus climbed into a sycamore tree to get a look at Jesus passing by. But Jesus stopped under the tree and looked up at him, which must have been an awkward moment for Zacchaeus. Jesus said, "Zacchaeus, make haste and come down; for I must stay at your house today."

Now it is time for the censing. Once again they make a procession through the entire apartment, this time with Fr. John leading the way, making the sign of the cross with the censer. As he follows, Paphnutius keeps continuously reading Psalm 100/101, which promises, "I will walk within my house with a perfect heart."

The four gather again in the living room for a few more prayers, then Fr. John pronounces a blessing on Paphnutius and Becky. While he sprinkles them with holy water, he and Presbytera Beth sing, "God grant you many years!"

The rite is finished, and as they stand around the dining table, Becky asks Fr. John to say the blessing. All turn to face a nearby icon of Christ. (When Orthodox hear "Let us pray," they stand up and look around for an icon.) They pray the Lord's Prayer, halting after "deliver us from evil." Fr. John then prays the conclusion, as the Orthodox render it: "For thine is the Kingdom, and the Power, and the Glory, of the Father and of the Son and of the Holy Spirit, both now and ever, and unto ages of ages." Everyone supplies the "Amen."

Then Paphnutius, Becky, and Beth say together, "Lord, have mercy. Lord, have mercy. Lord, have mercy. Father, bless." Fr. John makes the sign of the cross over the table while pronouncing the blessing that many Orthodox offer over every meal: "O Christ our God, bless the food and drink of your servants, multiplying it throughout the world in the houses of the poor, for you are blessed, now and ever and unto ages of ages. Amen."

When the prayer is finished they sit down, and Becky and Paphnutius ask some practical questions about this new church, the town, and the community. When the meal is over, they'll all stand again and Fr. John will pray, "We thank you, Christ our God, for providing us with your earthly gifts; deprive us not of your heavenly Kingdom. But as you entered among your disciples to give them peace, enter among us, and give us your peace, and save us. Amen."

As Presbytera Beth helps Paphnutius and Becky in the kitchen, Fr. John has his own tidying up to do; the candles, jars, bottles, incense, and everything else has to go back in its case. The table Paphnutius had set up for him looks as cluttered as the icon corner. Orthodoxy may be classed as a form of "spirituality," but there's sure a lot of tangible stuff to clean up.

24

"Those Who Have Fallen Asleep"

(1 Cor. 15:20)

Preparing the Body, Feast of the Dormition, Feast of the Transfiguration, Mercy Meal, The Funeral

Monday, August 4—Dormition Fast

ather John has been expecting this phone call for a few days. Kate died at home, as expected, fairly peacefully. So he heads out to chant the Trisagion prayers for the departed at her bedside; this is a brief set of prayers very similar to the Memorial Service offered at the end of a Sunday liturgy.

Ariel, Kate's middle-aged daughter, opens the door. A quiet, reticent person, she doesn't appear affected by a death that has been so long expected. They move into Kate's small bedroom, and as Fr. John prepares his censer, he notes the little icon corner across from the bed, with a small but very expressive icon of St. Taisia, Kate's patron.

The story goes that St. Taisia inherited much money while still young, and generously aided the Desert Fathers near her, a community that included St. John the Dwarf (AD 339–405). When her money ran out, she was counseled by "wicked men" to profit from her beauty and become a courtesan. Hearing of this, St. John said to his brothers, "While she could, she gave us charity. Now it is our turn to go to her aid, and offer her charity."

St. John went to her house and told her servants to take him to their mistress, for he had something valuable to give her. He was led to her bedroom, where she lay awaiting her next client.

"What have you got against Jesus that you behave this way?" he asked.

At his words, Taisia froze. St. John began weeping.

"Abba," she asked, "is it possible to repent?"

"Yes," he said.

"Take me wherever you wish," she said. Then she got up and prepared to leave. St. John noticed she gave no instructions to the servants about her house or possessions, as if she had already abandoned her earthly life.

The pair walked into the desert, and night fell. St. John gathered a pile of sand to create a pillow for Taisia's head, and traced the sign of the cross in the mound. He then walked a distance away and lay down to sleep. Some hours later he awoke, and saw a beam of light shining from heaven upon Taisia's body. He hurried to her and found she had died.

St. John prostrated himself before the body of a woman whose repentance had been so profound that it called down God's light. As he prayed he heard these words: "One single hour of repentance has brought her more than the penitence of many who persevere without showing such fervor."[102]

As Ariel bends her head to pray, Fr. John begins chanting the Trisagion prayers for the departed. He moves around the sides of the narrow hospital bed, censing the body, the husk, of a dependably lively and opinionated parishioner. Some months ago she had come to see Fr. John, to tell him she intended to have an earth-friendly burial. "Do you know how careful a funeral director has to be, to protect himself from those chemicals?" she asked. "Why would I want to turn my own body into toxic waste?" Fr. John had not heard of this, and liked the idea right away, though he wondered whether the idea was, in fact, practical. Every funeral he'd done had involved an embalmed body. (Orthodox do not use cremation; the ancient-world association is that burning is for garbage.)

Just as the Trisagion prayers are ending, the doorbell rings, and Ariel steps out to get it. Fr. John stands beside Kate's little body—so much smaller it seems, when unanimated!—and thinks about the dying of one of the Desert Fathers, Abba Sisoes (d. AD 429).

Sisoes had lived as a hermit in the cave of the great St. Anthony; he said, "In the cave of a lion, a fox makes his home." The ancient chronicle of his last hours tells the story like this:

> It was said of Abba Sisoes when he was at the point of death, while the Fathers [other monks] were sitting beside him, his face shone like the sun. He said to them, "Look, Abba Anthony is coming." A little later he said, "Look, the choir of prophets is coming." Again his countenance shone with brightness and he said, "Look, the choir of apostles is coming."
>
> His countenance increased in brightness and lo, he spoke with someone. Then the old men asked him, "With whom are you speaking, Father?" He said, "Look, the angels are coming to fetch me, and I am begging them to let me do a little penance." The old man said to him, "You have no need to do penance, Father." But [Sisoes] replied, "Truly, I do not think I have even made a beginning yet." Now they all knew that he was perfect.
>
> Once more his countenance suddenly became like the sun and they were all filled with fear. He said, "Look, the Lord is coming, and he's saying, 'Bring me the vessel from the desert.'" Then there was a flash as of lightning, and all the house was filled with a sweet odor.[113]

Kate and Ariel found a natural-burial ministry at a nearby Protestant church, and asked for someone from that team to prepare Kate's body when the time came. Ariel returns to Kate's bedside with Marjorie and Jane, and as Jane unpacks their kit onto a nearby table, Marjorie asks Ariel a few questions about Kate's last days. Jane sets out plain white soap and washcloths, essential oils, cotton balls and gauze, dried flowers and herbs, incense sticks, a candle. Also, hospital pads and latex gloves.[114]

Marjorie lights the candle and incense, and asks Ariel to bring a large bowl of warm water. Then, standing on opposite sides of the body, the two women deftly replace Kate's faded hospital gown with modestly placed lengths of white cloth. They begin washing the body, very gently, with soap and warm water. The atmosphere is peaceful and patient; it is as if they are handling a sleeping baby. Ariel opens the Bible Kate kept on her bedside table and, starting at the first chapter of the Gospel of John, begins reading in a quiet voice.

After washing her, the women clothe Kate in a simple white dress. When all is ready, they wheel the hospital bed out of the bedroom and over to the dining room, where a plain wooden coffin rests incongruously on the table. A sheet was in place beneath the body, and they use it to lift Kate's body from the bed and place it in the coffin. Then they put her well-worn prayer rope in her hand, and weave some dried flowers in her soft gray hair.

From here the body will go into Marjorie's station wagon, then directly to the church. Since Kate will be buried barely twenty-four hours after her death, there is no need for a funeral home. Marjorie tells Fr. John that, in light of the August heat, it would be a good idea to keep the church very cool. She also advises Ariel to keep some wrapped dry ice on Kate's abdomen, covered with a scarf or flowers.

Fr. John takes his leave to get to church for the evening service. Orthodox celebrate August 15 as the Feast of the Dormition of the

Theotokos; the term *dormition* indicates her "falling asleep" in death.* There is a first-century tomb outside Jerusalem that has long been said to be the Virgin's burial place, but the ancient belief is that it was found empty three days after her burial; she had been taken bodily to heaven, like Enoch (Gen. 5:24) and Elijah (2 Kgs. 2:11).

The icon of the Dormition shows Mary's body laid out on a bier, with the apostles standing around her, grieving. Unseen by them, Christ stands behind the body, within an oval formed of bands of deepening shades of blue. (This oval is called a *mandorla* and is meant to represent a full-body halo.) In his arms he holds a small figure of his mother, wrapped in white linen like a baby, like a corpse. It reverses the familiar image of Madonna and Child.

Every night of the Dormition Fast, there is at St. Felicity a prayer service called the *Paraklesis*, which honors Mary and asks for her prayers. The final hymn of the *Paraklesis* imagines the Virgin speaking to her Son's friends, who have come to her bedside from their far-flung mission fields.

> O you apostles, come from afar
> And now gathered in the village of Gethsemane,
> Give burial to my body,
> And you, my Son and my God,
> Receive my spirit.

After the service, Fr. John asks the small group of worshipers to stay for a moment. He tells them that Kate had reposed that morning, and that they are now going to bring her coffin into the church.

Dn. Andrew and a few others carry the casket into the nave and set it upon a makeshift bier, with Kate's feet toward the altar. Fr. John places a large standing candle at the head of the coffin, then opens the lid. Kate's determined face comes into view.

Fr. John places a hand cross on the pillow just above her head, and a small icon of Christ next to the prayer rope in her right hand. Then, as worshipers gather loosely around the bier, he repeats the

---

* In the West this is called the Feast of the Assumption, and commemorates her being "assumed," lifted by God, into heaven.

same Trisagion prayers for the departed that he said in her bedroom a few hours earlier, and censes around all sides of the coffin.

When this brief service is completed, Dn. Andrew asks those present to sign up to take part in the vigil: parishioners will be reading from the book of Psalms in pairs, an hour at a time, from now until the beginning of the funeral tomorrow morning.

Miriam and Despina take their place behind the chanters' stand and open the great book of the Psalter, taking the first shift. There will be continuous prayer surrounding Kate's body from this moment until it is laid in the ground.

The addition of a funeral makes Tuesday's schedule tight. That service will be in the morning, and it will be followed by the burial at the cemetery. Then the people will return to the church and gather in the parish hall for the "mercy meal." While there isn't a place in the Orthodox funeral service for people to deliver a eulogy or tell fond stories, this communal meal held after a funeral gives friends and family a chance to reminisce. Since they are in Dormition Fast the menu would have to be fasting; but fish is always served at a mercy meal because, after his resurrection, Jesus appeared on the seashore and ate fish cooked over a charcoal fire (John 21).

So Tuesday would bring a funeral, followed by the usual interment and mercy meal. What complicates the schedule is that the following day, Wednesday, is the Feast of the Transfiguration, one of the twelve great feasts of the Church. Its liturgy was scheduled for Tuesday night, right on the heels of the funeral.

This radiant and unimaginable event comes breaking into the quiet, poignant Dormition Fast every year. The troparion of the feast says,

> You were transfigured on the mountain,
> Christ our God,
> And revealed your glory to your disciples

As far as they could bear it.
Let your eternal light shine on us sinners,
Through the prayers of the Theotokos,
O Giver of Light, glory to you.

At the end of the Transfiguration liturgy there is the traditional thanksgiving for the fruits of the summer harvest, and parishioners bring platters and baskets of fruit to be blessed; after that there's a postliturgy potluck. So it promised to be a very busy day. The most pressing concern was the timing of the pre-Communion fast. The funeral, burial, and mercy meal would have to be finished by early afternoon, so everyone could begin the fast from food and drink before the Divine Liturgy that night.

Fr. John arrives at the church early the next morning, while the psalm-readers are completing their vigil. He is relieved to see that Kate looks the same as she did last night, as Marjorie had assured him she would. When the last pair of psalm-readers completes their hour, Fr. John stands before the iconostasis and begins the funeral service by proclaiming, "Blessed is our God, now and always and unto ages of ages. Amen."

Despina is back at the chanter's stand, and reads Psalm 90/91, that hymn of trust in the Lord's protection. Then the small choir begins to chant the *Evlogetaria*. It's a hymn with the refrain, "Blessed are you, O Lord; teach me your statutes," with verses that can vary depending on which service is being offered. Caitlin chants the verses that are appointed for a funeral.

You created me from nothingness and bestowed on me your divine image, but my sins have turned me again to the earth from which I was taken. Restore to me your likeness and reshape me in pristine beauty.

I bear the image of your ineffable glory, even though I bear the marks of sin. Show me your compassion, O Master, for I am your creation, and purify me by your loving-kindness. Bring me to the homeland of my heart's desire, and make me once again a citizen of Paradise.

Dn. Andrew leads a brief ektenia as Fr. John censes the body. He has censed this body a lot by now; there was probably a practical reason for this in the days before air conditioning.

Next the choir sings passages from the Canon for the Departed by St. Theophanes the Branded (AD 775–845). St. Theophanes was a Palestinian who had his initial formation as a monk in the monastery of Mar Sabas, outside Jerusalem. He and his brother and fellow monk Theodore were seized because they defended the use of icons in worship, and the Byzantine emperor Leo V ordered them to be branded on their faces with twelve lines of bad poetry ("badly composed," he stipulated).

St. Theophanes wrote, in this funeral hymn:

In truth, all is vanity, and life is but a shadow, a dream. In vain every citizen of earth troubles himself, as Scripture says. When we have gained the world we must go to dwell in the grave, where there is no distinction between king and beggar. Therefore give rest, Christ God, to the soul of your handmaid who has departed this life, for you love mankind.

You only are immortal, you who created and fashioned us. You made the human race of earth and to the same earth we must return, as you commanded when you fashioned me saying, Earth you are, and to the earth you shall return. There all we mortals make our way, offering as our funeral hymn the song: Alleluia.

The brief ektenia and censing done earlier are repeated here, and then comes the chanting of a powerful hymn by St. John of Damascus (AD 676–749). It is an *idiomela*, which means that it has its own unique structure and doesn't resemble other established hymn patterns. This hymn has eight verses, and each is chanted in one of the eight Tones, in order. It is a grim text, taking the opportunity of the funeral to remind those present that they are bound for the same fate, and must turn to God for salvation.

> What sweetness on earth is not mixed with sorrow? What glory on earth remains unchanged? All things fly like shadows, all things are illusions and dreams, for in a single moment death obliterates all. But give rest, O Christ, to her whom you have chosen, in the light of your countenance and the sweetness of your beauty, for you love mankind.
>
> Where now are earthly desires? Where is the vanity of wealthy display? Where are gold and silver? Where is the noise and bustle of household servants? All things are dust, all are ashes, all are shadows. Let us come to the deathless King and cry out, "O Lord, receive her who has departed from us; account her worthy of your eternal goodness, and give her rest in your blessedness which does not end."
>
> I weep and lament when I think of death, seeing our beauty, fashioned in the image of God, lying in the tomb deformed, disfigured, and dishonored. Look, and be amazed! What is this mystery that befalls us? Why are we given over to corruption? Why have we been betrothed to death? Truly, it is by the command of God, whom Scripture says gives rest to the departed.

Another story is told about Abba Sisoes, the Desert Father whose fellow monks saw him die in that extraordinary way. It is said that Sisoes saw the open tomb of Alexander the Great and looked upon his remains. There's no ancient documentation for this story, but the event is possibly historical, because during Sisoes's lifetime there were riots in Alexandria and pagan temples and tombs were destroyed.

The icon called "The Astonishment of Sisoes" first appears in the fifteenth century. It shows him looking into the broken tomb and seeing the bones lying there. This text is lettered onto the icon: "Sisoes, the great among ascetics, stood before the tomb of Alexander, Emperor of Greeks, who at one time had shone with glory. Astonished, he weeps for the inexorable passing of time and the transience of glory. He cries out with tears, 'Beholding you, O Tomb, I shed tears from my heart, and weep for the common debt of all mankind! How shall I bear this? O Death, who can escape you?'"

The unsettling yet irrefutable words of the hymn by St. John of Damascus are followed by the Beatitudes, which present blessedness—the Greek word, *makarios*, also contains the idea of joy—as something that is not dependent on earthly power or wealth. Jesus' words from the Sermon on the Mount alternate with verses that continue the theme of inexorable death and eternal life.

> You who reign over life and death, give rest among the saints to her whom you have taken away from earthly things, who cries to you, "Remember me when you come into your kingdom."
>
> Blessed are the peacemakers, for they shall be called the sons of God.
>
> May Christ give you rest in the land of the living, and may he open to you the gates of Paradise. May he make you a citizen of his Kingdom, and grant forgiveness of all things in which you sinned in this life, O you who love Christ.
>
> Blessed are those who are persecuted for righteousness' sake, for theirs is the kingdom of heaven. . . .
>
> Let us go to gaze into the tombs; there we will see that man is but bare bones, food for worms, and stench. Thus we learn the true end of wealth, strength, and earthly beauty.
>
> Rejoice and be exceedingly glad, for great is your reward in heaven.
>
> Let us hear the words of Almighty God: "Woe to you who long to behold the terrible day of the Lord! For it is darkness, and all things will be tried with fire" [Amos 5:18].

Ariel has asked Fr. John if she could read the Epistle today. She looks pale, but chants in a sweet, high voice that fills the room.

But we would not have you ignorant, brethren, concerning those who are asleep, that you may not grieve as others do who have no hope. For since we believe that Jesus died and rose again, even so, through Jesus, God will bring with him those who have fallen asleep. . . . For the Lord himself will descend from heaven with a cry of command, with the archangel's call, and with the sound of the trumpet of God. And the dead in Christ will rise first; then we who are alive, who are left, shall be caught up together with them in the clouds to meet the Lord in the air; and so we shall always be with the Lord. (1 Thess. 4:13–17)

Fr. John follows with the Gospel reading. It comes from the Gospel of John, and brings us Christ's words.

Truly, truly, I say to you, the hour is coming, and now is, when the dead will hear the voice of the Son of God, and those who hear will live. . . . Do not marvel at this; for the hour is coming when all who are in the tombs will hear his voice and come forth, those who have done good, to the resurrection of life, and those who have done evil, to the resurrection of judgment.

I can do nothing on my own authority; as I hear, I judge; and my judgment is just, because I seek not my own will but the will of him who sent me. (John 5:24–30)

After another brief ektenia and censing, Fr. John prays for the forgiveness of Kate's sins.

May the Lord Jesus Christ our God, who ordained that his holy disciples and apostles should bind and loose the sins of those who fall, and who has, through them, bestowed this command upon us; by that power my spiritual child Kate is absolved, through me a sinner, of all things in which she has sinned, whether in word or deed or thought, voluntary or involuntary, in knowledge or in ignorance. If she, as a mortal, was bound by any sins, but repented with her whole heart, she is now absolved, and may all that proceeded from her weak human nature be forgiven her, and consigned to oblivion.

As the funeral concludes those in the congregation line up and, one at a time, stand beside Kate's body and pray for her, an observance called the "Last Kiss." Some kiss the hand cross resting above her head or the icon in her hand, while others kiss their fingertips and then touch them to the icon or cross. During this time, the chanter sings:

> Let us give a farewell kiss to her who has gone forth from us. . . . She hastens to burial, no longer remembering the vanity of the world or the pains of the flesh. Assemble, all her friends and family. Now is the time of her departing. Let us pray to the Lord to give her rest.
>
> Look upon me now as I lie before you, deprived of breath, deprived of voice. Mourn for me, my friends and family, for yesterday I was with you, but now the hour of death has suddenly come. All who will miss me, come give me the parting kiss. I will not walk or speak with you again, for I am going to stand before the Judge, where no one can boast of her earthly status. There the servant and master stand together, the king and the warrior, rich and poor; in that place all are of equal rank. Each one shall be praised or blamed for her deeds alone. Pray for me to Christ our God, I beg you, that he will bring me into the Light of Life.

As the service ends and all prepare to depart for the cemetery, Fr. John checks the time; he's relieved to see that so far all is on schedule. Downstairs two parishioners are preparing the mercy meal, baking a salmon to be served with a mix of vegan mayonnaise and capers.

The graveside service is brief. Fr. John repeats the Trisagion memorial prayers—this is the third time—and sprinkles earth upon the coffin lid, saying, "The earth is the Lord's, and the fullness thereof; the world, and those who dwell therein" (Ps. 23/24:1). He recalls Kate's pointy, eager little face, and feels a sudden pang. Now the lid is shut, and he will never see it again in this life.

As he heads back to his car to return to the church, Fr. John checks the time on his phone. He notices that a text message came in while he had the ringer turned off for the service. It's from Beth's best friend, and it reads: "Contractions getting stronger. Meet us at the hospital NOW."

Conclusion: "Go and Do Likewise"

(Lĸ. 10:37)

Ever since I became a Christian, forty years ago, I have been longing to know the Lord better. That's all I want: to get closer to him, to be always in his presence, to see his work and know his will. I feel a strong connection with Christians everywhere who have this longing, no matter what church they attend. Drawing nearer to Jesus is the most important thing.

I had assumed that "more of Jesus" meant accumulating more emotional experiences. But as the years went by I kept getting *less* emotional. Christian faith kept getting less exciting; instead, I found, it was getting deeper, more wordless, more filled with awe.

Since I didn't know what Christian growth should look like, I feared that the diminishment of emotion was a bad thing—a sign that I was losing my "first love" (Rev. 2:4).

I didn't really want to be Orthodox. It was my husband's idea. I went along because he was so enthusiastic, without being enthusiastic myself. I learned Orthodoxy in the way I've tried to convey in this book, by living it, listening to worship, looking at icons, and talking to Orthodox people. Orthodox spirituality was like nothing else I'd encountered.

Till then, I had associated spirituality and mysticism with St. Teresa of Avila and St. John of the Cross; I thought of it as an esoteric and refined pursuit. But here it was simple and straightforward, expressed in terms that ordinary people leading their daily lives could understand and apply. And the love for Jesus was so evident, so simple and clear. I resonated with it deeply.

I eventually came to see that Orthodoxy is *all about* getting closer to Jesus. That's the whole point. It was everything my evangelical heart had longed for, and sought in ineffective, undirected, stop-and-go ways. I found in Orthodoxy a time-tested Way, one tried all over the world in many different cultures, that reliably brought about growth in Christ. It was what I had always longed for. Now I feel like my prayer life is actually going somewhere. Well, not "feel like"—I can see proof. It just keeps getting better.

You can think of me as being like somebody who is enthusiastic about a diet program, and promotes it with plenty of warnings that you have to follow it *exactly* or you won't lose weight. You can see that's not the case; in the case of a diet, if you adopt even a few of the elements, it's going to do *some* good. It's not all or nothing.

Likewise, if you adopt some of the elements of this early Christian Way, it will surely do you good. These resources aren't the private property of the Orthodox, because all Christians go back to the early church. That treasury belongs to all of us, and anyone can take from it whatever she likes. You can utilize only the things you like, and you'll surely see some benefit. But the results will be different than they would be if you were taking it all on, intact.

Here are three considerations. First, what you choose out of this treasury will inevitably be things you like. The things you already like are not going to change you. They'll confirm you in your comfortable places, and reinforce things you already understand. But the things that will actually change you may not be things you understand, at first. They may seem perplexing or unattractive. You come to understand them by doing them—hopefully, in the company of others who are on the same path, some of whom are further along and can guide you and answer your questions.

Second, the recent fascination with the early church has a lot to do with the quest for authenticity. We sense something simple and strong in the early church; there's something in its worship that seems fresh in comparison with even the most skillfully planned worship today. That authenticity comes directly from its "ancient-ness," the fact that it was intact and in practice long before our lives began. It's the work of an enormous community, stretching over lands and centuries; its roots are vast and deep. It wasn't packaged and marketed by someone living today. This makes it immensely attractive to use as a resource for worship and spiritual growth.

The catch is, when someone selects from this treasury the things he likes, he automatically *becomes* a modern-day marketer and pack-ager. When someone assumes the role of editor and curator of the early church, all that ancient authenticity gets reset to last week.

There's a third consideration. It's that the various parts of this ancient path fit together in an *organic* way. And when everything is in place together, something *happens*.

It's like a car's engine. If you happened across one and didn't know what it was, you might take out the parts that appeal to you—particularly shiny parts, or square ones. You could array them on black velvet, and they might well look beautiful and intriguing.

But they can't take you anywhere. It's when all the pieces are linked together in the right way that you start going places.

Still, it's perfectly all right for you to use only the pieces you like. This is your inheritance as much as any Christian's. I would just invite you to think about what might happen if instead you accepted it intact, and let it go to work.

Significant Feast Days

The twelve great feasts of the church are in regular typeface, and the five lesser feasts are in italics. Your local Orthodox church is likely to have services on the morning of these days, or the night before. (It's best to check their schedule.)

The church year begins September 1, which is called the "Indiction."

- The Nativity of the Theotokos (September 8)
- Exaltation of the Holy Cross (September 14)
- *The Protecting Veil of the Theotokos* (October 1)
- Presentation in the Temple of the Theotokos (November 21)
- The Nativity of Christ (December 25, preceded by forty days of fasting)
- *The Circumcision of Christ* (January 1)
- Theophany (January 6)
- The Presentation of Our Lord in the Temple (February 2)
- Annunciation of the Theotokos (March 25)
- The Entry of Our Lord into Jerusalem (Palm Sunday, a week before Pascha, and preceded by forty days of fasting)
- The Ascension (forty days after Pascha)
- Pentecost (fifty days after Pascha)
- *The Nativity of John the Forerunner* (June 24)
- *The Feast of Sts. Peter and Paul* (June 29, preceded by fasting that begins the eighth day, a Monday, after Pentecost)
- The Transfiguration of Our Lord and Savior Jesus Christ (August 6)
- The Dormition of the Theotokos (August 15, preceded by two weeks of fasting)
  - *The Beheading of St. John the Forerunner*

Holy Pascha is the feast of feasts, and not numbered among the twelve. (The date is moveable; the process for determining it each year is covered in chapter 13.)

Notes

1. "Enter His Gates"

1   *Will you escape notice:* Tertullian, *Second Letter to His Wife* 2.5.

2   *Let him who would test this by experience:* St. Athanasius, *On the Incarnation* 48.

3   *Let the Cross, as our seal:* St. Cyril of Jerusalem, *Catechetical Lectures* 13.36.

4   *After praying with an Orthodox sister:* Chuck Colson and Ellen Vaughn, *Being the Body* (Nashville: Thomas Nelson, 2003), 81.

5   *Some sit, some lie on their faces:* Quoted in Metropolitan Kallistos Ware, "C. S. Lewis, an 'Anonymous Orthodox'?," in *C. S. Lewis and the Church*, ed. Judith Wolfe and Brendan N. Wolfe (London: T&T Clark, 2011), 136. In the same essay, Met. Kallistos provides a second, similar quotation:
> "What pleased me most about a Greek Orthodox mass I once attended was that there seemed to be no prescribed behaviour for the congregation. Some stood, some knelt, some sat, some walked; one crawled about the floor like a caterpillar. And the beauty of it was that nobody took the slightest notice of what anyone else was doing."

Lewis's snapshot of Orthodox worship sounds more chaotic than it is in reality. I have never, for instance, seen anyone crawl like a caterpillar.

2. "The House of God"

6   *Eastward worship:* St. Basil the Great, *On the Holy Spirit* 27.

7   *Resembling a bonfire:* N. I. Brunov (in Russian), *Hram Vasilia Blazhennogo v Moskve* Храм Василия Блаженного в Москве. Покровский собор (Moscow: Iskusstvo, 1988), 100.

3. "So Great a Cloud"

8   *All possible care:* St. Vincent of Lérins, *The Commonitory* 2.6.

9   *Peter Damian, a saintly abbot:* Tim Perry, *Mary for Evangelicals* (Downers Grove, IL: InterVarsity Press, 2006), 182–83.

4. *"Upon This Rock"*

10   *Christians worshiped in Greek*: Johannes Emminghaus, *The Eucharist: Essence, Form, Celebration* (Collegeville, MN: Liturgical Press, 1997), 52.

5. *"A Sacrifice of Praise"*

11   *29 percent of the Greek Orthodox*: Nicole Neroullias, "Study Finds More Orthodox Christian Converts," *USA Today*, October 23, 2008, http://www.usatoday.com/news/religion/2008-10-23-orthodox-christians_N.htm.

12   *In the Antiochian Archdiocese*: Samuel Freedman, "More Protestants Find a home in the Orthodox Antioch Church," *New York Times*, October 2, 2009, http://www.nytimes.com/2009/10/03/us/03religion.html.

13   *Pliny the Younger*: Pliny the Younger, *Letters* 10.96–97.

14   *Seemed very long*: St. Nikolai Velimirovich, *The Prologue of Ochrid* (Alhambra, CA: Serbian Orthodox Diocese of Western America, 2002), 2:459.

15   *Fr. Roman Braga, a modern-day elder*: Fr. Roman Braga, *Exploring the Inner Universe* (Rives Junction, MI: HDM Press, 1996), 82–91.

6. *"Partakers of the Divine Nature"*

16   *He was made man*: St. Athanasius, *On the Incarnation* 54.3. St. Irenaeus of Lyons (AD 130–200) said much the same a century earlier, and repeatedly, though not as succinctly: *Against Heresies* 3.10.2; 3.18.7; 3.19.1; 3.33.4; 4.20.4; 5, preface.

17   *When iron is brought*: St. Cyril of Alexandria, *Commentary on St. Luke's Gospel*, Sermon 142.

18   *Are truly called*: St. John of Damascus, *On the Holy Images* 3.33.

19   *The kingdom of heaven is within you*: Though recent translations have rendered it "among you," it was understood as "inside you" or "within you" from ancient times; the Latin Vulgate, the King James Version, and Luther's 1545 German version all convey it in the sense of "within." The Greek preposition *entos* means "inside" or "within"—as in "clean the inside [*entos*] of the cup" (Matt. 23:36, its only other New Testament occurrence). When Luke meant "among," he used a different term: "For I am *en meso* you as one who serves" (Lk. 22:27). More on this at Ilaria Ramelli, "Luke 17:21: 'The Kingdom of God is inside you.' The Ancient Syriac Versions in Support of the Correct Translation," *Hugoye: Journal of Syriac Studies* 12, no. 2 (2009): 259–86, http://syrcom.cua.edu/Hugoye/Vol12No2/HV12N2Ramelli.pdf

20   *[He is] at peace in himself in such a way as to be peace*: Vasileios Gontikakis, *Hymn of Entry* (Crestwood, NY: St. Vladimir's Seminary Press, 1997), 126–31.

21   *Little by little the prayerful person will experience small and great divine events*: Elder
     Paisios of Mount Athos, *Epistles* (Thessaloniki, Greece: Holy Monastery of
     the Evangelist John the Theologian, 2002), 216.

22   *If ninety-nine of us*: St. Nikolai Velimirovi, *The Religious Spirit of the Slavs*
     (London: Macmillan, 1916), 38.

23   *Gently and without tumult*: Vasileos Gontikakis, *Hymn of Entry*, 126–31.

24   *He is weak, like a spider's web*: Vasileos Gontikakis, *Hymn of Entry*, 126–31.

25   *Material light pours*: St. Ambrose of Milan, *Isaac, or the Soul* 6.51.

26   *A clergyman from a Western denomination*: Fr. Roman Braga, *Exploring the Inner
     Universe* (Rives Junction, MI: HDM Press, 1996), 83.

27   *Pressed Elder Paisios to perform a miracle*: Priestmonk Christodoulos, *Elder Paisios
     of the Holy Mountain* (n.p.: Holy Mountain, 1998), 102.

7. "Christ and Him Crucified"

28   *That which could calm*: Leonid Ouspensky, *Theology of the Icon* (Crestwood,
     NY: St. Vladimir's Seminary Press, 1992), 1:78.

29   *Had been present in seed form*: Gustaf Aulén (*Christus Victor* [New York:
     Macmillan, 1969], 81–84) finds the concepts of both "merit" and "satis-
     faction" in Tertullian (*On Penance, 6*). He summarizes Tertullian's thought:
     "Penance [an act of penitence] is satisfaction, the acceptance of a temporal
     penalty to escape eternal loss," and "it is possible . . . to earn an overplus
     of merit" through "supererogatory" deeds that exceed the requirements.
     He finds that St. Cyprian of Carthage (*On Penance, 2*) also "begins to apply
     the principle [that superfluous merit can be transferred from one person
     to another] to the overplus of merit earned by Christ, and to interpret his
     work as a satisfaction." It's interesting that you can draw the line between
     Eastern and Western Christianity through North Africa, with mystical
     Alexandria of Egypt of the East, and Tertullian and St. Cyprian's Carthage
     (now in Libya) and St. Augustine's Hippo (now in Algeria) of the West.

30   *One who could freely offer*: St. Anselm, *Cur Deus Homo?* 2.19

31   *If imitation of a righteous man*: St. Augustine, *On Forgiveness of Sins and Baptism*
     1.19.

32   *Treasury of grace*: Pope Clement VI (AD 1291–1352) established that the
     resources of this "treasury of grace," administered by the Roman Catholic
     Church, could be applied in the form of "indulgences," to lighten the tem-
     poral punishment for sin. See also *Catechism of the Catholic Church*, §§1471,
     1478–79, 1498.

33   *Those who are punished in Gehenna*: St. Isaac of Syria, *The Ascetical Homilies* 28.141
     (Boston: Holy Transfiguration Monastery, 2011), 266.

8. *"Image of the Invisible God"*

34   *Treat the statue with respect:* St. John of Damascus, *On the Divine Images*, 2:66

35   *Friends and servants of God:* St. John of Damascus, *On the Divine Images* 1.13.

36   *If the two beams:* St. John of Damascus, *On the Divine Images* 2.19.

37   *Council of Trullo:* Also called the Quinisext Council, it met to formulate penalties for violating the theological decrees of the fifth and sixth ecumenical councils. The passage dealing with the image of the lamb is canon 82.

38   *Of old, God the incorporeal:* St. John of Damascus, *On the Divine Images* 1.16.

39   *Sight is the "noblest sense":* St. John of Damascus, *On the Divine Images* 1.17.

40   *The council ruled:* The Declaration of Faith of the Second Council of Nicaea.

41   *Not quite iconographic:* Irina Yazykova, *Hidden and Triumphant: The Underground Struggle to Save Russian Iconography* (Brewster, MA: Paraclete, 2010), 158.

9. *"Your Body Is a Temple"*

42   *Some may then ask:* St. Athanasius, *On the Incarnation* 43.1.

10. *"Into the Sanctuary"*

43   *Let no one do anything:* St. Ignatius of Antioch, *Epistle to the Smyrnaeans*, 8.

11. *"Reconciling the World"*

44   *Preserved free from all stain:* Pope Pius IX, *Encyclical Ineffabilis Deus*, December 1854.

45   *That which he has not assumed:* St. Gregory the Theologian, *Critique of Apollinarius*.

46   *Mildest condemnation of all:* St. Augustine of Hippo, *On the Forgiveness of Sins*, 21.

47   *Pope Benedict XVI:* "The Hope of Salvation for Infants Who Die Without Being Baptized," International Theological Commission, 2007, http://www.vatican.va/roman_curia/congregations/cfaith/cti_documents/rc_con_cfaith_doc_20070419_un-baptised-infants_en.html.

48   *What can we offer you, O Christ?:* Sticheron of Great Vespers, December 25.

49   *Act of reproduction:* St. Augustine, *On Forgiveness of Sins* 2.11.

50   *So it is with the King of all:* St. Athanasius, *On the Incarnation* 2.9.

51   *He has, in his work of recapitulation:* St. Irenaeus, *Against Heresies* 5.21.1. St. Irenaeus wrote in Greek, but only fragments remain, and his work is mostly available in Latin.

12. "Not Counting Their Trespasses"

52   *The understanding of salvation as rescue:* Gustaf Aulén, *Christus Victor* (New York: Macmillan, 1969).

53   *Fish swallowing a baited hook:* St. Gregory of Nyssa, *Great Catechism* 24. "In order to secure that the ransom in our behalf might be easily accepted by him who required it, the Deity was hidden under the veil of our nature, that so, as with ravenous fish, the hook of the Deity might be gulped down along with the bait of flesh."

54   *A mouse taking the bait:* St. Augustine, *Homilies* 261.1 (Benedictine numbering). "The devil jumped for joy when Christ died; and by the very death of Christ the devil was overcome: he took, as it were, the bait in the mousetrap. He rejoiced at the death, thinking himself death's commander. But that which caused his joy dangled the bait before him. The Lord's cross was the devil's mousetrap: the bait which caught him was the death of the Lord."

55   *To whom was that blood offered:* St. Gregory Nazianzus, *Oration* 45.22.

13. "The Lord Is King"

56   *Eternal punishment:* Catechism of the Catholic Church (Collegeville, MN: Liturgical Press, 1994), §§1472–73. The classic teaching has been that "God requires temporal punishment for sin to satisfy His justice, to teach us the great evil of sin, and to warn us not to sin again" (Baltimore Catechism, 1941 edition, http://www.catholicity.com/baltimore-catechism/lesson31.html). The more recent catechism (from which the quote comes) describes it as the need for purification from an "unhealthy attachment" to created things.

57   *Repentance is great understanding:* Hermas, *The Shepherd* 30.2.

58   *A stranger to any fall:* St. Ambrose of Milan, *Sermon* 20 (on Psalm 118).

14. "Lord, Have Mercy"

59   *Who was the author:* St. Basil the Great, *On the Spirit* 29.73.

60   *Strengthens the singers' recitation:* St. Basil the Great, *Letter* 207.3–4.

61   *No one would suggest:* James Bowman, *Honor: A History* (New York: Encounter, 2006), 59.

62   *Our offenses against God:* Scott Hahn, *Lord, Have Mercy* (New York: Doubleday, 2003), page NA.

63   *Do not call God just:* St. Isaac of Syria, *The Ascetical Homilies* 51.251 (Boston, MA: Holy Transfiguration Monastery, 2011), 387.

64   *A sin is classed as mortal:* Catechism of the Catholic Church (Collegeville, MN: Liturgical Press, 1994), §§1857–62.

65   *I saw that we all depend on each other:* Garrison Keillor, "Letter from Jim," *News from Lake Wobegon,* audio CD (High Bridge, 1990).

15. "Awake, Sleeper"

66   St. Justin the Martyr: St. Justin Martyr, *First Apologia*, 61. "Understanding" here is *dianoia*.

67   *The place in man*: Gerhard Kittel and Gerhard Friedrich, eds., *Theological Dictionary of the New Testament*, trans. Geoffrey W. Bromiley (Grand Rapids: Eerdmans, 1965), 3:611.

68   *When the mind is in the heart*: Quoted by Igumen Chariton, ed., *The Art of Prayer* (London: Faber & Faber, 1966), 157.

69   *The heart is a small vessel*: Macarius (usually called Pseudo-Macarius), *Fifty Spiritual Homilies* 43.7.

70   *Decent little cottage*: C. S. Lewis, *Mere Christianity* (New York: Touchstone, 1996), 176.

71   *Always in labor*: St. Gregory of Nyssa, *The Life of Moses*, 2:11.

72   *We theologize*: St. Gregory of Nazianzus, *Homilies* 23.12.

73   *Whatever things were rightly said*: St. Justin Martyr, *Second Apologia*, 13.

74   *The mind is fallen*: Fr. Thomas Hopko, "Christian Doctrine in an Age of Relativism," *Metropolitan Andrei Sheptytsky Institute Study Days* (Ottawa, Ontario, Canada, July 2, 2008).

75   *[The Byzantines] valued fidelity*: David Bradshaw, *Aristotle East and West: Metaphysics and the Division of Christendom* (Cambridge: Cambridge University Press, 2004), 221.

76   *It is a great evil*: Elder Isaac, *Elder Paisios of Mount Athos*, (Holy Monastery of the Evangelist John the Theologian, 2002), 215–16.

77   *We cannot use our intelligence*: St. Maximos the Confessor, *Various Texts on Theology, the Divine Economy, and Virtue and Vice* 4.31.

16. "Time for the Lord to Act"

78   *Martin Luther also recommended*: "Luther used also to discuss the eight church tones; giving the Epistle to the 8th tone and the Gospel to the 6th." Sir George Grove and John Alexander Fuller-Maitland, *Grove's Dictionary of Music and Musicians* (London: Macmillan, 1906), 2:788.

17. "Choose This Day"

79   *He is a man*: St. Nikolai Velimirovich, *The Prologue of Ochrid* (Alhambra, CA: Serbian Orthodox Diocese of Western America, 2002), 1:650.

80   *In early Christian symbolism*: John B. Dunlop, *Staretz Amvrosy: Model for Doestoevsky's Staretz Zossima* (Belmont, MA: Nordland, 1972), 19.

81   *Religious beliefs of American youth*: Christian Smith and Melinda Lundquist Denton, *Soul Searching: The Religious and Spiritual Lives of American Teenagers* (New York: Oxford University Press, 2005).

82 *If one were to summarize:* David Bradshaw, *Aristotle East and West: Metaphysics and the Division of Christendom* 264–65.

83 *Paphnutius pointed to the example:* St. John Cassian, *Conferences* 3.10–12.

84 *Just as a mother:* St. Isaac of Syria, *The Ascetical Homilies of St. Isaac the Syrian* 39.192 (Boston, MA: Holy Transfiguration Monastery, 2011), 323.

85 *When people are tortured by a specific passion:* Priestmonk Christodoulos, *Elder Paisios of the Holy Mountain* (n.p.: Holy Mountain, 1998) 49–50.

86 *What do you love?:* "The Life of Our Holy Father Saint Herman of Alaska," St. Herman of Alaska Brotherhood, http://www.pravoslavie.ru/english/47984 .htm.

18. "Where Two or Three Are Gathered"

87 *Dwell in one another:* St. John of Damascus, *The Orthodox Faith* 1.8.

19. "When You Fast"

88 *When I am here:* St. Augustine, *Letter* [to Casulanus] 36.31–32.

89 *Refers to this way of fasting as xerophagy:* Tertullian, *On Fasting,* 9.

90 *Abstaining from things:* Tertullian, *On Fasting,* 15.

91 *Fast on the fourth day:* Didache, 8.

92 *In 1893 there was a conference:* I was told this anecdote long ago and had been unable to substantiate it. This passage fills in a gap: "Towards the end of that same year [1892] Archimandrite Christopher Jabara also traveled from Syria to New York on his own initiative. The immigrant community welcomed the Archimandrite. . . . Shortly after his arrival, however, Archimandrite Christopher began to spread heretical opinions, scandalizing the Orthodox Syrians. When preaching on the subject of religious freedom, he declared that 'the religions of Christ, Moses, and Mohammed' are, in reality, one religion, and that the Gospel, the Torah, and the Quran are, in reality, one Scripture. At the Chicago Exposition Archimandrite Christopher addressed the International Congress of Religions [should be World's Congress of Religions] where he expounded these views, but they were not well-received. Compelled to leave the country, he eventually fled to Egypt, where he eventually died as a layman." Andre Issa, *Saint Raphael Hawaweeny* (Englewood, N.J.: Antakya Press, 2000), 24.

20. "Each Person Is Tempted"

93 *A scholar attracts:* St. Nikolai Velimirovich, *Kassiana: Lessons in Divine and Christian Love* (Seattle: St. Nectarios Press, 1995), 53.

22. "A Great Mystery"

94   *When the fiancé of St. Macrina:* These quotations from St. Macrina and St. John Chrysostom are cited in David Ford and Mary Ford, *Marriage as a Path to Holiness: Lives of Married Saints* (South Canaan, PA: St. Tikhon's Seminary Press, 1999), xxxiv–xxxv. The authors' introduction to this book is a rich essay on the meaning and spiritual power of marriage.

95   *You will depart:* St. John Chrysostom, *Letter to a Young Widow,* 3.

96   *Let the husband:* St. John Chrysostom, *Letter to a Young Widow,* 1

97   *You call my words immodest:* St. John Chrysostom, *Homilies on Colossians,* 12.

23. "Built His House upon a Rock"

98   *The haunts of the Britons:* Tertullian, *An Answer to the Jews* 7.4.

99   *Yupik Alaskan woman:* Retrieved from *Jacob's Well,* "Matushka Olga Michael: A Helper in Restoring the Work of God's Hands," http://www.jacwell.org/articles/1997-SPRING-Matushka_olga.htm on December 3 , 2012.

100   *Three times a day: Didache,* 8.

101   *Be careful not to squander:* Elder Paisios of Mount Athos, *Epistles* (Souroti, Greece: Holy Monastery of the Evangelist John the Theologian, 2002), 217.

24. "Those Who Have Fallen Asleep"

102   *St. Taisia inherited much money:* Benedicta Ward, trans., *The Sayings of the Desert Fathers* (Collegeville, MN: Cistercian Publications, 1975), 93–94.

103   *It was said of Abba Sisoes:* Ibid., 214–15.

104   *Unpacks their kit:* A similar kit is described in J. Mark and Elizabeth J. Barna, *A Christian Ending: A Handbook for Burial in the Ancient Christian Tradition* (Manton, CA: Divine Ascent Press, 2011).

Recommended Reading

Other Introductory Books

Clark Carlton. *The Faith: Understanding Orthodox Christianity*. Salisbury, MA: Regina Orthodox Press, 1997.

Fr. Anthony Coniaris. *Introducing the Orthodox Church*. Minneapolis: Light and Life, 2007.

Fr. Marc Dunaway. *What Is the Orthodox Church: A Brief Overview of Orthodoxy*. Ben Lomond, CA: Conciliar, 1995.

Matthew Gallatin. *Thirsting for God in a Land of Shallow Wells*. Ben Lomond, CA: Conciliar, 2002.

Fr. Peter Gillquist. *Becoming Orthodox: A Journey to the Ancient Christian Faith*. Ben Lomond, CA: Conciliar, 1989.

Fr. Peter Gillquist, ed. *Coming Home: Why Protestant Clergy Are Becoming Orthodox*. Ben Lomond, CA: Conciliar, 1992.

Fr. Michael Harper. *A Faith Fulfilled: Why Are Christians Across Great Britain Embracing Orthodoxy?* Ben Lomond, CA: Conciliar, 1999.

Fr. Thomas Hopko. *The Orthodox Faith: An Elementary Handbook on the Orthodox Church*. Vols. 1–4. New York: Orthodox Church in America, 1976.

Fr. John Meyendorff. *The Orthodox Church: Its Past and Its Role in the World Today*. Crestwood, NY: St. Vladimir's Seminary Press, 1981.

Virginia Nieuwsma, ed. *Our Hearts' True Home: Fourteen Warm, Inspiring Stories of Women Discovering the Ancient Christian Faith*. Ben Lomond, CA: Conciliar, 1996.

Archbishop Paul of Finland. *The Faith We Hold*. Crestwood, NY: St. Vladimir's Seminary Press, 1988.

Timothy Ware (Metropolitan Kallistos). *The Orthodox Church*. New York: Penguin, 1963.

Timothy Ware (Metropolitan Kallistos). *The Orthodox Way*. Crestwood, NY: St. Vladimir's Seminary Press, 1990).

Other Introductory Books by Frederica Mathewes-Green

At the Corner of East and Now: A Modern Life in Ancient Christian Orthodoxy. New York: Tarcher/Putnam, 1999.

Facing East: A Pilgrim's Journey into the Mysteries of Orthodoxy. San Francisco: Harper, 1997.

First Fruits of Prayer: A 40-day Journey through the Ancient Great Canon. Brewster, MA: Paraclete Press, 2008.

The Illumined Heart: Capture the Vibrant Faith of Ancient Christians. Brewster, MA: Paraclete Press, 2007.

The Jesus Prayer: The Ancient Desert Prayer That Tunes the Heart to God. Brewster, MA: Paraclete Press, 2009.

The Open Door: Entering the Sanctuary of Icons and Prayer. Brewster, MA: Paraclete Press, 2008).

Prayer Books: Pocket Sized

A Pocket Prayer Book for Orthodox Christians. Englewood, NJ: Antiochian Orthodox Christian Archdiocese. Often called "the little red prayer book."

The Hours and the Typica. South Canaan, PA: St. Tikhon's Monastery.

A Manual of the Hours of the Orthodox Church. Otego, NY: Holy Myrrhbearers Monastery.

Prayer Books: A Little Larger

A Prayer Book for Orthodox Christians. Boston, MA: Holy Transfiguration Monastery.

Prayer Book. Jordanville, NY: Holy Trinity Monastery. Often called "the Jordanville prayer book."

Service Book. Englewood Hills, NJ: Antiochian Orthodox Christian Archdiocese.

Prayer Books: Really Big

The Great Horologion [Book of Hours]. Boston, MA: Holy Transfiguration Monastery.

The Orthodox Study Bible. Nashville: Thomas Nelson. Includes brief morning and evening prayers in the back. The Old Testament is a new translation from the Septuagint.

The Bible and the Church Fathers

The Ancient Christian Commentary on Scripture. Downers Grove, IL: InterVarsity Press. A multivolume (and expensive) series of books of Scripture, with commentary by church fathers.

The Bible and the Holy Fathers for Orthodox. Crestwood, NY: St. Vladimir's Seminary Press. Contains the daily Scripture readings for the Orthodox church year. Each reading is followed by some commentary from the church fathers (length ranges from a paragraph to a couple of pages). I use this every day.

Index

About *Paraclete Press*

Who We Are

Paraclete Press is a publisher of books, recordings, and DVDs on Christian spirituality. Our publishing represents a full expression of Christian belief and practice—from Catholic to Evangelical, from Protestant to Orthodox.

We are the publishing arm of the Community of Jesus, an ecumenical monastic community in the Benedictine tradition. As such, we are uniquely positioned in the marketplace without connection to a large corporation and with informal relationships to many branches and denominations of faith.

What We Are Doing

PARACLETE PRESS BOOKS | Paraclete publishes books that show the richness and depth of what it means to be Christian. Although Benedictine spirituality is at the heart of all that we do, we publish books that reflect the Christian experience across many cultures, time periods, and houses of worship. We publish books that nourish the vibrant life of the church and its people—books about spiritual practice, formation, history, ideas, and customs.

We have several different series, including the best-selling Paraclete Essentials and Paraclete Giants series of classic texts in contemporary English; Voices from the Monastery—men and women monastics writing about living a spiritual life today; award-winning poetry; best-selling gift books for children on the occasions of baptism and first communion; and the Active Prayer Series that brings creativity and liveliness to any life of prayer.

MOUNT TABOR BOOKS | Paraclete's newest series, Mount Tabor Books, focuses on liturgical worship, art and art history, ecumenism, and the first millennium church, and was created in conjunction with the Mount Tabor Ecumenical Centre for Art and Spirituality in Barga, Italy.

PARACLETE RECORDINGS | From Gregorian chant to contemporary American choral works, our recordings celebrate the best of sacred choral music composed through the centuries that create a space for heaven and earth to intersect. Paraclete Recordings is the record label representing the internationally acclaimed choir Gloriæ Dei Cantores, praised for their "rapt and fathomless spiritual intensity" by *American Record Guide;* the Gloriæ Dei Cantores Schola, specializing in the study and performance of Gregorian chant; and the other instrumental artists of the Gloriæ Dei Artes Foundation.

Paraclete Press is also privileged to be the exclusive North American distributor of the recordings of the Monastic Choir of St. Peter's Abbey in Solesmes, France, long considered to be a leading authority on Gregorian chant.

PARACLETE VIDEO PRODUCTIONS | Our DVDs offer spiritual help, healing, and biblical guidance for life issues: grief and loss, marriage, forgiveness, anger management, facing death, and spiritual formation.

Learn more about us at our website:
www.paracletepress.com or phone us toll-free at 1.800.451.5006

SCAN
TO
READ
MORE